THE CATHOLIC ETHIC
AND GLOBAL CAPITALISM

The Catholic Ethic and Global Capitalism

BRYAN FIELDS

Routledge
Taylor & Francis Group

LONDON AND NEW YORK

First published 2003 by Ashgate Publishing

Reissued 2018 by Routledge
2 Park Square, Milton Park, Abingdon, Oxon OX14 4RN
711 Third Avenue, New York, NY 10017, USA

Routledge is an imprint of the Taylor & Francis Group, an informa business

A Library of Congress record exists under LC control number: 2003055319

ISBN 13: 978-1-138-71271-3 (hbk)
ISBN 13: 978-1-138-71269-0 (pbk)
ISBN 13: 978-1-315-19927-6 (ebk)

Contents

List of Tables

Preface

While this book is a study of the way one particular society has engaged with global capitalism, it is also an explicit acknowledgement that the insights gained into the nature of this engagement were only achieved by turning, or more correctly returning to the roots of sociology and in particular to the ideas and concepts of some of the classical sociologists. As they placed a premium on the socio-cultural context to inform their thinking and to ground the abstraction of their empirical evidence, it was no coincidence that their most robust sociological insights inevitably arose by studying a social fact from its beginning and then tracing how it evolved little by little until it reached its present form.

This back to basics approach seems almost tailor made to study economic development paths yet many authors often rely exclusively on presenting a descriptive and universal set of economic conditions derived from their present form as a blueprint for the dynamic of development and often premised on the so-called hard fact of economic life whereby all societies are eventually destined to be pulled relentlessly into the vortex of capitalism. Even the impact of sentiments such as religion and nationalism, it seems, is no match in the long run for the objective rational and acquisitive spirit of global capitalism.

As a counterbalance to the so-called benchmark advanced economies as the pre-eminent source for harvesting sociological insights, our study presents a micro-analysis of a small formerly colonised peripheral country on the western edge of Europe. From the perspective of the so-called miraculous Celtic Tiger we can provide a template to trace how these sentiments continue to shape a long standing economic disposition and how this disposition at the individual level continues to set the terms of reference for engagement with global capitalism.

While the Celtic Tiger may be small fry in global economic terms, it nevertheless harvests in sociological terms, a critical contribution to our understanding of the process of economic development. We believe that this study from a sociological standpoint makes a small but unique and original contribution to this understanding. It does this in a number of ways.

Firstly, it identifies two specific cultural factors, namely religion and nationalism and reveals their role in determining the nature of the economic disposition of Irish society. This economic orientation, which is characterised by individuals engaging in yet detached from the Celtic Tiger, simultaneously inhibits and assists with Irish economic development. Secondly, the profile of the research sample itself is, we believe, unmatched because it captures a range of contributions from the mosaic of Irish social life including some of the individuals responsible for the economic and the pastoral welfare of Irish society, senior executives and staff in a traditional and a recently arrived multi-national, some of the most efficient model farmers in Ireland, pre-labour market second level students completing their final year of the senior cycle, and a cross section of disadvantaged individuals in Irish society such as the homeless, the unemployed and one of the most disadvantaged groups in Europe, Irish Traveller women. Thirdly, the success of the research methodology, adopting as it does a multi-faceted tailor made approach to capture sensitive data about Irish society, is itself an exposé and commentary on the value of personal networking in Irish society and opens a window on the dominance of personal and sectional rather than national economic objectives in Irish life.

If the study proves anything, it is that to avoid falling into the trap of *describing* economic development by substituting a list of contributory causes for an analysis of how it happens, the economic data needs to be forged with an inventive and in-depth application of an array of sociological concepts to tackle the formidable challenges faced by the modern sociologist to adequately explain the underlining developmental dynamic. In other words, a study of this nature cannot be shaped by what we call theoretical cronyism i.e. we do not advance a particular sociological paradigm as a silver bullet to explain such a complex social phenomenon. Even though we reveal that religion and nationalism continue to exert a profound influence in the theatre of global capitalism it must not be assumed that they act out a zero sum game on the capitalist spirit. Each in their own way ebb and flow with the prevailing economic climate.

Furthermore, the study is at pains to avoid generalising from the specific, to avoid an error of logic frequently found in economic discourse. This logic maintains that a generalisation which is by and large true can always be applied to an accidental set of circumstances or that the reverse also holds true in that an accidental case can be presumed to apply to the majority of situations (Copi and Cohen 1998). This generalisation is often manifested by those who confidently continue to rely on mainstream advanced economies as landmarks to shape social and economic theory with the inference that less significant economies will eventually succumb to the conventional wisdom. Since the Celtic Tiger had a true accidental pedigree, it inadvertently provided a heaven sent opportunity, as it was actually happening, to check out the commonsense of some mainstream socio-economic thinking.

Consequently we concentrated our efforts on three research areas. Firstly, how was it possible that the emergence of the Celtic Tiger not only caught off guard every academic and economic commentator, even the government itself, but also flew in the face of well regarded economic developmental theories? Secondly, since the Irish economic disposition was regarded as the chief culprit of poor development in the past, was there now a fundamental shift in that disposition towards actively assisting economic development, providing yet again further confirmation of just another convert to global capitalism? Moreover, would that shift expose what many considered a necessary pre-requisite for development, namely a strong Protestant Ethic. Thirdly, could we rely on the insights of the so-called fathers of sociology namely, Marx, Weber, Durkheim, Freud, Elias, Parsons and Giddens, to make sense of the Celtic Tiger sporting its new economic disposition and if not, were we equipped to take a fresh look at how these insights could be made more relevant and inclusive to accommodate this new reality?

To address the first question, the study set out to trace the origins of the Celtic Tiger over a long-term period of economic development and to isolate recurring or durable patterns of economic behaviour. We then attempted to establish the extent and nature of the impact exerted by these patterns on the dynamic of Irish development before and during the Celtic Tiger. Following this particular line of enquiry then led to some revealing insights into the reasons for Irish society's contradictory choices such as rejecting some institutions like Protestantism while attracting its stable-mate capitalism, creating a compliant workforce as part of a highly competitive environment conducive to the growth of global capitalism, while simultaneously promoting equity as the number one national priority.

As this sociological study was conducted during such a dramatic improvement in Irish economic circumstances, it concurrently provided a golden opportunity to test a long-standing fact about the path of western economic development and Irish development in particular. Many commentators had connected Ireland's consistently poor record of development with Catholic religious beliefs and a colonial history, that made Irish society in general and workers in particular, indifferent at best and inimical at worst to economic development. The most obvious aggregate effect of these beliefs and this history could be seen, as many commentators argued in a general antipathy towards industry and a weak work ethic. The expectation was that when Irish workers would eventually internalise a more secular and acquisitive economic ethic, in other words a Protestant one, significant economic development would inevitably follow. We set out to construct a profile of the Irish economic disposition during this high performing phase of progress and compare the results against these expectations.

Finally, the Celtic Tiger provided one other not to be missed opportunity. We could re-visit and re-examine a largely forgotten and somewhat unfashionable sociological debate concerning the impact of religious beliefs on economic development and litmus test their universal mandate against one manifestation of global capitalism, namely the Celtic Tiger. Ever since Max Weber had isolated the complementarity of Protestantism and capitalism, it has been embedded in almost all sociological thought explaining social and economic progress. The importance of using the Celtic Tiger in this debate should not be underestimated, for as long as countries such as Ireland remained Catholic and poor, these long standing insights on the natural link between the Protestant ethic and capitalist development could not be challenged. However, if Ireland became wealthy while still remaining predominantly Catholic, how secure then would these insights remain? Furthermore, if it could be established that Catholicism was a key influence in shaping progressive socio-economic development before and during the Celtic Tiger, then Marx's economic relations model would also have its work cut out to stay theoretically relevant.

To address these important questions we adopted a fairly straightforward four-step approach. The first was to trace in some detail, the improbable origins of the accidental Celtic Tiger and this is outlined in chapters two, three and four. The second step was to conduct research on a representative mosaic of Irish social life and to construct a profile of the existing Irish economic disposition as it engaged with global capitalism. The results are presented in chapters five and six respectively. The third step tested the robustness of long standing sociological theory by going back to basics to explain the nature of that profile and the result of this approach is provided in chapters seven, eight and nine. Finally some of the universal sociological insights employed in the study were then refined to provide a more inclusive interpretation of the Irish economic disposition. The outcome of this revised interpretation is presented in our final chapter ten Conclusion : A Theory of Limits.

Finally I do hope that some of the ideas presented in this book will shed a little light on one of the most important and complex areas confronting sociology today, namely rising above the descriptive blueprints currently in vogue to explain the process of socio-economic development and to inform industrial policy.

Acknowledgements

This study could not have been completed without the assistance and support of many individuals and organizations and I would like to express my sincere appreciation to all those who have helped in its realization.

In particular my thanks to the Librarian and staff in the National Library Dublin, to the Librarian and staff of the Allen Library and to the Christian Brothers' Community, O'Connell Schools, North Richmond St., Dublin where the Library is housed, to the Librarian and voluntary staff of the Central Catholic Library, Dublin, to the Librarian and staff of the FÁS Technical Library who also processed my many requests for material housed in Trinity College Library, Dublin and the British Library, to the Librarian and staff of the Distance Learning Library at Leicester University and to the Librarian and staff of the Economic and Social Research Institute, Dublin.

For their helpful comments, suggestions and support, my thanks go to Professor David Ashton and to Dr. John Goodwin of the University of Leicester.

I am also greatly indebted to all those who were interviewed and gave so generously of their time when they had so many other pressing engagements. My thanks also to the multi-national companies for giving me access to their employees and treating me with much courtesy.

One could not have hoped to access such a broad and unique range of contributors without special assistance. A sincere thanks therefore go to Gráinne McBride, Aidan Flaherty, Ray Kelly, David O'Carroll, Marie-Therese Byrne, Shay Mulhall, Packenham Pim, Larry Lohan, Jim Bannon, Frank Nugent and Gerry Larkin.

Finally to my family, Gráinne, Caitríona, Brendan, Siobhán and Dylan thanks for your encouragement, patience and support.

Glossary of Terms

Throughout the study a number of terms are used to reflect the complexity of the Island of Ireland since the Island is politically divided into the Republic of Ireland and Northern Ireland. The purpose of the definitions is to describe important aspects of Irish culture, politics, people and events and clarify their application in this study.

The terms Rebellion of 1916, the 1916 Rising and the 1916 Revolution are used interchangeably to denote the insurrection of 1916 planned by the Irish Republican Brotherhood (IRB) which took place on Easter Monday 1916, where one thousand Volunteers and two hundred recruits of the Irish Citizen Army formed the backbone of the nationalist force against British Crown Forces. Padraig Pearse of the Volunteers and James Connolly of the Irish Citizen Army proclaimed an Irish Republic outside the General Post Office in Dublin. The rebellion which lasted from 24 to 29 April 1916 was in military terms a disaster and easily suppressed by British Crown Forces. The rebel leaders were subsequently executed. The 1916 Rising should to be seen in terms of a sacrifice or martyrdom for the nationalist cause and a critical juncture in the eventual attainment of the Irish Free State. It is also referred to as the Easter Rising.

The Anglo Irish War or the War of Independence was fought during the period 1919-1921 by Irish Republican Army (IRA) Volunteers against British Crown Forces. In 1920 the Government of Ireland Act partitioned the island of Ireland. This was followed by the Treaty of 1921 between the Provisional Irish Government and the British Government where partition was accepted by both sides. The Irish Civil War 1922-23 then followed between Old IRA - now incorporated into the new Free State Army who were Pro-Treaty - and IRA Irregulars who were part of a broad Republican front (Sinn Féin) led by Eamon De Valera who were Anti -Treaty.

The Pro-Treaty members of Sinn Féin became the core of Cumann na nGaedheal (Party of the Irish) founded in 1923 and became the government after the 1923 Free State elections. Fine Gael, Ireland's second largest political party was formed in September 1933 following an amalgamation of Cumann na nGaedheal, the Blueshirts and the National Centre Party (Farmers and Ratepayers League) to counteract the rise of Fianna Fáil. Fianna Fáil, (Soldiers of Destiny) was founded in May 1926 when Eamon De Valera withdrew his support for the Anti-Treaty Sinn Féin coalition due to tensions relating to the oath of allegiance to the British Crown given Ireland's dominion status. It quickly established itself in the 1932 Irish Free State elections as Ireland's largest political party, the Republican Party, when it immediately claimed jurisdiction over the entire island of Ireland.

The Irish Free State or Saorstát Éireann as it was known in Irish, was the first name of the Irish State in the period 1922-37 i.e. immediately after independence.

The 1937 Constitution superseded the 1922 Constitution of the Irish Free State, where the title Irish Free State was superseded by Éire (Ireland). It continues to be used today often derisively by both Unionists in Northern Ireland and Republicans in both northern and southern Ireland to refer to the southern Irish State. The name of the state is Éire or in the English language Ireland.

The 1937 Constitution of Ireland under article two defined the national territory as 'The Whole Island of Ireland' but in Article 3, jurisdiction was limited to the twenty six counties of southern Ireland. The southern Irish Government, acknowledged the *de facto* position of Northern Ireland as part of the United Kingdom but did not abandon its *de jure* claim to jurisdiction over Northern Ireland until 2 December 1999 following the coming into force of a referendum on 22 May 1998 simultaneously held in the Republic of Ireland and in Northern Ireland that eventually endorsed the British and Irish Good Friday Agreement.

The expression Republic of Ireland is not mentioned in the 1937 Constitution but in the Republic of Ireland Act 1948, No 22, and was designed to show that the twenty six county Free State had left the British Commonwealth and severed the final link with Britain. Remarkably, the name of the island of Ireland, namely Ireland is also the name of the part that excludes the territory of Northern Ireland. On the international stage such as the EU and UN, Ireland is used to refer to the political entity called the Republic of Ireland. The President of the Republic of Ireland is known as the President of Ireland, the Government as the Government of Ireland and Ambassadors are Ambassadors to Ireland.

In this study Ireland is used to refer to the Republic of Ireland. The terms Republic of Ireland, Northern Ireland, and Free State are used in this study to distinguish or emphasise a particular political entity or economic policy or context in a given era.

Although the term Nation is sometimes taken to mean those living in the Republic *and* in Northern Ireland together - who would then form the Irish nation - in this study the terms Nation and National Identity refer specifically to the Republic of Ireland.

The terms Nationalism and Nationalist are used to denote a political philosophy that declares that national identity is premised on the achievement of a nation state and is traced as a mass movement in Ireland from the 1790s. Irish national identity is characterized by a strong sense of a lost of ancestral rights for a Gaelic tradition to be recovered from British imperialism.

The Irish constitutional nationalist movement enjoyed a close working relationship with the Catholic Church, and Catholicism although rarely acknowledged is still the essence of the Irish nation. Irish nationalism differed from many continental nationalisms in that it did not have a strong basis in either language or culture until the late 1880s when it became associated with Irish cultural revivalism such as the Gaelic language. Irish identity became split into nationalist and unionist and was embodied in the partition of Ireland, i.e. the nationalist twenty six county south and the six county unionist north.

The term Republicanism is used to refer to a rejection of monarchy and aristocracy disseminated by the American and French Revolutions. Republicanism remained a minority force within Irish nationalism. The strong attachment of many Irish republicans to the concept of a republic that embodied an all Ireland rather than a twenty six county territory forced many to choose sides in the Irish Civil War, where the Anti -Treaty forces are identified even to this day as Republicans.

In article twenty-eight of the Constitution, the Taoiseach (Prime Minister) is unequivocally Head of Government, nominates the Tánaiste (see below) and Government Ministers who are then appointed by the President of Ireland on his or her advice and on the approval of Parliament (Dáil).

The Tánaiste is the Deputy Prime Minister under the Constitution of Ireland 1937, taken from Gaelic Ireland where the Tánaiste was designated successor to the king or chief, having been nominated during the Taoiseach's life time. The present Tánaiste is also the Minister for Enterprise, Trade and Employment.

Voting is by a system of single transferable voting where voters allocate their preference for candidates and a quota system determines the seats allocated to a particular constituency so that a single constituency will have representatives of different parties elected. First used in Irish local elections in 1919.

The term Celtic Tiger was first used in 1996 by Kevin Gardner, an economist with London stockbrokers Morgan Stanley Dean Whitter, comparing Ireland's economic performance with that of the Asian Tigers and publicised in Newsweek of 23 December 1996. However, Sweeney (1999) insists that the American David McWilliams was the first economist to coin the phrase Celtic Tiger from the term Asian Tiger which compared the economic turnaround in Ireland to the economic progress that had occurred in Thailand, Malaysia and Hong Kong in the late 1980s and first half of the 1990s. In our study the term Celtic Tiger refers to the economic turnaround and subsequent sustained growth experienced in the economy of the Republic of Ireland from 1993 to mid 2001.

The terms Social Partnership or Social Dialogue or Consensus came to prominence in 1987 when the economy was 'on its knees' and a partnership of interests such as the government, employers, trade unions and farmers negotiated the first Partnership agreement.[1] There have been six agreements to date, namely the Programme for National Recovery (PNR) 1987-1991, the Programme for Economic and Social Progress (PESP) 1991-1994, the Programme for Competitiveness and Work (PCW) 1994-1997, Partnership 2000 1997-2000, the Programme for Prosperity and Fairness (The PPF) 2000-2003 and the sixth

---

[1] At present the partners include the Government, Irish Business and Employers Confederation, the Irish Congress of Trade Unions, Construction Industry Federation, Irish Farmers' Association, Irish Creamery Milk Suppliers' Association, Irish Co-Operative Organisation Society Ltd., Macra na Feirme (Farmers), Irish National Organization for the Unemployed, Congress Centres for the Unemployed, Conference of Religious in Ireland, National Womens' Council of Ireland, National Youth Council of Ireland, Society of St. Vincent de Paul, Protestant Aid, Small Firms Association, Irish Exporters Association, Irish Tourist Industry Confederation, Chambers of Commerce of Ireland, and the Community Platform which itself includes twenty six participant organizations such as the National Traveller Womens' Forum, Simon Communities of Ireland, Womens' Aid, Forum of People with Disabilities, Gay and Lesbian Network, The Irish Commission for Prisoners Overseas.

agreement, Sustaining Progress 2003-2005 which was ratified by the Social Partners in early 2003. The agreements are formulated with the National Economic and Social Councils vision for Ireland as their aim, namely economic inclusion based on full employment, socially sustainable economic development, social inclusion and a commitment to social justice.

References

Casey, J. (1987), *Constitutional Law in Ireland*, Sweet and Maxwell, London, pp. 32-37.

Coakley, J. and Clear, C. (1998), 'Cumman na nGaedheal', and 'Fianna Fáil', S.J. Connolly (ed.), *The Oxford Companion to Irish History*, Oxford University Press, Oxford, p. 130, p. 191, p. 194.

Connolly, S.J. (1998), 'Nationalism', S.J. Connolly (ed.), *The Oxford Companion to Irish History*, Oxford University Press, Oxford, pp. 378-380, p. 533.

Curtis, E. (1995), *A History of Ireland*, Routledge, London, pp. 406-411.

Eaton, G. (1989), *Introducing Ireland - A Critical Guide with Biographies of over 450 Leaders*, Mercier Press, Dublin, p. 2.

Foster, R.F. (1989), *Modern Ireland 1600-1972*, Penguin, London, pp. 511-513.

Garnham, N. (1998), 'Republicanism', S.J. Connolly (ed.), *The Oxford Companion to Irish History*, Oxford University Press, Oxford, p. 483.

Government of Ireland, (1990), *Bunreacht na hÉireann - The Constitution of Ireland*, Government Publications Office, Dublin, pp. 4-56.

Government of Ireland, (2001), *Achievements in Implementation of the Good Friday Agreement - A Paper by the British and Irish Governments*, 14 July 2001, Government Press Office, Dublin.

Government of Ireland, (2003), *Sustaining Progress - Social Partnership Agreement 2003-2005*, Government Publications Office, Dublin.

Leddin, A. and Walsh, B. (1998), *The Macro Economy of Ireland*, Gill and Macmillan, Dublin, p. 27.

Litton, F. (1988), *The Constitution of Ireland 1937-1987*, Institute of Public Administration, Dublin, pp. 5-6, p. 39, p. 63.

McMahon, D. (1998), 'Constitution of Ireland', and 'Taoiseach', in S.J. Connolly (ed.), *The Oxford Companion to Irish History*, Oxford University Press, Oxford, pp. 112-113, p. 534.

Sweeney, A. (1999), *Irrational Exuberance - The Myth of the Celtic Tiger*, Blackhall Publishing, Dublin, p. 60, p. 94, p. 126.

Chapter 1

Introduction

Eire's 3 millions eke out an existence that would be considered
poverty this side of the Irish sea, unlike the English...they don't
normally want more than they have (Ireland in the Thirties -
MovieTone News 1999)

Introduction

While the analysis of the Celtic Tiger was expected to present difficulties from an
economic and historical perspective, an even more formidable challenge arose
given the sociological context of the study. There are two reasons for this. The
first concerns the political complexity of the island of Ireland which now exists as
two distinct yet interrelated societies, one in the north and the other in the south,
each having its own dominant tradition, world view and economic history. Our
study explores the economic disposition of one of these societies, namely the
Republic of Ireland. In order to place our exploration in this specific social
context, it has been necessary to deploy a number of historical, political and
economic backdrops to ground the abstraction of the theoretical analyses of the
economic profile undertaken in later chapters and to provide clarification on the
meaning of culture specific vocabulary used throughout this study, terms for
example such as Éire, Ireland, the Free State and the Celtic Tiger. Therefore a
comprehensive explanation of the many special terms used is provided in the
preface of this book.

The second reason concerns the nature of the sociological forum in Ireland.
According to Brewer (2001) the sociology community in the North and South of
Ireland is very small, parochial in focus, with little inter-university engagement on
the Island in the field of sociology. Apparently the same sociologists appear time
and time again resulting in the failure of sociology to interpret the daily
experiences of people living on the Island of Ireland even though the Northern part
is comparatively speaking the most studied place on earth.

As for the Republic of Ireland, there have been attempts at a sociological
interpretation of Celtic Tiger society such as the 'vox pop' contributions published
in the Sociological Chronicles of Ireland (1995-1996 and 1997-1998) again written
by a small cadre of individuals belonging to one Irish university (Brewer 2001). [1]
While they are good cultural studies featuring some examples of strong

---

[1] A two volume series of unorthodox essays edited by Eamon Slater and Michel Peillon with
an emphasis on understanding contemporary Ireland aimed mainly at the lay reader.

sociological reflection they fail nevertheless to include important sociological dimensions impacting on the topic area. Moreover, the really serious impact of Irish insularity is reflected in the lack of substantive debate on critically important ideologies. Ireland's Marxist historical tradition for example, has been so marginalised and neglected, encountering significant resistance within Irish historiography, that the Irish Marxist-Nationalist debate has prevented generalising models such as those of Wallerstein and Hirst to make *any* impression on Irish historical thinking (Brady 1999). Up to 1990 there was not even *one* successful application of a classical Marxist analysis to *any* component of Irish life (Akenson 1991). Our study will attempt to provide both an interpretation of the daily economic experience of Irish society and achieve it through the application of a number of sociological paradigms and ideologies.

As we will see later, the Irish sociological context is then confronted by a number of anomalies relating to the Tiger status of the modern Irish economy. Consequently, over reliance on some stereotypical views embedded in sociological discourse could easily lead to relatively mis-informed assumptions about Irish socio-economic matters in general and a faulty interpretation of the revealed profile of the Irish economic disposition in particular. An informed evaluation of the arguments and explorations that are presented in the early part of the study is therefore vital in developing an appreciation of the structure of the Irish economic disposition and to make transparent the application of the analyses of it that follow. Consequently the remainder of this introduction and much of the content of the subsequent three chapters are designed to equip the reader with essential data and an overview of important developmental debates to appreciate the Irish political, economic and cultural landscape, providing in genealogical terms, the family tree of the Celtic Tiger. The value of this approach is to reveal, in chapter six, the many elements that make up the Irish economic disposition as a natural outcome of two durable cultural forces shaping Irish socio-economic development.

Some Observations on the Post-Independent Irish Economic Context

In 1922, Ireland became one of the first nations in the twentieth century to secure its independence from a colonial power, Britain (Breen, Hannan, Rothman and Whelan 1990). Since then, the history of its economic performance can be divided into five distinct phases, namely the early period 1922-1939, the war and early post war period 1939-1957, the first recovery period 1958-1969, the set back period 1970-1986 and finally the second recovery period 1987-2001 where the latter includes the Celtic Tiger period from 1993 onwards (Whitaker 2001). The recent second recovery phase can be further sub divided into three periods, namely the upturn from 1987-1990 followed by sluggish growth from 1991-1993 and then a very significant spurt of growth from 1993-1999 (O'Connell 2000). Broadly speaking then, economic performance can be described as poor to the late 1950s, good to the mid 1970s, very poor to the early 1990s and then at last, the arrival of the belated golden age better known as the Celtic Tiger (O'Gráda 1997). This latter era saw a period of accelerated economic convergence where Ireland had finally moved on from centuries of the 'too many workers not enough jobs' dilemma (Duffy, Fitzgerald, Kearney, Hore and MacCoille 2001). The late catching up was due to an uninterrupted forty year strategy of global integration (Nolan, O'Connell and Whelan 2000) and increased educational participation (Nolan, O'Connell and Whelan 2000a).

This belated golden age was also distinguished by exceptionally high levels of economic performance. For example, the year 2000 was not only the seventh successive year of very strong economic growth, with GNP at 8.6 per cent in real terms, (Forfás 2001),[2] but during that period Ireland had the highest consecutive growth rates in all of the EU (Economist Intelligence Unit 2001). At the beginning of 2001 unemployment stood at its lowest level (3.7 per cent) in modern times (Central Statistics Office 2001) and a record trade surplus for the period Jan-Feb 2001 of £IR3,749m (£2,811m sterling) showed an increase of sixty seven per cent over the same period in 2000 (Central Statistics Office 2001a). The period 1994-1998 in particular had seen the most sustained period of rapid economic growth in the last fifty years giving rise to the label the Celtic Tiger (O'Hagan Murphy and Redmond 2000). Moreover, optimistic predictions were continuously made throughout this era about the on-going sustainability of economic development because there were no signs of the underlying growth forces abating, at least in the short term (Govt 2001). The literature was now resplendent with tidings of great joy. Strong competitive forces, and sound fundamentals had been firmly embedded in the economy (OECD 2001).[3]

In fact a good deal of the literature available explaining Irish economic development since independence and later examined in chapter three, stands in marked contrast to the observation of O'Malley (1989) that the Republic of Ireland in terms of either a nineteenth century latecomer or a twentieth century less developed country, had frequently been overlooked by both economists and sociologists. In particular the modernisation and the conflicting dependency approach were particular favourites used to explain economic development-underdevelopment in Ireland. The modernisation theory claimed that changes in the internal value system allowed entrepreneurship to flourish while the dependency theory focussed on the absence of the necessary indigenous capital for development due to colonialism. It is now increasingly obvious that no ideal one way of capitalist development actually exists (Allen 2000).

Moreover, another old chestnut, the regional convergence theory, arguing that free movement of goods and capital would inevitably find its way from the industrialised core to the under industrialised periphery has been found to be

---

[2] Forfás is the Policy and Advisory Board for Industrial Development in Ireland and advises the Minister for Enterprise Trade and Employment on matters relating to development of industry in the State. At present the Minister is also Tánaiste or Deputy Prime Minister.

[3] Despite the downturn in the IT sector in the first half of 2001, the Third Report of the Expert Group on Future Skills Needs in July 2001 was upbeat on the overall underlying strength of the Irish economy noting that employment in IT software in contrast to IT hardware sectors remained particularly strong thus requiring no downward revision of overall IT employment levels for the period 2001-2005.

erroneous. In contrast, Ireland has adapted to external and internal forces by using a mix of liberal and state economic controls, in other words had adopted a country specific rather than a generalised approach (Bradley 2000). Even as Leddin and Walsh (1998) admitted that the theoretical argument and empirical evidence to support convergence theory was rather mixed, they conceded that Ireland appeared to be a good example of a country whose living standards had *somehow* reached similar levels to those in advanced European economies. The implication was pretty clear, they were unsure how this development had occurred.

Yet even where a significant body of hard demographic evidence was gathered it tended, at least on the surface, to provide a strong correlation between poor Irish economic development and the Catholic belief system, yet it was, according to Akenson (1991), gathered by studying first generation ghetto Irish immigrants in Britain, Australia, and the US or other Irish emigrants living overseas but not actually in Ireland. The remarkable fact was, that the Weber-Tawney debate on the central role of religion as the fulcrum in indigenous Irish culture and economic life had started and finished in 1905 due to the sensitivity of the topic area.[4]

Nevertheless, nearly a century later, Garvin (2001) in a potted history of Irish economic development, still pointed to Catholicism as a factor in retarding Irish industrial development noting that Catholicism kept southern Europe poor while Protestantism made northern Europe rich. Even the Catholic theologian Kung (1999) cited Protestant Northern Ireland and the Catholic Republic of Ireland as examples where economic differences were associated with religious differences underlining the observation that poor countries tended to have a distinctly Catholic imprint. The Irish Catholic work ethic that had been attacked by Plunkett in 1905 was still regarded as problematic by Black (1994), who maintained that Irish competitiveness was seriously threatened because of the anti-industrial nature of Irish work values and attitudes, arguing that the Irish work commitment was still weaker than that of workers in Britain. Interestingly this observation was made at the very moment of the birth of the Celtic Tiger.

There are other puzzling labour market indicators surrounding the development of the Celtic Tiger. While it is recognised that there is no one pathway towards industrialisation, the Asian Tiger economies demonstrated that a successful economically integrated skill formation process was pivotal to economic success (Ashton and Sung 2000). Yet the Republic of Ireland lacked this very integration (Goodwin 1997) and the Third Report of the Expert Working Group on Future Skills Needs acknowledged that there still existed the fundamental mismatch

> between education and training sectors' ability to increase the number educated in a short timeframe. (Forfás 2001a: 69)

---

[4] In 1905 Sir Horace Plunkett a Protestant establishment champion of economic development and the Co-operative Movement in Ireland outlined various Irish (meaning Catholic and lazy) cultural practices inhibiting economic development. M. O'Riordan counter-argued against Plunkett's position and according to Akenson 'that was that ever since'.

Not alone was there a skills and educational mis-match but it had actually worsened in Ireland in the period from 1992-2000 while at the same time, the rate of human capital growth actually stagnated when compared to levels recorded in the 1980s giving Ireland the least efficient EU matching of education outputs with labour demand (European Commission 2002). By 2001 Irish firms were still under investing in training when compared to their EU counterparts (Duffy, Fitzgerald, Kearney, Hore and MacCoille 2001).

In fact the Celtic Tiger was characterised by both labour *and* skill shortages (Forfás 2000, Forfás 2001a). Forfás (2001b) also indicated that these labour shortages were a welcome change from previous years, although it had been pointed out that these shortages threatened the Republic's ability to sustain economic growth (FÁS 2000) and skills shortages in particular which became pervasive now posed a real threat to current and future economic development (Irish Competitiveness Council 2000). Furthermore while the potential for skills shortages to compel indigenous and foreign sectors to crowd out each other was very real, the issue still remained unresolved by policy makers (Barry, Bradley and O'Malley 1999).

While Denny, Harmon and O'Connell (2000) offered a suggested rather than a proven correlation between human capital formation, accumulation and economic growth based on US, German and Japanese studies, they nevertheless continued to argue that interventions of education and training underpinned Ireland's recent economic transformation. The Irish Government was also confident that investment in education and training was a primary contributor to the Celtic Tiger (Govt 2000a) and the OECD position was broadly in line with this assessment (OECD 2001). Yet research in this area still lacked a proven empirical correlation between education, training and competitiveness (Ashton and Green 1996), or between training and economic growth (Ashton and Sung 2001), or between the precise contribution human capital can make to economic development (Pissarides 2000, Bassanini and Scarpetta 2001). On top of that, little official data existed on the incidence of training in many Irish companies and even less for assuming a link between company specific training and higher productivity and competitiveness (CEDEFOP 1998).

The fact was, that practically no research existed that quantified the relationship between training and national economic growth and where research did exist, it actually pointed in the opposite direction, i.e. training may be an outcome rather than the cause of higher productivity (Machin and Vignoles 2001). Even overlooking the fact that the objectives for the future development of human capital in the Irish Governments National Development Plan 2000-2006 were not clearly formulated (IMF 2000), the reality was that Ireland had the lowest per cent of second level students in vocational education in the EU and an adult illiteracy rate of twenty five per cent of the adult population (OECD 1999). The assumption of a linkage between education, training and competitiveness should be seen therefore, as an expressed wish by human capital theorists and economists of what *ought* to be the case, in contrast to what business people actually saw as being the real cause of competitive advantage, namely acquisitions and mergers (Coleman and Keep 2001).

However, one atypical characteristic stood out above all others in the Irish socio-economic environment, namely the relatively low levels of secularisation and high levels of Catholic religiosity in Irish society at the very moment when the economy was at its height, even though Weber (1930) had argued that Catholic religious beliefs were the main reason why Catholics failed to develop an ethic conducive to economic development. He identified Protestantism as having this developmental capacity where his term, economic ethic, was defined as the religiously determined impulse to take rational economic action with the notion of salvation having a profound impact on this action (Weber 1969). While the economic ethic was not determined by religion alone, since history and geography also had an important role to play, the religious impact on practical economic behaviour nevertheless remained profound (Weber 1969). So the question that now arose was how could Catholicism co-exist and continue to flourish at the very pinnacle of modern Irish economic development in an era of global capitalism?

Some Observations on Irish Catholicism and Nationalism

The Irish Catholic Church has enjoyed an almost universal mandate actively assisting the new Irish Free State to develop in a Catholic fashion since 1922 and had

> a decisive influence over the hearts and minds of the majority of
> the Irish people…[wielded]…immense influence over not only
> its own flock but also over non adherents. (Morgan and Graham
> 2000: 5)

The Irish Republic remained a society along with Portugal, the least susceptible to secularisation in Western Europe with a Catholic affiliation rate of ninety one per cent (Corish 1996) on the eve of the birth of the Celtic Tiger. From 1891 to 1991 the Irish Roman Catholic population actually increased from eighty nine to ninety two per cent (Redmond and Heanue 2000). At the time of the demise of Celtic Tiger in 2002, while Catholic affiliation rates had decreased only marginally to just below ninety per cent of the population numbers actually increased by approximately one quarter of a million (Central Statistics Office 2003).

However, it would be a mistake to rely on rates of affiliation as the sole measure of religious commitment. Religious commitment has five dimensions, namely belief or holding a particular theological outlook which is the most important, followed by practice or religious rites and devotional acts, then experience or the feeling of communication with a divine essence, followed by knowledge or information on central tenets, and finally consequences or the impact of religious beliefs in everyday affairs (Stark and Glock 1969). Our study of course, has a particular interest in the first and fifth dimensions i.e. belief and its impact on everyday economic affairs.

In Ireland, the first two dimensions, belief and practice, remain quite strong although O'Toole (2000) argued that an increase in secularisation in Ireland had inevitably weakened religious attachment to the idea of summary justice at the end of life, namely Heaven or Hell. While the increase in secularisation was caused by instrumental rationality spilling over from industrial capitalism into all areas of Irish life, religious practice still remained extraordinarily high (Breen, Hannan, Rothman and Whelan 1990).

Whyte (1980) argued at the time that Ireland has an unusually high number of committed and practising Catholics and over a decade later, Hussey (1993) contended that as eighty two per cent of the Catholic population went to Mass once a week, it made them the most orthodox community in the western world. This level of Irish adherence was notable even by European standards (Connolly 1994) and the strength of the orthodoxy of Irish Catholics was beyond dispute (Nic Ghiolla Phádraig 1995, Humphreys 1997). Although Pope John Paul II acknowledged the low attendance at Mass in some Catholic countries, particularly at lower and upper social strata (Reuters 1998), there was ample evidence to maintain that religious values still occupied a central position in Irish society (Whelan 1994, Humphreys 1997, Conway 1998). The Bishop of Ferns Brendan Comiskey (1998) was confident that although religious practice has diminished, religious belief had remained secure.

For example, a study presented by pupils of Newtown School, County Waterford in the south east of Ireland, in the January 2000 ESAT Young Scientist of the Year Exhibition, indicated that between eighty and one hundred per cent of young people sampled between fourteen and sixteen years, attended religious service at least twice a month (Ahlstrom 2000). Although Donnelly (2000) argued that the Catholic Church in Ireland may have lost some moral credibility, with its political influence reaching its lowest level since the Famine of 1847, and despite the combined effects of materialism and clerical sex scandals revealed in the 1990s, more than two thirds of the population still attended Mass at least once a week, a remarkably high figure at the end of the millennium. Not only was there still a high level of confidence (seventy seven per cent) in the Irish Catholic Church but the most popular political parties with young people were the nationalist and republican parties of Fianna Fáil and Sinn Féin indicating the durability of a strong traditional Catholic *and* nationalist identity during the Celtic Tiger (O'Toole 2001).

Moreover, the nationalist sentiment was following an ever-present pattern. A three hundred year old tradition of nationalism in Ireland has continued very strong and durable (Cronin 1999). Nationalism, however, remains an ill-defined concept and does not easily lend itself to definition since it is a vision that mobilises an attachment of the majority to a particular imagined community, a feeling of a common heritage, an ethnic identification with a nation state (Hagendoorn and Pepels 2000). Nationalism is a programme of action built on the premise that national consciousness, a feeling of belonging to a particular nationality, only finds its true expression in the creation of a nation state (Connolly 1998). Moreover Ignatieff (2001) argued that identity only works when institutions such as education and religion collaborate to enable society to imagine a shared identity.

Yet the remarkable fact is, that while there are at least nine academic disciplines that develop theories of nationalism and nation states (Treanor 1997), sociology never actually developed an explicit theory of nationalism nor was nationalism central to the sociologies of either Marx, Weber or Durkheim (McCrone and Kiely 2000). While it is almost impossible to pin down any 'ism', colonialism and imperialism being difficult enough and nationalism particularly so, the tendency of Irish nationalism, namely political unity on the basis of nationality, to be almost exclusively directed against the forcible subjugation to or alliance with a stronger nation, namely imperialist Britain, gave the Irish nationalist independent intention its imprint and identified the act of subjugation by Britain as both colonialism and imperialism (Hobson 1988).

The durability of central Catholic beliefs is as marked as nationalist sentiment. In the early stages of the Celtic Tiger, Belief in God was measured at ninety eight per cent for Irish society and eighty nine per cent for British society (Whelan 1994). In the US the comparable figure was eighty per cent (Cox 1996). Belief in Heaven at eighty eight per cent for Irish Society can also be compared to the seventy five per cent level for Britain (Whelan 1994) and to the seventy one per cent level for the US (Fenwick 1996). Even as belief levels fall, it is important to remember that these lower figures tend to reflect an un-churched rather than a secular country (Davie 2000). Even where the figures indicate a rise in secularisation, Hamilton (1995) warned against equating the rise to the absence of religious commitment because even with low attendance levels, belief in the supernatural remains high.

In any event, secularisation is a self-limiting process and religion continues to be of central importance for individuals since only religion and not science can give meaning to life (Hamilton 1995). Even prominent members of the American and British scientific community are now beginning to question the validity of their own scientific claims to explain the natural world.[5] Not alone are they moving away from atheism, stating that physics is nowhere near explaining everything, they also note that these disciplines seem to get stuck explaining the origins of their own natural laws and so it now seems very plausible that the constant laws of nature could only have been fixed by God, the so called third explanation (Channel 4 2001).

Even when the numbers of conventional active Christians diminish, simple faith groups tend to flourish in their place (Foskett 1996). The relatively lower levels of institutional affiliation to Catholic and Anglican Churches for example, must be seen in the context of *increased* religious beliefs without belonging (Flanagan 2001).

In Ireland, Catholic religious beliefs have endured over recent decades. For example, in a 1962 survey of the attitudes of Dublin Catholics towards religion, ninety per cent of the sample endorsed the view that the Catholic Church was the greatest force for good in Irish society and today the Irish are still a religious and quite nationalistic people (Garvin 2000). Hornsby-Smith and Whelan (1994) later pointed out that there had been little change in traditional Christian values in or the religiosity of, Irish society. In the results of both the European Values Studies in

---

[5] Most notably J. Polkinghorn Professor of Theoretical Physics and Theology, Cambridge University, also R. Penrose, F. Tipler, P. Davies and N. Turok.

1981 and 1990 together with the 1991 and 1998 International Social Survey Programme 'Survey on Religion in Twenty Five European Countries', it has emerged that not only is there little if any change in basic religious beliefs in Ireland, with daily decisions still infused with religious considerations, but even more remarkable is the fact that the youngest cohort surveyed, namely those born after 1970, showed the strongest Catholic beliefs and identity and were therefore rightly regarded as the most Catholic of all cohorts surveyed (Greeley and Ward 2000).

The Second Social Survey Programme results which showed levels of belief in God at ninety four per cent and in Heaven at eighty five per cent – marginally less than the levels observed in Irish society in 1991 – also revealed that Ireland still had the highest Mass attendance levels anywhere in Europe (Greeley and Ward 2000). Most important of all was that it provided critical sociological analysis to disprove the common sense argument that the Celtic Tiger has transformed Irish society into a secular, materialist, consumer oriented and neo-pagan country when in fact the opposite was actually the case (Greeley and Ward 2000). The Census undertaken in 2002 confirmed that Catholic affiliation rates were still remarkably high at eighty eight per cent of the population. In fact the number of Catholics from beginning to end of the Celtic Tiger era had actually increased by over seven per cent, although the population increased at a higher eleven per cent rate thus giving the minus three per cent lower affiliation rate when compared to the 1991 rate (Central Statistics Office 2003). That Ireland remained the worlds most traditional rich country having one of the least secular societies was also confirmed with the publication of Michigan University's Third World Values Survey in January 2003. The most important component of that traditionalism was the influence of religion in peoples lives. The reality is that Irish people under twenty years of age who grew up amidst the affluence of the Celtic Tiger did not see economic growth as the be all and end all of their lives (Valarasan-Twoomey 1998).

These last observations are an important addition to the debate on the sociology of religion since Wilson (1969) argued that the significance of secularisation is that it provides de facto evidence that society does not now derive its values from religious preconceptions. Secularisation is not a harmonised model capable of cross cultural application in any age but is a historical process that ebbs and flows depending on other socio-cultural factors (Robinson 1999). As very few Christians regard secularisation as anything other than the diminution of religious commitment in favour of the secular (Parsons 1999a), it is not sustainable to hold that Ireland was a secular society during the Celtic Tiger. The fact is that even where a country's culture has become secularised, society's religious faith can actually become stronger (Mac Réamoinn 2000). Therefore, if a society's faith in central religious teachings makes them religious, then the Irish were still the least secularised and most religious nation in Europe (Greeley and Ward 2000). For example, religious pre-conceptions continued to infuse and dominate Irish education providing a clear example of the strength of Irish religious commitment (Clancy 1995). Even though weekly attendance at Mass had in modern times declined to fifty five per cent, there was still considerable institutional church power particularly in the educational development of the young (Allen 2000).

Moreover, Catholic beliefs inculcate a particular worldview towards economic matters and Catholic Social Teaching (CST) provides guidelines for economic engagement. According to Herr (1991), while CST declares that Catholics are duty bound to collaborate in economic development, there is no such thing as a Catholic economic blueprint. The emphasis in CST is on the development of the person who should be at the core of all economic activity, thereby necessarily dictating that labour is pre-eminent in any economic order. A social market economy where there is co-operation between capital and labour and where the needs and dignity of the individual worker remain paramount, is the preferred model that comes very close to the Catholic ideal (Herr 1991).

Catholicism has a different economic worldview to other non-Catholic but Christian Churches, and in particular Protestantism. For example the Catholic God is seen in everything (sacramental), and the material world is used (meditative) to bring about the unity of mankind (communion) where the use of reason is analogical i.e. the knowledge of God is achieved through the knowledge and experience of the created world (McBrien 1994). One particular aspect, that of Catholic charity, has been defined as a habit, desire or act of relieving the physical, mental, moral or spiritual stress of anybody without recompense, the motive being the love of God although seeking spiritual benefits from the act by the giver is a legitimate albeit second level form of charity (Ryan 1908). Catholic doctrine defines charity (good works being practical evidence of charity) as *the* substance of faith i.e. a manifestation of the love of God and one's neighbour and a sure way of securing salvation, whereas Protestant doctrine emphasised that charity contributed nothing to those who gave since they are already saved or doomed and therefore, according to Moehler (1894), good works and charity only secure a temporal advantage for the receiver and nothing for the Protestant giver.

While charity is a also central precept in Islam and its practice almost guarantees salvation (Cantor 1993), Catholic charity remained a superior form as Islamic charity (almsgiving) excluded non believers. Ryan (1908) also argued that charity in the Jewish religion only applied to Jews or their friends and in Buddhism one is exhorted not to hate enemies rather than to love them, thus establishing the inclusiveness and superiority of the Catholic version. He goes on to argue that the advent of Protestantism and political economy where compulsory self-reliance was seen as the key to developing the will for self support together with the increase in materialism, combined to almost destroy the Spirit of Charity throughout Europe (Ryan 1908). Originally the Spirit of Charity, which infused the newly developing economic life of Western Europe around the year 1000 based on money exchange, was the cornerstone of the Christian business ethic and this moral philosophy understood the poor as *helpless* victims of economic processes and therefore required assistance (charity) for the love of God (Duby 1974). The Spirit of

Charity was the unifying link between the realm of the religious life and the individual's involvement in this world (Peschke 1997).[6]

The importance of the Protestant notion of *conditional* charity is that it is calculated to promote a strong Protestant work ethic and industrialism and must be contrasted with the *unconditional* notion of charity that had existed in Irish Catholic culture and in particular among the poor (McHugh 1998). Catholic charity is distinguished by a detached love of one's neighbour so that everybody, irrespective of status is entitled to charitable thoughts and action, requiring no reciprocity and based on need and it is this use of preference of need which constitutes the proof of the love of God (Peschke 1997). In other words, the greater the need of one's neighbour the higher their preference rating for charitable intervention, although neglecting oneself in doing so is not permitted as it must be based on the individuals capacity to contribute.

Some Sociological Observations and this Study

In his review of the development of social science in Britain, Giddens (1996c) asserted that the great anthropologists of the nineteenth century never studied internal colonisation in Britain i.e. they never studied the Irish, Scots or Welsh, only cultures in distant lands. Furthermore most sociological thought is written on

> the side of the Protestants and Whigs rather than Catholics…to emphasise progress in the past and thus produce a story that glorifies the present. (Buxton 1985: 21)

Hickman (1995) maintained that Whiggism established the irrefutable link between progress and prosperity with Protestantism while according to Brady (1999) it also highlighted the natural or Providential nature of English progress towards this prosperity. So while there are numerous historical accounts of the Irish diaspora in Britain, little is known about their everyday experience in British society (Delaney 2000). It is also a remarkable fact that the historical study of emigration from Ireland to Britain and America in the twentieth century has remained largely 'terra incognita' despite the sheer scale of the movement (Delaney 2001). Even with a profusion of historical interest in recent times, the Irish were still a relatively little known ethnic group in British society (MacRaild 1999). Although they are the largest census defined ethnic minority in Britain, just ahead of the Indian population who number over eight hundred thousand, again little research has been conducted on the experiences of Irish born people living in Britain (Winston 2000).

Moreover, there appeared to be an understanding among many sociologists that the Irish had become naturally assimilated into British society because of their

---

[6] This is the very sentiment that we are seeking to measure through our own research. We are not stating that Irish society gives all of its possessions away but that it has developed a sense of the psychological and spiritual value of embracing a spirit of charity that works against the strengthening of the acquisitive impulse.

whiteness and were consequently 'airbrushed' out of the sociology of ethnicity at both the epistemological and policy level leaving just one published sociological text on the Irish in Britain in 1995 (Hickman 1995). Nor was this airbrushing confined solely to British commentaries. In a recently published text on European nationalism by European sociologists and political scientists, sixteen nations are examined including the four countries of Great Britain – England, Scotland, Wales and Northern Ireland. Yet the Republic of Ireland, one of the first colonised nations to achieve its independence in the twentieth century and from Great Britain, is nevertheless, overlooked by all twenty six contributors.[7]

In an industrial sense too the Irish were portrayed until very recently as possibly the greatest nuisance, so much so that in Victorian times the words slum and Irish were virtually interchangeable (MacRaild 1999). As history is written from the perspective of the victors and the strong, and the view of the defeated is seldom if ever included (Elias 1997), colonial countries such as Ireland where religion was central were often regarded as peripheral and marginal to the great industrial centres such as Britain and the US (Gilsenan 1982). The need therefore to proceed with caution in undertaking our sociological study was guided by the advice of Akenson (1991) who strongly recommended that in any study of Ireland and its religion, one should collect from as wide an evidentiary basis as possible because Ireland had probably the western world's most religiously sensitised society. The advice too by Fromm (1974), who argued that it is more appropriate when researching social issues involving human beings to use real situations rather than create an artificial environment is also reflected in the breadth of the research sample used. One of the main reasons for this sensitivity towards religion is that together with nationalism it forms one of the twin pillars of Irish identity, being

> the most conspicuously successful fusion of faith and identity
> anywhere in the British Isles…became deeply embedded in the
> social, political and cultural fabric of society and in the first half
> of the twentieth century was simply the worlds most devoutly
> Catholic country. (Hempton 1996: 72, 91, 143)

Hempton (1996) goes on to point out that the strength of this fusion not only weakened the impact of secularisation but actually strengthened Catholicism in the midst of rapid economic and social change and as a consequence, Irish identity can only be properly analysed with reference to religion.

It is a curious fact therefore, that the curricula of most sociology courses present religion as part of something else, such as the problem of secularisation or as part of the classical sociological heritage of Durkheim, Weber and Marx rather than holistically with its theology placed in a socio-cultural context (Flanagan 2001). Even a giant of sociology Norbert Elias, overlooked religious culture and

---

[7] See Cinnirella, M. (2000), 'A History of Four Nations' Louk Hagendoorn and György Csepeli and Henk Dekker and Russell Farnen (eds.), *European Nations and Nationalism*, Research and Migration and Ethnic Relations Series, Ashgate, Aldershot. Only the Northern Ireland 'Troubles' are briefly discussed.

Roman Catholicism in his study of the civilising process and in particular how Christianity shaped conscience in the history of western culture (Turner 1999). Moreover, the limitations of economics as a science alone to explain economic development in Ireland has been finally acknowledged with the result that the socio-cultural context in which this development occurs was only now beginning to be regarded as vital to the success or failure to generate the necessary growth (Fitzgerald 2000). In other words, country specific national sentiments such as religion and nationalism are re-emerging as important factors in modern economic development.

A unique study by Greenwood (2001) goes even further and equates the spirit of capitalism with the force and nature of a country's nationalism. In her study, she argued for example, that English nationalism evoked the idea that prosperity and economic growth were distinguishing features of the English nation and in the process wealth and those occupations pursuing profit were elevated to a pre-eminent place of honour in English consciousness. Prosperity was seen as a positive thing and this in turn committed the nation to constant growth because nationalism freed English society from the traditional ideological structures that inhibited economic development such as Christianity (Catholicism). Greenwood also argued very effectively that nationalism explained the economic development process of Germany, France, Holland, the US and Japan and because she avoids describing the conditions in favour of analysing the process of development with reference to the temper of each country's nationalism her contribution is all the more robust.

Our study on the other hand takes a completely different perspective. It is not a nationalism defined by some of the worlds leading economic and military nations nor is it distinguished by a strong imperial orientation, but from the vantage point of a small open economy that found itself, as it were, on the wrong end of the imperial sceptre. In fact the impact of English economic nationalism on Irish economic development was inextricably linked to the development of an Irish economic consciousness that defined itself by the very absence of both the capitalist spirit and material prosperity in marked contrast to those nation states examined by Greenwood.

A number of important sociological considerations now emerge. Firstly, Collingwood (1999) argued that there is no set of initial conditions which in themselves are sufficient to produce or cause a particular event but there is a certain regularity to patterns of behaviour or thought processes manifested in the basic concepts and conventions to which a society conforms and automatically follows as it attempts to make sense of its experiences and knowledge. Billington Hockey and Strawbridge (1998) call these patterns a durée or a structured and continuous flow of conduct that both reproduces and changes society. The commitment or compulsion to conform to these patterns comes with the territory of understanding within a particular discourse.

Collingwood called these durées, Absolute Pre-suppositions, themselves subject to modification but are never annihilated or eliminated. Even though economic development may signal a move from absolute to rational norms, the broad cultural heritage of a society such as its religion leaves an indelible mark on core values that endure despite the force of modernisation (Inglehart and Baker 2000). Even today, many economists still continue to underestimate the influence of faith on the way American society uses money and wealth (Wuthnow 1993) and this is an important oversight because the primary purpose of the Pre-supposition, religion, is to perpetuate behavioural and thought patterns expressed as core values, which then form the basis of a society's thought patterns (Collingwood 1999).

Moreover, the Irish Absolute Pre-suppositions of religion and nationalism (macro level) seem to be immune to change whereas the political elites (Meso level) and institutional arrangements such as education (Micro level) are more susceptible (Fitzgerald and Girvin 2000). The relationship between the three different levels of cultural values and economic opportunity is complex and it this interaction that gives a particular economic dynamic to society.

More importantly it is not fully understood exactly what effect the immunity enjoyed by these macro level Absolute Pre-suppositions has on economic activity (Fitzgerald and Girvin 2000). Trying to determine the effect of the national Absolute Pre-suppositions is further complicated because Swanson (1969) argued that each individual is also characterised by enduring values or dispositions that silently determine many of his/her activities including the economic and that religion is one of the most important of these values. Therefore, the Catholic religion, from the standpoint of our study remains doubly important, since it can exhibit parallel normative forces working on the economic behaviour at both the individual and national levels.

Secondly, it should be remembered that while Weber was clear about the negative impact of Catholicism on economic development, he and a number of other classical sociologists were not value neutral commentators on religion. For example, the founders of modern sociology, Freud, Durkheim and Weber were religious disbelievers, while Durkheim was a non practising Jew and regarded himself as belonging to the anti-clerical left in France (Parsons 1999a).[8] Weber, Marx and Durkheim treated religion as an illusion and wrong when measured against objective scientific criteria, but it is now evident that both the theological and subjective basis of religious beliefs as embodied in everyday action still remains a substantial sociological force within post modernity and requires further analysis and consideration (Flanagan 2001). Moreover, Freud (1991g) admitted that he could not understand the power of religious feelings and the human's natural aversion to work. Because contemporary sociology has inherited a reductionist framework i.e. religion is perceived as some other phenomenon, such as an ideology to validate class relations for Marx, or as an obsessional neurosis for Freud or as a form of self worship by society for Durkheim, the net result is that the sociology of religion is now regarded as a backwater to main stream sociology, presented as an epiphenomenon, an effect rather than a cause and almost devoid of independent impact (Aldridge 2000).

Thirdly, one notable consequence of this relegated role is that nothing is allowed to count against the secularisation thesis as it dogmatically withstands any

---

[8] Freud's contribution to the sociology of religion is acknowledged by both Robert Bocock and George Ritzer.

evidence to the contrary (Aldridge 2000). Sociologists, therefore, have failed to address the proposition that some generalised behavioural patterns in society, including economic ones, can be based on religious authorisations adopted by an individual. This fairly straightforward notion is not altogether easily perceived in a typical Western setting and as a consequence, much sociological theory organised to explain the interrelationships between different institutions such as the economy and religion has become fractured (Huff 1993). For example, Weber's insight into the relationship of the rise of capitalism in the West with the development of rational and ethical action by individuals is clouded by the absence of a definition of rationality and by his use of this concept as both cause and effect (Crone 1999).

Added to that we now have considerable disagreement among sociologists on sociological definitions, the basic tools of the trade as it were. For example, the terms, parts and relationship of parts in the discourse on social structure and the subjective-objective debate concerning the power of the individual (subject) to act on social structures (object) or visa versa, remains problematical (Mouzelis 2000). In the debate on the source of agency, Ritzer (1988) uses Weigert's definition of ethonomethodology to describe how society comes about by the practical action of rational people, whereas Craib (1992) identified in Althusserian social theory, the opposite cause whereby society is accomplished by individuals who are worked like puppets. Furthermore, if we take the so-called war of paradigms in the 1960s and 1970s that directly challenged Parson's functionalist and positivistic approach, the effect in the 1980s and 1990s was to compartmentalise sociology into discrete paradigms such as neo-marxism, non-conflict marxism, structuralism, and ethnomethodology, with each of course claiming absolute validity (Mouzelis 2000). A good example is reflected in the title of Arnason's (1997) 'Figurational Sociology as a Counter-Paradigm'. Other approaches such as Giddens' structuration theory (duality instead of dualism) then attempted to transcend the subjectivism-objectivism split in the social sciences (Mouzelis 2000).

Fourthly, the language, ideas and insights of sociology embedded a singularly masculine perspective on actors, events and ideas and then only discovered later that this discriminating approach had not been adequately addressed in the sociological literature so that women's disposition and identity required an array of new sociological concepts (Giddens 1997). In fact Siltanen and Stanworth (1984) had earlier pointed out that sociology contained a number of analytical weaknesses in this regard including the perception that most women can be classified as being more or less mindless matrons. Attempts to redress the sociological imbalance in advancing women's perspectives and insights still had to overcome the so-called standard of objectivity which had given rise to criticism of feminist sociological writing as narrative that is committed and well meaning but still showing weak objectivity (Elias and Dunning 1986). Goodwin (1999) then concluded that the gender argument had gone too far and had fallen into the trap of creating a sociological imbalance of the opposite kind, since an adequate analysis of men was a very rare topic in modern empirical gender-based sociology.

Although it may appear that we have been sidetracked with an equality debate, it is highly significant for our study of the Irish economic disposition. The embedded discrimination against one social group, in this case women, exposes the real nature of so-called common sense and well regarded Protestant economic developmental models (Leacock 1986). These models are by and large based on the subservience of women within the prevailing socio-economic order and, to counter it Leacock (1986) calls for a more substantial analysis of these models because

> a certain image of development in Europe as governed by the rational and scientific attitudes embodied in the Protestant ethic has been widely promulgated, along with the essentially racist inference that the central problem in a nation's development lies in achieving Western standards of scientific and technical knowledge and skill. (Leacock 1986: 224, 225)

We will be well rewarded indeed if this study is regarded as a small contribution in support of Leacock's call for this type of analytical approach.

Fifthly, social science theory is packed with ideology (Gulalp 1983). For example at a national level in relation to the two Ireland's, north and south, the concerns of social science are inextricably enmeshed in partisanship, with academics refusing to acknowledge the fact that truth not only becomes distorted but actively reconstructed (Coughlan 1994). On a global level, it appears that industrially advanced states are somehow more acceptable for sociological enquiry than peripheral ones such as Ireland. For example, Giddens (1987) defined sociology as that branch of social science that studied advanced or modern societies. Kilminister (1987) also contended that the emergence of Norbert Elias was also dependent on the advance of sociology in advanced countries. Even Elias and Scotson (1965) had already noticed that there was a general tendency within sociological studies, rightly or wrongly, to regard major societies as sociologically superior, more significant and more worthwhile than minority ones.

In the case of Ireland for example, Giddens (1996c) asserted that most authors overlooked an examination of internal colonialism within Britain itself, in favour of the study of colonised peoples in *distant* lands with the result that the Irish were simply regarded as British. The result of this, according to Littlewood (1996), has seen the categorisation of the Irish as a subdominant group in Western society and therefore open to forms of idiosyncratic communication due to the fact that life for subdominant groups is lived in a dual sense i.e. separate but within a dominant order. It is not surprising when Winston (2000) argued that Irish people placed a negative value on their Irishness and regarded their identity as peripheral and insignificant when interacting with more powerful ethnic groups such as the English. If that is the case, then attempts to explain sociological processes within so-called subdominant cultures may be fatally weakened by relying solely on taken for granted sociological concepts and terms which have evolved from studies of dominant and sociologically more 'worthy' societies.

Finally, the western fashion of segregating concepts into rational entities such as individual, state, society, self, that suit western sociological paradigms are almost useless to explain some equally significant cultures such as non western Islamic societies (Esmail 1996). In these societies, there is little or no dichotomy between matter and spirit and where the role of sacred imagination must be taken into account when studying the human condition instead of relying solely on narrow rationalism (Esmail 1996). The almost total reliance on these concepts is greatly aided and abetted by proscribing the pronoun 'I'. As social scientists naively accepted that their primary function was to follow the natural sciences and discover laws rather than generate meaning (Giddens 1996e), the convention of not using 'I' in sociological writing still remains paramount because it is perceived as personal and subjective. This has had the effect of turning reality into abstraction with the result that insightful issues disclosed in the study of the human condition, mainly in the interpretation of private lives, are rendered inferior and almost useless in sociological discourse (Ribbens 1993). Not only can the use of 'I' assist greatly with the individual's understanding of empirical reality (McGettigan 1999) but reliance on the objectivity benchmark can actually prevent the truth from being fully revealed since Fulford (1996) argued that the most objective of scientists, physicists, have all but rejected the exclusive positivist account of science as it prevents the emergence of the truth. So what then about a social scientific study into a deeply personal, private and subjective a matter as the individuals religious beliefs?

It should come as no surprise to learn that sociology finds great difficulty in devising a comprehensive definition of religion based on a single concept that tells us what religion is or what it does (Hamilton 1995). Definitions invariably create and set within the presented definition an agenda to establish pre-determined results in an empirical manner only (Hamilton 1995). This implies that what can be observed i.e. empirical data, is the only *true* measure of religiosity. Yet there can be no single agreed definition of religion because it constitutes a whole complexus of attitudes, emotions, beliefs and rituals by which we express our fundamental relationship with Reality or God and even though religion is an explicit manifestation of faith, it should be remembered that an implicit faith alone is enough to secure salvation (McBrien 1994). Consequently, sole reliance on empirical evidence i.e. numbers attending rituals of religion, could easily undervalue the depth of religious belief. Hamilton (1995) argued, that because religion was still used by people to give meaning to their lives and more especially in today's modern industrial society, scepticism regarding individual religious truths has not been able to completely anaesthetise the uncomfortable question relating to the existence or non-existence of a life after death. As a matter of *social fact* it is something that still continues to elude science.

The sociological guidelines used for presenting this study of the Irish economic disposition are based on Durkheim's (1964) insight that we need to build up an incremental and evolutionary picture of the linkages between economic and religious values

> Every time we undertake to explain something human taken at a given moment in history, be it a religious belief...or an economic system it is necessary to commence by going back to its most simple form...show how it developed and became complicated little by little and how it became that which it is at the moment in question. (Durkheim 1964: 3)

The whole study is therefore constructed around using this incremental approach. Therefore, as a single perspective such as the utilitarian theory of action is incapable of enabling us to understand the evolution of economic attitudes (Schlucter 1999), we employ a multi-dimensional approach both in our methodology and in the application of the theory to the research findings.

The study is organised under four themes, namely the economy, the profile of the economic disposition, the analyses of that disposition and finally the presentation of new sociological insights. More specifically chapter two provides background information on the Republic of Ireland, including physical features, population, constitution and government. Also provided is an economic overview of the Celtic Tiger using key indicators, and highlights of labour market developments and trends supported with relevant demographic data.

The development of the Irish economy is then placed in an historical context where we examine trends over a one hundred and fifty year period 1845-1995 that alerted us to three interlinked external events that have shaped both the definition of and subsequent response to Ireland's economic problems in the twentieth century and stamped their imprint on the nature and dynamic of the Irish economic disposition. Chapter three follows with an exploration and discussion of economic benchmarks to validate the Tiger status of the Irish economy. Theme one then concludes with a detailed analysis in chapter four of the debates, theories and models of Irish economic growth since independence.

The second theme opens in chapter five with an outline of the rationale for the research together with a description of the sample and a discussion of the methodological approach used. The approach was based on using an amalgam of interview methods in order to capture a set of views that would accurately reflect the mosaic that is Irish social life in the Celtic Tiger. The sample is made up of four domains or groupings of respondents each displaying a profile of typicality. In chapter six, we provide a summary and analysis of the main themes emerging from the contributions of each domain and these findings then inform the profile of the Irish economic disposition presented towards the end of the chapter.

The third theme is organised into three chapters where an array of sociological insights are deployed to explain the elements making up the profile of the Irish economic disposition. Our strategy was to employ whatever suite of insights that could potentially unravel the various complex configurations between religious beliefs and economic behaviour. Consequently, in chapter seven, Marx's concept of historical materialism, the economic relations model, is used as the main analytical tool to explore the role of religious and nationalist sentiment in shaping the Irish economic disposition. Then in chapter eight, an alternative to the so-called static Marxist economic relations model is used, namely Norbert Elias' figurational sociology. Here the emphasis is on pinpointing the changing dynamics inherent in the interdependent relationship of the Irish nation with Britain, its subsequent impact on Irish national consciousness and on the emergence of the Irish economic disposition that reflected this nationalist identity.

The final chapter nine employs a range of related classical and modern sociological insights in five sub sections, each contributing a specialised and complementary understanding of the impact of religion on the economic order. In section one, Weber's insights into the different economic outcomes induced by different world religions are explored. A comprehensive definition of and discussion on the Protestant Work Ethic is presented and his contention that Catholicism and industrial development remain incompatible is also addressed. In section two, a number of Freudian observations reveal how an economically repressive spirit can develop within the individual as a result of established sexual mores and we explore the consequences for the development of a capitalist economic disposition. The third section explores some of the insights of Durkheim regarding the role of religion in society and the potential to create happiness-unhappiness when it confronts the economic order particularly in periods of strong economic growth. Section four includes a number of key insights from Talcott Parsons to enable us explore the effects that norms and value systems such as religion can have on the individual's economic orientation. Finally, Giddens' structuration framework is discussed in section five as we explore the capability of individuals to knowingly take certain courses of action characteristic of their economic behaviour.

Our conclusions, presented under theme four in the final chapter ten, Conclusion : A Theory of Limits, are informed by both the strengths *and* weaknesses of the array of sociological insights employed in previous chapters as we attempt to make sense of the apparent contradiction inherent in the co-existence of low levels of secularisation and very high levels of economic development. An important contribution to this discussion comes from the study of Bertram Hutchinson (1964), who argued that the Irish economic disposition was inherently inimical to rational economic development. We present a new interpretation of his evidence.

Conclusion

This introductory section has defined the aims of the study, explored the Irish sociological context in which this study is placed, provided an overview of the broad phases of economic development since independence and discussed the nature of Irish Catholicism and Nationalism. The important but relatively unknown impact of Absolute Pre-suppositions in shaping the economic disposition was highlighted as a key area for our study. The move from suspecting to quantifying this impact now starts in earnest when in the next chapter we provide general background information on Ireland and place the development of the Irish economy in its historical context. This provides a strong platform to validate the Tiger status of the economy and conduct an assessment of the causes surrounding the developmental path taken by the economy that are presented in chapters two, three and four.

Chapter 2

Ireland in Profile :
An Improbable Tiger Habitat

Introduction

If the aim of much of theme one is to provide a socio-economic profile of Ireland, trace longer term patterns in Irish economic development and establish the origins and credentials of the Celtic Tiger, then chapter two makes a threefold contribution to this aim. Firstly, it acts as a fast track induction into the Irish socio-economic context by informing the reader of the main features of modern Irish political, demographic and economic life. Secondly, as it provides a brief but succinct outline of the main trends in Irish economic activity from the middle of the nineteenth century up to the new millennium, it reveals the improbable origins for the emergence of the Celtic Tiger. Finally it equips the reader to make an informed evaluation of the arguments presented later in chapter three when we examine the claim to Tiger status of the Irish economy and in chapter four when we determine the validity of the accidental nature of the Celtic Tiger.

Physical Features, Population and Literature

Ireland is a island lying on the western periphery of Europe located next to the UK and has a total area of eighty five thousand square kilometers with a central lowland and coastal mountains of which Carrantouhill in County Kerry in the southwest of the country, is the highest measuring approximately one thousand metres. Ireland is three fifths the size of England or in American terms four times the size of Massachusetts (Bottigheimer 1982) and is over one hundred and twenty times the size of another former British colony, the Asian Tiger, Singapore. Due to the Gulf stream Ireland enjoys a temperate climate where rain remains a feature of the weather throughout the year. Ireland is a politically divided island consisting of thirty-two counties, twenty-six of which are under the jurisdiction of the Republic of Ireland and the remainder, more commonly referred to as Northern Ireland, forms part of the UK. The population of the Republic in 2001 stood at 3.84 million, the highest level since the census of 1881 and was no longer classified as an emigrant country (Central Statistics Office 2001b). By contrast the population of the UK, Irelands nearest neighbour and the fourth largest economy in the world, is fifteen times greater. Little under one half of the Irish population is below the age of twenty five.

Ireland has been inhabited for approximately seven thousand years. Christianity was introduced in fifth century by Saint Patrick and in the sixth and seventh centuries centres of learning were established in many parts of Europe by Irish monks (Curtis 1936). Ireland has been subjected to two significant invasions, the Vikings and the Normans. Around the seventeenth century, the old English (Normans) and the Gaelic Irish were brought under the control of the English Crown where the Battle of the Boyne in 1690 marked a significant political and cultural watershed. The Act of Union in 1800 secured the full parliamentary union of Ireland and England. During World War One, a Republic was declared outside the general post office in O'Connell St. Dublin. An armed insurrection took place between republican insurgents and British crown forces. The insurrection failed with one thousand three hundred and six fatalities including one hundred and forty British soldiers, eighty insurrectionists and the remainder ordinary Dubliners (Stewart 1998). The leaders of the insurrection were executed by firing squad. After the War of Independence, the Irish Free State came into existence on 7 January 1922 (Curtis 1936). The Free State left the Commonwealth on 18 April 1949 and duly declared itself a Republic (Foster 1988).

There are two official languages, Irish the national language and English. Irish is rarely spoken although it is the first language used in some isolated districts called Gaeltachts particularly in the west regions of the country. A national radio and television service is available through the medium of the Irish language. A list of prominent Irish writers contributing to literature and drama in English is impressive: Jonathan Swift (1667-1745), Oliver Goldsmith (1728-74), Edmund Burke (1729-97), Oscar Wilde (1854-1900), George Bernard Shaw (1856-1950), William Butler Yeats (1865-1939), George Russell (1867-1935), James Joyce (1882-1941), Samuel Beckett (1906-89), Brendan Behan (1923-64), Seamus Heaney (b. 1939), John McGahern (b.1934) and Roddy Doyle (b.1958). The Nobel Prize for Literature has been awarded to Beckett, Shaw, Yeats and Heaney, the highest for any country in this category.[9] One interesting remark made by Congleton (1991) in relation to the correlation between storytelling and the lack of economic efficiency would suggest that the emergence of the Celtic Tiger, overcame a significant obstacle when he contended that a society that

> encourages honesty rather than creative storytelling may have a weaker literary sector but overall a more efficient economy because fewer resources are required to police contracts. (Congleton 1991: 366)

It would appear then that the Irish economy should have exhibited less efficiency than many other countries but as the study unfolds we will show that the opposite was actually the case. However, before addressing the question of economic efficiency a brief overview of the present political context is now provided.

---

[9] See 'Ireland in Brief', and 'Ireland-The National Flag, Arms and Anthem', Department of Foreign Affairs, Dublin, Fact Sheet No 3/96.

Constitution and Government

Ireland is a parliamentary democracy. The National Parliament consists of the President, the House of Representatives (Dáil Éireann) and the Senate (Seanad Éireann). There are one hundred and sixty six members of parliament (Dáil), elected by proportional representation (PR - single transfer voting system) from forty one constituencies. There are three main political parties, Fianna Fáil (the largest), Fine Gael, and Labour and a number of smaller parties including the Progressive Democrats, Sinn Féin, the Social Democratic Party, the Green Party, and Independents. Elections must take place at least once every five years. All laws enacted by the Government should conform to a written constitution, known in Gaelic as Bunreacht na hÉireann (Constitution of Ireland) adopted by a plebiscite in 1937 and supersedes two previous constitutions, namely the Constitution of Dáil Éireann (1919) and the Constitution of the Irish Free State (1922). The 1937 Constitution sets out the fundamental rights of each citizen in areas such as the family, education, and property etc.

Ireland has been a member of the European Union since 1973 and a willing signatory of both the Single European Act 1988 and the Maastricht Treaty 1992 (McQueen 1998) and ratified the Amsterdam Treaty in a 1998 referendum. Successive Irish Governments and the electorate are strongly committed to and supportive of EU integration. The narrow rejection of the Treaty of Nice by electorate in June 2001 was later overturned by a second referendum in October 2002. Not only has Irelands attractiveness to non EU multinationals become consolidated but direct funding from the EU to implement regional, social and structural policies was in the order of IR£21,000 million for the period 1973-1995 (Department of Foreign Affairs 1998).[10]

Longer Term Trends Evident in the Irish Economy

In order to trace the developmental path of the Irish economy and place the emergence of the Celtic Tiger in context, a brief exploration is now undertaken of the main trends in economic activity and employment that occurred from the middle of the nineteenth century up to and including the Celtic Tiger and the structural peculiarities characteristic of that development. Such peculiarities, which are a feature of the combined impact of de-industrialisation, the Famine of 1848 and the emergence of the Free State post 1922 that, given that the six counties of the industrial North of Ireland remained as part of the UK, had the overall effect of skewing the Irish economy to such extent that it lacked any significant industrial base when independence was eventually achieved. The sheer scale of this imbalance becomes clear in Table 2.1 below when the employment trends in each of eight economic sectors are examined for the period 1841-2001.

---

[10] For further official political information refer to 'Ireland-Constitution and Government', Dublin, Department of Foreign Affairs Fact Sheet No: 2/95 and 'Ireland and the European Union', Dublin, Department of Foreign Affairs, Fact Sheet No 4/96.

Table 2.1 Employment and Population 1841-2001 (Male and Female 000s)

Economic Sector	1841[a]	1851[a]	1926[b]	1960[b]	1975[c]	1997[d]	2001[e]
Agriculture/Forest Fishing	1852	1459	652	413	229	134	121
Mining/Quarrying	8	12	2	12	9	6	-
Manufacturing	1021	733	120	190	217	271	318
Construct/Elect Gas/Water	68	51	41	74	100	109	179
Transport/Comms Storage	21	51	47	55	68	84	107
Distribution	-	-	41	45	87	203	246
Finance/Profess/ Personal/Miscell	395	346	187	178	208	456	308
Public Admin/Defence	17	24	38	39	59	74	78
Total Labour Force	3475	2799	1305	-	1041	1399	1709
Total Population	8175	6552	2972	-	3115	3660	3840
Total Population less Northern Ire[f]	6526	-	2972	-	3115	3660	3840

[a] Geary, F. (1996), *Irish Historical Studies XXX*, No: 118, School of Public Policy Economics and Law, University of Ulster, Jordanstown, Nov 1996, Table 1, p. 172.
[b] Mahony, D. (1964), *The Irish Economy - An Introductory Description*, Cork University Press, Cork, Table II, Chapter 2, pp. 17-20, p. 30.
[c] Central Statistics Office (1975), *First Labour Force Survey*, The Stationery Office, Dublin, p. 1, p. 11.
[d] Central Statistics Office (1997), *The Labour Force Survey, 1997*, The Stationery Office, Dublin, p. 16, p. 31.
[e] Central Statistics Office (2001), *The Quarterly National Household Survey May 2001*, Central Statistics Office, Dublin, pp. 1-24.
[e] Central Statistics Office (2001), *Population and Migration Estimates*, Central Statistics Office, Dublin, August 2001 pp. 1-8.
[f] Kennedy, K. and Giblin, T. and McHugh, D. (1994), *The Economic Development of Ireland in the Twentieth Century*, Routledge, London, Chapter 5, Table 5.1, p. 99.

Note: Some rounding of figures and grouping of categories was necessary for clarity and convenience as new classifications and some discontinuities emerged in the period under examination.

Two trends are particularly noteworthy, namely dramatic decreases in both the population and in the labour force. The population figures for 1841 and 1851 show a significant decrease due to the Famine of 1847 and subsequent emigration levels. The population figures for 1841 and 1851 also include Northern Ireland, whereas the Free State figures for 1926 and subsequent years do not. In the periods 1841-1851 and 1851-1926 respectively, the employment levels in all sectors except Transport and Public Administration virtually collapsed. Not only was there a decrease of 0.5 million agricultural workers and a decrease of 0.3 million industrial workers but also a decline of over 1.5 million in the total population. By 1926 approximately three years into the early development of the new Free State, there was a decrease of approximately 1.2 million agricultural workers, one million industrial workers and quarter of a million professional-personal services workers recorded for the area corresponding to the present boundary of the Republic of Ireland. For the same boundary area, a sixty four per cent reduction in the general population is also recorded from 1841-1926 and its manufacturing base is calculated at only ten per cent of the industrial base existing in 1841 for the whole island of Ireland. While the labour force and the manufacturing sector in particular showed a slight recovery from 1926 to 2001, there was an inexorable decline in agriculture.

Yet despite the immediate post Famine decrease of thirty four per cent in agricultural employment and a forty per cent decrease in industrial employment, an increase of eighteen per cent in output in the former and a thirty per cent increase in output in latter was recorded. This 'productivity' cannot be explained by emigration and labour market globalisation alone, but only by a standard neo-classical growth accounting model (Geary and Stark 1996). This model identifies the growth arising from increases in capital and the resultant productivity, particularly the rise in capital to labour ratios. In the Irish case, capital accumulation, technical progress and subsequent productivity gains in industry followed from railways from 1841, from shipbuilding in Belfast from 1870 and from the fastest growing total factor productivity industries in the period from 1873-1913. These industries included Gas, Electricity and Water, which recorded a five hundred per cent employment increase, Electrical Engineering an increase of one hundred and six per cent, Vehicles a modest increase of eighteen per cent and Insurance and Banking in the Services Sector, where an increase of three hundred and forty per cent was recorded with Scientific Services increasing by more than half (Geary and Stark 1996). Broadly speaking then, the trends confirm the transition from a rural agricultural economy to a more globally integrated economy of industrial and services employment (Treacy and O'Connell 2000).

The figures for the period 1926-1996 appear to underline the on-going shift from agricultural employment, (down from fifty three per cent to ten per cent of total employment), to employment in services (up from thirty four to sixty three per cent of the total). At the same time manufacturing remained relatively constant and showed all the signs of a post-industrial economy in the Republic of Ireland (Madden 2000). By 2001 agriculture had declined to less than seven per cent of total employment whereas manufacturing doubled from nine per cent to eighteen per cent of total employment even with a rise in the total population. Construction actually recorded a rise of sixty per cent in the period 1997-2001. The overall trend from the late 1920s onwards shows a consistent decline in the agricultural labour force and even when forestry and fishing were included in the agricultural total, it still only managed to account for less than ten per cent of the total labour force in 1998 (Whelan 1998). Curiously Bielenberg (2001) noted that while the fastest growing sector from 1850 to 1920 was Services, it still remained neglected in terms of socio-economic study in favour of agriculture and industry.

In the light of the broad trends outlined above, the Famine now becomes crucial to appreciate how Irish Catholic society continued to engage with the prevailing economic order. The reason is, that it had the effect of substantially increasing the religious commitment of Catholics to their faith and reduced the possibility of the ascendancy of the rational and Protestant ethic. As Akenson (1991) argued, the Famine was not a Protestant event but was

> built into the Catholic sense of history...as an event of cosmic significance not merely a human conspiracy and from then on until well into the 20th century, Irish Catholics became more attached to their religious beliefs a religion where the heart dominated reason. (Akenson 1991: 144, 145)

The Famine can rightly be regarded as the great divide in Irish economic and political history (Haughton 1991). After this unparalleled nineteenth century disaster extensive economic growth (aggregate output) was precluded mainly due to high levels of emigration and as a consequence, intensive growth (increase in productivity) when it did occur was primarily based on decreasing numbers attempting to produce the same output (O'Gráda 1997). From that moment forward both the nature of the Irish economy and the scope of the definition of Irelands economic problems were shaped by the Famine and assisted by the process of de-industrialisation (Barry 1999).

Barry explained the long term effects of these deeply ingrained psychological events. Firstly, the strengthened propensity of the population to migrate to seek out better economic conditions to those existing in Ireland as a result of ordinary peoples experience of deprivation during the Famine, shaped Ireland as a regional rather than a national economy. Secondly, this peripheral context left the Irish economy exclusively dependent on the vagaries of other national economies. Thirdly, the British induced de-industrialisation of the Irish economy left a predominantly agriculturally based regional economy next door to an industrially advanced one, so that the regional economy was unlikely to improve due to a common problem encountered by agricultural economies of this nature, namely that the capital intensification effects on labour rules out *extensive* growth in GDP. The conclusion must be reached that the increases in GDP were almost entirely due to the presence of less people producing the same output (intensive output).

MacRaild (1999) pointed out that while the Famine is often seen as the trigger for consolidated trends in increased poverty this is not necessarily the case. Bankruptcies and emigration were already a feature of Irish economic life when the Famine arrived, indicating that a recessionary trend was well underway before the Famine yet the event still remains a central nationalist symbol in Ireland. Another significant consequence of emigration patterns was that all pressure to reform conservative and conformist social structures that were not conducive to capitalist innovation were once and for all removed (O'Gráda 1997). Therefore the capacity of the Famine to act as the great divide in Irish economic history and to condition social structures inimical to the development of capitalism is an important contribution for contextualising the debates on modern Irish economic development which follow in chapter four. That contribution is further enhanced by now presenting a brief discussion on the main demographic and social outcomes of the Famine.

Using a modern idiom, there was a population explosion prior to the Famine. Estimated at about four million at the time of the Union (1800) it was returned at just under seven million by the Census of 1821, and at fractionally under nine million by the census of 1841 and continued to grow until 'checked' by the Famine of 1846-47 (Chart 1920). During this time over one and half million died from starvation and disease and in the period 1851-1860 nearly one and quarter million emigrated (Chart 1920). O'Gráda (1995) confirming these remarkable increases in population also argued that the subsequent decline was unmatched in any other European country. Remarkably, prior to this decade the Irish economy proportionally speaking had actually supported double the numbers employed in British agriculture and the same number in manufacturing (Geary 1995). The potato blight and technological change in one industrial sector – the invention of wet spinning which hit the textile industry particularly hard – caused the majority of manufacturing job losses in the post Famine decade (Geary 1995, Geary 1996).

Emigration was also a key factor in the decline of the Irish population (O'Tuathaigh 1998). According to Ni Bhrolchain (1998) between 1801 and 1921 eight million people emigrated from Ireland confirming beyond doubt that it was

a truly massive exodus. (Ni Bhrolchain 1998: 27)

While Hickman (1998) agreed that Ireland stood out as a country having a history of substantial emigration, it was by no means the largest migrant source in Europe. Britain and Italy headed this table with eleven million and ten million respectively. Nevertheless no other country lost between ten and twenty per cent of its population in each decade (Ni Bhrolcain 1998). By 1890 only sixty per cent of those who were born in Ireland were actually living in the country (Daly 1994). Moreover, the loss was also distributed unevenly because, in the period 1851-1926 there was a forty two per cent decline in the population of what was to become the Irish Free State whereas the decline in Northern Ireland was only twelve per cent (O'Gráda 1995).

The table below summarises the flow from Ireland for the fifty years prior to independence and in the immediate post independence years.

**Table 2.2 Natural Increase, Change in Population, Net Emigration
between 1871-1926**

Period	Natural Increase	Change In Pop	Net Emigration
1871-1881	318,557	-183,167	501,724
1881-1891	195,999	-401,326	597,325
1891-1901	149,543	-246,871	396,414
1901-1911	179,404	-82,135	261,539
1911-1926	237,333	-167,696	405,029
TOTAL	1,080,836	-1,081,195	2,117031

Source: O'Mahony, D. (1964), *The Irish Economy: An Introductory Description*, Cork, University Press, Cork, Table II^A, p. 4.

Emigration was one of the most persistent features of Irish social life after independence and continued unabated right into the early 1990s. According to Drudy (1995) over one hundred and sixty thousand emigrated in the period 1926-1936 and over four hundred thousand in the period 1950-1959. Between 1951-1961 nearly half a million Irish migrants went to Britain and by 1971 the Irish population resident in Britain was approximately one million (Walter 1986). In the periods 1956-58 and 1962-64, over fifty thousand moved out of Agriculture, Forestry and Fishing, twenty thousand moved into Manufacturing and six thousand into Construction, yet the workforce decreased by nearly fifty thousand and with at least three quarters of these previously employed, it suggested that emigration was running at well over forty thousand per annum and was therefore the real cause of the numerical decrease in the employment figures (Firth 1967).

Even with a natural population increase of over one million the levels of emigration were such, that overall, a *decrease* of over one million was recorded for the period i.e. approximately two million emigrated from Ireland. Yet some commentators have put a beneficial 'spin' on emigration and on the Famine arguing that it generated positive economic outcomes.

For example, a combination of the effects of the Wyndham Act of 1903 and high emigration levels resulted in over sixty per cent of farmers securing possession of their holdings by 1914 (O'Tuathaigh 1998).[11] In the period 1850-1914, income per head grew faster in Ireland than in the UK and Irish economic performance for the whole of the twentieth century was equal to the average achieved for western Europe (Kennedy 1996d). Moreover thirty years after the Famine, Ireland had one of the richest economies in the world based on income per capita (Geary and Stark 1996) achieving a relatively respectable west European average living standard by the early twentieth century (Kennedy 1994).

---

[11] Where farmers were guaranteed repayments that were lower that previous rent levels.

Looking at the Irish economy in the early part of the twentieth century one can observe that it was almost totally agricultural based. Table 2.3 shows the scope and nature of Irish economic activity just three years before the Easter Rising in 1916.

Table 2.3 Comparison of Goods Imported and Exported from the Whole of Ireland (including Northern Ireland) in 1913 in £ Sterling

Items Exported	£ Sterling	Item Imported	£ Sterling
Live Animals	18,000,000	Drapery	6,000,000
Linen Yarn	16,000,000	Cotton Goods	5,000,000
Eggs and Poultry	4,000,000	Maize (15,000,000 cwts)	4,000,000
Bacon and Ham	3,700,000	Wheat (8,000,000 cwts)	3,300,000
Butter	3,700,000	Other Grains	1,000,000
Ships	3,100,000	Wheat Flour	2,600,000
Cotton Goods	2,700,000	Coal	3,200,000
Beer	2,200,000	Flax	2,300,000
Spirits	2,000,000	Bacon	2,000,000
Miscellaneous[a]	17,600,000	Miscellaneous	43,600,000
Hides		Boots and Shoes	
Corn		Machinery	
Flour		Steel	
Biscuits		Sugar	
Potatoes		Linen goods	
Fish		Raw Cotton	
Machinery		Timber	
Condensed Milk			
Rope/ Thread			
Tobacco			
Wool/Goods			
Drapery/Raw cotton			

Total: 73,000,000   **Total: 73,000,000**

Source: Chart, D.A. (1920), *An Economic History of Ireland Dublin*, Dublin, Talbot Press, and tabulated from statements pp. 137-142.

[a] No item more costing more than sterling £1,000,000.

According to Kennedy (1994) while the proportion of those working in industry in Ireland in 1911 was only a quarter of the British proportion, by 1914 the per capita income for the Republic increased to sixty per cent of the British level. This figure was comparable to the Nordic countries but slightly lower than Austria and higher that Portugal and Greece. Consequently there is some justification for claiming that a relatively good standard of living was achieved through low output *without* industrialisation. But the really important point about the economy is not the actual numbers emigrating but the consequential failure of the Irish economy to industrialise from 1850-1914 which left it for all intents and purposes as a pre-capitalist economy and Irish society itself as very much pre-modern (Girvin 1986). Indeed only much later in 1986 did Ireland experience its first recession as an *industrial* economy and then only as a partially industrialised one (Weinz 1986).

Exports were dominated by food items such as live animals, eggs, bacon and ham, butter, biscuits, flour and corn together with clothing and textiles. Where industrial activity was recorded, such as ship building, tobacco and rope manufacturing, it was again place restricted to specific areas of Northern Ireland and Belfast in particular. Imports are dominated by clothing such as drapery and cotton goods, and food such as maize, wheat, and wheat flour. Steel appears to be the only 'heavy' industrial product imported into Ireland.

High levels of agriculturally dominated economic activity continued to feature well into the middle of the twentieth century and it was only in the late 1990s when it receded. For example, in 1949 the total value in sterling pounds of exports from the Republic reached sixty one million, yet approximately sixty per cent or forty four million consisted of live animals and food but by 1998 when exports had reached over two billion Irish punts, food and meat accounted for as little as four per cent of the total (O'Hagan, Murphy and Redmond 2000).

The Modern Economy

The Irish economy is now an open economy with a small domestic market and a lack of resources requiring large importation of raw material and fuel. The two main sources of exports are both traditional and new, namely technology manufacturing and agricultural products. Over three hundred of the worlds leading electronics companies invested in Ireland between 1980 and 1997 where over forty per cent of all new US inward investment into the EU was located in the Republic of Ireland (Department of Foreign Affairs 1998). The labour force in 2000 which consisted of 1.7 million was up from a figure of 1.4 million in 1993, an increase of approximately twenty two per cent (FÁS 2000) and by mid 2001 had increased further to 1.86 million (Central Statistics Office 2001c). The three main sectors of the economy, namely agriculture, manufacturing-construction and services together with the underlying variations within each of the sectors at intervals during the period 1851-2000 are now presented in Table 2.4 below. A key trend within the figures is confirmation of a move from an agricultural to a services and manufacturing based economy with a decline of nearly ninety per cent in Agriculture. There was a significant increase of just over three hundred per cent in the Manufacturing sector although it is still lower in percentage and real terms than the increase recorded in the Services sector. This latter also shows a doubling of numbers approximately every seventy years with an average increase of ten per cent per annum recorded from 1996 onwards.

Table 2.4 Employment Trends in Economic Sectors 1851-2000

Sector	1851 [a]	1926 [b]	1996 [c]	1998 [d]	1999 [e]	2000 [f]
Agriculture	1,459,400	652,000	200,000	136,000	190,000	130,000
ManuConst	784,400	158,000	400,000	438,000	509,000	488,000
Services	291,100	408,000	800,000	921,000	1,001,000	1,075,000

[a] Geary, F. (1995), *De-Industrialisation in Ireland to 1851: Some Evidence from the Census*, Economic and Social Research Institute (ESRI), Dublin, Working Paper No 68, Table 2, p. 6.
[b] O'Mahony, D. (1964), *The Structure of the Irish Economy - An Introductory Description*, Cork University Press, Cork, Table II: p. 20.
[c] FÁS/ESRI, (1996), *Labour Market Report*, FÁS - The Training and Employment Authority Dublin, Issue 1, January 1996, pp. 1-6.
[d] Central Bank of Ireland, (2000), *Irish Economic Statistics*, Central Bank of Ireland, Dublin, Autumn 2000.
[e] FÁS, (2000), *Regional Aspects of Irelands Labour Market*, FÁS, Dublin, Labour Market Update Paper No 1, Table 8.
[f] Central Bank of Ireland, (2001), *Autumn Review 2001 - Labour Force Statistics*, Central Bank of Ireland, Dublin.

A further breakdown of the three main economic sectors into activity sub-sectors follows in Table 2.5. Production, Wholesale Retail, Education and Health and Financial and Other Business Services account for over sixty per cent of total employment. Manufacturing and Construction jointly account for just under thirty per cent. In contrast Agriculture, Forestry and Fishing employ less than seven per cent of the total workforce.

Table 2.5 Breakdown of Employment by Economic Sector in 2001

Sectors	000s	% Labour Force
Agriculture, Forestry and Fishing	121.7	7.1
Other Production Industries	318.3	19.0
Construction	179.9	10.5
Wholesale and Retail	246.5	14.5
Hotels and Restaurant	106.6	6.2
Transport Storage and Communication	107.2	6.2
Financial and Other Business Services	218.1	12.7
Public Administration and Defence	78.4	4.5
Education and Health	242.6	14.0
Other Services	90.7	5.3
TOTAL	1,710.0	100.0

Source: Central Statistics Office, (2001b), *Population and Migration Estimates*, Central Statistics Office, Dublin, August 2001, pp. 1-8.

If we now examine the Key Economic Statistics published by Ireland's Central Bank and compare Irish economic activity at the following three periodic intervals, 1988, 1998 and 2000, then the dramatic transformation of the nature and volume of Celtic Tiger economic activity can again be observed. The economic data includes the Gross National Product (GNP), National Income Levels, External Trade, Balance of Payments, Birth and Death Rates, and Migration Trends. The most significant trends are a two hundred and seventy per cent increase in Gross Domestic Product (GDP), a two hundred and fifty per cent increase in Gross National Product (GNP) and near threefold increase in industrial production.

Table 2.6 Key Economic Activity Data for 1988, 1998 and 2000

National Product (m)	1988 [a]	1998 [a]	2000 [b]
Gross National Product	20,056	52,183	68,600
Gross Domestic Product	22,718	59,637	81,472
Exports of Goods Services	13,634	50,305	59,958
Income			
National Income	15,540	39,620	51,077
Weekly earnings in industry where 1988 = 100	100	144	152.6
External Trade			
Imports	10,215	33,188	43,866
Exports	12,305	45,042	65,750
- Industrial		39,826	60,621 (92.2%)
- Agricultural		2,111	3,156 (4.8%)
Exports to E.U			40,765 (62.0%)
Of which to U.K			14,662 (22.3%)
Agriculture			
Gross Agricultural Product (GAP)	1,934	1,506	2,343
Balance of Payments			
Balance on Current Account	+62	+563	-537

Vital statistics (per 1000)	1981-86	1986-1991	1991-96	2000
Birth Rate	20.2	15.7	14.0	14.3
Death Rate	9.7	9.0	8.8	8.2
Net Migration	-4.1	-7.6	0.5	6.1
Net Increase in Pop	6.4	-0.9	5.7	11.4
Marriage Rate	5.9	5.1	4.6	5.1

[a] Central Bank of Ireland (2000), *The Central Bank of Ireland Autumn Review 2000*, Central Bank of Ireland, Dublin.
[b] Central Bank of Ireland, (2001), *The Central Bank of Ireland Autumn Review 2001*, Central Bank of Ireland, Dublin.

From the above data we can also observe that in the period 1994-1998, the annual average growth rate of GNP by volume was just under eight per cent. This level was in excess of twice the rate achieved in the previous thirty three year period (Walsh 1999). In the period 1988-2000 Gross Domestic Product increased by more than three hundred and fifty per cent, Gross National Product (GNP) by just less than three hundred and fifty per cent and the exports of goods and services by a factor of four. National Income also increased by a factor of three and average weekly earnings increased by approximately a half. Exports were one and half times the value of imports and while imports increased by over four hundred per cent, exports also increased by over five hundred per cent. The strong contribution of industrial exports, over ninety per cent, to the overall total export figure contrasts sharply with the less than five per cent contribution of agricultural exports. Gross Agricultural Product for 2000 showed an increase of over fifty per cent over the 1998 figure but a relatively modest increase of approximately twenty per cent over the 1988 total. Exports to the UK accounted for over twenty per cent of total exports while over two thirds were exported to other EU countries. While the balance of payments showed a surplus of £IR501m in 1998 compared to the relatively small surplus of £IR62m in 1988, yet by 2000 a deficit of £IR537m was recorded indicating a negative fluctuation of approximately one billion Irish punts for the period 1998-2000.

Important demographic changes in migration patterns and education levels are also captured in those Vital Statistics. In marked contrast to the traditional long standing outward net migration flows and population decreases, a reverse pattern was recorded resulting in a net inward migration rate in excess of six per cent of the total population while at the same time an eleven per cent net increase was recorded for the total population in the period 1981-2000. Approximately one quarter of that population were receiving full time education with approximately half attending primary schools, one third in secondary and the remainder in third level institutions.

Table 2.7 Primary, Secondary and Tertiary Educational Enrolments

School Levels	No of Schools[a]	No of Pupil[b]
Primary level	3,354[c]	451,000
Second level	796[d]	358,000
Third level	59[e]	122,000

[a] Department of Education (1999), *Statistical Report 1997/98*, Govt. of Ireland, Dublin, p. 10.
[b] Central Bank of Ireland (2001), *Irish Economic Statistics, Autumn Review 2001*, Central Bank of Ireland, Dublin.
[c] One hundred and nineteen special schools and forty nine non aided primary schools.
[d] Eighteen schools aided by other government departments such as Defence and Agriculture fifteen non-aided schools such as secretarial and commercial.
[e] Seven Universities and thirteen Institutes of Technology, ten religious institutions and seventeen others including Royal College of Surgeons in Ireland.

Since the mid 1960s there has been a continuous increase in the investment per pupil at both primary and secondary level. For example, in the period 1965-1997, expenditure per pupil at primary level had increased nearly four fold and more than doubled for each second level pupil (Dept of Education 2001). However, the more telling data concerns the per cent of GDP spent on education during the Celtic Tiger phase where it has consistently decreased from over six per cent in 1994 to less then four and three quarter per cent in 2000, one of lowest levels in the EU (European Commission 2002a). Completion rates for second level education calculated by the numbers completing their upper secondary level senior cycle has increased from twenty per cent in 1965 to seventy five per cent in 1997. Furthermore, the percentage of any age cohort transferring from second to third level has increased from ten per cent in 1965 to forty eight per cent in 1996 (Dept of Education 2001).

Summary

Ireland is a stable parliamentary democracy on the western edge of Europe with an open and strong economy. The underlying impact of The Great Famine and subsequent emigration patterns on the various sectors in the economy over a period of a century and a half was examined. The nature and durability of a de-industrialised and agricultural economy was a notable feature of this discussion where the Famine defined the nature of Irish economic problems for well over a century. It was here that we observed that it was not only a national disaster but from then on was imprinted on the Irish psyche as a particularly Catholic event. Running in parallel with the Famine, was another deeply ingrained demographic trend, namely emigration.

Our discussion noted that the very high and persistent emigration levels were, when measured as a per cent of population, one of the highest in Europe although other countries, notably Italy had higher numbers of individuals emigrating. The longer term dynamic of sectoral employment in the Irish economy underlined a move from agriculture to services economy together with an increase in both the volume and nature of national economic activity. Economic performance during the Celtic Tiger was characterised by spectacular increases in employment, in productivity and in the balance of payments surpluses.

We also noted how average weekly income increased by approximately on half in the decade 1988-1998. Not only did birth rates decrease, but so too did the death rate and together with a significant increase in population, pointed to a society that was experiencing all the signs of growth in employment and in real earnings. The most remarkable sign that the economy was beginning to turn in a dramatic way, can be gauged from the complete reversal of the long-standing trend in emigration, so much so, that Ireland now was no longer classified as an emigrant country.

The increase in infrastructural investment and the increased participation in education at primary secondary and tertiary levels were other key observations of an economy on the turn, although the per cent of GDP spend on education actually declined.

The data and commentaries in the earlier part of our discussion isolated the low industrial base and the high and constant emigration levels throughout the twentieth century as features of Irish economic development. It hardly seemed plausible then that this economic environment would almost overnight, be transformed into one of the most successful in the world. Was it possible then, that Ireland had actually given birth to a Tiger economy? In the following two chapters we will concentrate our efforts to answer this very question.

Chapter 3

Rich Man, Poor Man :
But is it a Tiger Economy?

Introduction

While chapter one painted broad brushstrokes of Ireland's economic development
and revealed the longer term sectoral trends and demographic changes that
characterised the Irish economy, the purpose of this chapter is to present and
discuss specific economic data to establish whether or not the Tiger status of the
economy was a deserved one. On the one hand, the data strongly suggests that
internationally accepted benchmarks were indeed achieved if not exceeded. On the
other, more data confirmed that by international standards high levels of poverty
featured prominently and where an unusually high risk of poverty for certain
disadvantaged social groups was to retain its presence in Irish society for the
duration of the Celtic Tiger.

How Loud was the Roar of the Tiger?

In economic discourse the terms economic growth, economic development and
industrial development tend to be used interchangeably but there can be significant
differences in their emphasis. Economic growth is defined as increasing total
output without a rise in living standards or increasing efficiency, whereas
development indicates a rise in productivity without a reduction in the numbers
working (Oser 1967). Moreover, development does not always imply an industrial
context because some economic development histories that occurred in the 1960s,
as in New Zealand for example, can just as easily be underpinned by an
agricultural rather than an industrial base provided that skill development and
social attitudes support appropriate growth strategies (Williams 1967).

Industrial development on the other hand, is defined as a process whereby
productive resources in a particular economy are used to generate higher quality
lower cost products than were previously available (O'Sullivan 1995). Economic
development is usually understood to mean that more individuals are better off in
conditions of a rising population, full employment and income growth (Haughton
1991), although the OECD (2001a) in a policy briefing document, still used the
terms economic performance, economic growth and economic development
interchangeably to refer to an increase in GDP figures. Yet it is also worth
remembering that economic development is not purely economic in the sense that

it also encompasses the concurrent development of internal social factors that assist economic development such as the decline in religious beliefs and the rising social esteem attached to economic success (Cairncross 1962). But as we already noted in chapter one, the advance of secularisation and the corrosion of religious beliefs and values in Irish society are not well supported in the literature. Yet Leitch (1998) continued to argue that internal social factors still generated ambivalent attitudes to economic development in the Republic stating that

> the south of Ireland at the present time is racing, hell-bent, to become part of that industrialised society. They spend all these centuries saying we don't want to be like these people, but they want to achieve what Britain did, in ten or fifteen years which is another of the great ironies. (Leitch 1998: 68)

By definition then Ireland has experienced both economic development and economic growth in the Celtic Tiger because output (GDP) for the period 1993-1998 more than doubled, employment levels increased and levels of private consumption was close to eighty per cent of the EU average. The gains in wealth, productivity and output created a more competitive economy than Japan and Britain despite reservations about EU subsidies and multinational tax dodges (Shuttleworth, Kitchen, Shirlow and McDonagh 2000). Further confirmation of the continued increase in Irish economic development and growth rates came from the IMF (2000) who pointed out that

> Ireland continues to achieve spectacular economic growth...reflects propitious policy decisions...[which]...has sparked a virtuous circle of rapidly rising incomes and employment and contributed to strong growth in private consumption and investment. (IMF 2000: 34)

As early as 1988, Ireland was already classified as a rich industrial country by the World Bank using the measure of Gross National Product per Capita and confirmed Ireland's twenty seventh position in a cohort of over one hundred countries surveyed (Haughton 1991).

The economic data available during the Celtic Tiger tended to underline an even higher economic status. For example, there were optimistic targets set for employment of 1.5million by 2003, for an unemployment rate of seven per cent by 2005 and for an economic growth rate of five per cent per annum for the early years of the twentieth first century (ESRI 1997). Yet as early as 1998 all targets were easily exceeded and where an annual increase of thirty thousand jobs was 'effortlessly' achieved (Sexton 1998). In fact the unemployment rate actually stood at just over four per cent at the end of 2000 (Central Statistics Office 2000a) and the revised unemployment targets of five per cent overall and two per cent for the long term unemployed, to be achieved by December 2000, had again been exceeded nine months earlier than expected (Govt 2001).

The underlying dynamic in the workforce, calculated on an ILO basis was very positive because total employment in the Irish economy increased by over a quarter of a million between April 1989 and April 1997 and was unmatched in the history of the state (Tansey 1998).

The sheer scale of the decrease in both the rate and number of registered unemployed from 1985 onwards can be observed in Table 3.1 below. A key feature is the general downward trend in both numbers and percentages, noting that the most significant variations had occurred in just the last ten years. By 2001 the actual unemployment rate was half the 1975 level notwithstanding substantial increases in the both the population in general and the labour force in particular.

Table 3.1 Levels of Unemployment 1975-2001

Year	Total	Rate
1975	85,000	7.3%[a]
1985	226,000	17.3%[a]
1995	192,000	13.3%[a]
1998	214,014	7.0%[b]
2000	152,871	4.4%[c]
2001	149,000	3.7%[d]
2001	154,100	4.1%[e]

[a] Tansey, P. (1998), *Ireland at Work-Economic Growth and the Labour Market 1987-1997*, Oak Tree Press, Dublin, Chapter 3, p. 52.
[b] Irish Times, (1999), Saturday, February 6th 1999, Business and Finance Section p. 18.
[c] Government of Ireland, (2000), 'Further Good News on the Unemployment Front, Tánaiste announces that Long Term Unemployment falls to under 30,000, - 270,000 extra at work', *Government Press Office*, Dublin, Friday, 4 August 2000.
[d] McCoy, D. and Duffy, D. and Hore, J. and MacCoille, C. (2001), *Quarterly Economic Commentary June 2001*, The Economic and Social Research Institute, Dublin, p. 1-8 and http://www.cso.ie
[e] Central Statistics Office, (2001), *CSO Live Register Statement November 2001*, Central Statistics Office, Dublin, Standardised Unemployment Rate for November 2001.

The dramatic improvement in economic performance during the early part of the Celtic Tiger era was also acknowledged by Baker, Duffy and Shortall (1998) of the ESRI who argued that on every relevant criterion the economy had performed exceptionally well. Their progmosis was confirmed in 1998 when the best ever exchequer returns for the first half of any year since the foundation of the state were reported by the Minister for Finance (McCreevy 1998). Moreover, the labour force had grown by over twenty per cent, employment by nearly forty per cent, unemployment decreased by more than a half, with numbers registered as long term unemployed i.e. those over one year on the Live Register, decreasing by nearly seventy per cent, while at the same time income levels per capita increased by over thirty per cent (FÁS 2000). The performance figures for the period 1993-1998 were of such a magnitude that they were deemed to constitute an economic miracle (Sweeney 1998).[12] By 2001 the population had increased to another record of 3.84 million, its highest in over a century and because Ireland still remained relatively under-populated at approximately one fifth of the density of the UK, it lead to the conclusion that the economy could potentially support an even higher population (Central Statistics Office 2001b).

So using annual benchmark economic indicators of levels of population, of employment, of unemployment, of GNP by volume and per capita, there had been significant improvements from 1994 to 2000 (Central Statistics Office 2000). Moreover, if the correct policies continued to be implemented then Ireland could look forward to continuing and impressive increases in its standard of living (OECD 2001). Speaking at the EU Summit in Nice, the Irish Prime Minister reminded the Irish people that for the first time in their history, the level of GNP achieved by his Party (Fianna Fáil) equaled the EU average (RTÉ 2000).

And it got even better! The record low levels of unemployment recorded in November 2000 stood at just under four per cent (Govt 2000c) and now became a positive economic problem because Forfás (2000) contended that the increase of approximately a half a million persons at work in the decade 1990-1999 had eventually precipitated both labour and skill shortages in the economy. Even so, when Irish income levels as measured per Head of Population were compared to those prevailing throughout the EU in July 2000, they were found to be second only to Luxembourg based on Gross Domestic Product (GDP), rather than GNP. However, GNP did not include profit repatriation by multinationals and had these figures been taken into account, then GNP would be fifteen per cent below the GDP level (European Commission 2000). It was also well known that GDP figures for Ireland were notoriously poor indicators of national income earned by productive Irish capital and labour and as a consequence, GDP totals over the last few years had averaged thirteen per cent above the more accurate GNP totals (Barry, Hannan, and Strobl 1999).

Nevertheless, even using the lower GNP figure as the real measure of economic growth, the Irish economy in terms of output growth, ranked first in the OECD in the 1990s and reached a point in 2000 where GNP was approximately ninety per cent of average EU levels, up from sixty per cent in 1993 (IMF 2000). By the end of 2000 the largest flow of portfolio capital in the world came into Ireland making it a leading financial services centre (ATKearney/Foreign Policy 2002). By the end of 2001 the debt to GDP ratio had fallen from approximately one hundred per cent in 1993 to slightly over the thirty per cent mark and GDP per head now exceeded both the German and UK levels.

Furthermore, as early as 1998 there was clear and consistent evidence that because of wage and employment levels in the economy, both intensive and

---

[12] The term miracle then become commonplace in official reports, in the media, in politics and in everyday conversation to describe the turnaround in Irish economic fortunes.

extensive economic development has occurred i.e. higher numbers working, earning higher wages, delivering higher productivity (Barry, Hannan and Strobl 1999). Even in the subsequent spiral of higher labour costs, higher wages, higher prices and higher inflation rates already evident by 2000, there was still 'extraordinary' productivity growth in the economy and most remarkably, competitiveness measured as unit labour costs in manufacturing actually improved during this time (OECD 2001). This happened even though calculated hours per week worked in full time jobs had on average decreased significantly from 1993 onwards for both men and women – from forty four hours in 1983 to thirty eight hours in 1999 – notwithstanding the false impression created by male managers that the opposite was the case, because their social position enabled them to 'talk loudest' (Wickham 2000). In other words, productivity increased even when both the cost base *increased* and the working week *decreased*.

Published data on industrial activity also confirmed that the economy had performed exceptionally well. For example, Ireland was unique in displaying an increase of just over seventeen per cent in manufacturing employment in the period 1988-1998 particularly when this rate is compared to the comparable figures in the same period for the industrially advanced economies of the US (-3.7 per cent), Japan (-9.1 per cent), Germany (-30 per cent), UK (3.9 per cent) and Sweden (-21 per cent). The Irish performance can be put down in the main, to its success in attracting foreign multinationals into Ireland (Forfás 1999). This success was built on the availability of national economic planning, management and implementation based on the social partnership consensus model (Travers 1999).

The multi-national dominance of the economy was a noteworthy feature of the Irish economy. Foreign owned companies accounted for just under fifty per cent of manufacturing employment and over half of total employment if internationally traded and financial services were included (Forfás 1999). They also accounted for two thirds of industrial output and over three quarters of industrial exports (Wren 2000). Approximately three quarters of all sales in the Manufacturing and Internationally Traded Services Industry was generated by multinationals (Forfás 2000a). They had a central role in the performance of the Irish economy (Kenny 1997) and were described by Suiter (2000) as

> the most powerful engine in the transformed economy of the Republic. (Suiter 2000: 1)

Though according to Keenan (2000) there was one worrying trend, namely the over-reliance on a small number of sectors and companies. Not only were the multi-national figures higher at three quarters of all manufacturing output but chemical and computer multinationals accounted for sixty per cent of all multinational exports, constituting over half of total exports, noting that both Dell and Intel alone accounted for over one half of the total output from the electronics sector. Another concern was that exports still showed a disproportionate reliance on the UK market which accounted for nearly half of all exports, with a third going to the rest of the EU and a fifth to the rest of the world (Forfás 2000a). Another concern was highlighted when the quality of key multi-national job opportunities provided by FDI was questioned by Barry, Bradley and O'Malley (1999) who highlighted the footloose nature of multinationals and the consequent potential for economic instability because the average duration of a multi-national manufacturing job in Ireland was thirteen years, well below the eighteen achieved in both the US and the UK.

However, the Globalisation Index showed that FDI inflows into Ireland increased from $3 billion per year in the mid 1990s to over $20 billion per year in 2000 which was more than three times the average amount of FDI per resident in Finland (A.T. Kearney/Foreign Policy Magazine 2002). The economic fundamentals were so good that the Irish Minister for Finance, echoing the former British Prime Minister Harold Macmillan, claimed that people in Ireland never had it so good (McCreevy 2000).

On the other hand, significant sections of Irish society never had it so bad during this belated golden age of development. The Government candidly conceded when it launched its RAPID initiative (Revitalising Areas by Planning, Investment and Development), that there were over one hundred and sixty five thousand individuals in twenty five of the country's most concentrated areas of disadvantage who had not benefited at all from the wealth generated by the Celtic Tiger (Govt 2001a).[13] Moreover, a street head count of the homeless in Dublin carried out between 15 and 21 October 2000 and undertaken jointly by Focus Ireland, Dublin Simon and Dublin Corporation, established that there were two hundred and two homeless individuals in Dublin which was more than the combined total of Manchester, Birmingham, Liverpool, Oxford and Nottingham and equated to almost two thirds of the London total (Irish Times 2000a).

According to the UN, Ireland had the highest levels of relative poverty in the industrialised world outside of the US and almost twenty three per cent of the Irish population was functionally illiterate unable to read for example labels on common packages of food or medication etc. (Cullen 1999). Despite the progress made in Ireland's Human Development Performance, being ranked twentieth from over one hundred and seventy countries, the Irish level still remained well below the average for industrialised countries (UN 1999).[14] The level of poverty in Ireland was high at eleven per cent of the population thus leaving Ireland in second last position from seventeen industrialised countries surveyed (UN 1999).[15] However, even the doubts expressed about the disproportionate weighting of some variables used to measure the Human Poverty Index (HPI) which left Ireland stuck in the second worst position of the seventeen richest countries even after the boom times of the Celtic Tiger, Irish society still continued to suffer from the most serious of social

---

[13] The most disadvantaged communities were prioritised using the Trutz-Hasse Social Deprivation Index that includes variables such as the unemployment rate per household, income level per household, family and social structure and high levels of rented public housing.

[14] Measured by school enrolments, GNP per capita and life expectancy since the 1980s.

[15] Measured by the per cent of the population below the median adjusted disposable personal income threshold.

deficits across a variety of areas of life (Nolan 2002). When measured as a per cent of the average equivalent household income in the EU, the numbers of individuals existing below the forty per cent poverty level was relatively low but when the fifty and sixty per cent threshold levels were combined they gave a rate comparable to the that existing in the UK, Greece and Spain with only Portugal of the remaining EU countries having higher rates of poverty (Callan and Nolan 1999). Moreover, increases in socio-economic well-being when they did occur were place restricted to Cork, Dublin, Limerick, Galway and Waterford leaving the remaining counties of the Republic lagging behind and reflected Ireland's position at the top of the table for the greatest social polarity in terms of income within the EU, with double the number of children living in poverty since 1971 and the largest differential in economic status between the sexes within the EU (Shuttelworth, Kitchin, Shirlow, and McDonagh 2000).

Following my own analysis of the official income tax receipts for 1998 as recorded in the Statistical Report of the Revenue Commissioners (Govt 2000b), some striking examples of income inequality can be observed. For example over sixty per cent of Ireland's 1.5 million taxpayers earned less than €15,000 gross per annum and accounted for only twenty eight per cent of the national income, while the top three per cent who earned more than €65,000 gross per annum, accounted for almost sixteen per cent of national income. If those earning more than €40,000 gross per annum are also included, then the top fifteen per cent of tax payers accounted for over half of total income. For example, the income earned by the top twenty five Irish businessmen and women in the tax year 1999-2000 exceeded €510 million (*Sunday Times* 2000). This level of income inequality had only marginally improved when compared to the position in the early 1980s, because Kenny (1984) contended at the time, that less than five per cent of the population owned between fifty seven and sixty three per cent of the national wealth whereas now, the figure had tripled to fifteen per cent of the population. According to Callan and Nolan (1999) the trend towards greater income inequality and poverty rates in Ireland had not generally re-occurred in other OECD countries with the exception of the UK and the US.

But it is at the individual level where the true extent of endemic poverty becomes apparent. As Table 3.2 now shows, at the outset of the Celtic Tiger in 1994 approximately one fifth of the population had an income below half of the average Irish household income level and were classified as poor using the Combat Poverty Agency's Poverty Qualification Threshold. This is a report by an individual household of an enforced lack one of the everyday eight items listed below.

Table 3.2 Household Poverty Levels using the Poverty Qualification Threshold

Deprivation Benchmark	*% Below 50% Poverty Line*
Getting into debt for everyday expenses	56.9
Went without main meal	23.4
Went without heat	23.4
Enforced lack of new clothes	38.3
Enforced lack of two pairs of shoes	33.9
Enforced lack of warm overcoat	28.5
Enforced lack of roast or equivalent per week	38.4
Enforced lack of meal without meat, fish equivalent	24.1

Source: Nolan, B. and Whelan, C.T. and Williams, J. (1998), *Where are the Poor Households? The Spatial Distribution of Poverty and Deprivation in Ireland*, Combat Poverty Agency, Research Report Series, Oak Tree Press, Dublin, p. 13, p. 15.

The figures indicate that about one in five households in Ireland experienced a lack of at least one of the eight indicators listed and over half of these poor households experienced debt difficulties to meet daily living expenses. Callan and Nolan (1999) concluded that the above table of eight categorical measurements was a better indicator of both the scale and trend in generalised deprivation than numbers and percentages above or below poverty lines or the oft quoted poverty threshold figures. Furthermore, these deprivation levels were not expected to improve significantly in the period 1999-2000 (Nolan 2000) i.e. at the maximum impact point of the Celtic Tiger.

In fact the Combat Poverty Agency (1999) indicated that there were worrying signs of a general tendency to stigmatise many of those in poverty and to label them according to two categories, namely deserving and undeserving poor, mainly as a result of the Irish society becoming atomised and individualised. Even though eight per cent of the population fell below the sixty per cent average income threshold and were therefore classified as experiencing basic deprivation, over half of the *single adult household* category experienced a poverty rate that was half of the average income, a figure over double the rate for the next category *2 adults with four or more children* (ESRI 2001). The risk of falling below the 50 per cent threshold was greatest for households where the reference person was *disabled* with a 72.6 per cent risk assessment, followed by an *unemployed* reference person with a 56.2 per cent risk assessment and 28.7 per cent risk assessment where the reference person was *retired* (ESRI 2001). According to a former Fine Gael Prime Minister, Dr. Garrett Fitzgerald (2001), Ireland had now become the most right wing country in Europe based on the per cent of resources allocated to poverty reduction and the most unequal society in Europe based on the after tax income of the rich measured against government resources allocated to social action.

Whatever way it was measured income inequality and social mobility had actually increased during the Celtic Tiger (Peillon 2003)

Summary

This chapter has presented details of the developmental dynamics of the Irish economy and complemented the discussions on the broad socio-economic profile presented in the previous chapter. Data on the nature and level of economic activity evident in the transformed modern Irish economy revealed high levels of sustained economic performance as a durable feature of the Celtic Tiger. The decline in unemployment from 1975 onwards marked a fundamental transformation of the Irish labour market.

A number of benchmarks were also examined that verified the Tiger status of the economy and from these results we can conclude that the Irish economy probably deserved the label of the Celtic Tiger. Yet despite strong underlying empirical support for confirming its Tiger status, the Government admitted that large sections of Irish society had still not benefited from the economic transformation. Further examination of the poverty data revealed that a significant section of Irish society experienced unusually high levels of deprivation in their daily lives.

While we can probably claim that the Celtic Tiger was more of a reality that a myth, we have not explored the reasons why or how it had become so at this particular juncture in Ireland's economic and social development. The exploration of the various debates that attempt to uncover the dynamic of Ireland's development including that of the Celtic Tiger, forms the central narrative of the next chapter.

Chapter 4

The Accidental Tiger

Introduction

In the previous chapter, the view of many commentators that the Irish economy met and at times easily exceeded Tiger performance benchmarks was upheld, notwithstanding of course the relatively high levels of sustained poverty. The purpose of this chapter is to try to establish how the economy came to be transformed so unexpectedly given the unlikely socio-economic backdrop depicted earlier in chapter two. To achieve this objective the debates on Irish economic development are divided into two categories where it then becomes possible to undertake a comparative analysis on the merits of the various arguments presented throughout these debates. Category One debates include explanations of poor development for the period 1922-1993, while Category Two presents hindsight explanations for the underlying cause(s) of strong development including attempts to explain the Celtic Tiger phase of development.

It is worth remembering that the much longer timeframe taken to achieve levels of economic development comparable to that achieved by other Tiger nation states was almost universally overlooked by many commentators. This oversight contrasted with the contention of Singh (1994) that even the extremely adverse conditions after colonial rule in the period 1950-1980 failed to prevent or dampen the golden age of economic development in South East Asia. Ironically this very colonial influence which places the ultimate cause within an imposed *external* framework is presented by many Irish commentators in Category One as prima facie evidence for the generally poor economic performance since independence.

Category One - External Factors Explaining Poor Economic Growth

As early as 1870, Ireland along with Spain and Portugal, appeared to possess the potential to become a first world industrial country but had not done so by the late 1980s, well over a hundred years later (Bradford De Long 1989).[16] The social capability and desire to accumulate through hard work i.e. an observable

---

[16] But he also cautioned that the Protestant option may have had serious repercussions on the levels of national well-being experienced in industrialised countries arguing that the lower levels experienced in less industrialised countries may have been a much more preferable option in the long term.

commitment to the Protestant Work Ethic, was highlighted as the key missing factor.

Girvin (1997) argued that Ireland was not in fact prepared to go this Protestant accumulative route due to the colonial factor i.e. it defined itself as Catholic and nationalist, while furthermore there was always the suspicion that Irish society had neither the inclination nor the will to industrialise because of the presence of certain behavioural features calculated to impede economic development.[17] In any event, nationalists preferred the achievement of an independent state to the almost guaranteed development of Irish material resources and the subsequent prosperity that was virtually guaranteed on foot of a genuine commitment to a union with an industrial supreme, Britain (Manseragh 1965c). Again and again this external colonial factor is cited in one form or another by many commentators.

O'Brien (1968) contended that the lack of Irish legislative independence after the 1800 Act of Union worked against an economic policy favourable to Irish circumstances.[18] However Johnson (1989) confirmed that from 1914 to 1920, the years immediately prior to independence, there was unprecedented economic prosperity in Ireland due to a rise in agricultural prices during World War One. However, because this boom was agricultural it consequently suppressed any desire to address issues relating to industrial development (Sweeney 1992) and Mjoset (1993) blamed overt British policies of de-industrialisation in Ireland prior to independence as the main reason why slow industrialisation occurred thereafter.

The whole debate on whether the Act of Union with Britain in 1800 debilitated or assisted Irish economic development has remained problematical, as two commentators insisted that the economic outcome for Ireland was ruinous, nine taking the opposite view, while a further nine remained neutral (Kennedy and Johnston 1996). Hickman (1995) however, had little doubt when arguing that Ireland was at the epicentre of capitalist industrialisation but in a colonial and subservient role, permitted to produce agricultural produce only and then on condition that it did not endanger British products. As a result, Ireland became an emigrant nursery to supply industrial workers from the thousands of its displaced agricultural labourers. There was some support for this view since Connolly (1996) contended that there was in effect a policy of excluding Ireland from British colonial commerce but without local compensatory action. The resultant lack of industrial development was a clear case of British mis-government (Kennedy 1995).

Moreover, Ireland had itself experienced considerable progress as an industrial and capitalist economy by the time of the Industrial Revolution, where six of the twenty six counties that later formed the Republic of Ireland actually had more people engaged in industry than in agriculture but that from 1800 to 1922 free operation of market forces within the union of Britain and Ireland had a catastrophic effect on Ireland's economy in the first ten years of independent

---

[17] We will of course address this issue later in chapter ten, Conclusion : A Theory of Limits.

[18] A measure on 1 January 1801, creating The United Kingdom of Great Britain and Ireland, with one hundred Irish MPs sitting in the British House of Commons. Both exchequers and tax systems were later unified.

government (O'Malley 1989). The reason was that the emphasis on *laissez-faire* policies within the Act of Union was responsible for the decline of Irish industry up to 1922, leaving a mere eight per cent of the workforce in industry and half that again in manufacturing (Fitzpatrick and Kelly 1985).

This meant that after independence Ireland had to start its industrialisation process from scratch and was unique insofar as it had from that moment, followed the received wisdom of developmental economics to the letter and for longer than anyone else namely, protectionist from the 1930s to the 1950s and outward, open and free market from the 1950s to the present, dependent on substantial FDI, and giving all the appearance of a successful economy (O'Malley 1989). Yet another interpretation highlights over-reliance on the UK market, where the state of the British economy continued to exert a very significant negative impact on Irish development and Burke (1995) maintained that the continued inertia in the Irish economy was due to the long-term decline evident in the British economy particularly in the latter half of the twentieth century.

Internal Factors Explaining Poor Economic Growth

Despite the prominence of colonial arguments some commentators placed a more important emphasis on internal factors. As was pointed out towards the latter part of chapter two, the Great Famine defined the nature and scope of Ireland's economic problems for most of the twentieth century. As a result of this, one crucial course of action was denied the Irish economy. The key strategy of comparative advantage used by late industrialisers such as Germany after the industrial revolution and the post World War Two Asian Tiger economies, was unavailable as an option to Ireland because emigration induced an artificially high minimum wage level throughout the Irish economy (Barry 1999).[19] The impact of emigration is also singled out by Leddin and Walsh (1998) because the resultant intensive inward orientation by Irish society contributed significantly to a poor record of economic development.

Eventually when independence was achieved, there was a lack of political will on the part of successive Irish governments to develop an integrated industrial base (Firth 1967). This left the Irish economy with a grossly underdeveloped industrial infrastructure and an anti-industrial ethos (O'Donnell 1979). Furthermore, protectionist policies adopted by Fianna Fáil when they attained power culminated in the economic war with Britain in the 1930s that resulted, until the mid 1950s, in a shortfall of twenty five per cent in the level of national income that the economy was actually capable of generating (Sweeney 1992). Moreover, from 1932 to 1966 the Irish economy was the most protected in the world and this, according to Leddin and Walsh (1998), was by far the most important reason for poor economic development.

---

[19] Where both economies concentrated on the development of low wage sectors to generate economic growth through human capital accumulation.

These protectionist policies from 1932 onward led to a decade of stagnation in the 1950s, policies implemented in the main due to the failure of export oriented internationally competitive indigenous industries to realise foreign exchange (Fitzgerald, Geary, Lalor, Nolan and O'Malley 1996). When employment growth eventually happened in the 1960s and 1970s, it was primarily recorded in *foreign* owned export oriented companies and this exposed just how weak the indigenous Irish industry really was. Little appeared to have changed over more recent decades because the increased skills evident in the workforce was a key factor but only in attracting foreign investment since industry still continued to suffer from a considerable absence of internationally competitive *indigenous* firms (Fitzgerald, Geary, Lalor, Nolan and O'Malley 1996).

Moreover, Irish outward FDI stock was less than thirty per cent of inward FDI stock and this ratio was very low compared to levels in other EU countries and even lower when compared to the one hundred and thirty per cent ratio in the OECD overall, although it did increase in the period 1985-2001 to the point where over sixty thousand were employed in the US by Irish companies compared with one hundred thousand employed in Ireland by US companies (Forfás 2001a). One of the probable causes of the lack of focus on indigenous industry was that the Irish political system ensured that politicians were enmeshed in patronage and backscratching, so that a hapless state bureaucracy was powerless to formulate let alone implement an appropriate economic policy so that the exclusive focus on FDI and the pressure relieving impact of emigration allowed state agencies to skirt around the problem of indigenous development (O'Riain 2001).

With emigration averaging out at approximately 10.6 per 1000 of population, it also induced attitudes of mind and patterns of behaviour that led to mental disorientation in the general population prejudicial to economic development (Fanning 1983a). This disorientation was re-enforced with the imposition by the industrial Protestant British of individualistic capitalism on a pastoral communal society such as Ireland, which inevitably led to an outcome of underdeveloped industrialism (Crotty 1986). Yet the very group that should have shown a positive disposition towards industrialism, namely employers, were also unwilling to change behavioural patterns inimical to economic development (Weinz 1986). This was not surprising since there was an endemic low value placed by Irish society on economic development (Kennedy 1992) that resulted in the absence of a culture conducive to the spirit of enterprise and was directly responsible for the poor performance of Irish industry (Bielenberg 1995).

According to Lee (1989) and echoing Plunkett, the so-called Irish culture that was not conducive to enterprise was simply the fact that the Irish had a lazy work ethic. This pre-disposed them to adopt and apply a possessor rather than a performance ethos because the tangible rewards to be gained by adopting such an approach in Irish society was quite significant. Laziness was also highlighted in the 1960s by the then Taoiseach, Seán Lemass, who was sternly rebuked by the opposition TD Mr. Donegan in the Dáil (Parliament), criticising Lemass' morose justification of his own economic policies by arguing that fun and games were equally valid political objectives (Dáil Éireann 1965).[20]

Regarding the drag of Roman Catholic doctrine on economic development, Inglis (1989) was confident that the Catholic Church's teaching against materialism in the schools and in the pulpit worked directly against the formation of an industrial ethos.   However, proof of this influence was quite tenuous (Kennedy 1996) and in any event European industrial development in general was not a particularly Protestant event (Haughton 1991).

Yet early in the twentieth century, Catholicism had been singled out as the most important factor in the lack of economic development in Ireland because it was diverting significant domestic capital from industrial into Catholic church-building projects in the late nineteenth century (Plunkett 1905). Yet there was counter evidence that at that time to show that church-building actually contributed to economic growth although it could be conceded that it was indeed a reflection of a social structure inimical to economic development (Kennedy 1996). What does appear to be undisputed however, is the energy of the clergy in promoting Danish style agricultural co-operative development in preference to the British industrial development approach (Kennedy 1996a).

Other observations included factors such as the vagaries of the Irish PR system of voting which ensured that it was almost impossible to pursue national over individual and sectional interests particularly in the economic field (Mair 1992). Consequently the immediate need of politicians remained firmly focussed on local clients and interest groups rather than on national aims and objectives (Kingston 1995). Nor was localism a peculiarly modern phenomenon because throughout the nineteenth century it superseded all national aspirations for the everyday attention of politicians (O'Tuathaigh 1999). It was all too evident in the Celtic Tiger where it was not uncommon for politicians to regularly interrupt their state work to attend to the individual needs of constituents such as fixing a back door on a council house and as a result major national issues such as reducing poverty never received enough attention (Donnycarney Unemployment Group 2001).   The contention of Bradford De Long (1989) that honest government[21] was required to generate the social capacity to undertake sustained economic development was, according to

---

[20] Again in chapter ten we will show that the emphasis on this-worldly enjoyment was not confined to the 1960s but also emerged in our own research because it is a valid Catholic worldview contrasting with the exclusive work emphasis of the Protestant Ethic (PWE).

[21] Still, Irish corruption levels are quite low by international standards being judged the fifteenth least corrupt society in a survey of eighty-eight countries, although many poorer Catholic countries are placed at the more corrupt end of the data set. There is some evidence to link higher GDP with lower corruption levels but because many countries with low GDP levels are also Catholic, it is then assumed that religion is directly responsible, but that correlation is not proven.   See Paldam, M. (1999), *The Big Pattern of Corruption: Economics, Culture and the Seesaw Dynamics*, Working Paper, Department of Economics, University of Aarhus, Denmark.

O'Toole (1999), largely absent in Ireland and allowed a culture of corruption to flourish throughout the 1970s and 1980s.

Another argument according to Kennedy Giblin and McHugh (1994) was that the lack of relevance of Irish Catholic education to the world of work and other inherited past attitudes inimical to economic dynamism, inculcated a strong preference for safe jobs in the professions and public service. Yet the religious ethos in Catholic schools in the US has been identified as the primary reason not only for the permanence of orthodox Catholic religious and moral values among Irish Catholics in the US but simultaneously responsible for the advancement of Irish Catholic American students into the top echelons of American society, second only to Jews in average annual income and educational attainment and third after Americans of British Protestant origin and Jews in occupational prestige (Murphy 1997).

Category Two - Debates Explaining the Emergence of the Celtic Tiger

It is worth remembering that the Celtic Tiger was not the first and only example of a high performing Irish phase of economic development. In the 1960s and 1970s, following the policy shift of the then Taoiseach, Sean Lemass from an inward protectionist to an outward open economy based on foreign direct investment, a measure of sustained growth was achieved that generated the highest GDP growth rate in the EU (Fitzpatrick and Kelly 1985). However, this short burst of growth was an exceptional one-off experience due to the success of the Irish Government in attracting a significant proportion of the available mobile global investment in those decades (O'Malley 1989).

O'Malley (1989) argued that the most significant difference in the industrial policy of Japan, Taiwan and South Korea – and to a lesser extent Singapore and Hong Kong, who used the same exclusive inward investment strategy policy as Ireland – was that they all departed from the orthodox view on industrial development, moved from the free operation of the markets – the very approach that dominated much of the thinking behind many Irish industrial policy makers since the 1950s – to protection and selective intervention in indigenous industries to overcome barriers to market entry experienced by latecomers. Another common economic development strategy of Asian Tigers was their adoption of an approach with a significant manufacturing orientation and it was this that enabled sustainable and superior economic growth to occur (Fingleton 1999). In contrast, many commentators on Celtic Tiger development highlighted quite different approaches.[22] The most notable are presented in Table 4.1 below.

---

[22] This is highly contested arena. Nobody has yet succeeded in establishing how development is caused by the combination of factors listed in the models. It now seems more likely that the push dynamic exerted by so-called leading factors is much weaker than the pull of the growth dynamic itself i.e. development growth may initiate the need for the conditions rather than the reverse.

Table 4.1 Celtic Tiger Economic Growth Models

Author	*Key Conditions-Variables Identified*
1. Sweeney[a]	FDI, Tight Fiscal Policy, Stable Macro Economic Policy, EU Transfers, Labour Market Flexibility.
2. O'Hearn[b]	Problematic Multiple Causes.
3. OECD[c]	Government Policy of De-Regulation, EU Transfers, Increased Labour Supply, Quality of Education and Skills.
4. Geoghegan[d]	FDI, Policy Consistency, EU Transfers, Demographics, Higher Levels of Education, Social Partnership.
5. Walsh[e]	FDI, Favourable Exchange Rates, Large Number of Unemployed Available, Social Partnership.
6. Barry[f]	FDI, Fiscal Stability in the 1980s, EU Transfers, Increased Level of Education in the Workforce.
7. Allen[g]	Tax Haven for American FDI Stable Pro-Business Political Climate, EU Transfers, Young Educated English Speaking and Cheapest Labour in EU, 'Coat Tailing' on US Economy.
8. Fitzgerald[h]	A Forty Year Strategy of FDI, Fiscal Stability in the 1980s, Policy Consistency, English Language, Concentration on the Core Employment of Sophisticated Services, Outward Looking Attitude most Important Factor in Economic Recovery.
9. Forfás[i]	Policy Decisions taken in the 1960s such as Education and Industry, Social Partnership, De-regulation, Investment in Human Capital, Globalisation of Investment, EU Membership, German Spending after Re-unification.

[a] Sweeney, P. (1998), *The Celtic Tiger: Ireland's Economic Miracle Explained*, Oak Tree Press, Dublin, p. 1, p. 203.

[b] O'Hearn, D. (1998), *Inside the Tiger: The Irish Economy and the Asian Model*, Pluto Press, London, p. 12.

[c] OECD (1999), *Economic Survey of Ireland - May 1999*, OECD, Paris, pp. 27-31.

[d] Geoghegan, B. (1999), 'Ireland - The Challenges of Success', Irish Business and Employers Association, Dublin, paper delivered in Halifax, Nova Scotia, May 1999, p. 2.

[e] Walsh, B. (1999a), 'The Persistence of High Unemployment in a Small Open Labour Market: The Irish Case', Frank Barry (ed.), *Understanding Ireland's Economic Growth*, Macmillan Press, London, p. 223.

[f] Barry, F. (1999), 'Irish Growth in Historical and Theoretical Perspective', Frank Barry(ed.), *Understanding Ireland's Economic Growth*, Macmillan Press, London, Essay 2, p. 1, pp. 25-26.

[g] Allen, K. (2000), *The Celtic Tiger - The Myth of Social Partnership in Ireland*, Manchester University Press, Manchester, pp. 16-19, pp. 25-27, p. 160, p. 174.

[h] Fitzgerald, J. (2000), 'The Story of Ireland's Failure-and Belated Success', Brian Nolan, Philip J. O'Connell and Christopher T. Whelan (eds.), *Bust or Boom - The Irish Experience of Growth and Inequality*, IPA, Dublin, p. 28, pp. 55-57.

[i] Forfás (2000b), *Enterprise 2010 - A New Strategy for the Promotion of Enterprise in Ireland in the 21ˢᵗ Century*, Forfás, Dublin, pp 1-4.

The wide array of variables cited in these mainly descriptive models highlights two important insights. The first is that they expose the weakness of the descriptive approach by providing a list of conditions deemed conducive for growth without explaining how all these variables generate the growth, i.e. there is a lack of focus on the process of development. Secondly, while there is some disagreement among experts on the precise origins of the Celtic Tiger they are not without generalising tendencies. For example FDI is included in models one, four, five, six, eight and nine. EU Structural Funds is included in models one, three, six, eight and nine while Education is cited in models four, five, six and nine. The correct Fiscal Policy is identified in models one, five, six and nine. In a telling assessment of the Celtic Tiger models one, two three and four in comparison to the Asian Tiger models, Goodwin (1999a) concluded that serious structural dissimilarities existed in the Irish case such as the absence of integrated human resource strategies situated as they were within a framework of sectional interests dominating national goals.

Commentators themselves differed even on identifying *the* most important of these factors. For example, the single most important factor identified for the emergence of the Celtic Tiger is membership of the EU where many global corporation have located in Ireland to service this wider EU market (Duffy, Fitzgerald, Kearney, Hore and MacCoill 2001). The perceived link between increased investment in education-training and economic growth in models three, four, six and nine was another identified by Leddin and Walsh (1998) as *the* key contributory factor to recent Irish economic growth. Another was that of Durkan, Fitzgerald and Harmon (1999) who argued that using the Solow growth model i.e. growth in labour and capital stock together with technical change to calculate the supply capacity of the economy, the human capital measure of the rising education levels in the workforce, namely the Education Adjusted Employment Level (EAL), had contributed nearly a third of the total GNP growth rate for the period 1991-1996. The direct contribution of education was estimated to have added as little as one half of one per cent to the average per annum four per cent GDP in the period 1980-1997 (Healy 2003).

O'Gráda's (1997) assessment was that the empirical literature had indeed uncovered a positive correlation between levels of investment and the economic growth rate and as the levels of capital and human resources invested in the Republic of Ireland up to the mid 1980s were well below other countries at a similar stage of development, growth rates were bound to be low.[23] Pissarides (2000) argued that a correlation of this type only existed theoretically and not empirically, since most economists relied on three narrow macroeconomic

---

[23] We have already argued that it is not feasible to rely on this assumption. For example education expansion at the three levels in Egypt from 1980 to 1995 was approximately equal to that of the Asian Tiger South Korea, yet Egypt actually dropped one place to forty eighth poorest with average growth rates of two per cent per annum in contrast to the seven per cent of South Korea. Switzerland has one of the lowest third level rates in the OECD yet has the second most competitive economy. See Wolf, A. (2002), *Does Education Matter? Myths about Education and Economic Growth*, Penguin Books, London, pp. 39-40.

aggregates of employment, schooling and participation rates to make their case. In fact there is now a growing scepticism that reliable and formal evidence exists on the precise impact of education on economic development and on the accumulation effects of human capital in particular and this is a correlation that remains extremely difficult to verify (OECD 1999b, European Commission 2002).

Nevertheless, Krugman (1997) argued that both the levels and quality of the investment in the Irish education system was *the* outstanding factor underpinning the success of the Celtic Tiger. However, Apple (1990) provided an instructive observation on the critical role of intellectuals in providing legitimacy for political and economic ideology when he stated that while they support the predominant political and economic ruling class the favour is returned when politicians and economists support the education system.

Notwithstanding the arguments above, nearly all theories concerning the Asian newly industrialising countries placed the accumulation of investments in physical and human capital at the core of any explanation of their success (Nelson and Pack 1997).[24] Yet as already noted in the opening section of the study, the IMF (2000) warned that the training and education objectives of the Irish National Development Plan 2000-2006 were not clearly formulated.

In 2000 a surprising new emphasis was noted in the explanations when Walsh (2000) exhorted other economists to come clean and own up to the fact that not alone was the Irish miracle unforeseen but its duration was actually beyond forecasting. As there was still no economic model which predicted the Celtic Tiger as late as 1990, most analysts therefore focussed on reasons for past economic failure implying that the Celtic Tiger was either an aberration or that all along from 1922 onwards, unknown sociological preconditions for economic development were being formed (O'Gráda 1997). Either way the previous scenarios precluded what was now beginning to be acknowledged i.e. the absence of rational and organised planning towards a pre-determined Tiger outcome. As a matter of fact, the Celtic Tiger was the least predicted phase of economic development while it went on to have *the* most dramatic transformation on the economy (Whitaker 2001). The unexpected nature of this transformation and the incredulity expressed at the level of Irish economic performance had the effect of making commentators and the general public wary that it would all end in failure due to the Irish inexperience of and poor preparation for, managing sustained and strong growth (Hannigan 2000).

The public's premonition appeared a sound one because quite suddenly the demise of the Celtic Tiger was officially announced (*Irish Times* 2001).[25] Just a day previously McCoy, Duffy, Hore and MacCoille (2001) of the Economic and Social Research Institute, stated in their Quarterly Economic Commentary that as a

---

[24] Other variables such as technology transfer, learning capability and the crucial aggressive ethos of entrepreneurship that develops in the absence of government interference are also taken into account.

[25] On 7 November 2001, the Governor of the Central Bank of Ireland, Maurice O'Connell declared to a joint Oireachtas (Legislature) Committee on Finance that the Celtic Tiger era was over.

result of the 11 September attacks and the Foot and Mouth Disease (FMD), the economy had moved into a new phase of lower below potential output growth. This was coupled with a significant deterioration in public finances, the re-emergence of a budget deficit and an end to a decade of declining unemployment. Moreover, they pointed out that first quarter GDP growth in 2001 of over thirteen per cent would be halved for the year, with a further sharp fall to just over three per cent predicted for 2002. Shortly after that announcement, the Central Statistics Office (2001c) confirmed that GNP had dropped from eleven per cent growth in the first quarter of 2001 to a mere one per cent in the second quarter and unemployment rose for the first time since 1996 from just over three per cent to just over four per cent.

Then in early December 2001 the CSO figures showed an increase of seven and half thousand in monthly seasonally adjusted unemployment figures (Central Statistics office 2001d). This was the largest increase ever recorded in the history of the state. By late December, Forfás (2001) stated that for the first time in over fifteen years employment had decreased in companies supported by the Industrial Development Authority where many multi-nationals were concentrated. An increase of just under fifteen thousand jobs in 2000 had turned into a net loss of just under four thousand jobs in 2001. A sense of déjà-vu descended when the World Economic Forum's Global Competitiveness Report for 2002-2003 placed Ireland as the twenty fourth most competitive economy, just two places above its twenty sixth position in the early stages of the Celtic Tiger and a long way from the heady fourth position achieved in 2000 (Cornelius 2002).

The accidental emergence and demise of the Celtic Tiger would appear to lend substance to O'Sullivan's (1995) argument that the 'Lap of the Gods' approach is just as valid as the so called empirical models on the basis that mainstream economists are regularly caught off guard, totally incapable of constructing a theory analysing the interrelationship between economic policy and performance with the result that they are not in any position to determine let alone provide a precise explanation of *how* the process of industrial development actually occurs.

Indeed a comparison of the development strategy and social preconditions between Ireland and Singapore are quite instructive.[26] Singapore too was a former British colony, became an independent democratic Republic in 1965, over forty

---

[26] The analytical weakness of relying on just one input factor, namely education, as the dynamic underpinning economic development is highlighted in the performance of eastern and western tiger economies. Although Ireland is placed ninth for third level density i.e. universities per head of population, against Singapore's fourteenth and while fifty per cent of the Irish workforce is educated below second level, the comparable figure in Singapore is higher at sixty five per cent, it is illuminating that Singapore has still managed to achieve a top ranking in competitiveness in the annual BERI Survey of forty nine of the worlds most developed economies for twenty one consecutive years since 1980. In this 'Labour Force Evaluation Measure Assessment' Ireland had achieved a fifth place in 2000 but only on one of the four criteria used i.e. productivity, but even here it had fallen back to fifteenth place by 2001. See *Ranking of Singapore's Workforce by BERI*, Development and Planning Centre, Productivity and Innovation Group, SPRING, Singapore. See also *Singapore's Manufacturing Miracle*, The Committee for Economic Development of Australia.

years later than Ireland, with a parliamentary system of government (Govt. of Singapore 2000). It had a highly educated workforce of 2.119 million (slightly larger than Ireland) with approximately forty per cent educated above second level although it was experiencing an unemployment crisis of 2.6 per cent (less than Ireland's 4.3 per cent) while it's Gross Domestic Product was down from 4.7 per cent in first quarter to -0.9 per cent in the second quarter of 2001 (Govt of Singapore 2001, Govt of Singapore 2001a).

Nevertheless, this rate is less than half of the Irish GDP decrease for the same period. Religiosity is also similar to Irish levels standing at eighty five per cent of the population but again is different in nature and denomination. Singapore is a multi racial society and religious affiliation is categorised as one third Buddhists, one fifth Taoists, one seventh Muslims, one eighth Christians of which one third are Roman Catholics, with the remainder being Hindu (Govt of Singapore 2000).

There are additional key institutional differences between Ireland and Singapore that impact of developmental progress. In Singapore one political party has maintained power since independence and government policy and implementation is highly interventionist, paternalist and with the overwhelming emphasis on matching outcomes of the education system to the objectives of manpower planning (Felstead, Ashton, Green and Sung 1994).[27] Manpower planning interventions are themselves guided by an industrial vision and strategy (Green and Sung 1997). There is a continuous process of structural adjustment to get the government's economic vision right (Ashton 1998) that is based on high levels of institutional integration (Ashton and Green 1996).

In contrast, Ireland is generally perceived to be a decentralist country with some centralist tendencies (Hardiman 1994) where the Irish government is subject to a pluralist play of interest groups (Pellion 1995). The emphasis on client needs at a local level take precedence over national issues, where a premium is placed on 'stroking' (Lee 1989) in a culture where truth and honesty are not valued.[28] The inevitable outcome is the inability to define long-term economic aims (Goodwin 1997). Moreover, the Irish education system is state funded and centralised and generally speaking Church controlled (Inglis 1998). Crucially, third level education is determined by government budgets rather than human resource needs in the marketplace (O'Hare 1999).

In their review of the literature on East Asia's Tigers and their miraculous economic growth rates, Haggard and Kim (2001) pointed out that while some

---

[27] Singaporean children were deemed the best educated in the World. Irish children were assessed well below the Singaporean level. See 'Special-Educational League Tables-Who's Top?' *The Economist*, 29 March 1997.

[28] Similar to the term 'blagging' used in the UK – conning or beating the system for personal gain – can also mean working while claiming the dole (social welfare payments) or using a small scam to get into an event or club without paying. John Giles former Leeds United and Republic of Ireland soccer footballer now sports broadcaster, insisted that stroking was widely admired in politics and business in Ireland and so why not in football approving the case for a footballer diving in the penalty area to cheat the referee (Giles 1998).

empirical evidence existed identifying a correlation between export oriented strategy and fast economic growth there was no clear understanding of *how* this happened as the nature of the relationship was unknown due to an absence of a strong explanatory theory. O'Hearn (1998), acknowledged that the Singaporean government was successful in implementing and co-ordinating economic policies, but he was compelled to offer guesswork rather than empirical solutions, pointing to a combination of both cultural and historical conditions conducive to economic development.

However, following their analysis of the literature on the sustainability of the Asian Tiger economies, Haggard and Kim (2001) proposed that the propensity for growth does not rest solely on open trade but on prior social foundations such as strong state intervention and relative social equity, factors that are not easily replicated in other states. Some years earlier Bradford and Chakwin (1993) had demonstrated that Asian Tigers' output growth was not caused by growth in exports due to increased openness and trade liberalisation as was commonly advanced in the literature, but by improved export capacity due to new and continuous human and capital investment.[29] The reason for the early and rapid industrialisation of Singapore and the other Tigers was that the social and historical foundations of the new state promoted the accumulation of capital through industrial development (Hamilton 1983). Fast paced accumulation was primarily due to the substantial inward direct investment by foreign multinationals in a narrow base of industries such as electronics, a process in stark contrast to the indigenously driven manufacturing expansion of Taiwan, Hong Kong and South Korea (Hamilton 1983). Whatever the secret of Singapores mix of variables and comparable levels of FDI penetration, the net manufacturing output and industrial exports achieved by Singapore thirteen years after independence were only achieved in Ireland twenty years later and seventy six years after its own independence. This much at least is captured in Table 4.2.

Table 4.2 Penetration of MNCs in Singapore, 1978 and Ireland, 1998

MNCs	*Singapore 1978* [a]	*Ireland 1998* [b]
Employment	52%	47%
Net Manufacturing Output	71%	77%
Industrial Exports	84%	84%

[a] Yoshihara, Kunio (1976), 'Foreign Investment and Domestic Response:A Study of Singapore's Industrialisation', Institute of Southeast Asian Studies, Eastern U.P, cited in Hamilton, C. (1983), 'Capitalist Industrialisation in the Four Little Tigers of East Asia', Peter Limqueco and Bruce McFarlane (eds.), *Neo-Marxist Theories of Development*, Croom Helm, London, ffn. 34, p. 178.
[b] OECD (1999), *OECD Economic Surveys Ireland:1998-1999*, OECD, Paris, p. 54.

---

[29] Their study presented investment as the primary cause of sustained high output growth.

From these figures we can see that multi-national industrial exports in 1998 measured as a per cent of total exports and net manufacturing output was only equal to comparable levels achieved in the Singaporean economy more than twenty years earlier. Moreover, in 1978 the Singaporean multi-national sector accounted for a higher proportion of total employment than that achieved in the same sector in the Irish economy in 1998. In 1998 Singapore's GDP rate still remained at a level that was sixty eight per cent greater than the Irish figure.

Although the World Competitiveness Report (1999) showed Tiger Ireland as the tenth most competitive economy, Singapore was still by far the most competitive, concluding that Ireland was strong on government, labour, technology and finance, but weak on infrastructure (IMI 1999). By 2002 Singapore had improved one position to the third most competitive economy whereas Ireland was moving in the opposite direction falling to twenty sixth position.

Table 4.3 GDP per Capita of Countries/Regions of Similar Size to Ireland

Country	Pop.	$US GDP per capita
Singapore	2.9m	32,436
Oregan USA	2.8m	26,554
Iowa, USA	2.8m	24,392
Schleswig Holstein (Ger)	2.8m	21,416
Aquitaine France	2.8m	19,662
Ireland	*3.6m*	*19,269*
New Zealand	3.5m	18,567
Britanny France	2.8m	18,430
Scotland	5.1m	15,981
Wales	2.9m	13,741
Saxony-Anhalt East Germany	2.7m	12,122

Source: Pathway to Prosperity a New Economic Agenda for Wales, The Welsh Office, 1998 Chapter 3, p. 8.

O'Riain (2001) noted that Irish state agencies have only recently begun to create a social world supportive of innovation, industry and growth, something long taken for granted in the Asian Tiger economies. The agencies have succeeded in this by embedding economic life in political and social relations and together with their own flexible organisational structures are now only *beginning* to manage the connections between local firms and the global economy by becoming a flexible developmental state. This means that the Irish government allows the global economy free reign, but at the same time ensures that local workers and firms connect with it and thereby avoid the more direct interventionist approach of the Singaporean government (O'Riain 2001).

An Accident of Birth!

Despite the many varied empirical accounts of development articulated in the above discussion and to counter the impression that models of Celtic Tiger development are presented as recognised formulae to safe crack or unlock the developmental mystery, it is worth reflecting on the observations of the OECD who pointed not to rational planning but to a mere fortunate conjunction of circumstances. In other words they nominated lady luck as a key influence in the Irish developmental process. While acknowledging the peerless performance of the economy, now by this time a world leader in a number of aspects of economic performance, the OECD (1999) maintained that Ireland had no silver bullet, was just plain lucky to undertake its fiscal correction in the presence of favourable world economic events.

Sweeney (1998) had previously argued that luck was indeed a factor and suggested that many economic, social and political forces unwittingly fell together by chance into the right configuration to allow the economy take off. Both Fitzgerald (1999) and Fitzgerald and Girvin (2000) also nominated luck albeit as one of the key factors enabling the dynamic of economic growth to gain momentum together with factors such as the social partnership consensus approach, multinational investment and rising education levels. O'Mahony (2000) too concluded that the Celtic Tiger was just sheer good luck rather than good management where complementary variables just happened to come together in the absence of government policy. Even the much lauded and so-called far sighted industrial planning of Lemass' First Programme for Economic Expansion of 1958 based primarily on seeking and securing inward investment and identified by some as *the* cause of spectacular economic growth in the early sixties, was hotly disputed by others who claimed that Lemass just got plain lucky (Lynch 1968). In her 2001 Oldcastle Lecture the present Tánaiste also spoke about how fortunate Irish society had been to have such a benign international environment that assisted with the emergence of the Celtic Tiger miracle (Harney 2001).

Nevertheless, some analysts rejected this lucky factor including the OECD who had previously endorsed it. They now provided a more traditional analysis by identifying the high technology multi-national investment sector as the key underlying dynamic and emphasised that it had not changed much since the 1960s (OECDa 1999). Another commentator Fitzgerald (2000) argued that the timing of Lemass' decision to introduce a sustained policy of substantial educational investment in 1967 together with his economic policy of FDI although twenty years behind most other European countries, were and still are well regarded as decisions crucial in creating the Celtic Tiger.

Of course the point about having a belief in luck or chance is that it indicates a well developed mindset that assigns to events a pre-determined supernatural outcome rather than relying on quantitative facts to explain effects (Veblen 1953). This belief directly affects all other habits of thought affecting the individuals life particularly in the economic sphere and runs directly counter to the industrially efficient consciousness that is a necessary pre-requisite for advanced industrial societies (Veblen 1953). However the diversity of explanations including those highlighting luck and put forward to explain the emergence of the Celtic Tiger leads to a strong suspicion that economists really do not understand the underlying processes although they invariably exclude religious and nationalist sentiments from their summaries.

The following is a brief list of the more important variables presented by both the International Monetary Fund and senior Irish government ministers as they struggled to explain the Irish economic miracle. The IMF (2000) provided the following seven interrelated reasons for the continued economic expansion that was happening at what they termed 'a torrid pace'

a) export oriented FDI
b) low cost English speaking workforce with links to American multinational decision makers through a history of migration,
c) EU structural funding
d) the fiscal crisis of 1987 which was addressed decisively
e) improved education and training standards
f) partnership models of social consensus
g) the early concentration FDI in high growth sectors which gave Ireland a competitive edge particularly in attracting a cluster of sectoral related multi-nationals.

Earlier the Tánaiste, identified a list of macro and structural factors underpinning economic success such as low inflation, moderate wage increases, prudent budgetary policies, low interest rates, and the falling tax burden on employees and companies and highlighted that

> these achievements are based on hard work and the commitment
> of people in all sectors of the economy and in all parts of the
> country. (Harney 1999: foreword)

Her statement is unique because it marks one of the few recorded acknowledgements of a positive correlation between the Irish work ethic and higher productivity and economic success. In other words, she acknowledged a socio-cultural factor that was usually overlooked in explanations of positive economic growth. Now the curious thing about that acknowledgement was, that while Catholicism was regarded as a significantly negative influence on the work ethic when development was poor (Plunkett 1905, Inglis 1989, Lee 1989, Lemass 1965), it must have disappeared before or during the Celtic Tiger – which we know was not the case – or that it was transformed into the Protestant one – something that we intended to establish from our research. Even as the labour contribution was recognised, it was done so only indirectly. For example, the National Competitiveness Council (1999) praised the structure of the social partnership consensus approach where the restraint of the greedy impulse by representatives and members of the Trade Unions was suppressed in favour of national interests. These partnerships were regarded as central to Ireland's economic success (IMF 2000), an important contributory factor to economic growth and job creation

(Hardiman 2000) and constituted *the* winning economic formula (MacSharry and White 2000).

However, two academics maintained, for opposing reasons, that social partnership should have been abandoned altogether. One claimed that the strength of the approach worked best to bring the economy to rather than maintain full employment but the fifth Partnership Agreement had given workers excessive wage increases leading to inflation (Leddin 2000).[30] The other claimed that the Celtic Tiger was only a myth because Irish labour had in fact fared much worse than either Irish or multi-national capital under these partnerships and a return to collective bargaining was recommended to address this imbalance (Allen 1999).

A call to re-evaluate the sustainability of the Celtic Tiger was also made by Anthony Sweeney (1999) who argued that the excessive growth of the Irish economy had distorted psychological perceptions where individuals and businesses abandoned fiscal prudence that in turn created conditions favourable for the usual boom-bust scenario characteristic of capitalism. He contended that all the Asian Tiger economies went bust in the 1990s and to regard Ireland as an exception to the rule only demonstrated the power of the myth surrounding the sustainability of the Celtic Tiger. Another critical factor then emerged in the shape of claims by some occupational groups that they had a pivotal role in the economic success of recent times and should be appropriately rewarded, such as the Association of Higher Civil and Public Servants (AHCPS 2000) and schoolteachers (RTÉ 2000, EL 2001).

Official Explanations for the Emergence of the Celtic Tiger

It is clear from the economic speeches and press briefings made from late 1998 to early 2001 by the Taoiseach, the Tánaiste and the Minister for Finance that the Government had only the flimsiest grasp of how the Celtic Tiger had emerged. Again and again they listed factors, often isolating and describing the principal ones deemed responsible, but provided little in the way of explaining the process of development.[31] For example social partnership and consensus was quoted as the most important factor in a number of speeches made by the Taoiseach on the economy. Other factors mentioned included education, FDI and technology transfer. Moreover, if one examines the speeches of the Tánaiste, as Minister for Enterprise Trade and Employment in the period 1998-2000 where she made remarks concerning the economy and the factors that she considered were crucial in making the Celtic Tiger a reality, the following factors were highlighted by her, namely fiscal and taxation policy (five speeches), social partnership (four speeches), education (four speeches), economic planning (four speeches), pay

---

[30] Programme for Prosperity and Fairness (The PPF) reached in February 2000.

[31] For example the Taoiseach's Address to Budapest University of Economic Sciences 'Ireland: From the Periphery to the Centre of Europe', 3 November 1999. His Address to The Irish Business Organisation of New York, Thursday, 11 November 1999. His Speech at a Dinner of the Ireland-Japan Association, 22 January 2000.

moderation (two speeches), economic liberalism (one speech), workforce skill development (one speech), flexible labour supply (one speech) and finally, the nature and diversification of current levels of international trade (one speech). For a full list of her 'economic' speeches examined please refer to Appendix A.

In these speeches there are over twelve all important macro economic variables that are deemed to provoke economic growth. Together with the common factors already noted in the nine Celtic Tiger models, the seven variables outlined by the IMF, the myriad of growth and non growth causes in the debates, it now seems that the Celtic Tiger was almost too well camouflaged to be visible. In fact, by attempting to isolate and prioritise a distinguishing subset of factors as the primary catalyst for the economic turnaround, the most expert economists have only added confusion to an area not well understood by overestimating the impact of some factors such as labour supply and underestimating others such as de-regulation (McAleese 2000).[32]   Only recently had Irish economists Fitzgerald and Girvin (2000) concluded that no one set of universal factors actually existed which were responsible for Irish economic growth, but on the contrary the answer *probably* lay in specific responses and adjustments to internal and external forces.

Haggard and Kew (2001) identified a useful framework used in their own explanatory models of Asian Tiger economies to rationalise a similar diversity of variables. They isolated key variables that contributed to factor accumulation as the main cause of sustained growth.[33] They then shifted their attention to supplementary factors thought to improve productivity such as tax and policy reform, openness to trade, de-regulation and flexibility. Yet even on the issue of openness to trade and economic growth, they warned that not only does the reverse causality exist between factor accumulation and growth, but that the direction of causality between economic openness and growth is highly problematical,[34] because the process of economic growth itself is not fully understood.[35] In Ireland this form of contested argument was often overlooked by the politicians.

The Tánaiste (2001) claimed that Ireland was the second most open economy in the world becoming the largest exporter of computer software in the world and manufacturing almost two thirds of all computers sold in Europe. The Globalisation Index of The Foreign Policy Magazine (2002) showed that in 2000

---

[32] The link between economic policy and growth.

[33] Human and physical capital, investment in plant and increases in education.

[34] Structural Vector AutoRegression Techniques (VAR) were used on panel data in an attempt to establish whether outward orientated export-led growth directly stimulates the economy or and whether investment-led output, mainly trade liberalisation, more competition and skill development were responsible.

[35] Generally the debates are divided into those emphasising investment of factors i.e. on factor inputs and those focusing on innovation, entrepreneurship and high performance organisation and work practices i.e. on maximising the factor mix. For an analysis on the effectiveness of the latter see Ashton, D. and Sung, J. (2002), *Supporting Workplace Learning for High Performance Working*, ILO, Geneva.

Ireland was the most global economy in the world.[36]   Yet the Report simultaneously acknowledged that many aspects of global integration including culture defy measurement. By 2003 it had been accepted that three quarters of the average per capita GDP growth rate of four percent in the period 1980-1997 could not be satisfactorily explained (Healy 2003). His use of the term 'contributory suspects' was very revealing. The Minister for Finance, in a radio interview with the broadcaster Eamonn Dunphy in 2000 appeared to have pre-empted this academic cul de sac when he verbalised in a forthright and public manner what many people were privately thinking. He just accepted the Celtic Tiger as a fact, exhorted everyone else just to get on with it and make the best of it while it lasted.

[transcript from broadcast tape]

> what we succeeded in doing from 1987 onwards is, whereas it might look very complicated is actually very, very simple...we've been able to give Irish business a competitive edge...by keeping down nominal wage increases, increasing productivity and that has allowed all those jobs which we've been speaking about...the reason we've been able to do this is we've been able to maintain our competitiveness...any sane person, on any side of the table, would have to say 'look we have found a successful formula for managing a small open economy like Ireland, why would you throw it away?' Did you ever know a manager of a successful team, whether you agreed with his tactics or not, and if they were winning, who changed them? when you do find a winning formula one is inclined to stick with it, and we have in Ireland found a winning formula. Now when history is written people have all kinds of views whether we came across the winning formula by accident or design, or through necessity or whatever it may be...but we *did* find it, and we should keep with it. (Minister for Finance: 2000a)

Yet even this winning and accidental formula was regarded as too aggressive by the Taoiseach and needed to be subject to the mediating and positive influence of Catholicism. In his reply to the Irish Catholic Bishops Letter 'Prosperity with a Purpose' Mr. Ahern (2000) described in his quest to achieve both a competitive economy *and* a caring society, how Catholicism could beneficially engage with sustained economic development particularly when it acted as both an antidote to selfish materialism and as a counter balance to the potential ravages of tooth and claw capitalism. The Prime Minister's approach also anticipated one aspect of a re-occurring theme that emerged from the analysis of the research responses to be presented later in chapter six, namely the proclivity of Irish society to concern

---

[36] Measured against benchmarks such as the use of technology, economic integration, political engagement with the outside world and travel, tourism and cross border transfers.

itself with the achievement of a balanced material and spiritual state of well-being.[37]

Conclusion of Theme One

The Weber-Tawney debate on the central role of religion as the key to understanding the dynamic of Irish economic development has been re-visited. The analytical weaknesses of many sociological insights as applied to the developmental processes in small post-colonial states such as Ireland, were discussed.

Then in chapter two, the developmental path of the Irish economy was placed in an historical context where a number of key events had such a profound impact on Irish social and economic structures that they determined both the nature and scope of Irish economic problems right up to the 1990s.

In chapter three data was presented that confirmed the status of Ireland's Tiger economy at a time when Irish Catholic religiosity in terms of belief and practice was universally high. The Celtic Tiger continued to be characterised by the presence of at least two durable normative forces, namely religion and nationalism. This threw doubt on the argument of Weber supporting the role of Protestantism in western economic development.

In the final chapter four, a comprehensive analysis and discussion on the debates surrounding the dynamic of Irish economic development since 1922 was presented. It was difficult not to conclude from that analysis that no one really understood what actually caused the Celtic Tiger to emerge. The term 'miracle' seemed very apt indeed. This accidental or miraculous explanation now provides a tip off on a line of enquiry that until now had appeared unproductive namely, the relatively unknown role of Absolute Pre-suppositions on individual economic behaviour and the subsequent effect that this behaviour may have on economic development. The results of this search over a four year period looking for the clues that would add to our understanding of the elusive developmental process is now presented under theme two in chapters five and six respectively.

---

[37] Not specifically the work/personal life balance that is currently in fashion as part of human resource management practices although we shall discuss it in chapter six as part of our research findings and more specifically in the Theory of Limits. Here, this philosophy sits within the fashionable quality of life debate that is itself informed by Enlightenment ideology. This thinking tries to ensure the greatest happiness for the greatest number by attacking ignorance, illness and poverty and then ensuring that a reasonable material standard of living is provided for all citizens who will then finally embed the practice of balanced good living in the wider society. See Veenhoven, R. (1998), 'Quality of Life and Happiness-Not Quite the Same', G. De Girolamo et al (eds), *Health and the Quality of Life*, Rome, Il Pensierro Scientificio. See
http://www.eur.nl/gsw/personnel/soc/veenhoven/Pub1990s/95b-ab.htm

Chapter 5

The Sample and the Methodological Approach

> Science cannot entertain the notion that there is any sort of difference which is inherently immeasurable i.e. there is a difference in kind as well as degree ...science by quantitative analysis can only deal with the skeleton not with the life that informs it...[can only]...furnish rules for the regular. (Hobson 1914: 154, 161)

Introduction

Under theme one we have provided a socio-economic profile of Ireland, traced the longer-term pattern of its economic development, validated its Tiger status and finally, established the accidental origins of the Celtic Tiger. In theme two, our aim is to provide a detailed presentation of and discussion on the research undertaken on a representative sample of the mosaic of Irish social life in the Celtic Tiger. This chapter contributes to this aim by providing a comprehensive description of the sample followed by a detailed discussion of the rationale and the research approach used, a description of and a discussion on, the design and implementation of a tailored research instrument. Specific methodological issues are also addressed, such as choice of methodology, pre-interview testing for the suitability of the research approach and instrument, interviewer engagement levels against a naturalistic background, truthfulness of responses, and finally some ethical considerations. We then follow our methodological discussion by providing some original extracts from the interviewees in chapter six. Finally towards the end of the chapter we present a profile of the Irish economic disposition that is informed by our research findings.

Initial Observations on the Sample and the Methodology

From the outset, it should be understood that in undertaking a study of this nature, namely to establish how religious beliefs shape both the nature and force of the Irish economic disposition, a unique set of research challenges had to be overcome. Both the nature and contrasting status of the respondents that represented the mosaic of Irish social life coupled with the sensitivity of the topic area demanded high levels of technical and social skills coupled with an ability to elicit information in a sensitive and flexible manner.

The sample profile was organised to reflect the macro economic stratification of the Irish economy i.e. it included contributions from the services, manufacturing and farming sectors of the economy. It did not however, rely on these three economic sectors but consisted of four groups or Domains of Contributors that would reflect and represent a more inclusive mosaic of Irish social life.

The first domain consisted of eight contributions from two strands of Irish life, one from those leading Irish economic affairs and from others leading the spiritual welfare of Irish society. The economic strand included two government ministers, a representative each from the Irish Business and Employers Confederation, the Irish Farmers Association and the Irish Congress of Trade Unions. The spiritual strand included contributions from, the Catholic Hierarchy, a senior representative of the Islamic community and a senior Anglican churchman the second largest Christian denomination in Ireland.

The second domain consisted of seven senior executives and managers in charge of Irish subsidiaries of two multinationals, one a unionised British manufacturing company and the other a non-unionised recently arrived American IT servicing company.

The third domain included seven contributions from a cross-section of staff working in both multi-nationals. This domain also included five contributions from nominated model farmers of the Irish Agricultural Advisory Research Service (Teagasc) including the Farmer of the Year.[38] The domain was completed by the inclusion of a number of Leaving Certificate students and some of their career guidance teachers.[39]

The fourth domain included contributions from four unemployed persons, a group of three homeless men, a national advocate of the homeless and a group of four Traveller women.

For convenience purposes the domains were labelled as follows, National Domain A (National and Religious Leaders), Executive Domain B (Senior Multi-national Executives), Labour Domain C (middle and junior management, technical,

---

[38] All were implementing the most modern farming techniques but some were part-time with another job off the farm and each hired seasonal labour when required. All farmed prime agricultural land in County Meath approximately thirty miles north of Dublin City or in County Kildare approximately thirty miles south of Dublin City. One was a dairy farmer with sixty acres, one a suckling farmer with eighty-five acres, one a dairy and beef farmer with sixty acres, one a tillage farmer with two hundred acres while another owned five hundred acres of mixed farming plus a thriving bed and breakfast adjacent to the farmhouse.

[39] The total number of pupils was one hundred and eighteen from six classes in four schools as follows: twenty from a mixed high ability class, twenty two from a mixed average ability class, twenty from a low ability class from the same north Dublin working and middle class secondary school run by the Dominican Nuns, fifteen of mixed ability in a boys secondary school in a north inner Dublin city school run by the Christian Brothers, twenty one from a south Dublin boys middle class secondary school run also by the Christian Brothers, twenty of mix ability from a north Dublin upper middle class girls secondary school run by the Holy Faith Nuns.

administrative, craft and operative levels plus farmers and students) and Disconnected Domain D (the homeless, Traveller women and the unemployed). Specific details of the sample, the unique but complementary contribution made by each Domain to the study and the issue of accessibility to individuals within each domain are now discussed.

Sample Profile

Two criteria were applied to the notion of typicality for inclusion in a domain. The first was the capacity of the occupational holder to determine the life chances of others to acquire material and or spiritual well-being. The second related to the concern in the research to establish attitudes and norms impacting on economic development. Therefore, social and psychological affinities were used because these affinities are to be found in the type of economic activity undertaken by individuals (Wright-Mill 1957). Individuals with similar economic functions were grouped together since the nature of this grouping can have an important role in the formation of an overall national economic disposition since the way a society produces its goods establishes its social and cultural shape (Storey 1993).

Multi-national companies were chosen because the data and debates in chapters three and four respectively had confirmed that they were the critical component underlying the dynamic of the Celtic Tiger. Both a services and a manufacturing multi-national were included to reflect the two most important economic sectors, one employing over two thousand staff while the other approximately seven hundred and fifty. The multi-nationals therefore, provided the managers and miracle workers driving the engine of the Celtic Tiger. Domain C we believe was also strengthened by the inclusion of the pupils and career guidance teachers for three reasons. Firstly, the school context is crucial for the development of cultural norms and behaviour (Vygotsky 1994) including economic ones. Secondly, we would be able to compare the nature and the level of students' economic disposition with other respondents to establish the stage of development of their economic disposition prior to labour market entry because this is the very cohort identified in the opening chapter of the study as the most religious cohort of all in Irish society. Finally, we could also determine the economic disposition of career guidance teachers because they influence and inform pupils' work related career options and these options as will be shown later can have an important bearing on the later development of adult workers' economic disposition.

The choice of school type was based on the fact that sixty per cent of all second level schools are of the secondary or grammar type followed by vocational with twenty seven per cent, community with ten per cent and finally comprehensive with three per cent (NCCA 1999). One school was of particular interest because many of its former pupils played a significant role in the 1916 Rising. One hundred and twenty of its past pupils took part and three of these, Con Colbert, Eamonn Ceannt, and Sean Hueston, were executed leaders of the 1916 Rising. Another of its past pupils was Sean Lemass, who as Minister for Industry and Commerce and later as Taoiseach, was credited with initiating Ireland's modern economic development programme under the First Programme for Economic Expansion in 1958 (Daly 1998).

We use the term disconnected to distinguish the fourth domain in the sense that these individuals were by choice or by circumstance marginally attached to mainstream economic activity. Nevertheless they formed an integral part of the mosaic of Irish life albeit one that lacked many of the economic benefits of the majority living in the Tiger economy. All the unemployed who were interviewed lived in Ballymun, a north Dublin suburb with a population exceeding sixteen thousand and one of the most concentrated areas of disadvantage in Ireland.

The Government (2001a) conceded that this community had not benefited at all from rising living standards generated by the Celtic Tiger. It also exhibited some of the worst deprivation in Ireland (The Ballymun Community Action Programme 2001) where nearly three thousand flats were divided into tower blocks of four, eight and fifteen stories, with another two and half thousand houses concentrated in an area of 1.5 sq. miles.[40] Over seventy per cent of those living in the tower flats were dependent on Social Welfare. With a high marital breakdown rate of approximately twenty per cent and a serious alcohol and drug problem, approximately fifty two per cent of tenants were single parent households and forty six per cent of all children in Ballymun were reared by lone parents. Less than one quarter of children from Ballymun completed second level schooling. At fifteen per cent, Ballymun had one of the highest unemployment rates of any community in Ireland, (Roynane 2001), was three times the national rate and over four times the Dublin region rate (WRC Social and Economic Consultants 2000).

The Traveller Women also made a unique contribution to the research in that they are the single most discriminated-against ethnic group in Europe.[41] According to the Report of the Task Force on the Travelling Community (1995), Traveller women not only contribute to the well-being of their community through their primary responsibility for rearing large families and to the Traveller economy of dealing and recycling, they also occupy a central position in maintaining Traveller culture and identity. This domain also included the contributions from a national advocate of the homeless who was also a member of the Irish Council of State,

---

[40] The Ballymun Re-Generation Project. The tower blocks are currently being demolished and the residents re-housed locally. A ten-year plan to re-build and re-vitalise the area is proceeding. A main street, entertainment centre, the Axis Centre (conference centre), offices, industry and professional practices are to be established.

[41] A 1991 EU Report published by the European Parliament Committee of Enquiry on Racism and Xenophobia, drew attention to the plight of Travellers in Ireland. See also Section H and p. 271 in particular for an outline of their economic role. The 1999 Health Statistics Report published by the Department of Health and Children, recorded nearly eleven thousand Travellers nationally for the year 1996. Approximately five thousand Travelling Community households or twenty three per cent of the national Traveller population was located in the Greater Dublin area alone. According to the National Traveller Accommodation Consultative Group, four hundred and eight families lived on unauthorised sites in Dublin City, (Irish Times 2000) although the Traveller Women in our research maintained that more than two thousand families nationally were living in unauthorised roadside campsites.

being a nominee of the President of Ireland. This particular contribution was deemed to speak on behalf of the homeless in Ireland.[42]

Access To The Sample

On the usual problem facing researchers, namely access to suitable respondents to conduct in-depth interviews (Pettigrew 1981), the researcher can use personal judgement as to who is suitable and so for this reason the group of respondents described above in the four Domains should be regarded as purposive samples. The principle of selection is the researchers judgement as to typicality (Robson 1995). The degree of typicality of respondents is measured against this subjective judgement. Due to the high level of personal networking enjoyed by the researcher, the respondents met the criteria of Robson for assigning the label of 'convenience' sampling to them in so far as they were handy and within easy reach. However, the terms convenience and handy could imply that almost anyone would have done, whereas specified groups were chosen for inclusion in the sample.[43]

Nevertheless there were terms and conditions imposed on the researcher in order to gain access to many of the respondents. For example, one respondent agreed to be interviewed provided the questions were sent in advance and written replies could then be discussed later during an interview. This of course worked against spontaneity during the interview. Most contributors however, did not request sight of the questions prior to the interview. Some potential interviewees directed my requests to their personal secretaries who would often refuse permission for an appointment. Only when a personal friend of the researcher by-passed the secretary and directly intervened with the prospective interviewee was progress made. Some would not allow tape recordings at all, usually those in the National Domain while others welcomed it and in particular some of those in the Disconnected Domain.[44]

Some National contributors advised the researcher to mention their name to other prospective national respondents indicating that this would have the desired effect of giving the research an aura of credibility by association and therefore they

---

[42] Article 31 of the Irish Constitution, Part 3 states 'Such other person if any, as may be appointed by the President under this article to be Members of the Council of State'. Ex-Officio Members of the Council include the Taoiseach, the Tánaiste, the Chief Justice, the President of the High Court, the Chairman of Dáil Éireann, the Chairman of Seanad Éireann and the Attorney General. The Council also includes former President(s), Prime Minister(s), Chief Justice(s) and the President of the Executive Council of the Irish Free State. For more information on roles and powers of state officials see Kelly, J.M. (1980), *The Irish Constitution*, Jurist Publishing, University College Dublin, Dublin, pp. 168-170.

[43] The label 'convenience' used in this discussion should be defined as a handiness and availability existing only through the researcher's particularly strong personal networking capability and is therefore only a variant of convenience sampling.

[44] They often remarked that this was the first and only time that anyone had spoken to them about their lives and their economic views.

would be more likely to collaborate.[45] This was good advice and provided a critical mass of well-regarded respondents with a highly visible national economic profile so that other individuals and groups in the other Domains when made aware of the national status of some contributors became only too willing to have their views included in what they concluded was an important research project.

The multi-nationals insisted that no details of their manufacturing process or products or services specification be allowed into the public arena. Nor was any detail of production specifications or processes to be shared however insignificant, with other non-company interviewees or work colleagues of a respondent participating in the research. An undertaking to assure total anonymity was key to gaining trust. A negotiated compromise saw, on the one hand the researcher prohibited from moving outside of stipulated areas on-site in both multi-nationals and on the other, employees who were nominated by their company as model workers across a range of functions and occupations were invited to be interviewed on company time, i.e. they were to be paid by the company for time at the interview.[46]

All of the farmers invited the researcher into their homes to conduct the interview, many late at night after all farm work was completed. Some of the interviews took place in the kitchen, others in the parlour while all provided refreshments and frequently a tour of the farm.

The school interviews were possible because a number of career guidance teachers were well disposed to the aim of the study and being professional colleagues of another friend of the interviewer readily agreed to collaborate.

Generally speaking then our experience contrasted somewhat with interviewers in a typical study who can choose their sample, decide on a suitable instrument to gather the data, usually with the emphasis on detachment, conduct the interviews as the objective researcher on the respondent(s) and then analyse and present objective findings. Such an approach reflects the controlling status of the interviewer throughout the research process. However, many atypical conditions prevailed in our research with the result that in many instances the control of the research process was a shared rather than an imposed experience between the researcher and the interviewee. The status of the researcher was transformed by the need to collaborate under agreed terms and conditions with each respondent to achieve the objective of the research.

Some examples of formal negotiated consensus occurred when interviewees or guardians of some interviewees exercised the power of veto on consent or content of questions permitted in the interview.[47] Moreover, many interviewees set their own time arrangements that also included the duration of their interview i.e. the time that they could spare for the research and as a result on a number of occasions

---

[45] Showed how tightly knit the social partnership community in Ireland actually was and how access to it was greatly assisted by the quality of the networking approach.

[46] This proved very helpful because it enabled those who were on the lowest rates of pay to participate. It must acknowledged that this was a generous gesture on behalf of both multi-nationals.

[47] When interviewing the traveller women in a traveller training facility.

the researcher had to respond almost immediately to an available window in their schedule.[48]

Secondly, the informal negotiation often occurred spontaneously when respondents who had agreed on the method for gathering their responses prior to the interview, e.g. tape recorder, or note taking, then changed their mind literally seconds before the interview commenced. In one case a respondent who had agreed to be taped then declined and switched to supervise the note taking of the researcher.

Thirdly, the interviewees or their guardians usually chose the location for the interview and this could vary from the Minister's offices to a farmhouse kitchen to a factory office, from a hotel lobby to sitting on a public thoroughfare with the homeless.

Fourthly, some of the sample automatically pre-selected itself, i.e. there was no alternative choice of respondent because only one of a kind existed, such as the respondents in Domain A.

Put simply then, it amounted on many occasions to their way or no way. This contrasts with the traditional approaches identified by Holloway and Jefferson (2000), where the researcher is still seen to set the agenda and in control of generating the information. In any event it was not possible to assume a completely detached role since each interview had to be based on trust, empathy and an ability to adapt to whatever unplanned circumstances that happened to present themselves outside of the agreed arrangements. The empathetic interaction with each participant required a flexible approach that would have to competently address each set of specific interviewee circumstances, withstand the necessary modifications as required while at the same time robustly conform to social scientific research principles.

The solution which is discussed in some detail later in the chapter was facilitated by openness, a characteristic of Irish society previously discussed in chapter four, where the existence of a culture of promoting group rather than national interests requires a willingness on the part of many individuals to constantly engage with different sections of Irish society. In choosing the sample and in designing the research tool, this openness to individual interests and the researcher's interests in particular was considerably enhanced by the quality and level of personal networking enjoyed by the researcher.

The Interview Method

A one-to-one interview was the technique used for most respondents with the exception of the students, the homeless and the Traveller women where a group interview was used. The reason for the student group interviews was both logistical and ethical i.e. the teachers agreed to give access to their pupils for a specific class period usually between three quarters and one hour. Secondly

---

[48] Mostly those from National Domain A and Executive Domain B and in particular government ministers and executives.

conducting a private interview with teenage boys and girls without the presence of another adult was deemed inappropriate and also the presence of a teacher was likely to inhibit full disclosure on the part of the student. Thirdly, as an independent researcher it made sense to use a format that would give access to a substantial number of students at any one time and maximize the flow of contributions.

In the case of the homeless, it was again deemed prudent to interview them in a group and in a public arena to safeguard the integrity of both the researcher and the interviewees. Interviewing homeless individuals was procedurally difficult given their usual location on a main Dublin thoroughfare with its potential for the usual interruptions and distractions.[49] Moreover, the homeless continued to beg while being interviewed and would randomly interrupt the flow of the interview to speak to a passer-by. Finally an either/or situation was presented to the researcher in the case of the Travellers. On the one hand they could be interviewed as a group on condition that the interview was monitored by their guardians sitting in one corner of the room to ensure that no advantage would be taken of the Travellers' vulnerable social and educational status. On the other hand, permission for the interview would be withdrawn is this was not acceptable. Obviously the first option was the acceptable one.

In summary then, the choice of structuring and recording the interview was on many occasions not determined by the researcher at all but by the occupational or personal or social circumstances of each particular respondent. In other words, the research methodology and instrument needed to have an in-built flexibility given the array of special circumstances and protocols pertaining to the diversity of contributors. Given the sample profile and the research aim of capturing attitudes to economic engagement it became obvious that a number of methodological issues would have to be successfully addressed and incorporated into the research.

Issue One - The Choice of Methodology

From the very outset it is important to declare that the research was intended to disclose the particular attitudes and beliefs that influenced the individual's economic behaviour and was therefore a matter of great sensitivity mainly because the responses included explanations of private and individual historical accounts that overlay deeply held religious convictions. One of our main concerns was to avoid creating any sense of unwelcome intrusion into the private arena, where any perception of a lack of sensitivity would have proved detrimental to the success of the research. High levels of trust were at a premium if the willingness of respondents to fully participate in the research was to be realised. A condition of that participation was that individuals who provided original qualitative contributions would not be identifiable in the public domain. Therefore, I am confident that the reader will appreciate that this imperative would determine the amount and content of the extracts that could eventually be presented to the reader.

---

[49] The interview was constantly interrupted by the Gárda (civilian police) as the contributors were also drinking beer from cans on the pavement and therefore breaking the bye-laws.

Moreover what we would eventually end up with was also strongly influenced by the qualitative versus quantitative debate.

We initially favoured the qualitative approach over the quantitative as it can facilitate the generation of sensitive responses (Mason 1996) where the emphasis is on interpreting those responses that help define the elements of an attitude rather than focussing on frequencies (Van Maanen 1979). However, Robson (1993) noted that attitude is a very fuzzy concept akin to opinion, belief or value and usually means the everyday definition assigned in a particular context. Nevertheless, Gagne and Medsker (1996) defined attitude as an internal state of mind that can be regarded as a singular influence on the subsequent choice of the individuals personal action. Hobson (1914) summarised the weakness of the quantitative approach when used to capture the essence of values and attitudes in both the economic and social contexts

> the economist can find the facts but he cannot find their human importance or value because assigning human value means referring to an extra-economic standard, one whose distinctive character consists in its being the expression and operation of the organic complex of forces composing the social personality. (Hobson 1914: 165)

Nonetheless it was also important to establish some measure of the economic disposition of these individuals because an empirical measure even if it only points in the general direction of a link between religiosity and economic engagement, could set the agenda to prioritise the issues to be addressed by the theoretical analyses presented later in chapters seven, eight and nine. Consequently, an integration of both the qualitative and the quantitative methodological approaches was deemed the most appropriate strategy since it presented significant advantages.

On the one hand, the qualitative approach had a particular advantage for eliciting responses because Bryman (1994) argued that since it concentrated on the point of view of those being interviewed it allowed theoretical ideas to emerge from the data. Open-ended questions also help the respondents to formulate and present their own point of view about the topic under discussion (Centre for Labour Market Studies 1998). On the other hand, the quantitative approach enabled certain attitudes to be quantified using measures such as means, variance and standard deviation and to gauge the extent of individual focus on this world as against the focus on the afterlife. Using such indicators it was then possible to connect stated attitudes to work with levels of religiosity and the subsequent importance that the individual attached to work as a means of achieving material and or religious objectives. This emphasis on measurement, the positivistic approach to the nature of knowledge being reductionist (Sapsford and Jupp 1996), allows explanations to follow from measurements when the various relationships within the whole are linked together by a 'scientific' researcher. Because qualitative analysis could also provide the basis to construct or amend a theory (Robson 1995), a research strategy incorporating both qualitative and quantitative approaches was finally adopted.

Since there is no harmonised suite of techniques appropriate for every phase in the research, it is valid therefore to construct a pastiche of procedures, instruments and particular theories to facilitate the emergence of creative research based on a strategic interplay between qualitative and quantitative methods (Strauss and Corbin 1998). The choice of a particular technique should allow the emergence of a central or core category with no forcing of data (Strauss and Corbin 1998). At the same time there was a requirement in the research to speculate on the relationship for example, between the degree of religiosity and the nature of principles governing economic behaviour. A focus on statistical probability was demanded (Centre for Labour Market Studies 2000) because we needed to ensure that both internal and external validation occurred to

> minimise the chances of ignoring contradictory propositions outside the theoretical scheme…allows an opportunity to try out alternative interpretations…where alternative explanations can be developed. (Burgess 1984: 160-161)

Our preferred integrated research approach also followed another recommendation of Robson (1995) that the researcher should address real world enquiry – the solving of a particular existing sociological problem – by adopting a multi-method, flexible and interactive approach towards the solution. Since no methodology is epistemologically superior to another, a multi-method approach is likely to minimise the failings of any one instrument and also guard against sole reliance on traditional notions of reliability and validity that may not be appropriate for assessing each criteria in a piece of scientific research (Johnson and Cassell 2001).

Issue Two - Testing and Validating the Research Instrument

Because of the need to attain honest communication if the true economic disposition was to be revealed, an initial pilot test was conducted to ascertain the most suitable and sensitive research instrument and interview procedure to achieve this. The test consisted of a comparison between the different responses elicited through a questionnaire on a specific yet sensitive subject matter, namely what it means to be feminine and responses elicited through an unstructured face to face interview based on a discussion of the questionnaire responses. Kvale (1996) calls this discussion a professional conversation i.e. a structured exchange of views with a specific purpose in mind. In this instance our aim was to compare the nature of these collaborative responses with those given by the same respondent through the initial questionnaire. The purpose of this professional conversation was to explore and reveal deeply held views, feelings and attitudes by probing about the experience of answering sensitive questions about femininity. The result of the professional conversation highlighted the superficial nature of the answers provided through the questionnaire.

During the professional interview a process of reflexivity occurred through the active participation of the interviewer whereby feelings, attitudes and beliefs were partially and then openly disclosed and a new and higher level of honest communication achieved. In fact the interviewees real understanding of the concept of femininity, namely love, was only disclosed during the latter stages of the conversation. The qualitative measure of success is reflected in a move from unacknowledged to acknowledged attitudes and beliefs. Moreover, an additional yet significant influence emerged, namely the occupational role of the interviewee, in this case an adult guidance counsellor.

Her occupational role seemed to determine the choice of answer given to a particular question. According to Huff (1993), Merton defined a role set as the human interactions peculiar to an individuals social status. In this instance, interactions with other counsellors, managers, lecturers, employers shaped the formal and moral nature of the adult counselling and guidance process to ensure socially acceptable happy rather than utilitarian outcomes for a client seeking advice.[50] When the transcript of the subsequent professional conversation was examined the concept of femininity captured in the questionnaire and defined by the impact of the interviewees counselling role set is seen to generate another meaning altogether, namely love, a sentiment never revealed in the original questionnaire responses. The active and subjective participation of the researcher was pivotal in achieving this higher level of disclosure.

The level of open communication required to reveal religious and economic attitudes was likely therefore to benefit from empathetic, reflexive, participative and informal exchanges. The reasoning behind this was that Irish culture tends to value processes that are informal and personal in nature (Tripoli 1998). These exchanges were unlikely to be facilitated by using structured interviews and questionnaires. Following the choice of an appropriate methodological approach, i.e. active participation of the researcher in a semi-structured interview, further tests were conducted using a revised Topic Guide where specific questions relating to the impact of religion on individual economic engagement were set. Piloting the suitability of the Topic Guides was conducted on a retired civil servant, a senior manager of a small to medium sized enterprise, two work colleagues and two unemployed persons undertaking skills training on a state supported training programme.[51]

However, it quickly emerged that questions relating to a national vision did not interest many respondents whereas the relatively long responses of the former civil servant on his national vision had to be eventually terminated after half an hour to address the other issues listed in the Topic Guide. All respondents provided interesting insights into their religious beliefs and their economic commitment and

---

[50] There was a perceived job requirement on the part of the guidance counsellor to provide empowered choices to females influenced by the over-riding need to achieve the happy norm for clients. In other words, the advice concerning the choice of career for a client is based primarily on its potential to provide happiness rather than wealth, with the understanding that wealth and happiness are usually incompatible.

[51] The draft Topic Guide originally consisted of twenty questions where ten core ones were supplemented by ten more to be used as backup when and if a suitable opportunity arose during the interview.

visibly relaxed when the researcher also disclosed some personal details about personal circumstances and religious views.

It also became evident that certain questions were more appropriate for addressing some issues and less so for others.[52] The outcome was the provision of a tailor made Topic Guide for each domain. Moreover, in Domain A, the objective was always to capture how religious beliefs informed policy and implementation regarding national economic development and this would necessarily demand a specialist emphasis that needed to be reflected in Topic Guide A. Four tailor made topic guides were therefore devised and formed the basis of the questions to be asked. Often additional questions flowed from particular responses given.

Topic Guide 1 - national 'economic' and national religious leaders

Q.1   What would you consider the ideal or target to be achieved in relation to the economic well being of the Irish people?
Q.2   What do you consider the main advantages-disadvantages of our democratic system to enable this ideal to be achieved?
Q.3   What strengths and weaknesses do you consider inherent in the disposition of the Irish workforce that would affect the likely success of achieving this outcome?
Q.4   Do you observe from your experience any evidence that the Irish workforce may not be fully committed to economic development?
Q.5   If Yes to Q. 4 could you outline the factors or reasons (political, religious etc.) that may be influential in this respect?
Q.6   What would you consider the main benefits or otherwise to individual workers in particular and Irish society in general from the recent rapid economic progress in the Celtic Tiger?

Topic Guide 2 was used for respondents in Domain B, Domain C and Domain D with the exception of the students in Domain C. Their Topic Guide did not include questions on work relationships. Topic Guide 2 was primarily constructed so that the different groups of occupations could be captured using this one guide.

---

[52] For example the importance of weather for farmers was almost irrelevant to many other respondents except of course for the homeless individuals where it had a direct bearing on the quality of their street life and their humour tended to fluctuate with the weather.

Topic Guide 2 - executives, staff of multi-nationals, farmers, unemployed
homeless, travellers

Q.1   Could you describe the type of lifestyle that you have at present?
Q.2   Could you describe the type of lifestyle that you would like to have?
Q.3   Could you indicate what are the factors preventing you achieving this
        lifestyle?
Q.4   Would you say that when you are working that you give everything to the
        job?
Q.5   Would you say that Irish people in general give everything to their job?
Q.6   What so you think happens to you when your life is over? Is there a
        heaven?
Q.7   Which do you think is more important - to be happy or rich or can you be
        both happy and rich?
Q.8   Do you think that hard work goes towards anything in the next life?
Q.9   Do you see any advantages-disadvantages with the Celtic Tiger?
Q.10   Could you place a mark on each of the first set of lines below on the Likert
        Scale. (Refer below for a sample Scale)

Topic Guide 3 - Leaving Certificate pupils

Q.1   How many of you go to Mass every Sunday and how go many sometimes?
Q.2   What is it that's important about work for you?
Q.3   Do Irish people work hard?
Q.4   Is it important to work hard?
Q.5   So what is it all about then – this life and work?
Q.6   Are you a better person if you work hard as against someone who
        doesn't work hard?
Q.7   Is it a problem for rich people to get to Heaven…do you believe in an
        afterlife, a Heaven?
Q.8   Is it better to rich or happy?
Q.9   So after secondary school what will you look for to make you rich or
        happy?
Q.10   Where would each of you put yourself on this line here and here and here
        and here i.e. on the four lines that I've drawn on the blackboard?
        (Replicating the Likert Scale)

Another tailored Topic Guide was used for the advocate of the Homeless since
her 'not for profit' work was deemed to be different to the business ethic informing
the multi-national and farming sectors.

Topic Guide 4 - advocate of the homeless

Q.1   How would you describe your work, your occupation if you like?
Q.2   What is your vision for Irish society, economically speaking that is?
Q.3   How near is Irish society to this ideal?
Q.4   Why is this the case?
Q.5   How is Irish society changing to industrialisation?
Q.6   Why are these connections not being made?
Q.7   What is the view of the homeless on the Celtic Tiger?
Q.8   Is there anything in Irish society's disposition that would assist or hinder in achieving your ideal?
Q.9   Could you place a mark on each of the first set of lines below (on the Likert Scale) indicating, where you believe the next life fits into your life and where you believe the next life fits into Irish peoples life. Secondly place a mark on the second set of lines below indicating the importance of work to you and then to Irish people in general?

As you can see, the last question in all Topic Guides with the exception of Topic Guide 1 for Domain A – who contributed a national rather than an organisational or individual perspective – included a request to rate on a modified Likert Scale, the respondents views in the following four areas

1.   The degree of self focus on 'This Life as against the Next Life'.
2.   The degree of focus that they believe Irish society has towards 'This Life as against the Next Life'.
3.   The degree of self focus on 'Work as the Most Useful Human Activity'.
4.   The degree of focus that they believe Irish society has on 'Work as the Most Useful Human Activity'.

These areas were of particular interest as they had the capacity to highlight a link between religious beliefs and the instrumental value of work exercised to exploit given economic opportunities presented in the Celtic Tiger. However, as one quarter of the Irish population was functionally illiterate, the usual Likert Scale format had the potential to disadvantage some respondents with literacy and or numeracy difficulties. Moreover, this modification was also deemed suitable to overcome problems encountered by any contributor with dyslexia who may have been embarrassed to disclose this disability. Consequently, a modified graphic integrating the usual measures used in language based Likert Scale questionnaires was devised following its testing on a number of individuals with low levels of literacy and or numeracy skills. This rating exercise always took place at the end of the interview when the four continua were revealed separately and in the same order. The minus figures (from 0 to –5) indicated a tendency towards the stated position to the left of the graphic with plus figures (from 0 to +5), indicating a tendency towards the right and opposite extreme of the continuum. Zero indicated an equal focus by the individual on both criteria. Irrespective of being positive or negative the numbers refer to a measure of the degree of commitment as follows:

1 = a slight tendency towards
2 = a definite tendency towards
3 = a stronger tendency towards
4 = a very strong tendency towards
5 = a total focus on the terminal point

Each continuum is divided into 11 segments i.e. zero and twin sets of measures either side from zero to 5 and from zero to -5. In a given sample below, three individuals A, B and C, complete the four continua and mark the lines as follows:

	Line 1	Line 2	Line 3	Line 4
Individual A:	-3.0	-1.0	4.0	2.0
Individual B:	1.0	-2.0	1.0	zero
Individual C:	-1.0	3.0	-1.0	1.0

In our example, Person A indicated that she had a strong tendency to focus on This Life (–3.0), while Person B indicated a slightly stronger tendency to focus on the Next Life as against This Life (+1.0), while Person C at (–1.0) had a slightly stronger tendency to focus on This Life as against the Next Life. The average rating for all three is calculated at (–1.0) and so the overall focus for the sample of three is measured as a slightly stronger focus on This Life as against the Next Life. The same exercise can be undertaken for the remaining three lines. See below for the modified Likert Scale representation for Person As ratings.

This part of the interview had the advantage of providing interest to respondents while allowing individual differentiation of views to be recorded and achieved the primary objective for the use of Likert Scales in interviews (Robson 1993). Likert Scales also enable the researcher to codify ordinal response rankings (Centre for Labour Market Studies 1998) and the above scale was formulated and designed to be user friendly and to prompt the respondent to ask questions and allow the researcher to check for understanding. The use of this rating exercise and the experience of validating the content of the Topic Guides only confirmed the high level of researcher engagement that was required to sensitively elicit the interviewees views and attitudes. Moreover, only used summary scores by domain were to support our conclusions because we adhered to a core principle of attitude measurement which, according to Duffy and Williams (2002), maintains that combined group scores are much more robust than individual ones.

In the case of the pupils individual scores in the first school A were combined into a class average and this score was used in the data set to calculate measurements presented later in the chapter. The same method was used for the remaining classes B-E where each class average was then combined to give one group result. It is this group result that is also used in the data set.

The Catholic Ethic and Global Capitalism

Sample Modified Likert Scale for Individual A

Line 1: Degree of Self-Focus

On This Life   **On The Next Life**

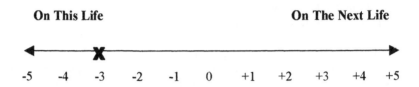

Line 2: Degree of Focus of Society

On This Life   **On The Next Life**

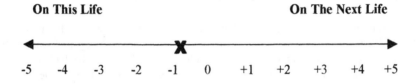

Line 3: Degree of Self-Focus

On Working to Live   **On Living to Work**

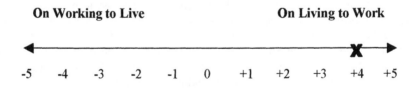

Line 4: Degree of Focus of Society

On Working to Live   **On Living to Work**

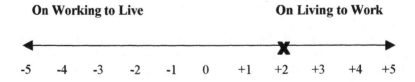

Issue Three - Level of Interviewer Engagement

Any research account can only be produced collaboratively where the interviewers questions are embedded in the entire interview and data analysis because both the researcher and interviewee are subject to the introduction of feelings and ideas by each other (Holloway and Jefferson 2000). The concept of reflexivity requires the researcher to become aware of the methodological implications of being positioned in the research field as much as the problems posed by very sensitive topics such as religion (Flanagan 2001). This requires disclosure or biography to be provided on the part of the researcher, namely stating where she is coming from and a duty to ensure that the little voices of the weak in society as well as the powerful are heard (Flanagan 2001). Nevertheless, the key reflexive criterion for all pieces of research is that the method(s) used to generate the data, such as the interview or questionnaire should reflect the epistemological assumptions underpinning the research approach (Johnson and Cassells 2001).

In this respect, the research according to Gephart's (2000) topology of paradigms was partly located within interpretivism because it was a search for meaning produced in natural contexts and partly located in critical theory-post positivism, since another important objective was to uncover hidden interests and values. Others, such as Guba and Lincoln (1994) would see a basis for placing the natural interview approach in the postpositive paradigm because it uses natural settings and solicits the views of people to determine the meaning they ascribe to their actions.

Because a respondent may be inhibited by a number of barriers including the inability to actually admit to holding certain attitudes, projective techniques can tap into a deeper level of conscious awareness (Oppenheim 1997). An effective projective or indirect method is called association which according to Oppenheim (1997) is the

> say-the-first-thing-that-comes-into-your-mind approach based on the assumption that a fast response to a stimulus, word, picture or question will be less guarded and more revealing of underlying attitudes and motives. (Oppenheim 1997: 212)

An important point to bear in mind is that subjective evaluation of states of mind cannot be measured objectively nor through external assessment but is best served by simple questioning in common survey interviews through the use of projective questions (Veenhoven 1997, Veenhoven 2000). Since humans are capable of overall appraisals of how well they are doing it is also valid to ask respondents to estimate or strike the balance of their life. Empirical studies show reasonable reliability levels in these self-reports (Veenhoven 2000).

Despite the advantages of applying a naturalistic research design to measure the impact of a religious belief system on the individual's economic disposition, the social scientists benchmarks of objectivity and reliability remained paramount concerns throughout the research process. However, both are themselves problematical issues in contemporary social science because the former is based on the belief that knowledge can be secured only when it corresponds with observed facts, while the latter applies to consistent and repeatable results (Holloway and Jefferson 2000). Even where objective data emerges we may have to concede that its interpretation cannot be objective. As psychoanalysis has recently conceded that the interpretation of data is not a science but an art form relying on intuition and because meanings are unique emerging as they do in situations under analysis, they are not therefore replicable (Holloway and Jefferson 2000).

Collins (1998) noted that Bourdieu regarded even the unstructured interview with its emphasis on objectivity and standing apart and aloof from the interviewee, as false, as it is only limited to capturing and relating the official account. On the same theme Polsky (1998) maintained that sociologists needed to abandon scientism i.e. the construction of social reality at several removes from the human being using scientific methods, because it provided the illusion that scientific sociologists only talked about people (hard quantitative methods) rather than feeling and thinking with them and listening to them in their natural habitat (soft qualitative methods). Furthermore, Stanley and Wise (1998) stated that the social sciences and conventional research methods claiming to provide objective knowledge independent of the personal situation of the social scientist led to misunderstanding and distortion of social facts. By tuning out personal experiences in conventional research the researcher is liable to miss important responses from the interviewee due to the failure of the researcher to share her own experiences during the interview (Kelly 1998).[53] Reflexivity requires a contribution to and an awareness and on-going evaluation of a piece of interaction as it happens (Potter 1996). In an epistemological sense Collins (1998) contended that Bourdieu warned that the process of disclosure required the interviewer to

> stand back and scrutinise the relationship between our methodology and the information it has enabled us to collect…[and how]…methodology and the kind of information collected determines the eventual form of our accounts. (Collins 1998: 2)

The fact is that there is a myth surrounding objective scientific observations because observations require an observer and observers have a point of view that implies that science could not possibly give an account of the world from a non point of view (Fulford 1996). In fact from the perspective of the religious frame of reference, namely having faith, the objective view actually impedes an understanding of the sacred imagination in society and this is quite unfortunate since a focus and concern with the sacred is immutable in the human condition (Esmail 1996). The bottom line is, that our objective world can only be experienced subjectively (Fenwick 1996).

Now given that the nature of the subject observed is changed by the very observation conducted by the observer (Fanning 1983), there is a falseness

---

[53] They fail to intuitively connect linked meanings due to a lack of reflexivity. This is precisely what we wanted to avoid in interpreting our research findings.

regarding two aspects of the debate surrounding structured and unstructured data collection methods and their objectivity. Firstly, there is no such event as an unstructured interview but ascending levels of structuredness where the higher the level the more reliable the results and where the lower the level, the more personal disclosure is likely to emerge (Wilson 1996). Secondly, all interviews require a certain degree of social interaction and that includes even the postal questionnaire (Wilson 1996). Giddens (1998) noted that a real problem was that the social scientist around could not gauge how much the interviewee knew about the intended outcome of their actions and the fact that this knowledgeability regularly shifted made it almost impossible for the researcher to measure subject matter in an objective sense.

In the controversy relating to subjectivity and objectivity inherent in the autobiography or personal interview, Ribbens (1993) held the view that socially patterned experiences such as class and ethnic grouping with their embedded psychical and common-sense nature could only be uncovered through the analysis of personal relationships and life courses. This approach required the interviewer not only to listen attentively but become actively engaged in the interview process. When that occurred linkages could then be very revealing. Feminist sociologists Cotterill and Letherby (1993) noted that Oakley also challenged the notion of proper interviewing techniques that placed a premium on detachment, control and objectivity since

> life histories tell it like it is...and do not fracture life experiences but make them relational to significant others highlighting the social construction of a lived experience. This should ensure that the values of society too are embedded in the narrative for analysis. (Cotterill and Letherby 1993: 74)

Since most unstructured personal interviews tend to uncover some elements of the interviewees life course, the researcher needs to be aware of the importance of this part of the disclosure for analytical purposes.

Therefore, the schedule of topics outlined in each of the four Topic Guides was structured with a three-phase interview process in mind, namely introducing the research, addressing general topics and finally eliciting very sensitive personal accounts of beliefs and meanings. This approach ultimately relied on unstructured naturalistic interviewing to create the illusion of a conversation, a technique that has been used very effectively in a study that elicited sensitive details from those in long term residential care (Wilson 1996).[54]

The first phase included the explanatory covering letter about the research and the schedule of questions that were forwarded days or even weeks prior to the interview. The simultaneous completion of phases one, two and three at one interview usually consisted in the sharing of a brief personal biography by both

---

[54] While the questions were integrated into the planned interview process in our study, they were not always effected in such a seamless manner in every single interview. In some instances another follow-up interview was required to complete the three-phases.

researcher and interviewee. This was followed by a move to general economic and religious concepts and topics. Using conversational episodes, phase three often took the form of a professional conversation. The analysis of the expressions and narrative of the third phase of the interview process sought to isolate recurring values and attitudes where the qualitative emphasis of the conversation would

> accurately reflect the meanings of those investigated...generalisations can be made...the emphasis here being on external validity...[consequently]...objectivity will be linked to certain values. (Williams and May 1996: 132)

In this respect a phenomenological inflection underpinned the research methodology because it enabled the respondent to set the course of the dialogue where personally relevant issues could then repeatedly emerge.

Moreover, phenomenology has an important influence on the sociology of religion as it provides concepts that gave meaning to existential problems of life, where human action is conscious and is therefore contrary to the idea that humans are the host bodies of all powerful social forces (Aldridge 2000). So the balance to be achieved in each interview was that the respondent set the course of dialogue while the researcher set the menu of issues to be addressed. This approach conforms to Kvale's (1996) argument that as phenomenology is the understanding of the world as it is experienced by individuals, then it this experienced reality that is the most important one and the job of the researcher is to find the common essence or constant nature of the individuals experienced reality.

However, it would be misleading if the above discussion gave even the slightest hint that the research was based on a schedule of Do-It-Yourself-Science highlighted by Heller (1986) where scientific principles are abandoned. In our study a systematic process of enquiry with approved techniques and strategies was implemented and despite the unusual challenges presented to the researcher, it was still possible to consistently implement the phasing of the interview structure and to manage to follow the topic schedule throughout all four domains. An objective research principle was rigidly applied, namely to follow an approved systematic methodological approach at all times.

While the integrated research approach and the level of personal networking facilitated a high degree of open disclosure by respondents, the very strength of this openness became a concern about validity. However, while the researcher may know the participants at one or two removes, validity can still be ensured because biographical similarities or common ground can actually assist the researcher to generate higher levels of analysis by intuitively noticing inferred meaning in the respondent's narrative (Holloway and Jefferson 2000). For example, Ellingson (1988) used her own experience of being a cancer patient to produce unique insights into other cancer patients' experiences of treatment procedures.

We are confident then that the collaborative approach adopted in the research, the pre-tested instrument and the interview phasing satisfactorily addressed concerns about validity. From an analysis of the naturalistic interview, a model of the social world can then be constructed on the basis that meanings are a product of history and social structure (Sapsford and Jupp 1996). This of course gave us even more confidence that the integration of a particular historical backdrop into the analyses of the Irish economic disposition that follows in chapters seven, eight and nine would pay dividends by grounding the abstraction of the paradigms in real people and through their observed behaviour. Yet in so far as the results of the findings justified the emphasis placed on having naturalistic settings for all respondents, this very strategy alerted us to yet another concern, namely to generate truthful responses in such settings.[55]

Issue Four - Improving Open Communication

Our questions in the various topic guides reflected the warnings of some commentators to be aware of the real possibility that weak intrinsic truth can be generated in many responses. Goffman (1955) argued that the replies that an individual used enabled them to have control over how they presented themselves to others i.e. as a matter of course individuals tended to give low levels of self-disclosure. This is known as the dramaturgical approach, namely an analyses of the socialisation process through the concept of a drama or play and it is essentially impression management i.e. putting the most appropriate face forward by masking or suppressing facts about the individual which would be contrary to the impression actually presented. Masking is very effective in civilised contexts and only in barbaric conditions is there any guarantee that the real self will emerge (Hart 1991).[56]

One of the problems encountered in unmasking is that the dramaturgical approach is based on a modern western social norm of endemic deceit in social activity which is highly instrumental (Baert 1998). Individuals protect vulnerable aspects of themselves, are motivated to disguise their feelings and are comfortable managing deceitful self-impressions to maximise their self-interest (Holloway and Jefferson 2000). Research methodology such as questionnaires and structured interviews tend to facilitate the presentation of the superficial and observable self described by Jung (1985) as

> the principle of a persona projected to conceal the true personality used for adaptive or convenience purpose. (Jung 1987: 32)

---

[55] Ironically while familiar surroundings allowed many respondents to relax and be natural it sometimes had the opposite effect on the researcher. For example the surroundings and formality of the Ministers' offices, the Catholic Presbytery, the offices of the multi-national employees and the city streets were, in their own way, quite intimidating locations to conduct a face to face interview.

[56] Here now is the third reason why the conflict generated in the process of early Irish state formation, the 1916 Rising, is selected as a suitable context in later chapters for grounding the abstraction of the analyses in real people and events.

However, the instrumental approach is also based on allowing a free play of inferences to optimise our understanding of meaning and consciousness and as a consequence, Thomas (1951) stated that it was vital to grasp that individuals lived their lives and made decisions by inference and not statistically or scientifically. However, the use of inference by individuals or concluding from the facts is itself problematical.

Husserl's phenomenological perspective of consciousness stated that the systematic analysis of things external and internal to ourselves that we experience constituted the real world for the individual (Magee 1998). Because individuals are unaware that they are ordering the social world and accepted it as already pre-structured, the key task of the researcher was to penetrate the various layers constructed by individuals to access the essential structure of their consciousness (Ritzer 1988). This interpretative process becomes inseparable from and subject to the language culture (Pollio, Henley, and Thompson 1997). Esmail (1996) argued for the crucial importance of language as follows

> language does not just express the mind...it conditions the mind...the terms in which a problem is stated amount to a constitution of the very problem being described...for this reason critical attention to language is of the utmost importance in understanding society. (Esmail 1996: 146)

According to Laney (1999), Garfinkel maintained that there are undertones in any conversation that are not always verbalised and until these are exposed then honest communication is virtually impossible. Garfinkel (1967) asserted that people refuse to permit each other to understand what they are really talking about in a purely rational discourse.

What was required then from the point of view of our own interview structure and process was to facilitate an exchange of honest communication with attention paid by the researcher to the words used and in particular to metaphors, because as Sandford (1987) argued metaphors are the tracks along which thoughts and beliefs tend to run. Metaphors are comparisons that cannot be taken literally but used to make a correspondence between qualities in this world with the primary subject under consideration (Mezirow 1990). Metaphors are crucial therefore, in verifying and interpreting respondents attitudes with regard to their engagement with the economic environment. Moreover, metaphors become even more important in an Irish context because Jeanrond (2001) argued that Catholic beliefs and teachings rely heavily on metaphors and narratives as a meaning-making tools and as Robson (1995) contended the structured interview does not facilitate this use of narrative. Actually this framing of meaning is much more important in social science than the discovery of laws (Giddens 1996e).

Particular attention therefore was paid throughout each interview to record any metaphors and narrative used by respondents to describe their attitudes and views and the inferred meanings expressed in their everyday language. Paraphrasing what had been said, namely checking the meaning of the metaphor and narrative without actually recording the response at the moment it was spoken, provided the key to the research because respondents usually gave unguarded statements to begin with, in addition to intended disclosures and then returned and discussed the unguarded statements i.e. higher levels of open communication were achieved. To enable inferred meanings emerge and be linked with other responses required the building up of trust and empathy and sensitivity to each of the respondent's particular set of circumstances. This required a sharing of private life histories and belief systems by both respondent and researcher and this sharing demanded strict adherence to ethical guidelines.

Issue Five - Ethical Issues

Subjective engagement in the research approach lends itself to understanding real time human behaviour as in vivo and not in vitro i.e. in the real process of living and not in the laboratory (Fromm 1974). Yet when respondents are unaware of the real nature of the interview, ethical questions such as consent may arise (Holdaway 1998). The issue of autobiographical consent has been addressed by Harrison and Lyon (1993) who argued that consent could easily defeat the purpose of autobiography which is to present the real self as experienced by the respondent. However, the basic ethical principle of total protection of the respondent, namely that no harm is done to her on foot of the interview (Sapsford and Abbott 1996, Oppenheim 1997) applied at all times before, during and after our research.

The recommended adherence to ethical guidelines was upheld in the research by always providing the aims and purpose of the research either in written format and or verbally to each respondent or group of respondents as well as assuring anonymity prior to and during the interview (Centre for Labour Market Studies 2000). The primary concerns such as consent and confidentiality were addressed and specific steps taken to protect each contributor such as coding of respondents. All participants were also informed that they could pull out of the research before and during the interview. Sometimes the questions that would be asked at the interview were sent in advance following a request made by a particular participants such as the politicians. At other times there were guardians present such as those working with the Traveller Women. Anonymity was important for all respondents, because even though the responses of individuals holding high public office or those working in the multi-nationals could potentially place them in a vulnerable situation, other groups such as the unemployed and Travellers were equally so, particularly when they shared views and details of circumstances that could have brought them to the attention of the authorities and where sanctions could be then applied retrospectively.[57] The Ethical Principles for Conducting Research with Human Participants published by the British Psychological Society (Robson 1995) at all times informed the ethical code of conduct implemented in the research approach.[58]

---

[57] For example unemployed persons doing 'nixers' i.e. working in the black economy while claiming social welfare payments which can carry heavy fines and sometimes imprisonment.

[58] These Guidelines have recently been up-dated and where the protection of respondents is, if anything, emphasised even more strongly than in the previous guidelines.

Yet despite all these precautions, a unique problem arose for maintaining the anonymity of respondents in Domain A. Because they held high profile positions, their very unique responses could easily alert an informed reader to the identity of the contributor. Consequently only the combined summary views from this Domain complemented by some brief extracts of unlabelled material is provided. The overriding objective here was not to violate Ethical Guideline No 8, Protection of Participants. In the other domains it was much more feasible to provide contributions in the knowledge that anonymity would remain intact.[59]

The approach used to collate the emerging themes was by categorisation, an effective tool used by researchers to integrate qualitative and quantitative data for analytical purposes and is based on themes and statements where similar or related expressed values by individuals provide a valid measure (Dey 1993). The post modern sociological concern of ensuring that sociological studies attend to individual subjectivity and short term small durable theories rather than grand, unitary and objective explanations (Billington, Hockney and Strawbridge 1998) was also an important objective influencing the presentation format of the contributions. The Theory of Limits that is presented in the final chapter ten is formulated as a result of applying sociological theory to the findings of our research and as such attends to this concern.

Finally we should also mention that the presentation of the findings with the exception of Domain A followed Christian's (1994) approach of providing minimum commentary which had previously been used very effectively by Goodwin (1999b) in his presentation of sensitive and personal face to face research conducted on working class men in Dublin in the late 1990s. In that instance he let the interviewees as it were, speak for themselves. Also by including the questions asked of our respondents we too are able to place the narrative in context for the reader and make the whole interview process as transparent as possible.

All the original responses were inputted into a Dell Laptop Computer in Microsoft Word format including the professional interview conducted with the Career Guidance teachers when no note-book or tape recording was used. This approach can legitimately form part of a valid research methodology. Polsky (1988) argued that memorised accounts can

> be written up fully and accurately after you get home at the end of the day…[since]…historians accept an account by a disinterested eye-witness written immediately after the event as decent evidence even when by an untrained observer (Polsky 1988: 326)

---

[59] Two further points about the presentation format of the findings should be borne in mind. Firstly, the domains are presented in alphabetical order with no implied priority assigned to that order. Each respondent brings equally valid contributions to the research. Secondly, the sum total of the contributions presents an insight that is greater than the aggregate of the individual parts. This becomes possible because our research is the first to include such a unique mix of contributors and as a result, the profile of the economic disposition is we believe a truer representation of the mosaic of Irish society.

Finally, respect for individuals, their particular circumstances and status was always observed by a sensitive awareness and conformance by the researcher to each interviewee's expectations of acceptable dress code.[60]

Managing the Data

It should be pointed out that the universal Catholic profile of the sample (only four non Catholics present) was but an accidental outcome of other criteria of typicality used for inclusion in each Domain. The categorisation of each respondent's level of Catholic religiosity was based on the topology of Fulton, Abela, Borowik, Dowling, Long, Marler and Tomasi (2000) who subdivided respondents into three types as follows

1.   Core Catholics who practice on a regular basis, and this level is indicated by the number three in the summary statistical tables in chapter six
2.   Intermediate Catholics who range from those who do not attend regularly but often, to those who only attend intermittently and this level is indicated by the number two
3.   Lapsed Catholics who do not *now* attend to their religious duties but once did, and the number one is assigned to these respondents.

Here representatives of the other two world salvation religions namely, Islam and Protestantism, are also assigned the number three, since similarities exist between their beliefs and Catholicism in relation to Heaven and this linkage between Islam, Protestantism and Catholicism is an important contribution to the analyses of the profile of the Irish economic disposition presented in chapter six.

To track the emerging themes and categories of themes identified in the interviews each line of statement by a respondent was tagged, i.e. preceded by a special code. The coding acted as a referencing system for the data and allowed each statement to be crosschecked and grouped into a specific category. This coding is presented in many of the labelled extracts in the next chapter. Two qualitative research (QRS) software packages were chosen for the purposes of categorisation and modelling, namely NVIVO and QSRNUD*IST 4. The former allowed field notes and commentary to be incorporated into the coding of text by the use of a chosen node. An example of a node label for capturing a re-occurring theme in the research was the word Jesuits, since reference to this religious order was made by both the Congress of Trade Unions representative and by one of the homeless individuals. The modeller feature of this software generated groups of linkages with a format similar to mind mapping but it proved to be a complex function and only partially successful. It failed to establish several crucial links

---

[60] For example we had noticed that politicians and executives tended to dress formally, whereas the homeless and unemployed did not. The idea was to signal respect for each individual and group circumstance and be sensitive to expectations and thus help put them and the interviewer at ease with the entire interview process.

between related values that were obvious to the researcher in the reading of the responses.

The reason for this oversight was that the package was not sufficiently sensitive to the style of language used in the narrative of the majority of respondents. For example insights such as 'I'm not into that' with reference to Mass-going, implied that they still believed, had faith but did not now attend Mass and other rituals but this was not picked up. Of course these and other statements are central for an understanding of the link between the various respondents' belief systems and their impact on subsequent economic behaviour. In short only the culturally sensitized human researcher was adequately equipped to make many important connections from the narratives.

The second software package proved much more useful in highlighting re-occurring phrases and patterns particularly word frequency lists. It quickly emerged that phrases referring to happiness levels were easily identified. The line coding allowed the respondents to be immediately identified by domain. However, the researcher could not avoid the old fashioned approach of examining each recorded line from all the responses within each domain. Here categories of themes were noted and potential links between religious beliefs and economic objectives were identified. These links were then inputted into a separate MS Word document.

Overall then little or no data reduction resulted from using this approach. The challenges presented in analysing the research findings, i.e. making culturally sensitive linkages to emerging themes, suggested that Holloway and Jefferson (2000) had indeed identified a significant weakness in packages such as Nud*ist. These IT based qualitative packages are necessarily based on the fragmentation of data in code yet it is this very fragmentation that prevents the data from being held as a whole in the mind, de-contextualises it and then hides links that can only be interpreted with reference to the whole and then mainly by the researcher's intuition.

All the Likert Scale ratings on the four continua which were completed by the respondents at the end of each interview in Domains B, C and D were collated and analysed using the appropriate Microsoft data statistical analysis functions on each of the specified arrays. The appropriate arrays, coding and correlation are presented as a summary table later in chapter six. The subsequent correlation between religiosity and individual indicators of economic engagement are then used to support a number of conclusions which in turn form the basis to construct the profile of the Catholic economic disposition with some confidence.[61] This profile then acts as a benchmark to engage with the universality of the sociological insights later employed under theme three. The results of our analyses and our subsequent conclusions are then used to ground a small theory explaining the Irish economic disposition.

---

[61] We do not use correlation as proof of the relationship but as indicative of holding an attitude that tends towards one or other of the stated positions on the continuum i.e. a stronger or weaker indication that it may exist.

Summary

This chapter has provided a description of a representative sample of the mosaic of Irish social life and grouped the respondents into four domains of contributors. This was followed by an outline of the rationale and purpose of the study. The methodology incorporated both qualitative and quantitative approaches and armed the study with instruments designed to secure full and honest participation of respondents.

A comprehensive description of the methodology and a discussion of design issues were also presented. The process of piloting and validating a tailored research instrument was described where a number of specific methodological issues relating to the sample, to the status of the interviewees and to the scientific role of the researcher were addressed noting that the implementation of the interview guidelines also gave rise to some concerns around the atypical nature of the research approach. A number of problematical issues such as interviewer engagement levels, informality, the naturalistic setting, truthfulness of responses and ethical guidelines were also addressed. We now open the next chapter with a discussion of the themes emerging from each of the four domains.

Chapter 6

A Profile of the Irish
Economic Disposition

Introduction

A culturally sensitive and tailor made methodological approach enabled us to capture a broad range of contributions that reflected the mosaic of Irish social life. An interview strategy, informed by both qualitative and quantitative methods and underpinned by a phenomenological paradigm facilitated the emergence of a number of key themes that shed light on the nature of the Irish economic disposition. The purpose of this chapter is to present these themes and synthesise them into an informed profile of the Irish economic disposition.

The chapter is divided into three parts. The first discusses the emerging themes from Domain A only. Being vigilant about adhering to previously discussed ethical issues we only provide a limited number of unlabelled extracts to supplement the thematic summary presented in Table 6.1. The presentation format of these extracts includes the question bounded by the brackets [...], followed by a selection of unlabelled responses made by a number of different contributors and where the response of each individual contributor is bounded by the symbols < >.

This is followed in the second part by a presentation of the findings from the other three Domains B, C and D where we provide a number of more comprehensive extracts with the confidence that contributors will retain their anonymity. Here the emerging themes are again thematically collated into two sub-sections. The first sub-section treats these three domains as if they were a single group for the purposes of obtaining the more valid group measurements.[62] The statistical summary presented in Table 6.2 provides each respondent's four individual ratings marked on the modified Likert Scale plus religious status, identification of the presence of the Spirit of Charity and their stated economic target so that individual contributions can be noted and compared. This is followed with a number of group statistical measurements and correlations presented in Table 6.3.[63] These group calculations are intended to provide indicators or

---

[62] To provide an overview of emerging norms and patterns reflected in the majority of contributions making up the mosaic of Irish social life.

[63] Nevertheless the correlations are strongly supported by the actual responses of the contributors who point out that their faith compels them to adopt a particular yet common line of economic behaviour i.e. there is evidence of a religiously influenced durée.

approximations of the strength of religious beliefs and work attitude and the degree of impact that religion is thought to exercise on the selected variables.

In the second sub-section, Domains B, C and D are re-constituted back into their original single domains where a similar set of individual ratings can be compared. Calculations for each domain are then presented in Tables 6.4, 6.5 and 6.6 respectively. The purpose of taking this individual domain approach is to identify where and why there may be differences in the coefficients of the stated variables.

The final section links the emerging themes from the four domains and using this information we then construct a profile of the Celtic Tiger economic disposition which is then presented towards the end of the chapter.

Part 1-Short Unlabelled Extracts from National Domain A

Unlabelled Extracts

[What would you consider the ideal or target to be achieved in relation to the economic well-being of the Irish people?]

<...Build on current wave of success...Create new synergies with countries of the Pacific Rim, particularly China, Japan, Korea, Malaysia...provide employment for all who seek it...invest in world class education and training particularly in information technology...devise innovative solutions to maintain family life on farms... encourage and facilitate more foreign and indigenous investment in Ireland...To tackle disadvantage and the causes of disadvantage...>

<...Well...we should have standards of living among the best in Europe...the best in the world...equality of opportunity...in every aspect the basis of life difference would be reduced...probably...economically...aiming to maintain the vibrancy present at the moment...Putting in policies to sustain that...maybe a trade off between self reliance and equality...>

<...I suppose it would be...eh... well...eh...well to increase GNP per capita...I suppose to have the highest in Europe...our GNP isn't the same as our GDP...as you know there's fourteen per cent in the difference, so I suppose if we get the two of them the same...I suppose... the second thing, is to end the alienation in Irish society...there's huge prosperity in the country at the moment, yet there's huge unemployment black spots, so we need to turn the tide on third generation unemployed...now it will require a huge effort...the third thing, I'd like to see more regional development...giving people a good reason to live in their local community. Next there's a tragedy not to avail of this prosperity, the work ethic is not there for these families, I think....there's a culture of unemployment in these areas, and apart from anything else it's a very slow process, turning this around...>

<...Is the aim to optimise growth? I think this is what it should be...growth is not the aim year on and year on ...but to optimise the growth...>

<...I suppose a bit of balance...a combination I suppose...living standards...I presume that they would be the typical standards of Europe...in broad terms comparable to the EU...clearly a lot of things come from that...Redistribution in the level or spread of income...social inclusion is part of the package...the level of social spending and safety nets...There should be social solidarity in the broad sense...equal opportunities...access to education...even though not everybody is going to achieve the same there should be still equal access to education...>

<...Economic well-being is not an end in itself...the important thing is the way you achieve wealth... it is very good if you use it for the community (i.e. parish not EU)...>

[What do you consider the main advantage-disadvantage of our democratic system to enable you to achieve this ideal?]

<...Well we don't have any other system broadly speaking so it's just a matter of getting on with it...The essence of the job is getting out to meet people in their workplace, in their clubs, in resident groups, in their professional groups and lobby groups and to listen to them and build your policies and action plans on that...>

<...Democracy in Ireland tends to be Liberal Pluralism...tends to undermine objective truth and is therefore, suspect...how do we see society...as a hospital or a jungle...one, the emphasis is on strength, the other on sickest...Thatcher focussed on society as a jungle...the poor and weak would not survive...we are beginning to do that now...>

<...the ideal would of course be that everyone would have a job and would be needed...take a role in society...some job is better than no job...if you don't work its bad for your character...>

<...Every political party in Ireland now is possibly lying centrist...from a lobby point of view the PR multi-seat constituency offers its attractions...I agree that it is not the most efficient system...politicians are focussed on doing favours...but if the hard question is asked do we want change?...no!...so the PR system puts manners on them (politicians)...it gives us clout...big clout...>

[Outside of economic imperatives, what value(s) would you consider ordinary people place on the role of work in their lives i.e. the Irish work ethic?]

<...The concept of a 'fair day's pay for a fair day's work' probably encapsulates the dominant view...Irish people generally expect to have a meaningful role at work where their contribution is acknowledged, their opinions are valued and their efforts are rewarded not only in financial terms...The willingness of Irish people to

emigrate to find work over the decades and the extent to which long-term unemployed people have responded to opportunities in the social economy in recent years demonstrate the importance attached to work...>

<...People do not see work and the incomes derived from it as the sole basis for dignity...on the contrary there is strong ethical conviction that people's dignity is independent of the type of work or the level of income which they enjoy...equally they believe that people must make a contribution to society in accordance with their capacity...>

<...I never had any interest in money...the sun will shine in Florida anyway...I tell her (wife) that we'll be long enough dead...so off she's gone to the Patrick's day parade in New York with her sisters...Holiday in Florida is better that accumulating it...my father liked to enjoy himself...Most people know that they can't have everything... they would like to have the good life but they know they can't have it...peoples horizons are to get a house, a holiday not entrepreneurial...they like to work for others...don't like responsibility...us Irish aren't like that...don't like taking responsibility...because the nation was dominated for centuries...>

<...The work ethic is getting stronger...trying to jettison the laid back approach...but the old one is still very much there...>

[Do you see any evidence to suggest that peoples belief or unbelief in an afterlife influences their total commitment to industrialisation?]

<...The social philosophy associated with religious belief, particularly the development of Catholic Social Teaching over the past century has had an effect which is discernible in our approach to industrial relations...>

<...Social partnership embodies concerns about equity and distribution and the right to participate, which would be central themes of that social teaching...These are embedded in our political and civic culture, as well as being an explicit aspect of the belief system of the majority...>

<...What defines Irish people in Ireland and abroad?...Catholicism in ninety five per cent of cases...They are gregarious, fun loving, articulate, easy going and friendly...on the Island you can contrast the Catholic here with the North...you can scale back the adjectives...you know hard working orderly, sets of regulations...I cannot put my finger on it...Catholicism is more directive...it emphasises the individual...Almost in a perverse way we are happy to let the Church look after the absolutes...so we have a good advantage...we have the capacity...the capacity of the Irish to deal with change is probably better against someone who alone is responsible for certainties and absolutes...like the Protestant...There are certainly advantages...the real winner takes both...don't take the super conservativeness of

the Protestant but do take the more likely one to succeed...hard work and planning...>

<...I am a Catholic and Mass going...I am what you could describe as an overt Catholic...I am very close to the Jesuits over the years...I was trained by the Jesuits when they were the Panzer Corps of the Church...they picked out people like me...to lead in my area...and so you conduct business in this life with a view to the afterlife...>

[If Yes to question four could you outline the factors or reasons (political, religious etc.) that may be influential in this respect?]

<...We would also be at the higher end of church attenders[sic]...belonging to Church groups and collecting at the church gate...that sort of thing...no...I don't think that we want to go top of the league...go totally industrialised...most Irish people are individualists...the Japanese and Germans may blindly follow orders but not us...There's more to life than work...the demands of modern family life ...they seek lifestyle...good house...two cars...it comes from our history...we're nearly all first or second generation workers... we are a lot more balanced in our outlook than modern Europeans...>

<...Industrial progress dehumanises us...makes us into robots...I never bring work home with me anymore...I just do enough... just enough...>

<...Worship the Almighty...everything else is secondary...the Almighty will judge...He will be more merciful on those rich who have accumulated by lawful means...being rich is a very big onus on the individual...it is very difficult to get rich lawfully...as you can see with the tribunals (corruption tribunals in the planning process in Dublin)...>

<...Leading a good life means a balance between wealth and happiness...giving to the poor...everybody needs goods and property yet shouldn't take over one...the balance is don't get rich and don't glorify poverty...be wary of wealth...acquiring wealth is not morally wrong...it is wrong when speculating...when it is got at the expense of poorer people or using it in a destructive manner....this balance leads to happiness here and good morality...>

<...The ideal set for human happiness is when you have enough...Aristotle says that virtue is a balance between two extremes...laziness versus workaholic... in-between is the ideal...>

<...My experience is that Ireland is still a Catholic country...as for stroking...we are not totally against it, each individual case must be examined...always remember...action in this life must be based on the afterlife...>

<...Well I'm big into that myself as you know!...wealth isn't everything...it isn't really...>

[What would you consider the main benefits and damage to individual workers in particular and Irish society in general from the recent rapid economic progress (The Celtic Tiger)?]

<...There were Scandinavians with me recently examining the Celtic Tiger phenomenon...I was conscious that they were held up as the as the model of economic success...although they are still very wealthy...they are experiencing severe structural problems and severe dissatisfaction with their lot...that's beginning to happen to us...>

<...The Celtic Tiger has become particularly significant in the last two years...many workers said...'I've had an inadequate income particularly with dependants'...then the wife gets a job and they can double their income...>

<...No correlation between wealth and happiness...Sweden an engineered society...were very unhappy...always unhappy...>

<...Now they'll need to get used to the idea that people will be working in several different jobs, and having one job will be the exception rather than the rule...I've just come back from Singapore last week, and there is a mindset on retraining...that's one of the key differences...>

<...About wealth...the most discontented people are in the best jobs...>

<...The work ethic at high level in the country is 'how to make money without working for it'...>

[end]

Discussion

Some key influences impacted on the substance of each economic vision. A number of respondents believed that Catholic Social Teaching embodied in the social partnership approach still had the capacity to achieve the balance between equity and competitiveness. A number of contributors did not regard wealth as a key personal priority. The religious leaders tended to focus mainly on the equity objective whereas the economic leaders assigned a higher preference for competitiveness as a way of achieving equity. Some claimed that the absence of Socialism and the consolidation of stable centrist political ideology underpinned the economic climate and this absence was a key attraction for multi-national corporations. Others were quick to point out that strong lobby groups play off the main political parties against each other in advancement of their own interests.

The absence of Socialism as a political force also left little subliminal or ideological baggage carried by the Irish workforce. Socialism was not recognized by any of the contributors as an appropriate framework to shed light on Irish economic development nor was it perceived to be an appropriate framework to inform individual or national strategies in securing material well-being. The importance of partnership consensus in assisting with economic development,. was paramount. Some argued that unlike the Protestant, the Irish Catholic worker was freed from the burden of finding answers to ultimate questions and as this function fell within the remit of the priest it enabled workers to focus their attention on work. This norm could be interpreted as a national competitive advantage. Moreover, some understood national strategy in terms of optimising rather than maximizing growth. In other words, there is a broad consensus that an optimum limit of enough development to secure the desired material and equitable outcomes at national level is the most preferable of economic targets.

The religious contributors stated that economic development must be for the greater good and that wealth can endanger both the individual's and society's search for truth. Furthermore, the greater good cannot be served by either Marxism or Capitalism, where the Catholic ideal is for a *social* free market. The Church of Ireland and the Islamic Community also held similar economic positions. Undoubtedly one remarkable finding was the revelation that one of the economic contributors was placed by the Jesuits into the elite strata of Irish society unaware that was happening until some time later. He acknowledged that his work philosophy had been subsequently governed by Jesuit psychology.

The disclosure by all respondents of an acceptable national and individual measure of economic success, namely enough, is another feature of Domain A responses where a balance between wealth and a good lifestyle for all was an important aim of economic policy. The table below summarises these and other themes that emerged.

Table 6.1 Thematic Summary of Findings - Domain A

C1	*C2*	*C3*	*C4*	*C5*
Contributor	*Key Elements of Economic Vision*	*Key Influence(s) on Vision*	*Hoped for Outcome*	*Measure of Success*
1	Four priority areas (mainly aspirational)	Catholic Social Teaching	Re-distribution of wealth through partnership	Enough for all citizens
2	Higher living standards ('I suppose')	Absence of Socialism and Marxism	Equality of income	Unemployment eliminated
3	Optimise not maximize growth	Catholic workers worldview	Equal opportunities for all	Optimise wealth creation
4	Full employment	Jesuit psychology	Access to free health and education	Enough for all citizens
5	Higher living standards ('I suppose')	Playing off the political parties for own gain	Equal distribution of income and opportunity	Enough for all
6	Opposed to Capitalism and Socialism	Official Catholic teaching on wealth	Equal distribution and Re-distribution of wealth	Enough for all is the ideal
7	Against a freely industrialisng System	God's will must be done	Sharing with the community	Enough for everybody
8	Welfare of individual is paramount	Economic development must be for common good	Re-distribution of wealth	Lack of profit incentive a sole motivator for wealth creation

Part 2: Sub-Section One

Labelled Extracts and Themes from a Selection of Respondents in Domains B-D

As previously discussed in chapter five, the approach we adopted for the presentation of the data was that the respondents would speak for themselves. Because we are confident of maintaining confidentiality in this instance, we can provide much more comprehensive individual and group extracts as representative examples of the contributions in each of the three domains, including the line coding and a brief explanatory narrative on some culture specific idioms and statements embedded in a number of these extracts. We start with the contribution from a senior executive, followed by a non-management multi-national employee, a farmer, second level pupils, their career guidance teachers and finally a group of women Travellers.

Domain B - The Multi-National Executive

[what kind of lifestyle do you have?]

Line 1: I spend a lot of hours at work…it wouldn't be unusual to have to spend ten to eleven hours a day in XXX department…
Line 2: I work harder because I'm a young woman…I have to work really hard at being acceptable to the men…
Line 3: I stop and think all the time the way I say things…female anguish is acceptable you know…it's okay to cry…I laugh when the fellas are going for a pint, they say ''XXX' has to go home and iron the clothes'…it's okay for me to be a senior manager but I don't get invited to the golf…I'm different…I play golf regularly yet they invite a guy who only tips around…

[what kind of lifestyle would you like to have?]

Line 4: my father died when I was young and we couldn't afford money to buy things…
Line 5: this job…I have money for clothes, holiday, golf, no doubt about that… I have a luxury apartment…
Line 6: I wouldn't have an aspiration for loads of money…just enough…
Line 7: I'm not pushed about material things…eventually I'd like to get married and have children…eventually I might get a job which gives me more time…
Line 8: I don't expect to be working my ass off forever…If I got money through the lottery or something, I'd leave straightaway…you know I'd like to get into a situation where it wouldn't be necessary to work that hard…
Line 9: I have a real duty thing to (the company)…
Line 10: I have a drive because I'm young… you feel you need to earn every penny you get…
Line 11: I've never been out sick…ever!…

Line 12: it's not good, but I have to drive myself...I would try any job they gave me...I'd even try sales... It's a Catholic guilt, I think...it rings a bell, what I'm saying...I'm just thinking about it now, as I speak to you...y'know if someone pays, then you must work hard to earn it, yeah...I think it's a Catholic thing...

This latter comment highlights the presence of a Catholic vocational conscience i.e. one that enforces continuous high levels of commitment to work. Although she admits that while men can underachieve by thirty per cent and still receive a hundred per cent reward, women must work to hundred per cent and consequently men tend to have a more balanced life (Line 16).

[would you say that the Irish generally give everything they've got to their work?]

Line 13: no...I would not!
Line 14: some have a slightly more balanced approach than I have...
Line 15: females, they have to do too much...
Line 16: men can say to themselves 'ah, I'll just do fuckin' seventy per cent, and it'll get me 100 per cent reward'...women can't do that...and you [men] are probably more balanced because of that...
Line 17: we're not Japanese types...but some people will be workaholic types, you know...

She observes that most Irish workers do not totally commit themselves to their work and agrees that money is a secondary objective a means to an end.

[when you reflect on your working life, what do you think?]

Line 18: there's more to life than work...
Line 19: work generates money, and I want to do things well...
Line 20: I do something active, like the football, it gets you away from all the pressures...
Line 21: money is the key...not the job...my enjoyment is crucial...I have a self-discipline, you have to when you study like I did...no one pushing you...

She re-emphasises her ideal and sets out her position regarding wealth and money by once more identifying the target of enough.

[which is more important to you, to be rich or to be happy?]

Line 22: happy, definitely...I'm not rich...relatively speaking though, I am...
Line 23: there's not much point in having lots of money without my having golf and sports...
Line 24: other things really don't matter...it won't matter if you're happy...a bigger car would not improve my situation...
Line 25: I'm not hugely materialistic...
Line 26: money is not the be all and end all...

Line 27: I give regular charitable donations, believe it or not...
Line 28: I don't really accumulate money, as long as I have enough to do what I want...

The Spirit of Charity is the most important aspect of an individual's behaviour in this life. She strongly believes in the existence of Heaven and it is important for her to secure Heaven. Moreover, she highlights the insignificant role of both work effort and work excellence in securing this afterlife. She also relates how her management style reflects this charitable ethos since the real benchmark is how you treat individuals.

Line 29: I believe in the afterlife...
Line 30: the way I treat people is the most important thing...
Line 31: I don't think how hard I work will give me the keys to the Kingdom of Heaven...
Line 32: you need to be a more decent type of person, not focus on somebody doing something wrong...you know everybody does something wrong...being a decent person is more important...
Line 33: if your ass is kicked, like in here, you shouldn't also kick ass...it's not an achievement philosophy, but I feel it's right...
Line 34: I just try to be decent, and as right as I can be...at the end of the day it won't be 'how well did you meet your budgets?'...'how well did you manage the stock?'...no definitely not...
Line 35: how well did I treat this person...or that person...yes...if you do something good someday it will come back...
Line 36: if I was being assessed (by the company) they would say I'm a charitable type...you know...a woman...soft wimpy side...too people conscious...not hard... you know?...but hey... *fuck* them!...

Work is a means to an end yet at the same time she has to commit her self to the job in hand and not lose sight of the importance of the afterlife. She sees most of Irish society in the same frame of mind i.e. trying to do well at work in order to secure the means to live at a comfortable level while simultaneously interacting with others within a charitable framework to secure Heaven. This instrumental view of work is the dominant one taken by most individuals in this Domain.

Domain C - The Multi-National Non-Management Employee

This contributor expresses his satisfaction with his personal circumstances and he provides a description of the enough target very early in the interview.

[what kind of lifestyle do you have?]

Line 1: I have a good lifestyle...we're on a really good salary and we have bonuses and shares as well...my family have grown up...some are working and one is just finishing his Leaving Cert....(state examination for end of senior cycle secondary education)...

Line 2:I have a car, a holiday, me few jars (drinks)...

Line 3: the house is practically paid for...

Line 4: I have anything within reason, really...

[what kind of lifestyle would you like to have?]

Line 5: nothing in particular, really...no, I'm happy enough with things...

He describes the psychological contract or 'deal' he has internalised between his family and the company.

[would you say you give everything you've got to the job?]

Line 6: no!...

Line 7: I make a good effort...

Line 8: no...I give a hundred per cent more to family than to the company...even though that's not always possible...but I think I'm changing...

Line 9: remember I told you I had a problem with XXX ? (family member) ...yeah...well...I chose a compromise...I chose a compromise...I took a half day to go to the doctor with him this morning, and now I'm seeing you this afternoon...and then going straight back to work...

Not only do other workers adopt the same approach but the company only requires a good effort from each employee.

[would you say the Irish generally give everything they've got to their work?]

Line 10: in general they would have the same approach as myself...

Line 11: Irish workers abroad are more concerned about getting on...they have to put in a real hard effort to get on...

Line 12: it's more relaxed here, you only have to put in a *good* effort...that's all...

This is an interesting observation as the implied standard required by the company is less than one hundred per cent work commitment, and is precisely the one expressed by executives in Domain B. He points out that many staff are purchasing Additional Voluntary Contributions (AVCs) in order to retire earlier to enjoy life but at the same standard of living that they would have enjoyed if they had remained working.

[when you reflect on your working life, what do you think?]

Line 13: generally speaking, it has been a good experience...

Line 14: the trend now, here, is to finish work earlier...Pensions [dept] are inundated with people to get out at fifty five...they have this guy, he is the pensions liaison officer and it's his job to answer all questions and make decisions about their pension and their future...and every day you'll see people talking to him about getting out...what do I need?...how many AVCs will I need?...He can't cope with the amount of questions he's getting...

Line 15: I probably feel the same myself...didn't, though, ten years ago...

Line 16: I've seen people work till sixty five and they haven't lasted too long after that...

Line 17: the quality of life...I would hope to retire at fifty seven, maybe earlier, and enjoy life...I think I'll be near enough to the standard of living I have now, and I'll be able to enjoy life...get out and enjoy life...that's what's important...

Line 18: even the younger guys now tend to retire early...

Line 19: I think people want to enjoy life more...more time to relax, play golf, y'know...do whatever they want...it's the complete opposite to years ago...y'know everyone then was going up to personnel looking for extensions to *stay on*...that was the norm then...

The affluence of the Celtic Tiger now makes it possible to stop working much earlier.

[which is more important to you, to be rich or to be happy?]

Line 22: from my experience anyway, all the money in the world...what good is it to you?...I'd say I'm comparatively rich from some people's point of view...yeah... I could be rich...

He regards work as almost irrelevant to secure the afterlife and states like many other respondents that the Spirit of Charity and practical generosity are more important.

[do you think this hard work goes towards anything or is it all over when you die?]

Line 23: well I think there's a better life when you die...I believe...yes...I believe in an afterlife...a Heaven if you like...

Line 24: work could help achieve this, but I think in the main, treating other people properly is the main thing...being good to people...so work, in that sense does not necessarily work!...people who have not worked...it affects them negatively alright...not able to cope, y'know...the 70's (1970s) really knocked the stuffing out of them...they found it hard to relate to others...y'know?...so work can actually screw you up if you don't have it...but as for anything to do with Heaven ...no...nothing...nothing at all...

Line 25: I have a clear conscience... I would work quite well...

Line 26: I believe in an afterlife...

Line 27: your body dies, but your spirit lives on...there's something   there alright...

Line 28: hard work doesn't affect this...

Line 29: it's how you live your life that counts...

Line 30: as I said before I am a Catholic, being decent to people, treat people well...as I said though I don't know if work'll help you into Heaven...

Line 31: I don't think it's to do with your work ethic...no...I don't think you'll be judged on that...

Line 32: I *do* think you'll be judged on how you treat people...I pray at Mass...I'm not a devout Catholic I'm a Christian and there's definitely a next life alright...so you've got to be charitable...

[what quality-strength of the workforce do you think contributes to profitability?]

Line 33: people are always happy to work, and if they're not happy you don't get the productivity...so I think they're happy here...

Line 34: some are unhappy on the floor...production are unhappy, they feel hard done by...the biggest problem is disgruntled workers...

Line 35: my contribution?...I would say was getting a good deal for my colleagues ...so, I got the lads to agree to it, and it's been good for us...we have it handy now...real handy...

Domain C - The Farmer

[how would you describe your lifestyle?]

Line 1: busy...we both (myself and my wife) work well under pressure...we need a goal to work towards...I couldn't just be a farmer...but you can't dwell on the negative...I have a good lifestyle, I enjoy what I do...

Line 2: I have other interests outside farming of course...I am involved with the GAA (Gaelic Athletic Association, promotes Gaelic games and is one of the largest sports organisations in Ireland) and I train the under tens in hurling...(game played with a long stick and a leather ball)...and football on a Saturday morning...I am on the parish council and we are both very active in the local community...(wife) teaches full time as well you know, she is on the board of management of the school, and she is also on the executive of the local Rural Women's Group...I'll show you the letter...(leaves momentarily and goes into adjoining kitchen...returns shortly accompanied by his wife who has the letter...I read the letter...congratulations and smiles all round).

[would you say you give everything to the job?]

Line 3: yes...100 per cent...you have to do it right, there's only two ways to do things, wrong or right...in fact, we're both perfectionists...

Line 4: when we started our B and B in 1992, we went for Bórd Fáilte (Irish Tourist Board) approval immediately...wouldn't start without it...By 1993 we had seen the wisdom of getting into agri-tourism so we got a contract with CIE (Irish Transport Company) to host bus tours of Americans...In XXX year we won the Regional Family Farm of the Year...we actually doubled our throughput in the B and B (bed and breakfast) between 1992 and 1996...Do you know that when it

peaked, we took in a huge number on the buses and nearly the same in the B and B over a seven month period?...We now have two full-time and one part-time staff in the B and B...
Line 5: we're always looking for goals...we're building on an extra four bedrooms at the moment, and we've got a contract for four night stays with Irish Ferries...I myself network with the local B and B's and pass on the overflow of clients to them...this year, we again won the Regional award for B and B of the Year and we're in for the national award for Family Farm of the Year.

He states that he is rich and successful because of hard work.

Line 6: well, I left school with two empty pockets, and to-day I have an asset base worth over 'X' million pounds...

Being a Core Catholic he sees work as a punishment for this life and is convinced that by being charitable to others he will almost guarantee himself a place in Heaven. Hard work has no relevance whatsoever in securing Heaven.

[what's the point of it all?]

Line 7: leave something good for my two sons...I had a hard childhood, but I always said I would make it...
Line 8: I know where I came from...and I appreciate what I've got...I've more than enough to keep me comfortable for the rest of my life...I worked for it...I'd like to leave land for my sons, I can't take it with me...I'd like to retire at fifty five and do some travelling or something like that...even have a weekend away...it's a dream at the moment...Just say you've lived thirteen thousand eight hundred and seventy two days by the time you're forty two years of age...it's all about time, isn't it...it's a state of mind...a friend of mine died yesterday, only thirty eight years old...it's times like that you ask yourself what's it all for?..
Line 9: I believe there's a Heaven and a God and a thereafter...but I don't know what they're like...and I believe you should have a purpose, y'know like earn by the sweat of your brow...a fella who has the use of his hands can do something...I go to Mass, say my night prayers and grace before meals (prayer)...and I firmly believe I'll be rewarded for my good living...doing good to others, but whether I work hard, or half as hard, I'll have the same chance of getting it as someone who dosses around (lazy)...a lazy fella who doesn't work but lives a good life...y'know is good to others...well he'll go to Heaven the same as a hard worker...no difference!...

[what makes you unique do you think?]

Line 10: my environment and my family influence...the kind of mentality I have...I couldn't draw Social Welfare when I'm healthy and can work...none of the twelve of us ever did...it's the family influence, though, children don't suddenly become disruptive at fifteen or sixteen years of age...they learn the difference between right and wrong when they are young...

[what disadvantages do you see to the Celtic Tiger?]

Line 11: it's not a boom for farmers you know, eighty per cent of farmers are not doing well...prices are worse now than ten years ago, but fertiliser and meal etc. has gone up...only the strong will survive...twelve thousand farmers have left farming over the past three years...we're a society of old priests, old nuns, and old farmers...no one is going into it...the youth are not following into farming...well the hours are bad with no return...a man works with me...I pay him £40 a day...he'd probably earn more somewhere else but he's with me years and he likes it...
Line 12: all facets of society are not benefiting from the Celtic Tiger...I'm cost effective with my B and B and my agri-tourism...and I put in the hours...but I wouldn't be in farming without my two other incomes...
Line 13: there's also been a drop-off in morality in the last five years...*we* were more morally responsible at eighteen...society has accepted looser morals...look at the important divorce referendum...people talk about partners now, never husbands and wives...you are more 'devil-may-care' when you have money...it can become a god...people think 'I can do what *I* want'...ah...I suppose it would have happened anyhow...
Line 14: but I definitely see a relationship between the economic success of the Celtic Tiger and a reduction in morals...they don't realise there are more things than having wealth...they can't take it with them...its really foolish on their part thinking this life is the only life they'll have...

[to sum up then, what would you say is your key personal quality which made you so successful?]

Line 15: honesty!...I've always been honest in all my dealings, I don't owe anything and I never 'did' anyone [cheat]...you can't live without charity, though, do you know that when it snowed really heavily here a few years ago, I got out my four-wheel drive and cleared the driveways all along here...the neighbours couldn't get over it!...I would look after people...they'd pay you back in kind...

In the final extracts he states that he will have to forfeit all of his wealth when he dies so it is irrational to focus exclusively on work as the most useful human activity.

Domain C - The Career Guidance Teacher

The Career Guidance teacher neatly summarised the unintended nature of the Celtic Tiger and then followed this with a statement outlining his belief that most Irish people eventually calculate the odds in favour of the existence of an afterlife and then act accordingly.

[what do you think about the economic situation at the moment...how did it happen?]

Line 1: I don't know...I don't think anyone knows...its just a set of circumstances that happened to arrive in Ireland...a bit like a snowball on the top of a hill...when it gets tipped over it just gets to be a critical mass and goes faster and faster, gets bigger and bigger...
Line 2: they're just after a good time (the pupils) wine, women and song but as they get a little older they'll wise up and they'll see that there is a strong possibility that there is an afterlife...the older you get the stronger the possibility becomes...then they'll catch on...they won't chance it that there isn't an afterlife...they'll hedge their bets on that one...most Irish people do that...won't chance it that there's nothing...eh...listen...mmm...[looking at his watch]...I'm a bit tied for time...

The teacher stated that there appeared to be an agenda to redirect the ethos of schools away from the holistic approach of educating the whole person, towards a narrower more vocational outcome. By vocational was meant a more business and scientific curriculum. This has happened as a consequence of collusion between the Department of Education and Science and employers with the sole intention of manipulating education almost exclusively for their own advantage. The introduction of performance assessment management techniques into schools was particularly irksome and reflected the supremacy of the new business ethos in the Celtic Tiger filtering into all sections of education. The link between education and business was clearly to be seen in the university sector. An example was cited of the outgoing Head of Dublin City University, who claimed that ninety five per cent of his time was spent securing funding for the University. Other examples of the O'Reilly and Smurfit business schools in Trinity College and University College Dublin respectively were also offered as clear indicators that

Line 3: education is now big business...if that trend continued, then there would be no place for the weaker student.

Line 4: the humanities was only a poor second rate option for third level students despite that fact that it provided opportunities for a more liberal educational approach as the counterbalancing antithesis of the economic imperatives now becoming ingrained in the education system...this business influence must be seen as a particularly dangerous trend for the future of education...already, it was

noticeable that business had attracted high calibre graduates that traditionally found their way into teaching...now only pass graduates apply for teaching posts...
Line 5: the pastoral care of pupils was an extremely important role for the teacher, but again the overriding objective now is to focus on the economic and a sense of amorality...

Although, most pupils saw work as an attraction

Line 6: they nevertheless, are made to understand [by the teachers] that their life was a transitory journey and this is the reason that the school should resist the economic ethos for the liberal educational one...

Nowadays, the more holistic approach of integrating pastoral, physical, and knowledge subjects was vital to develop maturity. Although the school itself is the victim of the economic ethos, compelling the teachers to 'hard sell' their own school at open evenings in the face of intense local competition from other schools, they have found that by adopting a more student centred approach for the benefit of the average student, their enrolments have stabilised. This was ironically, a telling reminder to the business community and the Department of Education in particular, that there was still a significant demand for the holistic personal development approach in education. The teacher indicated that she had a balanced view on the need to live a full holistic life now while preparing well for the next one.

Domain C - The Pupils

Not one pupil in the five classes said that they never go to Mass nor on the other hand did they declare that they regularly attended Mass. However their strength of belief in the afterlife was strong since over ninety per cent of pupils believed that it existed. Of those who did believe, eighty per cent said that the afterlife was a Heaven and regarded it as a place or location where life was happy and one would be re-united with family and friends. Every pupil regarded working hard or easy as irrelevant in achieving the goal of Heaven and approximately ninety per cent maintained that

Line 1: being good to people being nice to people...is what's important...

The focus for eighty five per cent of all pupils sampled was to

Line 2: have enough of the things of this life to enjoy life like a car, house, drink, holidays, clothes and craic (fun)...

This position is consistent with their approach of enjoying life now together with the objective of being happy. Yet they were also aware that this life was transient and was followed by another and better life, a Heaven. On the other hand they acknowledged that Irish society has a stronger focus on the after life with the rating on this continuum more evenly distributed towards the middle or zero range of marks. Since eighty five per cent of pupils maintained that there is a positive correlation between wealth and unhappiness, they then concluded that

Line 3: it stands to reason that as long as you have enough you'll be happiest…

Approximately fifty per cent of pupils regarded the accumulation of wealth as indicative of

Line 4: being a greedy person…

Consequently there was an element of undesirability about 'going after' wealth. The remaining fifty per cent were equally divided among those that regarded happiness as solely derived from wealth and enjoying it, to those supporting the use of wealth for the benefit of others. Almost all (ninety five per cent) maintained that the focus of their work would be exclusively instrumental i.e. to get something else and the popular view was that work was

Line 5: to enable you enjoy life outside of work…

Exploration of this theme uncovered the low intrinsic value of work regardless of income earned inasmuch as it is not possible for work to contribute to individual self-development other than as a means of securing

Line 6: the-where-with-all to have a life…

Over ninety per cent of pupils found it almost incomprehensible that one would focus one's life on living to work.

Line 7: it doesn't make any sense to do that…

Almost seventy five per cent of pupils indicated that everybody was doing well from the Celtic Tiger and the remainder felt that the politicians and the rich were getting much richer than ordinary individuals.

Line 8: ordinary people were only mugs, we're being 'fleeced by the bastards'…

Approximately five per cent of pupils said that they could not be bothered with examining or analysing the pros and cons of the Irish economic system nor its capacity to deliver a good quality life for all. It was simply a matter of

Line 9: just getting on with it and doing your best…

In other words there was a strong focus on this life and a very strong focus on the instrumental value of work.

Domain D - A Group of Four Women Travellers

[how would you describe your lifestyle?]

Line TravA 1: travelling around, it was more like a holiday when I think of it now...we would be camping down the road, and we would be camping in different places...it was a pure scenery place...between Kerry, Clare, Meath and Westmeath (counties in the south, west, east and midlands of Ireland)...it was nearly a holiday at that time, yet we didn't take any heed of it, y'know what I mean...we didn't appreciate it as much as we should...when we were travelling...because we were travelling to all them scenery places...them lakes...big mountains and things like that...we used to camp and live in those caravans...and the freedom that we had meant a lot to us...it was as good as a holiday to us...it's now we miss it...

[what kind of lifestyle would you like?]

Line TravB 2: my wish would be going back out to the rural part of the country...get every Traveller out from every house in Dublin, and get them back travelling...have our freedom back...when I was young myself thirty years ago, that'd be my wish...
Line TravC 3: don't think I'd like that...I'd like to settle...I don't think I'd like to start travelling...
Line TravD 4: I wouldn't travel, not at my age now...I worked all my life trying to rear my children...I'd like to go down to Mullingar and light a fire...there's no fires now...

[what's stopping you from having this lifestyle?]

Line TravA 5: what's stopping us? [yeah] when all the trades...the tinsmithin' went we had to go on the dole...when they went on the dole they had to have proper addresses, even though they hadn't proper addresses, they had to come out of a city or town...and if they weren't near enough to a city or town, they stuffed them into a field like animals...and blocked the road and blocked the camps that the Travellers used to camp in...and they wouldn't give them the dole except that they were near a town...I think that used happen...you had to have a fixed address...[64]

[I want to talk to you about your Religion – I'm a Roman Catholic myself]

Line TravA 6: *you're* a Catholic?

---

[64] Tinsmithing was the repair of tin implements and the chief source of work of the male Traveller from the nineteenth century onwards together with chimney sweeping, peddling and occasional farm labouring. Male labouring was supplemented by wives and children begging in towns and cities. The modern Traveller deals mainly in used cars and scrap metal.

[oh yes I am...just like you...why?... did you think that I was something else!]
Line TravB 7: kinda...[pause and smile]...our religion is very strong...
[I just manage to hold on to it!]
Line TravB 8: ha ha...(laughing)...

[Can you just talk to me about your religion, what it means to you?]

Line TravB 9: yeah...I think it would probably be a bit different...than the settled community...a lot of Roman Catholic settled people wouldn't go, wouldn't really be bothered in going to wells (holy wells) [65]...you will get people that do it, but not as much as a Traveller or a priest, if a priest, if there's a good priest that we know that is real religious and he'd go there and he's blessing you, he's praying over you and he's getting a crucifix...we know that he's down to earth religious, we'd go to him...Travellers make a big deal, like Fr. McDonagh now...Lord Rest Him (they make the sign of cross)...he was a...what do you call that College? (asking a fellow Traveller in the group)...Warrenstown College and every Traveller used to go to him, and he did cure me because I had a very strong belief in him...and now that he's dead they still pray to him...and...they got eh...they paid a few pound...all the Travellers throughout Ireland, and they got his head, just down to his waist, about to there (pointing just below the waist)...and they went down the country and got it done...now he is a priest that we remember, he is...you know you'd know straight away that it's him, and even to this day now there's people getting cured...

[a statue of him, is it?]

Line TravB 10: yeah...a statue on a grave...there's a grave where he's buried...Travellers still go there...I was there about two weeks ago as well...
Line TravC 11: he's only about twenty years dead, and we knew him when he was alive...y'know...he was a great friend of ours...we used to keep going to him...
Line TravB 12: if were any of the children were sick now, we'd rather bring the child to the priest, rather than the doctor...we'd have more belief because the priest does the blessing of the child and the child would get better...
Line TravC 13: we knew that Jesus and Our Lady the Blessed Virgin was above him...but the way we looked at it was, that he was so religious that God... he

---

[65] Thousands of Catholics travel to holy places of pilgrimage and penance such as Lough Derg (St Patrick's Purgatory) in County Donegal in the northwest of Ireland between June and August each year. Another is Croagh Patrick, a nine hundred metre high mountain in County Mayo in the west of Ireland associated with St. Patrick's fast for forty days. Some pilgrims climb the mountain barefoot as a higher form of penitential rite. St. Patrick is Ireland's patron Saint and a festival (St Patrick's Day) is held on 17 March each year. What is more remarkable is that nearly two thirds of the Irish population visited and prayed at the relics of St. Therése of Lisieux when it toured Ireland in 2001 at the very moment when the Celtic Tiger was coming to its finale and when one would have expected secularisation to be very widespread.

prayed to God and His Mother...to the Blessed Virgin...that they *had* to give it to him...y'know what I mean...that you were gettin' better, you know what I mean...they'd answer him (the priest) for you...

Line TravD 14: and another thing Travellers believe dearly is the man and woman whose living together and not married, there wouldn't be an hours luck on that road...and yet they'd be living in mortal sin (if you die in this state you go to Hell)...which is true...yet a lot of people thought that Travellers didn't get married, didn't get their childer baptised or didn't get their childer First Holy Communion and Confirmation...there's people like that...yet...the travelling people get their childer baptised before they're a week old, you know I have a son and he was baptised on the very exact day he was born...the eighteenth May...because the Travelling women wanted that...very particular about that...baptised on the day he was born...now the mother couldn't get ready the food, or handle the food...had to be churched by the priest, to take the sin of the birth of the child out of her [66]...

Line TravB 15: the most important thing to Travellers today, the most important thing that's in their life is to make sure that a child is christened, when it comes to the age it gets First Holy Communion, and Confirmation, right?...marriage then... make sure to get the family married, and not have to say you do your best...not to have a boy and girl living together that wanted to be married...and another thing if a person is sick and they're dying, that we'll get a priest...

Line TravD 16: unless that it's a sudden death...

[let me ask you about Heaven, tell me first, do you believe in Heaven?]

Line TravC 17: you were saying earlier about a wish...I live in a house in X, and my trailer is in Y, and so I'm caught between the two families...now my kids are mixing with the settled community, and when someone dies belonging to me they

---

[66] According to the Catholic Encyclopedia (1908) the term churching refers to a blessing given by the Catholic Church to mothers after recovery from childbirth. Only a legitimately married Catholic woman was able to receive this blessing. It is not a Church precept but a pious custom from early Christian times (Rituale Romanum). The woman presented herself to give thanks to God for a happy delivery. The mother carried a lighted candle and the priest blessed her with holy water in the form of a cross. Keith (1997) noted that it took on a semi-magical significance in popular estimation following from the Jewish ritual of Purification where the sin of childbirth was washed away. Catholic churching was deemed important by a simple people in that is was generally accepted that sexual intercourse tarnished a woman's purity and was therefore, unholy or unclean due to childbirth because both virginity and sexual abstinence were commonly equated with holiness. A taboo regarding the handling of food was also commonly upheld after childbirth. For example until a mother was redeemed through churching she could not take up a knife and cut bread i.e. prepare any food for the family lest she contaminate it (Kearns 1996). The reason for having children baptised so quickly was that if they died without being baptised or christened they would not go to Heaven but to another place called Limbo. (Encyclopedia 1908), literally the border place, although they will eventually leave and enjoy a perfect state of natural happiness in Heaven. Churching had died out in modern Ireland.

don't bother at all, yet when some one of their friends dies, they rush to it…I'd like them to admit they're Travellers, I'm a Traveller and I always will be, it's in your blood…even though you're living in a house you're still a Traveller…

[what makes you a traveller?]

Line Trav A 18: you can't choose to be a Traveller or a settled person, you're born that way, and there's nothing going to change, nothing going to change her (Traveller C's) childer…the other thing that I think that if her childer are as she said, what happened to them is that they got in, they got mixed up with some settled people, and there was some discrimination going on, maybe in the schools, and they just, they *want* to change, they can't change…what they are, they cannot change…
Line TravC 19: they're hiding their identity…
Line TravA 20: yeah, my brother is in England and his childer were never married, he was getting several houses, he has his own site in England, his childer, it's hard to believe they're in London…they have to speak Irish and they are Travellers…they call themselves Travellers and they were never in Ireland…it's the child that's hiding their identity, they want to be a Traveller deep down, you never change…
Line TravB 21: no matter how much of a generation you go back, or go on ahead, say grandchildren in the next fifty or sixty year and they're living in houses, their parents and grandparents living in houses all their life, you're still a Traveller, you can't…you know what I mean, you can't turn a cabbage into a cauliflower, can't turn an onion into a carrot, you are what you are and that's it…
Line TravD 22: I'm a Traveller, I was born and reared a Traveller and I'll always *be* a Traveller, now my children don't like me saying that…
Line TravB 23: it's just that they want to hide their identity…
Line TravD 24: because they were born and reared in a house…I'm living two lives at the moment, I'm living in XXX and I have a trailer in YYY and the rest of the family are in YYY, so I'm between the two…it's very hard to kind of watch the house, watch what's going on…it's kind of two homes…and you're trying to run your own life as well, it's complicated…he worked here for years (my son), he won trophies and all, they're all over the building…I hate it…
Line TravA 25: I say let them live their own lives…

[so if I can ask you about Heaven, then?…could you tell me if you all believe that there is a Heaven?]

Line TravA 26: yeah we do of course! (all nod)

[could you tell me what you think it is?]

Line TravA 27: I think Heaven is a beautiful place, with lovely green trees…ah…flowers all the people that's dead and gone belonging to everybody that goes to Heaven, sitting in those chairs…all dressed in white, clouds is low, floating, a lot of angels, Our Lord sitting up on the big throne, what do you call it …crown…Our Lady beside him, that's the way I picture it…

Line TravB 28: someone comes to the door and takes you in, there's a place for everyone…anyhow we're all going there…

Line TravC 29: I think the same, I think much like you (B), I think it's an awful hard place to get to…I know like even if you're a good living person, and personally even if there's nothing wrong in your life, it's a terrible hard place to get to…

Line TravB 30: it's hard to get to Heaven…I can imagine it up, I think if I died and went to Heaven… I'm not going to die and go straight to Heaven, I'd be years and years and years waiting to get in…I think you have to go through Purgatory [67] you're then taken into Heaven…I don't think it's a place at all…you can hear voices but you can't associate them with people…

[how do I get there? What is the something that you must do?]

Line TravA 31: I suppose, you're not suppose to, if you can live a good life, and not harm people…not do any harm at all to people…only helping people as much as you can, praying for people, things like that…I think when you die, if you're a good person when you die, that you're just taken…you go to Heaven…straight when you die…Our Lady and Our Lord promised you when you die…

[what do you think is the value of working hard in getting to Heaven?]

Line TravA 32: it has good value, if you work hard and you're a good provider for your family you're a good person, look after your childer [children] and look after your work, whatever you're working at, and you really want to get there, like you're preparing for something…if you're doing well in work and you're good at it, and you're interested in it, it is yeah…and ones who don't (work)…He'd (God) probably give them a little bit of punishment, but He will forgive them…He forgives everyone…

Line TravC 33: some people only helps their own…some only believe in helping their own, their own family…another poor 'craythur' (creature) maybe that wants a bit of help, well they'd ignore that person…they'd pass them by…everyone should be helped, you know anyone that needs it…

The benchmark that you work hard to provide for the family and where work is always seen as a preparation for the next life. The Spirit of Charity as explained by the Archbishop's Representative is also articulated by the Traveller Women whereby everyone is entitled to be helped if they require it without recompense, thus echoing the Catholic rather than Protestant emphasis of charity. The principle

---

[67] Purgatory is a place to purify the soul, a temporal place of punishment for souls who have transgressed God's law with venial faults that have not been repented. The penalty is a temporary banishment before entering Heaven. Prayers by the living and indulgences gained on behalf of the souls in purgatory can shorten a soul's stay in Purgatory (Catholic Encyclopaedia 1911).

and measure of enough also features in their narrative. Wealth is identified as a real danger to secure Heaven.

[what would you say to me if I said to you that there are some people who believe that the more wealthier, the richer you get, the more likely it is that you'll get to Heaven and be saved?]

Line TravD 34: I wouldn't think great wealthy people...I often heard that the poorer man has a better chance of getting into Heaven...[would you say it's true?]...Yeah, I'd say it's true...I think that everyone's entitled to be rich or poor, no matter who they are they should be treated equally, because money won't really won't make them any worse, won't make them any better...do you know what I mean?...money on the earth, it'll do you good, but once you die it's no good to you...
Line TravB 35: you have to be poor to go to Heaven...you have to give what you have, give everything away everything to the poor people...you can keep nothing for yourself...and I knew a priest one time that took the boots off his feet and gave them to a travelling man...
Line TravA 36: well, you couldn't give *everythin'* that you have, I think if a person has a good heart, a happy person, good to people and does them no harm, well, not doing a lot of harm, you know...

This last statement is an excellent example of the interpretation of the Spirit of Charity as it applies to everyday life.

[what about being wealthy and happy in this economic boom?]

Line TravC 37: the thing about the Celtic Tiger, is the people in power is the people with...[sic]...the rich people makes more money out of the Celtic Tiger than the poor people...
Line TravD 38: I've never been asked that question before...(Heaven)...I don't think much about it, I just do the best for me childer...there is people who don't think about it at all...
Line TravA 39: pray before I go to bed and I pray when I get up in the morning...

[what about at the moment, do you think your life is better because of this economic boom?...do you have more material things?]

Line TravA 40: do I have more money to spend?...I do have more material things...in a Traveller's life there's more material things than ever before...is that what you mean?...[yeah, over the last few years]...no...everything you buy has gone up...the money is alright, you get enough...you manage on what you get, but everything you buy in the shop has gone up...the money has gone up, but you are still managing the way you did...
Line TravB 41: I think anyone with childer (sic) can hardly manage at all...you're spending a lot more on food...(interjection by TravC) that's what I'm

saying...anyone with children is worse...you get a rise in the allowance, they're giving it to you with one hand, and taking it away with the other...do you know what I mean?...they are giving it to you with this hand, then you're going into the shops and paying it out...everything's gone up...they said last year with the Celtic Tiger that the pensioners was going to get this...a raise in their allowance, but there isn't three pounds of an increase...so like, how can you manage... they give you eight pounds for gas, and it's thirteen pounds a bottle...if they gave you a bottle of gas, at least you'd have the bottle of gas...but there's nothing...there is for the rich, only for the rich...nothing for people that is struggling...

Line TravA 42: If you go out to sites there, people are discriminated against because they're dirty, so what I...well I have another wish, and I wish to God to have this wish...is to put a wealthy, one of the people who has power and put them out to a site where the Travellers stay for one month and see what would they do...where there would be thirty families, maybe with one tap between them...one, what do you call it, portaloo toilet, which would get cleaned out maybe once in a month...right...a skip left for them to throw the rubbish into...that's left there maybe...could be the guts of a month there without getting took away...no way of washing their clothes...no real way of bathing theirselves [sic]...no heating...no lights...I only wish to God that I could put a person, a politician or someone from the Government just put them in there for one month that would be my wish...and put them in it for life, some of them...[laughs]

[why do you think they don't do something about it, when there's loads of money?]

Line TravC 43: because they'll say that if Travellers wants to live that way, then let them...their way of life, that's Travellers...this is what people, what the council what the Government think...they look down us the travelling people...the filth and dirt...way of life that's they want to live...there was twelve houses built up in Villa Park, isn't that right? (asking the other women)...There was about thirty families all looking to get one...they say they're going to have them all housed but I can't see that...

Line TravA 44: they say we're filthy and dirty, but you could go to a terrace of settled houses some you wouldn't take a drink of water out of...rubbish up to their back windows...some of the Travellers, they have houses and they are absolutely lovely...spotless clean...

[would you say that Irish people work really hard?]

Line TravB 45: I do yeah, the ones that want to...there's a lot of Travellers just don't get the chance...settled people can learn an awful lot from Travellers...provided they get that chance...they're good workers if they get that chance...

[If you could get the money you were looking for, how much would you be talking about…what would you say would be appropriate the right amount of wealth for you to have?]

Line TravA 46: I think if you have your health, you have enough…if you can walk around…

Line TravB 47: enough to survive every day if you have your health and you're happy, and your childer are healthy and everything else is going well… you're in a bit of a good job or any kind of a job as long as you're doing a bit of work and you have a bit of money to spare to buy something nice for yourself, treat your children to something…that would be good…I wouldn't be thinking about saving, saving all the time…it would be nice to be able to do it but it would be a bit greedy too…I think once you're making enough…if you died you can't bring the money to Heaven…

Line TravA 48: I remember this poor man, he was dying, and he has bags of money, and he was staring at the money and our Lord was standing on this side and Our Lord wanted him to turn his head to him, but he wouldn't turn his head because he couldn't take his eyes off his money…

Line TravB 49: money problems is the root of all evil…so I think too much money is…money can cause an awful lot of money…and you wouldn't work if you have too much money you'd be sitting down there in the trailer very boring…

Line TravA 50: I think making something of yourself is more important than the money you're getting…

[would you rather be happy or rich?]

Line TravC 51: I'd rather be happy…I think happiness comes first…I don't think you could be very rich and happy…if you were very rich God knows what you would do…too much power…look at the way the Government of Ireland is forgetting about the people…they want it all for theirselves [sic]…

They remain unsure whether it was actually possible for an individual to be both rich and happy.

[end of transcript]

Table 6.2 Thematic Summary of Findings - Compressed Domains B-D

C1	C2	C3	C4	C5	C6	C7	C8
Domain B							
Executive	2	-3.0	-2.0	-0.5	2.0	1	1
Executive	2	-3.5	1.0	-4.0	2.0	1	1
Executive	3	-3.5	-3.5	0.5	0.0	1	1
Manager	2	-2.0	-2.5	-4.0	0.0	1	1
Manager	0	-3.5	-4.0	1.5	-4.0	0	0
Manager	2	-2.5	-2.5	-2.0	-1.5	1	1
Manager	3	-3.9	-0.5	0.0	0.0	1	1
Domain C							
Craft 1	2	-4.5	-2.5	1.0	0.0	1	1
Admin	2	0.5	-2.0	0.0	2.0	1	1
Operative	3	-3.0	-3.0	-2.0	-1.0	1	1
Technical	2	-1.0	-2.5	-4.0	0.0	1	1
Support	0	-5.0	2.5	-2.5	-2.0	1	1
Craft 2	2	1.0	-2.0	-0.5	0.0	1	1
Support	2	-2.0	-2.5	-4.0	-0.5	1	1
Farmer	2	-2.5	-2.0	-3.0	-1.0	1	1
Farmer	3	-3.5	-3.0	1.0	-1.0	1	1
Farmer	3	0.0	-0.5	3.0	-3.0	1	1
Farmer	3	1.0	-1.0	-2.5	-1.5	1	1
Farmer	2	-1.5	-1.0	2.0	0.0	1	1
School A	2	-2.0	-1.0	-3.0	-3.0	1	1
Schools B-E	2	-2.5	-1.5	-4.0	-1.5	1	1
Teacher	3	0.0	-2.0	0.0	-2.0	1	1
Teacher	3	0.0	1.5	0.0	-2.0	1	1
Domain D							
Unemployed	1	0.0	-1.5	-4.0	0.5	1	1
Unemployed	3	-1.0	-2.0	0.0	1.0	1	1
Unemployed	2	-1.0	-1.0	-0.5	-2.0	1	1
Unemployed	1	-1.0	-3.0	-2.5	-2.0	1	1
Traveller	3	-3.0	-3.5	-3.0	-2.5	1	1
Traveller	3	-2.0	-2.5	-2.0	-2.0	1	1
Traveller	3	-1.0	1.5	-0.5	-1.0	1	1
Traveller	3	2.0	0.0	1.0	0.0	1	1
Advocate	3	-1.0	-2.0	-1.0	0.0	1	1
Homeless	0	0.0	-2.0	2.0	-2.0	1	1
Homeless	2	2.0	-2.5	2.0	-2.0	1	1

Key

$C2$ = Level of Religiosity where 1 = Devout, 2 = Intermediate, 3 = Lapsed

$C3$ = Self-Focus On This Life -5.0, On Heaven +5.0

$C4$ = Society Focus On This Life -5.0, On Heaven +5.0

$C5$ = Self-Focus On Living to Work -5.0, On Working to Live +5.0

$C6$ = Society Focus On Living to Work -5.0, On Working to Live +5.0

$C7$ = Charity, Distribution or Redistribution expressed, if yes then 1, if no then 0

$C8$ = Enough or equity expressed as the stated target, if yes then 1, if no then 0

The findings reveal a number of re-occurring key themes. The charitable disposition is a distinguishing feature of suitable economic behaviour and the conduit leading to Heaven. With two notable exceptions, namely Manager Two in Domain B and the Support Worker in Domain C, there is a universal religious bias within the sample. Furthermore with the exception of just one of these occupations, all respondents expressed the guiding principle of charity in their economic and personal lives and stated that their economic target was enough. Many were also able to define enough as a quantifiable measure of wealth such as a car, holiday, a round of golf, and a 'jar' (alcohol). Their responses implied that their measure was defined, individually tailored and limited to the economic possibilities given their particular set of circumstances. Moreover, while contributors worked extremely hard, a fact acknowledged by the multi-nationals, they were also keenly aware that this industrious ethic had little or nothing to do with salvation.

The data analysis in Table 6.3 below includes the mean or arithmetic average of responses, the median, the mode and the standard deviation by category for the responses of the compressed Domains B-D, where we treated the three domains as if they were one group to calculate the more valid measurements. It also includes correlation coefficients indicating a relationship between the independent variable Religiosity and the dependent variables listed in Columns C3-C8 in Table 6.2. This includes nominal or categorical data such as domain and occupation, ordinal or ranked data such as religiosity and interval data such as the rating or scores on the four continua. The latter is strictly speaking ordinal data since the real distances between numbers are not equal i.e. an individual marking +2 on the scale may not be twice as focused on this life as the individual who marks +1 on the same scale. The assumption for statistical research is that they are in fact equal measurements and this is a valid approach (Sapsford 1996). For the purposes of correlation, nominal or categorical data cannot be used since they are labels and not numbers capable of being a ratio measurement (Calder and Sapsford 1996). This means that Column 2 *Occupation* proves unsuitable for calculating degree of relationships although calculations and functions have been completed on the measurements in the remaining columns.

Table 6.3 Compressed Domains B, C, D - the measurement data

C1 Function	C2 Rel	C3 Self Focus This Life -5.0 'Heaven' +5.0	C4 Society Focus This Life -5.0 'Heaven'+5.0	C5 Self Focus Living to Work -5.0 Working to Live +5.0	C6 Society Focus Living to Work -5.0 Working to Live +5.0
Mean	2.15	-1.575757	-1.712121	-1.075757	-0.848484
Median	2.00	-2.000000	-2.000000	-0.500000	-1.000000
Mode	2.00	-1.000000	-2.000000	-4.000000	0.000000
Std. Deviation	0.90	1.781507	1.425385	2.121766	1.465674

C1 contd Function	C7 Charity Expressed	C8 Enough Expressed	Correlation	Coefficient
Mean	0.969696	0.969696	C2 and C3	0.152614
Median	1.000000	1.000000	C2 and C4	-0.046952
Mode	1.000000	1.000000	C2 and C5	0.071216
Std. Dev.	0.174077	0.174077	C2 and C6	0.205832
			C2 and C7	0.426505
			C2 and C8	0.426505

The average degree of religiosity for compressed Domains B-D is 2.15 which is slightly higher than Intermediate Catholic status with the typical value half way from lowest and highest values where the median equals 2.0. The most commonly expressed value (mode) is also 2.0, namely Intermediate Catholic status. The standard deviation is calculated at 0.90558 so that there is never more than an average of one level of religiosity from the mean value 2.0 i.e. Intermediate Catholic status.

A summary of scores representing the self focus on *This Life-Afterlife* by each respondent (C3) shows a mean of − 1.5 namely, a relatively stronger disposition towards *This Life* as opposed to *The Afterlife*. Irish society is perceived as having a slightly stronger focus on this life as expressed by the mean value of − 1.7. The individual commitment to *Working to Live* was relatively strong evoking a disposition with a value of − 1.0757. A slightly weaker value was recorded for the perceived disposition of Irish society towards *Working to Live* and was calculated at − 0.848.

The most frequent score recorded by individuals in the rating exercises for C5 was − 4.0, indicating a strong disposition towards *Working to Live*. This suggests a strong commitment to preferences other than work i.e. they placed a high instrumental value on work. The measurement of enough and the principle of charity were both calculated as having a theoretical mean of 0.9696 i.e. they are universally present throughout all three domains. The relatively high standard deviation values for C3, C4, C5 and C6 ranging from 2.1 to 0.17 are in close proximity to zero on the rating scale of –5.0 to +5.0. For example there is less than one level of religiosity separating all the respondents in the three domains. Less than two units of measure separate the highest recorded value for *Focus on This Life-Afterlife* and less than two units of measure separate the highest recorded value for the focus on *Working to Live-Living to Work* in all three domains. While the general disposition of the compressed Domains B-D is moving towards a 'Focus on this Life' (see C3 and a co-efficient score of – 1.5757), this does not reflect in itself a parallel increase in the *Focus on Work*. Rather the opposite may be more likely where a value of – 1.07575758 indicates a move towards zero or an equal focus on *Working to Live* and *Living to Work*. This reflects the view of the career guidance teacher and the Ballymun unemployed person who stated that most Irish people hedge their bets against the existence of Heaven.

The correlation between the level of religiosity in Column C2 and the *Focus on this Life* and the *After Life* in C3, gives a coefficient value 0.15 indicating a weak positive correlation thereby suggesting that bets are hedged by all respondents irrespective of their religiosity. The degree of focus on *This Life-After Life* by Irish society C4 is close to zero with a calculated coefficient of – 0.0469 i.e. a very weak negative correlation also suggesting the adoption of a hedging approach. A similarly low coefficient of 0.0712 is also recorded for C2 and C5 that suggests that a weak positive relationship exists between Religion and *Focus on Work to Live*. The coefficients for C2 and C6 i.e. focus on *Living to Work* by Irish society again indicates that a weak relationship exists between religion and work. This suggests that there is little if any intrinsic value in work. On the other hand the correlation for C2 and C7 (religion and charity) and for C2 and C8, (religion and enough) indicate a fair degree of relationship. A similar set of data analysis to that presented for compressed Domains B-D above is now presented for each stand alone Domain B, Domain C and Domain D in Table 6.4, Table 6.5, and Table 6.6 respectively.

Part 2: Sub Section Two - Comparison of Indicators within each Domain B-D

There is little or no difference in the degree of religiosity declared by the executive respondents within Domain B although on average they display a relatively strong focus on *This Life-Afterlife* which is calculated at – 3.0 for C4. Their assessment of the degree of focus of Irish society on *This Life-Afterlife* in C5 is calculated at – 2.0. There is a stronger correlation between C3 (religion) and C5 (focus on this life-afterlife) in Domain B than for its equivalent correlation in the compressed Domains B-D. The focus of Irish society on *Working to Live -Living to Work* for Domain B is calculated at – 0.2142, where it is significantly close to zero, so that there is an indication of the existence of a true balance between the intrinsic and the instrumental work value. There is also a moderate to good relationship between C3 and C7, i.e. religion and work, and a strong relationship between C3 and C8 (religion and charity) and between C3 and C9 (religion and enough).

Table 6.4 Domain B Only - the measurement data

C1 Function	C2 Rel	C3 Self Focus This Life -5.0 'Heaven' +5.0	C4 Society Focus This Life -5.0 'Heaven'+5.0	C5 Self Focus Living to Work -5.0 Working to Live +5.0	C6 Society Focus Living to Work -5.0 Working to Live +5.0
Mean	2.00	-3.000000	-2.000000	-1.214285	-0.214285
Median	2.00	-3.000000	-2.500000	-0.500000	0.000000
Mode	2.00	-3.500000	-2.500000	-4.000000	0.000000
Std. Deviation	1.00	0.577350	1.732050	2.121761	2.078804

C1 contd Function	C7 Charity Expressed	C8 Enough Expressed	Correlation	Coefficient
Mean	0.857142	0.969696	C2 and C3	0.160816
Median	1.000000	1.000000	C2 and C4	0.261006
Mode	1.000000	1.000000	C2 and C5	-0.344723
Std. Dev.	0.377964	0.377964	C2 and C6	0.693007
			C2 and C7	0.913500
			C2 and C8	0.913500

Labour Domain C displays a slightly higher mean level of religiosity of +2.2. Furthermore all the averages remain remarkably similar to the corresponding values of the compressed Domains B-D. However, unlike the Executive Domain B, Labour Domain C exhibits a fair degree of relationship between C3 and C4 (0.4597) i.e. a higher self focus on *This Life-Afterlife*. A fair degree of relationship is displayed between C3 and C6 (0.3268) i.e. religion and a focus on *Working to Live* by self. A significant negative correlation exists between C3 and C5 *Focus on This Life by Society* calculated at − 0.655. Here the influence of religion appears to be moderate to high when compared to the average figures for the compressed Domains B-D and suggests that for C5 the absence of religion would strengthen the disposition towards a focus on *This Life* i.e. move it towards the extreme − 5.0 rating.

Table 6.5 Domain C Only - the measurement data

C1 Function	C2 Rel	C3 Self Focus This Life -5.0 'Heaven' +5.0	C4 Society Focus This Life -5.0 'Heaven'+5.0	C5 Self Focus Living to Work -5.0 Working to Live +5.0	C6 Society Focus Living to Work -5.0 Working to Live +5.0
Mean	2.20	-1.600000	-1.600000	-1.230000	-0.960000
Median	2.00	-2.000000	-2.000000	-2.000000	-1.000000
Mode	2.00	1.000000	-2.000000	-4.000000	0.000000
Std. Deviation	0.77	1.905505	1.365388	2.313521	1.302013

C1 contd Function	C7 Charity Expressed	C8 Enough Expressed	Correlation	Coefficient
Mean	1.000000	1.000000	C2 and C3	0.349131
Median	1.000000	1.000000	C2 and C4	-0.564414
Mode	1.000000	1.000000	C2 and C5	0.326841
Std. Deviation	0.000000	0.000000	C2 and C6	-2.184217
			C2 and C7	NA
			C2 and C8	NA

The highest level of mean religiosity calculated at +2.18 is to be found in the Disconnected Domain D, and suggests that respondents with the lowest level of material well-being display a higher Catholic status than Domains B and C. The mean figure calculated for the intensity of focus on *This Life-Afterlife* is calculated at − 0.54545. This suggests that Domain D has by far the weakest disposition towards a focus on *This Life* and the strongest orientation towards a focus on *The Afterlife*. This would also suggest that those with the least material well-being have the strongest concern for the Afterlife.

In Domain D the respondents perceive that Irish society has the weakest focus on *This Life* calculated at -1.68 and where the respondents themselves have the weakest disposition towards *Working to Live* calculated at − 0.7727. The disposition of Irish society for *Working to Live*, calculated at 1.09009 remains the strongest of all Domains. These last two variables suggest that while those with the least wealth are more focussed on *The Afterlife* than those in either Domain B or C, they see others in society more attuned to *Living to Work*. They also perceive that Irish society is more interested in the intrinsic rather than the instrumental value of work. Another observation is that individual responses in this Domain D are almost identical. The Homeless, the Travellers and the Unemployed have similar and on occasions matching self-perceptions and ratings on the degree of focus displayed by Irish society on the after life.

Table 6.6 Domain D Only - the measurement data

C1 Function	C2 Rel	C3 Self Focus This Life -5.0 'Heaven' +5.0	C4 Society Focus This Life -5.0 'Heaven' +5.0	C5 Self Focus Living to Work -5.0 Working to Live +5.0	C6 Society Focus Living to Work -5.0 Working to Live +5.0
Mean	2.18	-0.540000	-1.681818	-0.772727	-1.090909
Median	3.00	-1.000000	-2.000000	-0.500000	-2.000000
Mode	3.00	-1.000000	-2.000000	-0.500000	-2.000000
Std. Deviation	1.07	1.507556	1.419026	1.979439	1.241333

C1 contd Function	C7 Charity Expressed	C8 Enough Expressed	Correlation	Coefficient
Mean	1.000000	1.000000	C2 and C3	-0.208524
Median	1.000000	1.000000	C2 and C4	0.198524
Mode	1.000000	1.000000	C2 and C5	-0.039663
Std. Deviation	0.000000	0.000000	C2 and C6	0.177648

Part 3: Presentation of the Profile of the Irish Economic Disposition

Themes to Emerge from Domains A, B, C and D

The inclusion of the religious and economic leaders in Domain A provided insights into the link between macro economic policy and Catholic social teaching. We also noted the similarity of both Anglicanism and Islam to Catholicism regarding the central objective of securing salvation in the next life. The Spirit of Charity or the so-called equity imperative featured prominently as did the measurement of enough material well-being as a preferred national economic objective.

There is evidence that Catholic social teaching informs national economic policy. Many of the respondents professed their Catholicism and the equity imperative was an important economic objective. No specific hard economic targets such as the highest average income per capita in the world by 2005, were articulated in their economic aims. In fact many observed an apparent correlation between increased prosperity and increased unhappiness. Most wished to create a macro economic environment whereby the opportunity would exist for all individuals to achieve their individualised measure of enough material well-being. In this respect a disposition that can achieve a balance between national and individual material well-being and spiritual happiness appears to be best served by a Catholic disposition as revealed by the individuals in the research. The limit of enough appears to successfully address the tension between living in this world and creating the opportunity to achieve acceptable levels of material well-being, levels that do not endanger the ultimate objective of Heaven. Moreover, the target of optimisation rather than the maximisation of economic growth was very influential. These attitudes and views became the first set to be affixed to a profile grid of the Irish economic disposition.

The narratives in Executive Domain B confirmed the presence of the Spirit of Charity at the multi-national senior management level and was also a notable feature of the contributions examined in Domain A. They also confirmed the preference of a measure of an individualised economic target of enough complementing the national target of enough cited in the contributions of National Domain A. These responses were the second set of attitudes affixed to the profile grid.

The main themes to emerge from Labour Domain C included the articulation of the enough measurement, the instrumental and less than total commitment to work and the central role of charity in establishing moral and economic standards when dealing with others. Almost all respondents use work to secure the means to enjoy life. Specific measures of enough are clearly articulated by the respondents and many of them nominated enough as their individualised objective or target for material wealth, and identified the same items and indicators declared by others in Domains A and B.

In the case of the multinational employees the elements of this individualised economic target are similar to those in Domain B such as a holiday, golf, and a jar etc. Moreover, a vocational conscience has again emerged in the narrative of three respondents as a factor in maintaining a strong commitment to work. Many employees believed in an afterlife and pointed out that generosity and charity are key attributes in securing Heaven. Work commitment is less than a hundred per cent where many seek to enjoy life now or retire early to do so.

Farmers work long hours and many did not have the opportunity to go on holidays. All five farmers believed in Heaven and were convinced that charity is the way to secure it. In the main they were happy with their circumstances and two were still seeking their measure of enough. Many do not see farming as a well regarded way of life anymore but as a business, and so acted accordingly to generate farm subsidies i.e. farm in such a way as to focus on the area of greatest returns, such as subsidies and sometimes this would mean little or no work effort. The richest farmer did not regard his wealth as important in itself since it will be of little use in the next life while others insisted that they do not give everything to farming but hold back for family and the community.

It is also clear that the existence of a measure of enough and the charitable disposition, namely the Spirit of Charity, together with a belief in Heaven have also been revealed in the responses of the pupils and the career guidance teachers in their approach to economic matters. This suggests that the prevalent economic disposition and the instrumental emphasis on work are already formed in pupils even before many of them enter into the adult labour market. The link between religious beliefs and the economic engagement of Domain C was revealed and this subsequently enabled us to affix a third set of attitudes and views to the profile grid of the Irish economic disposition.

The unemployed, the advocate of the homeless, the homeless persons and the Traveller women display a conditional attitude towards acquiring wealth and a conditional work commitment similar to other respondents in Domains A, B and C. They indicated that work effort has little or no value in achieving the afterlife but that charity is the key to Heaven. While the unemployed persons had a strong focus on this life in order to survive they are trying to become economically active to achieve their objective of enough. They see official employment such as that enjoyed by those in Domains A, B and C as a step in the right direction. Their economic objective is relative insofar as they want to secure the equivalent measure of enough enjoyed by those in Domain A, B and C.

On the other hand, the homeless do not hold official employment in high esteem but provided one of the best examples of higher order Catholic charity namely, they share their meagre possessions such as beer or cigarettes without looking for a return. Once they have enough they too maintained that they were happy. In relative terms, their definition of enough such as cigarettes, beer and a meal can be as difficult to acquire as the house and car for other respondents.

All respondents believed in Heaven and were adamant that possessing a charitable ethos was a sure way of getting there. While the aspirations are different in relative preferences, the principle of enough is identified as a universal feature throughout all Domains and this stated limit of material well-being is relative to the possibilities given individual economic circumstances.

The Traveller Women believed in the power of holy priests and wells to cure illnesses rather than the lay doctor. Their beliefs appear more innocent in as much as they implicitly trust in a loving and forgiving God. Their vision of Heaven is a simple one with clouds and angels. They are particularly sure that the only way to achieve Heaven is to give everything away and be charitable at all times i.e. the opposite sentiment to the acquisitive impulse. Yet the women also maintained that Travellers in general work very hard and that their economic objective too is enough. While they are the most discriminated group in Europe, Travellers appear to exhibit the strongest faith of all respondents, while at the same time their enough objective is quite similar to other respondents. The contributions from this domain now close the loop as it completes the mosaic that is Irish social life. The profile of the Irish economic disposition can now be presented on the basis of using a set of inclusive accounts that reflects the complexity of the mosaic of Irish social life during the Celtic Tiger.

Linking the Themes

The analysis of the both the empirical and qualitative suggests that within Domains B, C, and D there are only minor differences in the degree of individual belief in charity as the most influential principle that guides engagement in economic matters. Moreover, each individual who declared a strong religiosity also regarded the objective of achieving enough as the main successful legitimate measure of material well-being. The ultimate objective of individuals in Domains B, C and D is to achieve Heaven and this almost pre-determined their less than fully committed approach to economic life. Almost all give what is required to their work in terms of energy and commitment but little more. These results highlight an important approach to economic life. Almost all give what is required to their work in terms of energy and commitment but little more. These results highlight an important strategy of individuals who hedge their bets against the existence of Heaven.[68] Individuals also appear to accept the economic circumstances confronting them with only the unemployed group exhibiting some level of dissatisfaction with their socio-economic circumstances. On only one occasion did a respondent suggest violent action to redress inequality. The statistical analysis appeared to confirm that religious beliefs are strong across the Domains B, C and D. The presence of a Catholic vocational rather than sexual conscience compels the individual to exert work effort to avoid guilt.

Moreover, the common themes which emerged within all four domains point to a generalised pattern of behaviour, a dureé of economic engagement that enabled us to construct a profile containing that part of the economic disposition containing the *revealed* influences on this engagement. The evidence suggests that the central role of the Absolute Pre-supposition of Catholicism remains especially important in understanding how a configuration of internal socio-cultural variables determines the economic disposition at a national and individual level.

The weak inclination towards committing oneself too strongly to material things and the attachment to privatism, namely to keep back the best part of oneself for the individual's private world after work such as the family, are elements that are identical to the basic tenets of Stoicism. According to Cantor (1993) Stoicism is one of the ancient world's most influential and conservative philosophies that together with Platonism infuses much of the Christian morality found in the New Testament.[69] This idea appealed to early Christians and the evidence in our research strongly suggests that a degree of Stoicism and Platonism *still informs the economic world view of Celtic Tiger society.*

We are now in a position to present the profile of the Irish economic disposition in Table 6.7. It contains four aspects or emphases that draw heavily on the Catholic worldview. The first aspect confirms the existence of the Absolute Pre-supposition Catholicism-nationalism. The second is a statement describing the sociological patterns we observe due to the presence of the Absolute Pre-supposition. The third aspect identifies the revealed variables of the Catholic Work Ethic (CWE), while the fourth and final aspect describes the corresponding derived behaviours and attitudes that characterise the Irish economic disposition.

---

[68] They calculate the odds in favour of a strong possibility that Heaven exists and behave accordingly working on the principle that it is better to prepare for its existence even if there is some doubt, rather than being caught out with dire consequences if it actually does exist.

[69] According to Cantor (1993), Stoicism's emphasis on enough has transcended the ancient, the Roman, the mediaeval and industrial epochs while Platonism denigrated the material world in favour of attending to the spiritual requirements of the soul in order to attain salvation. Technically speaking Stoicism is a hybrid of Platonism, the most influential of ancient world philosophies. Aristotle's position was to adopt a scientific and empirical basis for understanding reality by relying on facts rather than ideas to inform this understanding. On the other hand, Plato believed that man had two aspects, the transient and the eternal and this insight is the origin of the philosophical distinction between the body and soul. The most important aspect for Catholics is the soul.

Table 6.7 A Profile of the Irish Economic Disposition

Aspect 1	*Aspect 2*
Known Ultimate Normative Force	*Revealed Patterns*
Absolute Pre-Supposition (Religion-nationalism)	The main force or durée in a constellation of internal factors impacting on national policy and on the individual's attitude to economic opportunity, namely Catholic Economic Ethic (CWE)

Aspect 3	*Aspect 4*
Variables within CWE	*Revealed Attitudes and Behaviours*
Belief in Heaven.	Main religious objective to secure Heaven.
Catholic Spirit of Charity.	Main principle governing code of conduct in daily economic and personal life.
Vocational Conscience.	Control of deviation from Spirit of Charity in relation to work effort.
Capitalism versus Catholicism (national level).	Norm of competitiveness but also equity.
Capitalism versus Catholicism (Individual level).	Individualised measure of enough material well-being.
Limit of enough on the acquisitive impulse.	The absence of specific national economic targets, instead better than the previous year is the target.
Happy with enough.	Acceptance of economic and political systems.
Experience of this world and enjoyment of life.	The accepted norm of the most useful human activity.
Instrumental approach to work.	Norm of displaying a Protestant Work Ethic up to a point where enough is achieved when commitment is transferred to maintain enough rather than seek unlimited wealth.
Tension between material and spiritual well-being	High levels of anomie and higher levels of unhappiness and suicide. 'In' but not 'of' the economic order distinguished by a norm of employing an adaptive and reactionary engagement rather than proactive participation in that order. Conditional assistance follows. Acknowledgement across all sections of society of accidental nature of Celtic Tiger.

One of the striking features of this profile in the revealed attitudes and behaviours is the limit of enough on the acquisitive impulse. It highlights the higher preference to enjoy this life over work as the most useful human activity. Work is used as an instrument to achieve these higher preferences. Consequently, an individualised measure of enough economic well-being is the maximum target set by the individual. While a strong work ethic is a feature of the individual's commitment to achieve this measure, it subsequently diminishes significantly after the economic measure of enough has been attained. Because of the presence of another element, namely the Spirit of Charity, the acquisitive impulse is weakened to the point where active and full participation is rejected in favour of giving conditional assistance to the economic order. As belief in the existence of Heaven is also strong then the most rational behaviour possible is not to jeopardise its achievement by deviating from the charitable principle. Hence the emphasis at an individual and national level on equity, distribution and re-distribution.

This 'proven' existence of the CWE contrasts with the PWE deemed by Weber to be responsible for the economic development of the west. So while some success has been achieved insofar as the configurations between religion and economic engagement have been identified in the above profile, it still does not explain how the configurations actually engage with each other i.e. it does not define the precise relationship between the Absolute Pre-supposition, the economic disposition and economic development. In the analyses of the profile that follows in chapters seven eight and nine, many important and diverse sociological insights are enlisted in an effort to address this very question.

Chapter 7

Explaining the Profile using Marx's Historical Materialism

> Freedom alone substitutes from time to time for the love of material comfort, more powerful and more lofty passions, it alone supplies ambition with greater objectives than the acquisition of riches. (De Tocqueville 1856)

Introduction

From the analysis of the research findings we were able to build up a profile of the Irish economic disposition. Here the Absolute Pre-supposition, religion was seen to generate an adaptive yet detached approach on the part of the individual when confronted with economic opportunity. The purpose of these next three chapters is to explain how that disposition has developed and consider how the configuration of elements profiled in the disposition influences economic behaviour. The approach draws on a suite of primary and secondary sources, then places them in a specific 'fiery' historical context and employs an alliance of sociological insights calculated to improve our chances of comprehending how the disposition is built up little by little until it arrives at its present form.

The first sociological contribution comes from Marx's insights on historical materialism. This is complemented in chapter eight by the use of an alternative interpretation of social development, namely Norbert Elias' figurational sociology. In the final chapter, a composite of the insights of Weber, Durkheim, Freud, Parsons and Giddens is deployed to build on the strengths of both Marx and Elias because many of these insights specialise in interpreting the religious and economic nexus in society.

Of course the specific challenge presented to all of these insights was always present, namely to explain the impact of the Absolute Pre-supposition, namely religion and nationalism on the Irish economic disposition as it leaves a specifically Catholic imprint on it at a time of very low secularisation and sustained Tiger performance. The inclusion of an alliance of insights also follows the advice of Akenson outlined in chapter one, namely to use as wide an evidentiary base as possible when studying the mosaic that is Irish social life, an approach, in the first instance, that proved to be quite effective in exposing the configuration of elements that constituted the Celtic Tiger economic disposition.

Moreover, by grounding the analyses in a specific historical war period and in specific individuals and groups of combatants it will reveal according to Hart (1991), normally latent sentiments because they become fired up during war and we therefore anticipate a greater chance of capturing the incremental development of the full force of the exposed sentiment.

We begin our analysis by exploring how the Absolute Pre-supposition infused Irish society with sentiments that have been successfully mobilised against any ideology deemed to challenge the essence of Irish Catholic identity including both left and right 'isms'. This particular capability is shown to shape a specific Catholic ethic of economic behaviour. The analysis of this capability is divided into two sections. Section A includes an examination of the national religious and class context confronting Marxist ideology in Ireland at the time of state formation and the emergence and eventual rejection of an Irish or green version of Marxism as championed by James Connolly.

Section B then focusses at the individual level on the occupational profile of the revolutionary fighters and their leaders and the key craftworker group, where we begin to unravel a profile of their economic disposition as an outcome of their religious-nationalist ideals. We expose how their ideals were shaped by a number of interconnecting strands such as the religious sentiment within the Irish workforce, the ethos of the school curriculum, the exhortations of the Catholic Church and post-revolutionary conservative economic policies. We will then compare these same sentiments with the configurations revealed in our own research on the mosaic of Irish social life that was the Celtic Tiger.

A number of observations are now made on some Marxist ideology to prepare the groundwork by which we can benchmark the relevancy of them to explain the Irish economic disposition. According to Morrison (1995) a central tenet of Marx's theory is that the state itself has a material origin and is dependent on the economic structure obtaining at that time. Morrison (1995) explained that Marx understood that the material world preceded the world of ideas and that the change dynamic in society was derived through the structure of economic relationships and therefore rejected Hegel's belief that the principles of social development (Contradiction, Affirmation, Negation, and Negation of the Negation) were manifested in historical ideas. In its place Marx preferred the concept of the dialectic to explain social development.

Ritzer (1988) described the dialectic as a non linear cause and effect dynamic initiated by the interaction of connected but conflicting parts of the social world and while one factor may influence a second, the second may also influence the first i.e. there is reciprocal causality. The Hegelian philosophical perspective maintains that reciprocal causality is the basis of the governing law of the dialectic and insists therefore that reality is an on-going historical process. According to Marx, this process can only be understood by identifying the historical causes (historical materialism) of the present situation and the need to change it and this insight forms the basis of all Marxist sociological insights (Magee 1998).

According to Marx (1857) the basis of all social interaction is material production. Marx (1857) maintained that men were treated like machines and called for labour to rise up against owners of capital when the subsequent dialectical interaction would determine the outcome in their favour. The socialist objective of Marx was to transform the capitalist economic system so that the surplus value of the work performed by an individual should then go to that individual and not to the capitalist (Veblen 1906). However, Schumpter (1908) contended that nobody could get all that his productive contribution was worth, namely its total value because while the work itself may be very useful the profit generated by this work may be insignificant. Nevertheless the outcome of dialectical interaction could only be achieved through a class struggle because the nature of capitalism with its cycles of boom and bust worked against labour, and therefore the working class would eventually initiate a revolutionary movement in defence of its own interests. The core of historical materialism insisted that labour and nature and not religion were the true basis of society since existence comes before consciousness (materialistic approach) and social evolution is determined by the constant struggle of conflicting forces of capital and labour (Trotsky 1939).

Three working definitions act as benchmarks to evaluate the premise that religion is not the true basis of Irish social development but on the contrary, the class struggle explains in a more comprehensive fashion one of the key Irish developmental conflicts, namely the 1916 Rising.[70] From a Communist perspective history therefore can only be explained in terms of a class conflict rather than idealism and the validity of this argument again forms a central focus for the exploration running through this chapter. Moreover the use of the word 'any' in the definitions of Communism and Socialism would suggest that local variations such as Irish Marxism were acceptable. This too is examined in Section A.

---

[70] Marxism

   an economic and political theory and practice originated by Karl Marx and Fredrick Engels that holds that actions and human institutions are economically determined, that the class struggle is the basic agency of historical change and that capitalism will ultimately be superseded by communism.

Socialism

   any of the various social and economic theories or movements in which the common welfare is to be achieved through the establishment of a socialist economic system.

Communism

   the advocacy of a classless society in which private ownership has been abolished....[and]...any social economic or political movement or doctrine aimed at achieving such a society...[and]...a political movement based upon the writings of Marx that considers history in terms of a class conflict and a revolutionary struggle (Collins English Dictionary 1999).

SECTION A

Strand 1: The Religious Context Confronting Marxism

Viney and Dudley Edwards (1968) argued that Marxism, Socialism and Communism were often regarded in Ireland as one and same thing because Catholic attitudes often precluded open discussion about them. As we shall see from Table 7.1 approximately ninety per cent of the Republic's population at the time of its state formation was Roman Catholic and positioned on an upward trend from just below ninety per cent in 1881 to just below ninety five per cent in 1961. Even after the Celtic Tiger era it still exceeded eighty eight per cent affiliation. By any standards what confronted Marxism then was a very durable universally Catholic society. It was highly unlikely that there was informed debate on any of these ideological 'isms'.

Table 7.1 The Catholic Population 1861-1991 Calculated as a per cent of the Population within the Boundary Area of the Republic of Ireland

Year	1861	1911	1936	1961	1981	1991	2002
%	89.4	89.6	93.5	94.9	93.0	91.6	88.4

[a] For 1861-1991 see Inglis, T. (1998), *Moral Monopoly The Rise and Fall of the Catholic Church in Modern Ireland*, Dublin, Gill and MacMillan, Table 1, p. 19.
[b] For 2002 see Central Statistics Office (2003), 'Commentary to Principal Demographic Results', *Census 2002*, Government Publications Office, Dublin, p. 20.

Moreover the ordinary Catholic in Ireland at this time could have had very few doubts concerning the evils of the noxious 'isms'. A series of condemnations of Socialism, Communism and Marxism was issued by a number of Popes to Catholics worldwide. In the mid 1860s bans on each were unequivocal. For example, Pius IX (1864) condemned, reprobated and proscribed both ideologies and commanded all Catholics to reject them outright. According to Leo XIII (1878) materialism was responsible for the manifold evils of the time causing a rejection of the teachings and institutions of the Church. He argued that this rejection was foolhardy, even in a selfish material sense, because there was a positive correlation between obedience to the Church and a nation's prosperity. This exhortation appears to support Hickman's (1995) argument that Catholicism was promoted as a counter culture as being materially on par with the aspirations of both capitalism and Socialism. In another encyclical Leo XIII (1878a) declared that the promoters and followers of these 'isms' were

> the deadly plague that is creeping into the very fibres of human
> society and leading it on to the verge of destruction...We speak
> of that sect of men who, under various and almost barbarous

> names   are   called   socialists,   communists   or
> nihilists...[planning]...the   overthrow   of   all   civil   society
> whatsoever. (Leo XIII 1878a: 1)

Leo XIII (1878a) promised a heavenly reward for the poor and warned artisans – who as we shall see later, were at the very core of the Irish state formation process – to be especially vigilant regarding the lure of Socialism. Moreover, the Catholic Church actively supported anyone fighting for the formation of a Catholic national independent state (Pope Leo XIII 1888). In another encyclical Pope Leo XIII (1888a) maintained that both greed and over-reliance by individuals and societies on reason alone at the expense of divine faith endangered eternal life which in turn led to the rise of

> poisonous doctrines...rationalism, materialism, atheism, [which]
> have   begotten   socialism,   communism,   nihilism...evil
> principles... [whereas]...the whole essence of a Christian life is
> to reject the corruption of the world and to oppose any
> indulgence in it [since] ...the soul must be fortified against the
> dangerous snares of riches...lest the soul should loose the
> treasure in heaven which faileth not. (Leo XIII 1888a: 3-4)

Later, Leo XIII (1889) again warned artisans to model themselves on St. Joseph the Worker and not to listen to these noxious and seditious doctrines. Leo XIII (1891) then attacked socialism noting that a limit or enough of wealth, namely a moderate livelihood achieved through charity would almost single-handedly guarantee the afterlife for the individual.[71]

Then in the early years of the development of the new Irish state, Pius XI (1931) maintained the right to pronounce with supreme authority upon social and economic matters and warned the rich to practice almsgiving i.e. observable charity. Later still Pius XI (1937) attacked atheistic Communism stating that it was intrinsically wrong and banned any Catholic from becoming involved with it in any way. Pope John XXIII (1961) declared that economic development and the betterment of material conditions were not the ultimate values to be prized by individuals.

Nevertheless there was some inconsistency in the messages of the Popes. Schuck (1991) points out that while Communism and Socialism were deemed intrinsically wrong and capitalism criticised, the Popes significantly failed to condemn the market system. The real reason that official Catholicism galvanised itself against the Marxist enemy was not that it was merely atheistic but more importantly it had much in common with Catholicism, such as its focus across all social levels, its idealism and altruism and had therefore the ever present potential to compete with and fatally damage the Church (Kenny 1997).

At local parish level the Irish Catholic Church galvanised itself by instituting the Marian cult to offset the noxious 'isms' of Communism and Socialism

---

[71] This of course was one of the key findings from our own research.

(Donnelly 2000). It structured Roman devotional practices under Cardinal Paul Cullen to suppress authentic Irish Catholicism that was dominated by the laity (Conway 2000) such visits to holy wells, to one controlled by a priestly hierarchy (Donnelly 2000a).[72] The type of religious disposition imposed on Irish society was not only Roman devotionalism but Jesuit in its ethos and thereby imbued it with a particularly other-worldly religious focus.[73] The Jesuits, a religious order founded by St. Ignatius of Loyola had devised a counter-reformation catechism for the instruction of the Catholic faithful particularly in the school and this Ignatian blueprint infused Irish Catechisms from the early eighteenth until the middle of the twentieth century and Tynan (1985) described the catechisms overall impact on religious formation where it

> was to have an extraordinary influence on our [Irish Catholic] society...our people were impregnated by Ignatian thinking, they came to be steeped in its spirit and proved so consistent in reproducing it that...they stood alone as a kind of affront to contemporary living in the West. (Tynan 1985: 13)

According to the Jesuits, complete unselfishness was the aim of this-worldly living (Nash 1956). For example, the religious Exercises of St Ignatius which have enjoyed successive papal approvals have had the primary objective of inculcating the ascendancy of the hereafter over this temporal world and as De Bernoville (1937) highlighted, the essence of the exercises was characterised by anti-materialism whereby riches should not be desired in preference to poverty. The Exercises were seen to have considerable social impact for good when they were grounded in the support of Trade Unionism and anti-Communism (Lafarge 1928) and hence the comments made by one of the National Domain A contributors concerning Jesuit secrecy at the highest level.

Furthermore local Irish diocesan clergy who were highly influential in the community accepted and promoted a harmonious and interdependent social stratification model in direct contrast to the Marxist class conflict model (Kennedy 1996a).[74] The reality of social stratification was not only recognised and accepted by them but conceived of as a system of interlocking mutually independent parts that functioned smoothly in the interests of all and was a harmony model of society. This was directly opposed to a Marxist conflict model and challenged the universality of the Marxist economic and political approach to absorb local, regional and national cultures and still remain effective (Williams 1987). Moreover the local Irish culture had evolved out of the resistance of Gaelic Ireland to the imposition of Protestantism and thus placed Catholicism in the forefront of

---

[72] The type of 'magic' Catholicism described by the Travellers in the research.

[73] A good example of Jesuit influence at work at high levels in Irish society was provided by a contributor in Domain A.

[74] Priests not usually belonging to a monastic order such as the Jesuits or Franciscans but living and working in a parish within a particular diocese ministering to the laity and reporting directly to the local bishop i.e. diocesan or parish clergy.

the fight for freedom from English and later British oppression, so that an Irish consciousness developed that fused religious, political and cultural elements to the extent that the cultural identity one professed was determined by one's religion (Williams 1999).[75]

Yet Marx did not appear to fully appreciate the impact that religious beliefs exercised on social and economic development since Giddens (1995b) noted that Marx did not study religion in any detail and was also criticised by Weber for overlooking the impact of religious beliefs to set acceptable levels of economic behaviour. Given the absolute and unquestioning faith of many Catholics in the period after the Famine and well into the twentieth century, where the faithful 'gladly' submitted themselves to the control of the priest (Connell 1968), this subservience to the priestly class was bound to present a formidable barrier to the successful implantation of Marxist ideas in Irish society. An indication of Marx's lack of sensitivity to the loyalty of the Catholic laity to their clergy can be seen in a letter from Marx to Engels in 1869 where he called for priests to be attacked because

> The dogs (for example Bishop Ketteler[76] in Mainz,), the priests
> of the Dusseldorf Congress are flirting where they find it suitable
> to do so with the labor question [sic]. (Marx 1869: 590)

This would hardly have gone down too well with Irish Catholics and labourers in particular. Because Marxism is the most conspicuous grand scale anti-religious movement that ever existed, its *raison d'être* was to attack religion (Parsons 1999), it therefore unwittingly attacked the essence of Irish identity and by implication attempted to undermine the Absolute Pre-supposition religion. Moreover his position on religion was pretty selective.

Because material progress was regarded as a fundamental basis for securing happiness for all, religion that defended those who exploited the working class must be attacked (Lenin 1909, Lenin 1909a, Trotsky 1937).[77] Marx noted that religion was a protest against suffering and was de facto, itself an expression of suffering (Marx 1844) implying that religion, far from being a device to trick and subdue people, was actually a structure to meet the emotional needs of those who may be suffering deprivation. Catholicism was seen by Marx as an oppression against labour. In contrast, Marx (1844) thought highly of Luther's Protestantism since it freed man from the external control of Catholic rituals and teachings thus making individual conscience supreme. Man became alienated from himself by the subservient relationship that he accepted between himself and the Catholic priest as mediator (Marx 1844a), whereas Socialist man sees man and nature and

---

[75] This is why we maintain that Catholicism and nationalism cannot be separated and examined as two separate forces and therefore nominate Catholicism-nationalism as one Absolute Pre-supposition.

[76] Founded the Catholic Social Teaching Movement to promote harmony among the social classes.

[77] Catholicism was perceived to support the status quo, 'servant obey thy master'.

not God as the true reality (1844a). As only matter can be perceived, God cannot therefore be known since He is not material (Marx 1845).

These principles of Marx appear to support Protestantism and so it is not surprising that Connolly (1998a) highlighted that Communism has never attracted significant electoral or popular support in Ireland. Nor indeed did Socialism fare much better where it too came unstuck in the Irish social environment. For example, when Fianna Fáil was first inaugurated in 1926 as a political party, its third and seventh aims of policy stated that the resources and wealth of Ireland should be subservient to the needs and welfare of all the people. This implied a very socialist economic approach and yet by the 1950s, following periods in government, this approach was totally reversed (Coakley 1998). Even the Irish Labour Party which adopted a new more Marxist constitution in 1936, had to formally retract it in 1939 because of the anti-communist directives of both the Catholic Hierarchy but more importantly, its own party members demanded religious conformity and forced more conventional and conservative policies infused with Catholic Social Teaching to be adopted (McGarry 2001).

Then in the 1940s a small political party called Clann na Poblachta (Family of Republicans) was part of an anti-Fianna Fáil coalition government where one of its leading members the socialist Dr. Noel Brown, was appointed as Minister for Health. However, he backed down in face of very strong criticism by the Irish Pharmaceutical Association and the Catholic Hierarchy against his socialised medical reforms, when he attempted to implement the provisions of the Fianna Fáil Health Act of 1947, thereby making his socialist principles subservient to the moral authority of the Catholic Church and acknowledged as much in his resignation speech in the Dáil (Horgan 2000).[78]

Dr. Browne had a social vision but was a mere pawn in the Archbishop of Dublin's (John Charles McQuaid) personal crusade against Communism and its milder form, disguised as socialised medicine spreading into Northern Ireland and the UK under the auspices of the welfare state and so in a sense he could be called Irelands first socialist martyr of the modern era (Cooney 1999). The Catholic Church at the time was solidly opposed to the growth of the state, saw communistic tendencies behind the Mother and Child scheme where the moral law

---

[78] Clan na Poblachta (Party of Republicans) was formed in 1946 and came to power on a programme similar to Fianna Fáil in 1932 i.e. radical republicanism and social and economic reform. They attracted all types including Blueshirts (Facists), dissident Fianna Fáilers, Catholic intellectuals and seen as an alternative approach to the bipartisan treaty parties. They formed part of a Coalition government that put out Fianna Fáil in the 1948 Red Scare elections joining with Fine Gael, Labour, National Labour, Clann na Talmhan (Farmers-Land Party) and independents. Dr. Noel Browne of Clann na Poblachta was appointed Minister for Health in that inter-party government and implemented the provisions of the Health Act of 1947 enacted by Fianna Fáil giving free maternity care to mothers and medical attention for all under sixteen years of age (The Mother and Child Scheme). The failure of the scheme resulted in a catastrophic decline in the Party's fortunes in the 1951 election, when its support collapsed from thirteen to four per cent. See Murphy, J. (1978), *Ireland in the Twentieth Century*, Gill and MacMillan, Dublin, p. 117, pp. 132-135.

had to triumph over the threat of the socialist agenda (Kenny 1997). Then the broad Socialist Left alliance of Labour, some Trade Unions and the Irish Communist Party was almost fatally weakened when another member, Saor Éire (A Free Ireland) the political arm of the IRA, was denounced as Communist by the Bishops who maintained that it was in league with the Third International intending to set up a soviet style republic (Cronin 1999). In 1951, the Archbishop of Dublin John Charles McQuaid declared it a mortal sin under pain of eternal damnation for Catholics to vote for Red O'Riordan in the 1951 General Election (O'Riordan 2000).[79] When Fianna Fáil regained power they adopted a policy of more centralisation seeking out beneficial social outcomes rather than implementing out and out socialist policies (Horgan 1997).

Furthermore, the focus on the noxious 'isms' of Socialism, Communism and Marxism should not be taken to mean that right wing ones were better supported by the Church. On the contrary, while Ireland may have had its own form of continental style national socialism or Facism popular in the 1930s, it nevertheless experienced a similar fate to the left 'isms' amidst Ireland's strong socio-religious context. Sharing a common philosophy of corporatism based on the Christian notion of fostering harmony among the social classes as an answer to the class war, Mussolini's Facism and O'Duffy's Blueshirts (O'Duffyism) were also like minded with the Church in their antipathy towards Communism and both of these common objectives were singularly advocated by the Papal Encyclical Quadragesimo Anno (Kenny 1997, Coakley 1998).[80] Yet this holy and green version of Facism was also short lived.

The first reason was that although the Blueshirts appeared as a Facist style organisation opposing socialist republicans, the specifically Irish context of a three hundred year long tradition of nationalism compelled all political organisations to enshrine nationalism as a central message in their policies and this quickly sidelined one of the essential platforms of the forty eight thousand strong Blueshirt movement (Cronin 1999). Secondly, the Church regarded Facism as excessive nationalism and opposed it on the grounds that it was not an acceptable form of *patriotism* because nationalist principles should always be subservient to Church law (Kenny 1997). Thirdly, in deference to the Church, all mainstream political parties were compelled to attack Communism and this removed the second core aim of the Blueshirts (Cronin 1999).

---

[79] He later became General Secretary of the Irish Communist Party.

[80] Eoin O'Duffy, former Garda (Police) Commissioner was dismissed by De Valera and was subsequently elected leader of the Army Comrades Association. He changed its name to the National Guard. When the Anti-Treaty De Valera came to power in 1932, Pro-Treaty Cumann na nGaedhael supporters joined its ranks. It took on the trappings of continental Facist movements including a distinctive blueshirt and a salute. Outlawed by De Valera in 1933 after it took on his Government in a show of strength and lost, it merged with Cumann na nGaedhael and the Centre Party to form Fine Gael and faded away in the late 1930s. See Fine Gael web site http://www.finegael.ie and Boylan, H. (1998), *A Dictionary of Irish Biography*, Gill and MacMillan, Dublin. See also Manning, M. (1970), *The Blueshirts*, Gill and MacMillan, Dublin, and in particular chapters XIII-XV.

The question of whether Irish Facism was in fact true Facism remained an open question as the real enemy of the Blueshirts were the socialist leaning IRA elements within Fianna Fáil and not the Communists per se (Foster 1988). The obsessive fear of Communism in Ireland (Manning 1970) and created by the Catholic hierarchy (Cronin 1999) resulted in a successful manoeuvre against all 'isms' in the 1930s. According to Manning (1970), the nationalism of the Blueshirts was actually less severe than either Fianna Fáil or the IRA, so much so that it was a regarded as a respectable thing to be a member of the Blueshirts because of its deference to the Catholic Church and its anti-communist stance. Yet fewer than five thousand votes were cast nationally for the Communists in the 1932 election (Manning 1970), showing that the threat of Communism was more mythical than real.

In the final analysis, the Blueshirt movement had much of the trappings and style but little of the substance of continental Facism (Manning 1970). Moreover the deeply divided Socialist Republicans preached a gospel as alien as Facist rhetoric to the Irish people (Cronin 1999). Yet the Blueshirt episode may have been the nearest thing to a class war that Ireland ever experienced, with the Blueshirts supported by the middle class, farmers and merchants against Fianna Fáil and the IRA who were supported by those with little or no property (Manning 1970). Overall then the conclusion must be that the conservative Catholic ethos of Irish social life (the Absolute Pre-supposition) remained strong enough to repel all 'isms' that threatened both religion and patriotic nationalism. This implied that the anti-materialist and moderate economic disposition outlined by the Popes was all the more likely to have remained intact or even strengthened.

Strand 2: The Class Context Confronting Marxism

There was evidence of socially ingrained anti-Irish racism across the spectrum of British society from left to right and Marx and Engels were no exception, since little difference distinguished the writings of Engels from the anti-Irish sentiments expressed in the Times (Hickman 1995). [81] Marx and Engels saw the question of Irish self determination as subservient to the class struggle, exhorting the Irish proletariat to work closely with the English working class to counter the forced immigration of impoverished Irish into England which generated severe

---

[81] For example, 'These people [the Irish] have grown up almost without civilisation, whenever a district is distinguished for especial filth and especial ruinousness the explorer may safely count upon meeting chiefly those Celtic faces...The Irish have discovered the lack of cleanliness which is the Irishman's second nature deposits all garbage and filth before his house. He eats and sleeps with it [the pig] his children ride upon it roll in the dirt with it. The Irishman revels in drink. The Irish man's crudity places him but little above the savage...[Irish migrant worker] who have grown up among Irish filth the degrading position of the English workers has been still more degraded by the presence of the Irish competition'. See Engels, F. (1993), *The Condition of the Working Class in England*, Oxford University Press, Oxford, and in particular chapter 4.

antagonism between the Irish and English worker (Woods and Grant 2001). Nevertheless some significant partisanship can be observed in Engels' writing on the Irish working class in England.

Engels castigated Catholic Irishmen, women and children for degrading the English working class (Engels 1993). He simultaneously espoused the cause of the universal working man (Engels 1935) insisting that while the British working class may not want a socialist outcome they just needed to be galvanised into achieving it (Engels 1913). Yet the archetypal squalor of the Little Ireland of Engels' Manchester conveniently overlooked the evidence of the enormous contribution that Irish citizens made to the economic and social development of Manchester and its environs in addition to supplying the usual unskilled and casual labour (McBride 1999).

Moreover the Irish class system itself appeared to be an atypical one. Sullivan (1968) contended that before Karl Marx set foot in the British Museum, the Irish were already a classless society due to centuries of British misrule with a very small middle class only appearing late in the nineteenth century. Manseragh (1965) concurred, stating that at least two classes were present and one absent in the time of Marx, namely the landlord (ascendancy) and the desperately poor peasant class while the social intermediary middle class were non existent. On the other hand, O'Malley (1989) disagreed, arguing that an important indigenous Irish middle class had existed in the eighteenth century.

Nevertheless, Marx explained the Great Famine of 1847 as a struggle just between two classes, the bourgeois and proletariat, claiming that the former starved the latter into submission (Marx 1849). The working class in the south of Ireland (now the Republic of Ireland) were in his view victims of agricultural capitalists where the conflict over tenancy rights (the land question) was simply a clash between workers and aristocratic capitalists (Marx 1864). Marx recommended a plan of campaign which included an agrarian revolution, self government and independence from and protective tariffs against England. Moreover Marx requested all Communists to side with the Irish in their struggle for independence from England (Marx 1870) and three of his recommended actions eventually came to pass, namely the 1916 Proclamation, independence in 1922 and the imposition in 1932 of protective tariffs at the commencement of the six-year economic war with Britain. Yet Manseragh (1965a) notes that Marx was relatively uninformed on Ireland whereas Engels was not, having the deeper insight into the Irish national sentiment and acknowledged

> the profound distaste for the Communist doctrine that existed in Ireland...the Holy Isle...[whereas]...Marx simply did not understand the conservative, the fanatical character and emotional side of Irish nationalism. (Manseragh 1965a: 99, 108)

Marx eventually acknowledged the unique cultural context of the Irish land question when he recognised that it was more national than economic because Irish landlords were hated as foreign oppressors, unlike England where they embodied national ideals (Woods and Grant 2001).

However, even the hoped for Irish worker revolution to achieve independence from England was not the class based revolutionary one as anticipated by Marx. As early as 1913, the playwright Sean O'Casey identified a completely different dynamic motivating the independence movement in Ireland when he argued that it was the Gaelic ideal alone that would compel individuals to take up arms and fight (Berresford Ellis 1996). This was an ideal based on recapturing a pre-English identity which would *coincidentally* glue together a wide variety of workers and other occupations under a common nationalist sentiment. Although Marx and Engels were familiar with the Irish class system and used Ireland to develop their theory of Imperialism, only Engels fully recognised the primacy of the Irish nationalist over the internationalist cause (Coughlan 1999). Moreover the level of existing nationalist sentiment actually precluded a workers revolution in Ireland and Shaw, who converted to Marxism and favoured a gradual rather than cataclysmic socialist revolution (Peters 1996), noted that the main Irish political parties regarded nationalism and separatism as their *raison d'être* and consequently had very little interest in the class war (Shaw 1920).

On the other hand, James Connolly (1908) anticipated a Workers' or Socialist Republic. However he appeared to have overlooked one important point. Historically the task of the bourgeois was one of national liberation through revolution. This liberation was a pre-requisite for the socialist revolution, namely the class struggle against the local ruling class *provided* though that there were socialists who would fight (Browett 1983). In the Irish case this absence proved to be a decisive factor.

The reason is, that Irish revolutionaries were not Bolsheviks but nationalists and products of the dynamics of three emotional stimuli, namely religion, nationality and land and were in effect the antithesis of the worker-owner, urban-rural and clerical-state cleavages that determined continental revolutionary outcomes (Coakley 1986). Whereas the Irish revolution was similar to the French revolution insofar as the outcomes favoured the bourgeois, the new Irish elite of farmers, professionals and merchants accepted the socio-political legacy of the political outcomes with aplomb and this was possible because the Irish are very adept at accepting the social and economic status quo ensuring that radical ideas and policies were almost totally absent from independent Ireland (Lynch 1968).

The rise to power of De Valera's Fianna Fáil in 1932, far from delivering on economic and social reform for all the people as promised in its 1926 policy document, was in fact the culmination of the bourgeois national revolution bringing in the rule of the last capitalist class, namely landless peasants who had evolved into farmers (The British and Irish Communist Organisation 1977). When Sean Lemass succeeded De Valera as Taoiseach in the mid 1960s, he never formulated or openly declared his economic philosophy although it is generally regarded as a mix of both private and state capitalism but still very far removed from Connolly's Socialism (Lynch 1968). Marx's correct appraisal that the nationalist Irish bourgeoisie always adapted themselves to the prevailing socio-economic conditions in their own interests can also be seen in their betrayal of the struggle for independence by agreeing to partition in 1922 (Woods and Grant 2001).[82]

In relation to the working class, who were expected by Connolly to form the backbone of the Irish revolution, Girvan (1984) pointed out that they were small and often the object of change and so despite the theoretical attractions of Socialism they frequently responded in a conservative and traditional manner. The nationalist issue also compelled the Irish Labour Party to face an impossible task during the Irish revolutionary period by making its objective of uniting northern Protestant and southern Catholic worker almost irrelevant in the universally Catholic environment of the Free State (Coakley 1986). Moreover Dublin working class cohesiveness that Connolly depended upon to carry the socialist revolt was very weak.

For example, Jim Larkin leader of the Irish Transport and General Workers Union (IT and GWU) who with Connolly unsuccessfully took on the employers in the Dublin Lock-Out of 1913 was vilified by the strongly nationalist Liberator newspaper using the tactic of driving home his socialist credentials thus equating him with atheism and Satan (Newsinger 1993). The more extreme newsletter The Toiler also attacked Larkin, although it neatly side-stepped the fact that he was not only an advanced nationalist but also a devout Roman Catholic and this type of personal attack only demonstrated the intensity of the inter-working class struggle in Ireland just three years prior to the Rising of 1916 (Newsinger 1995). The slander in these papers indicated a strong and endemic anti-socialist sentiment throughout the Irish labour class (Newsinger 1993). Moreover there was also a strong imperialist rather than socialist disposition in the Irish middle and upper classes. Kennedy (1996c) maintained that

> the middle classes and gentry in Ireland participated in the administration of the imperial system world wide...Ireland was a junior partner in that vast exploitative enterprise known as the British Empire)...[therefore]...1916 was not an uprising but secession. (Kennedy 1996c: 176, 177)

Yet despite the presence of the imperialist disposition, Williams (1999) highlighted the strong link between nationalism and Catholicism among all classes including the upper class and Coakley (1986) argued that Irish revolutionaries were *natural* products of emotional attachments to their religion and nationalism.

These emotions are almost always associated with sentiments and feelings for a common heritage of religion and fate together with a much sought after national state (Hagendoorn and Pepels 2000). The strength of these sentiments, and nationalism in particular is so strong that it can transform society, motivating all types of individuals in a communal spirit in a kind of social fever where they gel in a united manner against the enemy (Hagendoorn and Pepels 2000).

---

[82] This capacity of modern Irish society to take a pragmatic approach in dealing with the prevailing political and economic environment has of course already been established in our research.

Because the history of the Irish nationalist independence movement was not based on inter-class but inter-community conflict – Protestant and Catholic – it demonstrated that religious sentiments are more powerful than sectional interests and exposed a critical weakness in Marx's contention that materialism and its relations underpin social and political history (Manseragh 1965b). Even the two most famous examples of Irish Soviets, namely the 1919 Limerick Workers' and Soldiers' Council and the 1920 Knocklong Soviet Creameries were handed back by worker occupiers to their owners in exchange for higher wages, only underlined the absence within the short lived Irish soviet movement of any inclination to revolutionise capitalist management practices let alone initiate a socialist revolution (Fitzpatrick 1998).

Strand 3: A Green Version Of Marxism

The approach adopted by Ireland's leading Marxist, Edinburgh born Catholic James Connolly, one of the most important figures in the world labour movement, was to attempt to reconcile the socialist and nationalist ideal in Ireland by organising and partaking in a *Catholic nationalist* revolution as a preliminary to securing a socialist state (Greaves 1986). His involvement as a leading revolutionary in the 1916 Rising reflected Marx's view that Ireland needed to achieve political independence to deal satisfactorily with its own problems (Coughlan 1999). This approach of Connolly had one key supporter. Although Dudley-Edwards (1998) maintained that Lenin never knew of Connolly, there were some ideological similarities between both in relation to nationalism and imperialism and on the role of an oppressed nation in the rise of capitalism. For example, Lenin (1929) identified the exploitation of colonised workers, the Irish, as distinct from the labour of the British workers for the rise of British capitalism. Although Socialism needed to become the political aim of the working class (Lenin 1896), Lenin regarded culturally specific Marxism, for example the approach taken by James Connolly in Ireland, to be an appropriate model (Gibbons 1996).[83] However, because of this local focus by Connolly his influence was essentially nationalist and local rather than socialist and internationalist (Weinz 1986).

Connolly regarded British imperialism as not only an armed occupation but a highly developed form of capitalism and regarded historical materialism as the only way to comprehend the morass of unconnected historical facts, massacres, rebellions and apparently purposeless strife that was Irish history (Coughlan 1999).

Nevertheless Connolly (1898) showed the influence of the Communist Manifesto on his political philosophy Hibernicised Marxism, when he outlined his

---

[83] Marx did not and was opposed to this type of open-ended idealist or nationalist approach. Curry, J. (1997), 'The Dialectic of Knowledge-in-Production: Value Creation in Late Capitalism and the Rise of Knowledge-Centred Production' *Electronic Journal of Sociology 199*, ISSN 1176, 7323, p. 3.

ten point political and economic programme.[84] Connolly (1911) stipulated that the objective of the Socialist Party of Ireland was to bring about the common ownership of all the means of production and distribution.[85] He also maintained that the real re-conquest of Ireland was to free the Irish worker from the slavery of the capitalist system (Connolly 1914).

Connolly's (1941) idea of a free nation included economic sovereignty, prohibition of the sale of foreign goods and the supremacy of the State to alter laws against private property. The re-conquest of Ireland was possible only through the Labour Movement which was to be far more than just replacing a British with an Irish government (Connolly 1934). Connolly (1910) attempted to show that common rather than private ownership of land was the natural order of Irish life under the old Gaelic Brehon system and that the Irish working class had been effectively tricked into developing a foreign character by middle class ecclesiastics and politicians. Connolly believed that the Irish revolution was a fight for the mastery of the means of production by the workers (Connolly 1910).

The replies of Connolly to the Lenten Discourses on Socialism by Fr. Robert Kane S.J. in Gardiner St. Church, Dublin open a window on the content of the response of local clergy who argued against him. In reply to one of these sermons given at Mass, Connolly (1910a) highlighted a number of erroneous arguments made by Father Kane. These included a claim that the Materialist Conception of History denied God, that Surplus Value is not the property of the Workman, that Social and Christian Democracy are opposites and that no Catholic can hold Socialist views. Connolly's answer was to show that throughout Irish history the Catholic Hierarchy, the Popes and politicians sided with the English authorities against the nationalist people of Ireland and he gave thirteen examples to support his claim.

Connolly (1909) also put on record his views on religion and marriage when he asserted that he did not attack Catholic religion or its theology because religion was not an essential principle of Marxism.[86] Connolly was the only Socialist among the leaders of militant Irish nationalism and was clearly influenced in his early years by Marx and Engels' Communist Manifesto but the advance of national aims depended on the socialist agenda and thereby making the struggle economic in character, and this scenario was unlikely to be acceptable to Irish society (Ryan 1948). Nevertheless Connolly's credibility was undermined when he verbally assaulted certain clergy and the hierarchy. The subtlety that he was not actually

---

[84] Included a forty-eight hour week and a minimum wage, public ownership of utilities and national schools controlled by elected boards, free primary education, child maintenance and graduated income tax.

[85] Reflected in the opening lines of the third paragraph of Proclamation of the Republic 1916. The previous Proclamation of 1867 also demanded the same. While in the latter Church State separation was demanded , in the former it is totally omitted.

[86] This was contrary to what Marx had written. It also appears that religion was not discussed, or if it was, then not recorded at meetings of Irish Republican Socialist Party when Connolly acted as Secretary because not one entry of religious or moral issues is to be found in the Party's 1896 Minute Book.

criticising ordinary Catholics was totally lost on the public (Countess De Markievicz 1920).   However, despite his public stance against the Catholic hierarchy he chose to be received back into the Catholic Church before his execution where he made his final Confession and received Holy Communion (Hyland 1997, Kenny 1997, Dudley-Edwards 1998).[87]

Connolly held a heterodox position by adapting Marxism to local culture and traditions, maintaining that it had nothing to do with religion and therefore achieved his greatest intellectual feat, Hibernicised Marxism, where he reconciled Socialism with Irish Republicanism (Dudley Edwards 1997).   Others maintain that it was essentially a British import by Connolly and as a consequence it suffered from almost total nationalist isolation and he was then compelled to merge it with Catholic nationalism by developing a mythology concerning the origins of Marxism in Irish History (The British and Irish Communist Organisation 1977). Also Connolly's belief that a communal social system existed in Ireland prior to colonisation was clearly at odds with early mediaeval Ireland.   Here a rigid hierarchical tripartite social structure existed consisting of priests, lords and commoners (Richter 1988, Powell 1995, Curtis 1995).

In any event it seemed that local conditions in Dublin were just manifestations of a global pattern of capitalist development.   Sombart (1967) maintained that the rise of cities to over 100,000 in the eighteenth century including Dublin – which at this time was as big as Moscow or St. Petersburg or Vienna – was not brought about by trade but by consumption and this occurred due to the pressure of the germinating capitalistic system irrespective of the peculiarities of the country. This made the luxury industry that consumed the most goods more susceptible and more adaptable to capitalism because of the compelling need to have production efficiencies and speed to the marketplace when making valuable goods.

According to Dickson (1987) the scale of Dublin's growth from sixty thousand residents in 1700 to a quarter of a million in 1821 can only be understood in terms of the Irish social system where the rural landlords need for luxury goods was evident in Dublin's commerce which centred on the importation of wine, sugar, fine cloth and as Dickson (1987) noted, a vast array of specialist craftsmen-artisans became totally dependent on the consumption and purchasing of this landed class. This meant that many Dublin craftworkers and labourers, the very ones on whom Connolly depended to take up arms had a vested interest in and were dependent for their livelihood on, the on-going development of the capitalist system.

SECTION B

Strand 4: Profile of Key Combatant and Leadership Occupations

Having outlined a macro perspective of the prevailing religious and class context of Irish society, we now explore the profile of the combatants and leaders who

---

[87] Like most Catholics, confessed his sins to a priest, asked for forgiveness, was given absolution and therefore could look forward to entering Heaven when he died.

were directly responsible for Irish state formation. The pivotal position of the craftworker occupation in that fiery conflict is also established. We rely on two primary documents from that time which list the occupations of those detained and captured in the 1916 Rising together with a company of active IRA Volunteers in the War of Independence. Please refer to Appendix B for the occupational profile of these captured combatants.

As Hickey and Doherty (1987) give a total figure of two thousand captured in the Rising, then the combined totals of columns C2, C3 and C4 in Appendix B may constitute approximately forty per cent of all those captured in 1916. The most prominent combatant occupations for both 1916 and the War of Independence are in descending order, two hundred and thirty two craftworkers including eight apprentices, two hundred and twenty four miscellaneous, one hundred and thirty three labourers, eighty seven shop assistants, eighty five clerks and fifty three farmers. In categorizing the occupations we follow Prothero (1997) who maintained that titles such as artisan, craftworker, mechanic, and apprentice were used interchangeably to denote a highly skilled traditional craftworker or skilled machinist. The following definitions were used to put some order and structure on the myriad of stated combatant occupations.

Table 7.2 Definitions Used to Group Sample Combatant Occupations

Craftworker The stated industrial occupation listed as painter, electrician, carpenter, plumber, coach-builder, wagon-builder, tailor, mechanic, skilled machinist but not baker or jeweler
Labourer The stated occupation of men available for labouring, includes labouring of a permanent nature such as carter, driver, railway worker, also agricultural labourer
Merchant The stated occupation of a selling-trader, including publican, hardware, coal and building merchant, but not in small shops
Shopkeeper The stated occupation of small shop owners, shop assistants, messengers, including drapery, tobacconist and general grocer, but excluding publican
Politician No other occupation stated but where primary activity is in full-time political activity such as City Councillor or MP
Unstated No occupation or status is listed against this person and again the definition presumes the person to be unemployed or a non-political criminal.
Farmer with not more than 30 acres
Miscellaneous Unskilled or semi-skilled, but so varied, that it does not fall into any previous category, such as, gas lamp lighter, tea packer, but not labourer etc.

The value of these definitions is that the profile of unskilled, semi-skilled, skilled professional and aristocratic occupations emerges and fails to underline a working class movement. This becomes even more apparent when all the stated occupations are compressed into one of six social class categories using the recently developed Irish Social Class Scale in an attempt to collate and structure the diversity of those occupations. The advantage of this census based scale[88] is that it provides an ordinal grading of occupations corresponding to the social class structure, replacing the old (1951) CSO socio-economic grouping of eleven categories and one residual and where the new scale is based on grouping individuals who use similar resources to generate an income and share similar situations and backgrounds (O'Hare Whelan, and Commins 1991).[89]

The second step was to re-classify the collapsed occupational categories together with any residual stand-alone occupations such as chemist, into this new Irish social class scale. From table 7.3 we can now observe that all six social classes are involved with social classes three, four, five and six being the most prominent. Within these latter classes the craftworker in class four with two hundred and thirty two craftworkers listed from a total of two hundred and forty five combatants, constitutes the largest occupational group of combatants.

Table 7.3 Re-classification of Combatant Occupations into the Irish Social Class Scale

Class	Description of Occupations	NO.
1	accountant, engineer, private means, professional	8
2	banker, builder, chemist, druggist, farm manager, foreman, garage owner, merchant, pharmacist, surveyor, teacher, third level student, , undertaker	41
3	book-keeper, cinematograph operator, civil servant, grocer/assistant, clerk, insurance inspector, inspector of telephones, ex-policeman, journalist, newspaper reporter	183
4	apprentice, artist, craftsman, forester, glazier, skilled worker, tailor	245
5	baker, butcher, farmer, gardener, groom, labourer, machinist, postman, seaman, van/car driver, waiter	229
6	miscellaneous, tea packer, unstated	226

The third and final step was to establish the proportional degree of participation by craftworkers and the other occupations when measured against the labour force profile i.e. to establish the relative importance of this occupation in bringing about social change. Using Cullen's (1995) estimation of All Ireland National Income in

---

[88] Class 1 includes higher professional, managerial and proprietors and farmers owning two hundred or more acres. Class 2 includes lower professional, managerial, proprietors and farmers owning between one hundred and two hundred acres. Class 3 includes other non manual and farmers owning between fifty and one hundred acres. Class 4 includes skilled manual workers and farmers owning between thirty and fifty acres. Class 5 includes semi-skilled manual workers and farmers owning less than thirty acres. Class 6 includes unskilled manual workers.

[89] The unstated category is a special category noted by the Irish Times of 5 December 1918 p. 5, as indicating that the person was unemployed or a non political criminal.

1911, the most numerous occupations in descending order were farmer, industrial wage earner, miscellaneous, industrial labourer, agricultural performers, self employed, police, soldiers and teachers and a low national figure of just under two and half thousand craftworkers and just under one thousand apprentices.[90] Nevertheless when the most prominent Dublin combatant occupations of craftsperson, clerk, farmer, labourer and teacher are calculated as a per cent of the total Dublin workforce using the more reliable 1926 figures, the relative density of revolutionary participation can then be presented in Table 7.4

Table 7.4 Combatant Occupations as a per cent of the Dublin Workforce

Occupation	As a % of Dublin Workforce in 1926 and from Dublin only	% of Combatants who took part in 1916 Rising and War of Independence	As a % of National Workforce
Craftworker	8.00	3.45	3.45
Farmer	0.24	1.21	5.00
Labourers	9.00	15.60	1.73
Clerk	6.50	10.40	1.60
Shop Assistant	6.30	7.70	1.22
Teacher	1.25	0.40	3.12

At eight per cent of the Dublin workforce, craftworkers, still accounted for more than one quarter of all combatants and their participation rate is calculated at approximately three and half times their workforce rate. Dublin manual labourers, on the other hand, who formed a larger section of the workforce still only accounted for less than one fifth of all combatants with a participation rate of one and one half their workforce rate. Clerks and shop assistants have almost identical workforce levels although clerks have the higher participation rate in the revolution. While farmers were a minority in the Dublin workforce their revolutionary participation rate is calculated at five times their workforce rate although if calculated in absolute numbers they then emerge as one of the smallest

---

[90] However the estimate of two thousand two hundred and twenty one craftworkers calculated for 1911 may be understating the numbers because the 1926 Census of Population calculated the number of skilled craftworkers at ten thousand. Ryan (1995) arrived at a similar figure using technical educational records and applying a 7:1 apprentice to craftsperson ratio. Yet it seems unlikely that the number of craftworkers increased from two and a half to ten thousand in the period 1911-1923 given that the industrial North remained in the UK following Irish independence in 1922. One possible explanation is that in 1911 a substantial number of individuals who did craftwork or mechanical work categorised themselves as industrial workers or farmers or agricultural workers since the Census looked for their *main* occupation only.

combatant groups. Teacher is the only occupation listed which has a lower combatant participation level than its workforce rate.

The social class profile of the combatant occupations also points to the collaborative approach of craftworkers with both higher and lower class occupations. Mercier (1783) noted that craftworker's economic well-being was acutely dependent on all classes. Prothero (1997) in his study of English and French radical artisans in the nineteenth century, maintained that they were the leading group in political radicalism and were very prominent in popular or plebian forms of radicalism together with other workers and especially with the lower middle class occupations of shopkeeper, small dealer and professionals. In Ireland, craftworkers' reliance on full and part-time farmers was due to the weakening of consumer demand coming from small industrial urban centres and because shopkeepers and the professions also took to becoming land graziers renting on the eleven month system (Kennedy 1996b).

Craftworkers had both the individual and collective capacity to enter into collaborative radical political action due to these economic linkages, helped also by the nature of the work and club structure of craftworker life where benefit, trade, educational, and convivial clubs all catered for their work and social needs (Prothero 1997). Moreover their political activity often led to political alliances that were not predetermined by class and included alliances with non manual occupations where radical craftworkers typically saw themselves as patriots willing to work alongside like minded individuals.

Now radicalism always had a religious content in religious countries and so religion was always an important motivating factor in radicalism (Prothero 1997) and we know from Christopher (1997) that the majority of Dublin craftworkers had a Catholic disposition[91] where, on average, they declared a higher Catholic affiliation rate than either teachers, clerks or shop assistants who themselves were slightly below the national average and this strongly suggests that an anti-socialist, anti-communist moderate lifestyle would have been the norm among any of these groups.

Furthermore, Irish craftworkers tended to be better educated than most other workers but they had a notorious reputation for the 'bottle' (drinking) and as consequence, their capacity to form a broad social artisan radical consensus was weakened and their potentially cohesive and effective leadership disposition was greatly diminished (McHugh 1998). Given that there was one Dublin tavern and alehouse for every thirty inhabitants in 1750 (O'Carroll 1987) and by the end of the nineteenth century approximately sixty hundred and sixty of Dublin's seven hundred and sixty five public houses were visited at least once by almost half of Dublin's population on a Sunday, i.e. by approximately one hundred and twenty

---

[91] Although only seventy eight per cent of the population of greater Dublin area were Roman Catholic, the rate in city wards was higher including the North City at nearly ninety two per cent, Rotunda at just under eighty nine per cent, North Dock at eighty five per cent. Only one of the thirty three Dublin Electoral Divisions were non Catholics in the majority. Some of the highest Catholic affiliation rates are therefore recorded in the same electoral ward areas where most of the craft combatants as listed in Appendix 1 lived.

three thousand customers, it now seems feasible that like minded patriots could easily and legitimately congregate. Moreover, a substantial number of these pubs were owned by nationalist publicans who were also local leaders and who permitted nationalist meetings to take place in and placards to be displayed on, their premises (Malcolm 1986).[92] A example of this cross class radical collaboration can be seen in the aftermath of the failed United Irishman's Rebellion of 1798 where craftworkers joined with labourers, grain producers and drink sellers and where blacksmiths and carpenters were tortured along with owners of alehouses, the former for making pikes and the latter for storing them (Malcolm 1986). In this rebellion Presbyterians, aristocracy and gentry fought alongside the Catholic and Protestant middle classes and craftworkers particularly in Dublin (Connolly 1998b).

Historically then craftworkers emphasised their citizenship and formed political alliances with different groups against the powerful. There is no simple reason or explanation why craftworkers became radical, because their action is triggered not only by material concerns but also by notions of fairness and freedom (Prothero 1997). A strong idealistic basis appears to inform their actions. Yet unlike the majority of Irish craftworkers Rorabugh (1986) stated that their American counterparts rose to prominence in politics and the military after the American Revolution, allowing their parents explore different priorities for their children and take advantage of the new fluid social structure to fully develop their business potential.

Even where an Irish craftworker such as Arthur Griffith became a political leader he epitomised Irish Catholic nationalist and economic conservatism inherent in the nature of Irish craftworker radicalism. He was a co-founder in 1905 with Bulmer Hobson of the radical nationalist party Sinn Féin (Ourselves) and was heavily influenced by the German economist Friedrich List whose writings informed the basis of the party's ideology of equal partner dual monarchy independence i.e. same king but with independent parliaments (Davis 1976). A protectionist economic programme, advocating *passive* resistance characterised Sinn Féin's ideology (Augusteijn 1998). More importantly, Griffith also followed the teachings and ideals of Pope Leo XIII, particularly those set out in the Encyclical Rerum Novarum on Socialism and the Worker and relied on the new nationalist state to resolve the class issue. As a consequence, the moderate Griffith was regarded as a pro-capitalist conservative Uncle Tom by James Connolly and many other left wing commentators (Davis 1976).

Collaborative and conservative craftworker radicalism was not only confined to Dublin. For example, the secret police report on the election of the Mid Cork Sinn Féin Executive on the 25 October 1917, revealed that the occupational profile of

---

[92] In fact we may be using a very conservative figure. Kearns (1996) states that in the late 1870s, Dublin had one thousand and six public houses, three hundred and ten spirit grocers, one hundred and thirty seven beer dealers and two hundred and nine unlicenced drinking houses or 'sheebens' and quotes a Dublin magistrate who stated, that 'Dublin was saturated with drink…every third or fourth house deals in drink'.

the officers and committee was a carbon copy of Dublin combatants.[93] Yet the relatively high proportion of direct combatant involvement by social classes three, four, five and six masks the reality that socialist movements generated only token support in Dublin. Not only was a small group of socialist artisans, who worked in Dublin from 1841-43, forced out of existence due to attacks from the supporters of Daniel O'Connell the Catholic Emancipator but the membership for other socialist groups such as the Dublin Democratic Association, the Socialist League, the Irish Socialist League, the National Labour League and the Irish Socialist Republican Party never exceeded sixty in number (Lane 1997).[94] Their overall lack of numbers may reflect the laconic nature of Dubliners who have, according to Plunkett (1968), a sense of accepting things, as they come and are happy and content if they have among other things their pint of Guinness (beer) and the assurance of a better life hereafter.[95]

On the other hand, the social class structure of the 1916 leadership was by and large inversely proportional to that of the combatants. The occupational profile and educational background of a selection of the nationalist leadership including sixteen of those executed, is presented below. If the same Irish Social Class Scale applied to the analysis of the occupational classification of the fighters is now used to classify the executed leaders then the following social class profile emerges.

Table 7.5 Occupational Profile of a Sample of Executed 1916 Leaders

Class	Occupation	No
1	academic, diplomat, lecturer, nobleman	4
2	assayer, teacher, tobacconist, writer	4
3	barman, clerk (4), land agitator, soldier, union organiser	8
4	no occupations listed	nil
5	stonework-labourer	1
6	no occupations	nil

Source: Hickey, D.J. and Doherty J.E. (1987), *A Dictionary of Irish History 1800-1980*, Gill and Macmillan, Dublin.

In Table 7.6, a comparison of the Social Class profile of the combatants and leaders is now possible and it shows that leaders broadly speaking, belong to the

---

[93] Stewart, A. (1997), *Michael Collins, The Secret File*, Public Record Office, Blackstaff Press, Belfast, Document Number 23, pp. 69-71.

[94] Was one of the most prominent Irish MPs in Pre-Independence Ireland who worked for the repeal of the Act of Union and Catholic Emancipation through mass demonstrations. Made alliances with the Catholic clergy and funded the opening of the O'Connell's Christian Brothers School in Dublin, where we interviewed a class of Leaving Certificate pupils as part of our research.

[95] These are precisely the sentiments expressed in the Celtic Tiger profile of the economic disposition.

social classes one, two and three while the combatants belong to social classes four, five and six.

Table 7.6 A Comparison of the Social Class of Fighters and Leaders of 1916

Social Class	% Leaders from this class	% Combatants from this class
1	25	nil
2	25	nil
3	48	21
4	nil	28
5	nil	26
6	2	25
TOTAL	100	100

Two observations are worth noting about the comparison of social class. Firstly, James Connolly was the only socialist among the revolutionary leadership which itself had a strongly professional bias with writers, teachers, academics and the legal profession being the most prominent. Secondly, according to Hagendoorf and Pepels (2000), these professional occupations are the very ones that gravitate towards nationalism in an effort to secure social and economic advantage that is normally denied them i.e. they have a mainly economic and political objective in contrast to the craftworker for example, who is driven by a more egalitarian sentiment of patriotism. We now look at the economic sentiment of the more egalitarian craftworker.

Strand 5: The Economic Sentiment of the Craftworker

Marx (1963) maintained that the craftworker is

> cut up into two persons…as owner of the means of production he is capitalist…[and simultaneously]…he exploits himself as wage labourer…[since]…he as capitalist employs himself as wage-labourer…[eventually he]…will either gradually be transformed into a small capitalist…or he will suffer the loss of his means of production…and be transformed into a wage-labourer. (Marx 1963: 398)

Lenin (1929) identified craft workers as aristocratic labour susceptible to economic bribery who were, for all intents and purposes, part of the bourgeoisie i.e. they are enemies of the proletariat. James Connolly (1914a) had also previously pointed out that the craft unions had already succumbed to capitalism. Their very disposition was both conservative and moderate (Hyland 1997). Craft unions served as paragons of moderation for most of their existence and Dublin craftworkers were often in the better off sections of society (Lane 1997).[96] Craftworkers were traditionally a well-to-do group especially before the collapse of the textile industry in Dublin in 1826 when almost ten per cent of the city's population was affected and subsequently had to go on public relief schemes (O'Toole 1987). Skilled workers in Ireland earned an average of thirty four shillings and nine pence per week almost as much as their British counterparts and nearly twice as much as a male Irish labourer and three times as much as a female one (O'Gráda 1998). Some craftworkers such as printers were particularly well paid experiencing a two hundred and sixty five per cent increase in wages between 1913 and 1920 (Malcolm 1998). From an examination of wage levels provided by Cullen (1995), it can be seen that craftworker income per week was higher than any industrial or agricultural labourer.

Moreover, craftworkers had the least amount of automation and alienation compared with other occupations and their work was intrinsically more artistic than routine labouring jobs (Hobson 1914). They always fought against labour to preserve their middle class status because their orientation was inherently conservative and reactionary rather than revolutionary (Marx 1998). Although in capitalism the larger and more powerful landowners attempted to pauperise small farmers, shopkeepers and craftworkers (Trotsky 1939), Republicanism nevertheless depended for its vitality on farmers and shopkeepers – key economic collaborators with craftworkers – the very ones who were opposed to social revolution since it was anathema to them, and as a result they directed their republican and nationalist sentiments towards social conservatism and away from the socialist radicalism of a 'small clique of city men' in Dublin (Fitzpatrick 1998).

Dublin craftsmen were also the occupational group least affected by post Famine emigration (O Gráda 1998). Emigrants were made up of two very different groups at the top and bottom of the occupational ladder, namely the usual unskilled and the professional and well educated, where over capacity in the labour market restricted employment opportunities for lawyers, doctors and clergy (Daly 1994). Craftsmen must also have commanded a form of wage premium because the division of labour was practically unknown outside of the cities where the shortage of craftworkers and business people was seriously inhibiting industrial development in rural areas (O'Brien 1918). Furthermore entry to apprenticeship was restricted to an immediate relative (Daly 1994). Considering that the predominant occupations in Dublin City were general labourers, carters, messengers and porters (Chart 1920) and given the control on the supply of craftworkers just mentioned, an upward pressure on craft wage levels was almost inevitable. Indeed demand for their skills must have been further strengthened in the newly developing industries from 1841 to 1926 where new job opportunities emerged for fitter, up from twenty four to approximately one thousand two hundred, for fitter-turner up from one hundred and forty five to over one thousand

---

[96] For example, the early part of the nineteenth century saw George Steward, a carpenter and Alexander Thompson, a plumber, both living in the most prestigious aristocratic neighbourhood in Dublin city, namely Sackville Mall, now O'Connell St. (Walsh 1987).

two hundred, for electrical fitter up from zero to nearly one thousand four hundred and for motor mechanic up from zero to approximately one thousand two hundred. These new occupations underlined the changing profile of the Irish Labour force in the period 1841-1926.[97] More importantly these new crafts also had a Catholic affiliation rate of eighty five per cent and a conservative Catholic economic disposition was most likely to exist in these newly emerging industrial occupations.

Strand 6: The Catholic Disposition of the National Workforce

When affiliation rates of the Irish workforce recorded in the 1926 Free State Census are examined an exceptionally high average Catholic affiliation rate of nearly ninety three per cent can be observed. The unskilled or semi skilled occupations such as factory worker, newspaper seller and building labourer have the highest rates. Even where an Owner Manager Group has one of the lowest Catholic affiliation rates of fifty four per cent, for example in Print and Paper Episcopalians were the second most prominent group at twenty nine per cent followed by Presbyterians at seven per cent, Jews at one per cent and the remaining nine per cent equally divided between Methodists and Others. The importance of the number of Episcopalians i.e. Church of Ireland, is that they form the largest Protestant Church in the Republic of Ireland and as a member of the world-wide Anglican community they share a number of key theological principles with Roman Catholicism (Ford and Milne 1998). Given the combined level of Catholicism and Anglicanism, the overall capitalist influence of the Puritan acquisitive orientation highlighted by Weber must have been almost non-existent. In some rural areas the number of adherents to other religions was minuscule.[98]

Using Microsoft's Statistical/Correlation $f_x$unctions on two arrays of data, the correlation between the percentage religious affiliation and social class for the occupations listed was calculated at 0.849185425.[99] This suggests a positive

---

[97] Clarkson, L.A. and Crawford, E.M. and Litvack, M.A. (1995), *Database of Irish Historical Statistics*, Queens University Belfast, Department of Economic and Social History, Publication Number 1. p. III, and pp. 17-33. First Source for 1926: *Department of Industry and Commerce, 1928: Census of Population 1926, Volume 2, Dublin Occupations of Males and Females in each Province, County, County Borough, Urban and Rural District*, Stationery Office, Dublin, pp. 1-13 and pp. 96-119. Second Source for 1926 *Religious Affiliation: Department of Industry and Commerce, 1929:Census of Population 1926*, Volume 3, Part 1 Religions, Part 2 Birthplaces, Stationery Office, Dublin pp. 110-129.

[98] For example in County Clare on the West Coast of Ireland in 1911, there were over one thousand seven hundred or 1.7 per cent of Episcopalians, one hundred and sixty six or 0.1 per cent of Presbyterians, thirty eight Methodists and nineteen other non-Catholic recorded compared with over one hundred thousand Roman Catholics (Fitzpatrick 1998).

[99] Using the 1928 Department of Industry and Commerce, *Census of Population 1926, Volume 2, Occupations of Males and Females in each Province, County, County Borough, Urban and Rural District*, and the 1929 Department of Industry and Commerce, *Census of Population 1926 Volume 3, Part 1 Religious Affiliation*, pp. 114-120.

correlation between affiliation rates and social class number with the lower occupational skills and social classes showing the higher affiliation to Catholicism. Universal Catholic affiliation within the three main employment sectors of agriculture, manufacturing and services shortly after independence, can be observed in Table 7.7.

Table 7.7 Number and per cent of Catholics, Presbyterians and Jews in Agriculture, Manufacturing and Services in 1926

Sector	Catholics NO. and (%)	Presbyterian NO. and (%)	Jews NO. and (%)
Agriculture (All)	664,046 (98.8%)	8,083 (1.2%)	9
Producers, Makers, Repairers	867,098 (98.3%)	9,746 (1.2%)	406 (0.5%)
Commercial, Insurance, Finance	85,008 (97.1%)	1,641 (1.9%)	780 (1.0%)

There are just nine Jewish individuals recorded for the entire agricultural sector and only four hundred and six in the largest employment sector of Producer. The highest recorded Presbyterian level was in the Commercial and Finance sector yet they still only accounted for two per cent of the entire workforce in that sector. While the overall national Catholic affiliation rate increased by two per cent in the hundred year period 1881-1991, the Church of Ireland population decreased by five per cent giving a national affiliation rate of just over two per cent in 1991 (Central Statistics Office 1999). Presbyterianism also decreased from one and a half per cent to less than a half per cent in the same period, a decrease of nearly three quarters in absolute numbers, while Methodist numbers decreased by two thirds. The importance of the religious stratification is that it shows the absence of secularisation and the economically favourable Protestantism or Judaism. Moreover, the Catholic Church supported the nationalist Sinn Féin party in its struggle for independence and they sanctified this struggle in preference to the Irish Parliamentary Party (Stewart 1997).[100] Therefore the recommended economic objective of moderate or enough wealth for Catholics which was clearly articulated by the Papacy and in particular by Leo XIII in 1891 was unlikely therefore to be ignored by the Catholic nationalists acting as combatants or leaders.

Because Irish nationalism is a specifically Catholic phenomenon (Girvin 1986), we can now directly link it to the moderate economic objective as set out by the Catholic Church and the Popes in particular. This Catholic nationalist marriage also prevented the development of political forces within the island that could, according to Girvan (1986a) appeal across religious boundaries, although for

---

[100] The Nationalist Party was the generic term for the Irish Parliamentary Party in the British House of Commons. It vote collapsed in 1918 from seventy to six Westminster seats. The Irish Catholic Church suspected it of anti-clerical intentions, switching support to Sinn Féin.

example, farmers did not always vote their own class into power even though they had the potential to over-arch this narrow appeal (Kennedy 1996b). The implication of this marriage for our benchmarks on Marxism, Communism and Socialism, which we set out at the beginning of this chapter, is that Irish radicalism was confronted by three main obstacles which it never overcame. Firstly, it failed to address nationalism which subordinated working class interests to the nationalist interest secondly, the power of the Catholic Church remained intact as most devout Catholics supported the view that it was their duty to reject Socialism and Communism and thirdly, the land question where a narrow industrial base did not make Ireland susceptible to a national conversion to Socialism (Lane 1997).

The strength of this Catholic nationalist marriage to reject radicalism as an important personal and national goal can been gleaned from the prison poetry of captured combatants.[101]   Prison has produced much poetry that has been used successfully to analyse subjective experiences of imprisonment because those awaiting death or execution place a premium on truth and honesty (Jupp 1996, Bould 1991). This form of primary data is consistent with both qualitative and naturalistic research methodology particularly when it is genuine, original and representative (Jupp 1996). In other words, honest communication tends to be at a premium in this prison poetry.

Even before 1916, White (1998) drew attention to the fact that Irish prisoners in London were deeply committed to their religion and separated themselves from the Protestant Ordinary and other non-Catholic prisoners at the scaffold in the eighteenth century.   In the poetry of both the 1916 Rising and War of Independence prisoners, there is universal use of allegorical imagery and terms relating to death such as martyr, sacrifice and resurrection draw heavily on glorious Catholic devotional imagery. It is used mainly to liken the Catholic nationalist role of patriot and martyr to the death and resurrection of Jesus Christ, where the triumph of Ireland over British Crown Forces would be as inevitable as the Resurrection was after Jesus' triumph over death through the crucifixion.

Irish Example	*German Example*
For Ireland, the sacred fire of Ireland burst into flame	It is all a Swindle:
Renew the failing lamp within their souls	The War is for the Wealthy
Youthful one lie riddled by English bullets	The Middle Class must give way
God's angels there keep guard	The People provide the corpses
They would press through to join the host of God	
Nor should they fear the foe's revengeful might	
Powerless as Roman tortures affright	
The Fishers of the Galilean Lake	
Ireland over all	
Author: W.L. Cole	*Author: Anonymous*

---

[101] Forty-one diaries belonging to nationalist prisoners were examined. The prisoners were held in Dublin Castle, Red Cross Hospital, Rebel Ward 1916, Dublin, in Knutsford and Frongach Prison Camps 1916 Wales, in Galway Gaol 1916 Galway, in Mountjoy Jail Hunger Strikers 1917, and in Kilmainham Jail, Dublin, 1921. See *Prison Autograph Books, Box 1, No 189, and Box 2, No 190*, Allen Library, Dublin.

The Irish poetry is characterised by an absence of any reference to the class conflict in contrast to the poetry of deserting German soldiers in Belgium in 1918 where the class based nature of the conflict is evident.[102] The expressed sentiments marks out the Irish nationalist conflict as a religious war.

The Irish poetry also differs in emphasis from the poetry of other prisoner nationalities in other barbaric events and conflicts. For example, the prison poetry of Edith Cavel, who was executed by the Germans in 1915, which was collated by Bould (1991) focussed on a sense of loyalty and a duty to the existing state. In an examination of over one hundred extracts of Allied World War Two prisoner of war writings compiled by Bassett (1978) only one composition could be categorised as Jesus focussed, that of Danish sailor Kim Malthe-Bruun. Saving one's life and escape was a top priority expressed in the poetry of American soldiers incarcerated in World War Two Japanese prisoner of war camps and collected by McKendree (1995). Another modern selection of prison poetry collected by Marsha Hunt (1999) included contributions by nineteen drug offenders in Dublin's Mountjoy Jail where only two references to God by Fiddler (1999) and Francis (1999) are featured and these are negative ones reprimanding God for forgetting them. It appears that different prisoner groupings such as the 1916 Irish, the American POWs and the Dublin junkies express different sentiments that are uppermost in their minds at that time. The evidence suggests that the Irish revolutionary prisoners did not have a class-based motivation for their actions, but a religious and nationalist one.

These very sentiments also reflected the ethos of many of the schools attended by the combatants. Durkheim (1998) argued that teachers were the social representatives and intermediaries of society and that teaching fashioned the individual to reflect the basic values of society. A significant number of fighters, two hundred and nine, who took part in 1916 were from just four Christian Brothers Schools in Dublin city center, being part of a long history by this particular Catholic teaching order of turning out well educated young men with a passion for nationalism and ripe for republican volunteer armies (O'Herlihy, Griffin, O Donnell and Devereaux 1995). Moreover, Catholic pupils were well motivated to accept the guidance and exhortations of the Religious in the schools to ensure life after death and as a substitute badge of ethnicity which limited the sphere of influence of the Protestant establishment and its core values mainly by linking the acquisitive and greedy impulse of the Protestant to the rise of Communism (Nic Ghiolla Phadraig 1995).

Some examples of this link are revealed in the twentieth edition of the textbook Christian Politeness and Counsels for Youth, where in the chapter titled General Observations, the Christian disposition is characterised by a strong sentiment of charity towards others (Christian Brothers 1934). In another textbook, Fortifying Youth, the chapter on Economics and the Social Crisis highlights both the error of

---

[102] Howard, N. (1999), 'The German Revolution defeated and facism deferred: the servicemen's revolt and social democracy at the end of the First World War 1918-1920', Tim Kirk and Anthony McElligott (eds.), *Opposing Facism*, Cambridge University Press, Cambridge, pp. 12-32.

striving to achieve economic wealth and then compounding that error by equating wealth with personal happiness. It was then quickly pointed out that the pursuit of both by Protestants had given rise to the twin evils of capitalism and Communism. In chapter twenty even, Progress and the Dark Ages, Material Wealth Overrated, Communism was regarded as a natural outcome of the Protestant Reformation because wealth and greed inevitably and naturally fostered the environment in the first place thereby provoking it to take hold in the poorest sections of society. Moreover, the accumulation of riches was anything but a sign of salvation because God reserved riches for his greatest enemies. For example a single sheet revision examination on areas of Catholic social doctrine called Social Crisis enquired

> What do you understand by the term Social Crisis? Trace the development of present day social crises to the advent of Communism and describe the part played by Karl Marx. What are the fundamental errors in Communism? How are they directly opposed to the teaching of the Church?

The model answers declare

> The cause of this evil is the universal illusion that more and more money means more and more happiness, though saints and sages have been exposing it since the world began...for this deplorable apostasy [The Reformation] freed its victims from those wholesome restraints which keep the passions of pride and avarice in check. (Christian Brothers 1946: 100-101)

The connection between acquisitiveness and evil is clear and the implication is that Catholicism mediated the extravagance of Protestant greed, the cause of the excesses of capitalism.[103]

In 1949 the authorities of the deeply Catholic University College Dublin (UCD) were 'outcatholicked' by the student body who complained about the low Mass attendance of their lecturers. Then the university authorities banned the UCD Literary and Historical Society and special guest Dr. Owen Sheehy Skeffington from debating the merits for humanity of the ideals outlined in the Communist Manifesto (Myers 1999). Again, up to the late 1960s and early 1970s, in an approved Department of Education primary level civics textbook of twenty five short lessons and written by secular teacher Liam Gaynor (no date of publication presumably late 1960s), community values are seen to have been replaced by the selfish individualism imposed by a foreign and Protestant power, namely Britain. The lessons implied that the Irish nationalist values of charity and community were more suited to a Catholic society.

---

[103] This is precisely the view of a number of contributors in National Domain A in our research and was the sentiment highlighted by the Taoiseach to the Bishops as noted in the latter sections of chapter four.

Strand 7: The Post Revolutionary Conservative Ethos

The assertion of Marx that the ruling ideas of any epoch are the ideas of the ruling class (Giddens 1971) is particularly insightful in terms of the Irish nationalist leadership and the prevailing socio-economic disposition of Irish society. The Irish leaders were nationalist revolutionaries with nothing else in mind except freedom, yet even at twenty five years of age, they were deeply conservative (Fitzgerald 2000a). Social, political and economic conservative policies became the hallmark of the nationalist leaders who prided themselves as the most conservative revolutionaries in history (Breen, Hannan, Rottman and Whelan 1990). This was no surprise since the fledgling Irish government had many farmers and professions supporting it (Kennedy 1971). Even after a bitter struggle against the British administration, the pragmatic and opportunistic Irish revolutionary leadership adopted the familiar and acceptable Westminster constitutional model (Dinan 1986) and followed orthodox economic policies common at that time, namely balancing the books (Manseragh 1997). These policies were cautious, and focussed almost exclusively on agriculture (Neary and O'Grada 1991).

Conservatism was the dominant social perspective not only in Government but across all strata of Irish society and had the effect of enabling successive Irish governments to successfully restrict social and institutional change (Fitzpatrick 1998). Daly (1994) also highlighted the Catholic and conservative orientation of the ruling administrative elite in the new Irish civil service where almost all of the forty eight heads of departments came from Ireland and approximately half of these were Catholic. Moreover, with twenty one thousand individuals transferring from the British administration into the new Irish Civil Service and with only one hundred and thirty one individuals recruited from the original revolutionary administration of Dáil Éireann, an administrative post-independence revolution was prevented and continuity of the old conservative policies assured (Daly 1994).

Marx (1843) had already noted that politics and the Christian religion tended to be inextricably linked. Lee (1989) maintained that the two largest political parties in Ireland, Fianna Fáil and Fine Gael, both shared strong Catholic and anti-Communist sentiments and that the general population equated Communism with atheism and regarded the crusade against it as a religious rather than a class war. Broderick (1994) noted that in the 1930s, Irish society perceived that a Marxist revolution was a real threat to the new state and De Valera maintained that Socialism was not only anathema to Irish Catholicism but to the personality of the Irish and to the whole Irish way of life (Milotte 1984).

Moreover in that climate, the label of Communist carried more that just a potential violent threat (Hanley 1999).[104] The reason for the participation of twenty Irish students between 1927 and 1935 at the Comitern's International Lenin School ILS – Moscow's foremost academy for the training of foreign revolutionaries – was as a reaction to the very poor showing of the Irish Communist movement in the Ireland of the 1920s (McLoughlin 1999). The

---

[104] Widespread attacks were carried out by gangs on Communists and communist property in the 1930s following clerical sermons in Dublin's Catholic Pro-Cathedral.

combined red scare propaganda of the Church and State in the 1930s and early 1940s helped marginalise all socialist and communist revolutionary groups (Collins 1998) and in the 1950s all the political parties asserted that Communism and Socialism were incompatible with Christianity and democracy (Manning 1999).

Cairns and Richards (1988) explained that Catholic nationalist leaders in the new Free State saw the desires of the body as a menace to achieving Heaven and therefore gave priority to the needs of the soul, and as farmers embodied this national ideal it ensured that other group interests were subservient to those of the farmers.   Connolly (1994) argued that the power of the Catholic Church to inculcate this anti-materialist economic ethos with a special status reserved for the poor stemmed from the fact that the Church was not drawn from the social elite and was helped by the creation of a myth concerning long standing Irish national Catholic devotion and piety.[105]   Marx (1846) was quick to point out how religion supported and justified the capitalist economic relations of the day and this according to Arkins (1994) was precisely the relationship existing in the Free State where the clergy in conjunction with the civil service, businessmen and small to medium sized farmers formed a particularly strong Irish bourgeois alliance at the expense of the proletariat.

It is not really surprising then that the Irish Labour Party has never been a potent political force in Ireland because both Fianna Fáil and Fine Gael dominated the socio-political landscape so much. The Irish Labour Party was mostly a peripheral entity except in some modern coalition governments where it held the balance of power. This phenomenon seems remarkable when over sixty per cent of the Irish population classified themselves as working class (Breen, Hannan, Rottman, and Whelan 1990). In twenty five elections since 1922, the per cent of seats held by Labour has fluctuated from a low of just under five per cent in 1932 to a high of nineteen per cent in 1992 (Govt 1997). As Breen and Whelan (1994) noted, class influence on voting preferences was exceptionally weak in Ireland and this was reflected in across the board support for the republican Fianna Fáil leaving Fine Gael and Labour as minor parties in the scheme of things. The preference for the nationalist and republican Fianna Fáil can clearly be seen from the figures for voting preferences presented in Table 7.8 below. The total intermediate and non-skilled working class vote for Fianna Fáil exceeds the combined total of votes for all other political parties from these two categories of voter. In the professional-managerial class nearly half of all votes are also cast for Fianna Fáil.

---

[105] The first of the eight Beatitudes 'Blessed are the poor in spirit for theirs is the Kingdom of Heaven' (Matthew:5 3-10), where the common meaning attached to poor is economic distress, although scholars insist that the Heavenly Kingdom is not bestowed on the condition of poverty but on the willingness to bear this condition and so a very rich man can be poor in spirit. See *Catholic Encyclopaedia Volume II* (1907), Appleton and Co., New York.

Table 7.8 Voting Preferences for Irish Political Parties by Occupational Classification

Political Party	Professional/ Managerial	Intermediate	Un-Skilled Working Class
Fianna Fáil	49	54	56
Fine Gael	31	23	14
The Left	6	11	19
Others	14	12	11
TOTAL	100	100	100

Source: Breen, R. and Whelan, C.T. (1994), *Social Class, Class Origins and Political Partisanship in the Republic of Ireland*, reprinted from European Journal of Political Research 26, pp. 117-133, Dublin, ESRI Reprint Series, No 102, Table 1, p. 123.

There is further evidence that approximately fifty per cent of those holding left wing economic values in all three occupational categories voted for Fianna Fáil whereas only fourteen per cent of the professional-managerial, eleven per cent of the Intermediate and twenty one per cent of the non-skilled groups voted for Labour (Hardiman and Whelan 1994). The reason that class partisanship had been successfully avoided is through a combination of the PR system, which has allowed ideologies to develop that denied the importance of class conflict and by the catch all Fianna Fáil strategy of submerging class conflict in the call for territorial and social unity together with their policy of generating economic growth with minimum conflict (Hardiman and Whelan 1994). Furthemore the Trade Union movement was also dominated by sectional interests and a restricted frame of reference which focussed on comparability issues among the same occupation thus leading to an absence of class consciousness which left any co-ordinated development of a worker ideology with weak foundations (Breen, Hannan, Rottman and Whelan 1990).

This continuing problem of attempting to modify Marx's insights[106] without damping down the revolutionary call for social justice in capitalist economies gave rise to a number of modified Marxist perspectives all of which appear to be strong on aspiration but weak on observation (Gorman 1982). In Ireland, revisionist Marxist history writing is scholastic Marxism written by academics for journals rather than an action based guide for old fashioned working class political Marxists and acts as an apologia for British involvement in Irish affairs (Coughlan 1999). Moreover along the way it conveniently ignored the fact that a central tenet of

---

[106] Gorman discusses the range of unsatisfactory ideological answers to the problem including A Priori Marxism or Orthodox Materialism, Experiential Marxism where the focus is on individual rationality and its effect on the socio-historical process, Empirical Marxism which focuses on a verifiable revolutionary hypothesis, Critical Theory maintaining that individuals are unable to act authentically within the socio-historical process and the New Left concentrating on whatever works politically.

classical Marxism was embodied and actioned in Connolly's national struggle for independence namely, an attempt to subordinate the interest of capital to the working class (Coughlan 1999). Given that the collapse of the Soviet Union was regarded as definitive proof of failure of Communism and the ideas of Marx, the promise held out that technological advancement would be harnessed to minimise the working day and provide the materialist basis for advancement of human civilisation had been totally undermined by the mediation of Social Democracy in capitalist economies (Woods and Grant 1994). In this regard Ireland was no exception because

> in the world wide retreat from socialism in the 1990s Ireland has
> had a lot less distance to travel than most countries. (Collins
> 1998: 518)

Conclusion of Theme Two

The above exploration of the forces shaping the profile of the Irish economic disposition has benefited from using the concept of Historical Materialism. It has allowed us to reveal a coalition of socio-cultural strands programmed by the Absolute Pre-supposition religion and nationalism to protect and adapt the Catholic ethos to the prevailing or changing socio-economic conditions. This can be seen in the failure of green versions of both right and left leaning 'isms' such as O'Duffyism and Hibernicised Marxism. The direct action of the Catholic Hierarchy who sent consistent messages through the pulpit, and of the religious who inculcated Catholic nationalist sentiments in their pupils and of the workers themselves who for example, as members of the Labour Party demanded stronger Catholic Social Teaching principles in more of the Party's policies, marked out all the 'isms' for special attention.

The papal directives on legitimate economic engagement levels consistently articulated a charitable and moderate ethic. The disposition of one of the key occupational groups in that revolution, namely craftsmen, following a tradition of European and American craftworker radicalism is seen to be an almost universal Catholic one. This disposition is characterised by a configuration of anti-materialist, anti-Protestant, moderate and charitable sentiments. These religious sentiments are precisely the ones displayed in the profile of the Irish economic disposition revealed earlier in the research findings. The anti-industrial and conservative temperament of revolutionary leaders and early Irish governments was also revealed.

In conclusion then Marx appears to have overestimated the explanatory capacity of historical materialism since religion is a powerful cultural variable capable of profound positive and negative societal change which is independent from the change dynamic springing from material relations i.e. the economic structure (McGuire 1992). Our research suggests that this religious variable is the pre-eminent internal force shaping the economic disposition during the Celtic Tiger. Catholic nationalist consciousness had been characterised by extreme conservatism together with a long standing and deeply felt antipathy towards the Soviet Union (Manseragh 1997a). The remarkable fact is that it is possible for Irish society to hold extreme nationalist and conservative social views while simultaneously distancing the nationalist left from the socialist left (Manseragh 1997b).

The 1916 Rising was not a class revolution in the Marxist sense but a conflict between factions supporting different degrees of nationalism (O'Malley 1989). Moreover the formation of the Free State can be interpreted as a move to assist capitalism to take a stronger foothold in Ireland because national economic determination is a feature or safety valve within the capitalist system to prevent explosive revolutionary situations from developing such as that which occurred in Russia. In addition, by assisting with economic self-determination the capitalist system is actually being strengthened in the longer term (Fanning and McCarthy 1983). The critical weakness in maintaining that materialism and its relations underpin social and political history is exposed in the case of Ireland (Manseragh 1965b), where the Absolute Pre-supposition religion-nationalism has been revealed as the durée responsible for shaping the Irish economic disposition.

Chapter 8

Explaining the Profile using Elias' Figurational Sociology

From childhood, I was aware that there were two separate and immiscible kinds of citizens: the Catholics, of whom I was one and the Protestants, who were as remote and different from us as if they had been blacks and we whites. We were not acquainted with Protestants but we knew that they were there, a hostile element in the community vaguely menacing us with horrors as Mrs Smylie's home for orphans where children might be brought and turned into Protestants. While we Catholics varied socially among ourselves we all had the most common bond whatever our economic condition, of being second class citizens. (Andrews 1979)

Introduction

In chapter seven the Absolute Pre-supposition, namely religion-nationalism was seen to exert a profound influence on the socio-economic context, on the 'fire' of the individual's consciousness and on the nature of the derived economic behaviour. Moreover, the use of a stranding approach played a significant part in unraveling the nature of the linkages between the various socio-cultural factors that determined the essence of that disposition. This same stranding approach is again particularly useful to draw out the longer term dynamic of social development driven by the changing relationship between individuals and groups, a central theme in Figurational Sociology. Its deployment in our analysis adds a different rather than an opposing emphasis to the so-called static Marxist economic relations model. By focusing on the dynamic of changing relationships, it becomes easier to comprehend the underlying regularity of the Irish economic disposition as part and parcel of a longer term process of western development which Elias calls the civilising process. Moreover, by placing the nationalist aspect of the Absolute Pre-supposition within this civilising process and then by employing concepts such as Insider-Outsider, a number of apparent contradictions manifested in recurring patterns of Irish economic behaviour are seen to come more and more within the sphere of influence of nationalist sentiment. Here again the Irish state formation period and some of the main protagonists which were used successfully to ground the sociological insights of Marx, this time generate additional perspectives on the configuration of variables using five strands of analysis.

The first strand employs the concept of national identity to explore how group membership criteria and subsequent economic behaviour act as a re-enforcement of that identity. In the second strand, the rise of specific occupations during the formation and development of the Irish state is explored and the subsequent impact of this changing social structure on the development of the Irish economic disposition is discussed. In the third strand, the impact of farmers and teachers worldview on the national economic disposition is outlined. In the fourth strand, we examine the vocational rather than the sexual locus of conscience given the number of respondents in our research who alerted us to its influence in their working lives and attempt to establish how it shapes economic behaviour. In the final strand, we discuss the nature of the Irish-British colonial relationship where the grievance sentiment infusing the Irish psyche almost pre-determined the development of an anti-industrial disposition. These new strands help to contribute to a more informed understanding of the nature of the constellation of socio-cultural factors impacting on the Irish economic disposition. Central to this contribution is the concept of figurational sociology.

Figurational Sociology

There is no mention of Norbert Elias in modern sociological textbooks such as Ritzer (1988), Craib (1992) or Baert (1998). Yet he is one of the most penetrating and original sociological thinkers who rejected many traditional assumptions of sociology (Mennel 1997). In particular he rejected the notion of the individual and society as disparate entities. Van Krieken (1997) pointed out that the concept of figurational sociology deemed that social life can only be understood by defining the individual as part of a collective, as part of a constellation of dependent relationships i.e. within a figuration. According to Elias (1996)

> the image of man as a closed personality is replaced by the image of an 'open personality' fundamentally oriented towards and dependent on other people throughout his life. (Elias 1996: 213)

The simpler terms of interdependency, network and configuration are more workable than the term figurational (Fletcher 1997). Over time there was a noticeable change of emphasis by Elias in the concept of dependency from intra to inter-state societal processes, tracing a move from internal conquest and victory with the concomitant social disturbance and power relations, to a focus on relationships with other states (Haferkamp 1987).

Elias (1969) argued that industrialisation and nation building should be perceived as two distinct elements of the same transformation connected by the changing distribution of power relations in society and symbolically epitomised in the emergence of mass parties. Earlier Tawney (1921) maintained that western industrial development and nationalism which came to a climax in the period 1870-1914 was just one expression of individualism freed from a central source of communal authority. However, nationalism rather than industrialisation had by far the greater impact on the development of Ireland in the twentieth century (Girvin 1984). In other words, the Absolute Pre-supposition of religion-*nationalism*, remains one of the most important durées in Irish developmental dynamics and Elias (1939) highlighted the pivotal role of a durée to set the agenda for sociological enquiry exhorting researchers to focus on the

> penetrating underlying regularities by which people in a certain society are bound over and over again to particular patterns of conduct. (Elias 1996: 489)

The durability of a three hundred year old tradition of Irish Nationalism marks it out as an especially important force in Irish socio-economic life. As Irish nationalism has been shaped by the interdependency of Ireland and Britain within a colonial context, the importance of this figuration for explaining Irish economic behaviour is now the central focus of this chapter.

Strand 1: The Concept of Irish National Identity within a Colonial Relationship

Nationalism is a consciousness that envisages a sovereign community where members are equal as a nation and the most common type of nationalism is collectivistic-ethnic where community as a unit is combined with inherently genetic characteristics that define membership of the community (Greenwood 2001). National identities form through the power relationships between different states and in the case of England and Ireland, the former's stereotypical view of the latter may in itself have been evidence of an oppressive colonial relationship (Billington, Hockney and Strawbridge 1998). The important point is that during oppression or ethnic and political domination a close relationship between religious commitment and nationalism always develops (Hornsby-Smith and Whelan 1994).

The creation of a homogeneous nation is always the objective of nationalism when the intention is secession or independence from a stronger nation (Hagendoorf and Pepels 2000). Yet the Irish were not a homogenous group because a succession of colonisers from Norman lords, Scots planters and Victorian civil servants gave rise to a number of competing identities such as old Irish, old English, Scotch Irish and Irish Catholic (MacRaild 1999). Yet in the end, Catholics became the only meaningful and distinct Irish race because Catholicism and Irishness were both interlinked with nationalism and meaningful race meant 'bad' to the British (MacRaild 1999).

Nationalism in Ireland meant the restoration of independence to a mother country long under British subjugation and was symbolised in the concept of a republic (Manseragh 1997c) and this new republic could not be dominion in spirit

(Manseragh 1997a). Even when independence eventually arrived it was not a smooth but messy business leading to a civil war, where the Provisional Government simply consisted of

> eight young men in the City Hall standing amidst the ruins of
> one administration, with the foundations of another not yet laid,
> and with wild men screaming through the keyhole. (Fine Gael
> 1997: 7)

When the Republic was eventually declared in 1949 it seceded from the British Commonwealth unlike India who acceded, since the status of republic was tantamount to independence in Ireland whereas in India it was merely incidental to the independence movement (Manseragh 1997).

Rex (1996) described identity not as differentiation of one state and its people from others but more of a semi-sacred emotional attachment or feeling of being part of a nation. He asserted that one of the strongest mechanisms to engender this feeling of belonging was the ideology of nationalism with its attendant moral significance which *superceded class consciousness* and denied the authority of the State to its legitimate monopoly of violence which according to Weber (1968) was *the* mark of a state. Ellis (1991) however highlighted the illusion of past Irish sovereignty and although the Republic of Ireland ascribed to Catholic, Gaelic, nationalist and republican values, Ireland never actually existed as a unitary sovereign state. Because there had been little empirical research on the development of national identity in the Republic, since most research on Irish identity was conducted on Northern Ireland (Devine-Wright and Lyons 1997), it is not surprising that this ideal of recovering former unification had been taken for granted in much nationalist discourse.

Nic Ghiolla Phadraig (1995) argued that Irish Catholicism was deemed a powerful ethnic identity marker because it was nationalist in sentiment. While this ethic marker defined Irishness, the exclusion of some from the community was a necessary pre-requisite for the process of uniting and including the rest (McDevitt 1997). National uniqueness then consisted of invoking an identity based on membership of a particular national community and continuously affirming the ties that the individual had, to that community (Gray 1999). However, Delanty (1996a) maintained that Habermas offered one of the most devastating critiques of nationalism when he pointed out that European integration, supra national military alliances and globalisation made the process of integration at the level of nation state almost irrelevant. However, this very integration of smaller states such as Ireland into the EU, is also a key characteristic figuration of the longer term development of societies (Kilminister 1987).

In their appraisal of Colley's (1992) discussion on the notion of Britishness, McCrone and Kiely (2000) noted the British ambivalence towards Irish national identity. Although the Other was perceived to be the French or Catholicism or both in whatever guise they appeared, Britishness provided a catch all identity for the English, Scots and Welsh, whereas the Irish were never considered to be 'properly' British. According to Murphy (1999) the Irish never really sat neatly into the subject position of the Other allocated to them in English colonial discourse. The reason for this is that ever since the Act of Union in 1800, when Irish Catholics became citizens of Britain, they were discriminated against both economically and culturally and stamped as such, since Irish society represented the most powerful incarnation of the Other and so Irish Catholics were ruled as an internal colony (Hickman 1995). It was to be the most significant and long lasting colonial relationship anywhere in the world where nationalism and Catholicism identified the colonised and by their absence the coloniser (Christopher 1997). Underpinning this colonial relationship was the perceived true characteristic of the British Other, namely the lack of the Protestant Work Ethic, compounded by the belief that the degeneracy of the Irish embodied the absence of a civilising disposition (Hickman 1995). The Victorian image of the Irish equated them with decaying moral values and this provided a persistent stereotype of an *alien* Catholic presence among the British, characterised by poverty, immorality and drunkenness and had the effect of hiding the actual reality of their lived experience (MacRaild 1999).[107]

In relation to the concept of Insider-Outsider and its requisite membership values, Elias and Scotson (1965) described the process initiated by the Insiders of establishing identifiable benchmark attitudes and behaviours deemed characteristic of Outsiders as follows

> [the established]…can often enough induce the outsiders to accept an image of themselves which is modelled on a 'minority of the worst'…can often impose the belief that they are not only inferior in power but inferior by nature. (Elias and Scotson 1965: 159)

Elias and Scotson (1965) explained this power relationship as one group (insiders or established) having the opportunity to exercise power over another group (outsiders) who are totally or partially excluded from opportunity. The monopoly of the insider group is the prime source of their distinction over the outsider group, who themselves require the consent of the insider group to access these power chances. Insider and outsider groups can be only be studied effectively when they are seen in relation to the whole configuration or set of interdependencies in which both groups are situated. Hence the exploration of the British-Irish colonial relationship underlining this analysis.

Murphy (1999) warned that while there may be a powerful statistical argument to affix the term colonial to Ireland based on land transfers through dispossession and domination from the Irish Catholic to the English Protestant in the seventeenth century, it remains different from the colonisation of the New World. London's policy for Irish colonisation was based on assimilation and civilisation of the native population. He noted that unlike the American Indian, the Irish were incorporated as full subjects of the Crown where Gaelic Chiefs were given feudal titles and those who rebelled were tried and executed in London. In contrast, the North

---

[107] We have previously brought attention to this alien status in the writings of Engels.

American colonists not only succeeded in imposing their own culture and administrative structure on the native population like Ireland, the key difference here was that unlike in Ireland, they eventually outnumbered and marginalised them politically and economically (Ellis 1991). A similar pattern of British colonisation in New Zealand, Australia and the West Indies was also different to that in Ireland because these states attained their independence from a mother country whereas in Ireland the majority community sided with a native Gaelic rather than colonial past to *retrieve* a mother country (Ellis 1991). Furthermore Stewart (1998) argued that Irish colonisation outcomes were very far removed from those of Third World colonies of the nineteenth century, as it was not a culture brutally controlled by an outsider but on the contrary, democratic freedoms were very advanced by continental standards.

Nevertheless, attempts to explain economic development in Ireland in the many traditional hypotheses of English commentators exposed a pattern relying on racial and national characteristics, where for example, Ireland's misery in the Famine era was put down almost entirely to character traits within her Celtic identity (De Nie, 1998). Curtis (1995) stated that the 1840s saw the acceptance of popular racialist theories such as physiognomy among the educated British public and this position only re-enforced the perception that the Irish were a distinct alien race who lived and died inside the Union but intellectually, economically and culturally were deemed to exist outside the English pale (De Nie 1998). Furthermore, when the immigrant Irish came into Britain in the nineteenth century they were seen to threaten the body politic there and consequently Irish cultural and social habits and its political traditions were regarded as 'contagious as a virus' (Hickman 1994).

Brabazon and Stock (1999) contended that differences in identity are based on differences that are constructed in history and language. The British used two representations of the Irish from the twelfth to the twentieth century, namely barbarous-violent and inferior-stupid to generate the myth of the superiority of British civilisation but was nothing less than racism of the Other (Hickman 1995).[108] Gaynor (1999) argued that Irish cultural identity was still measured against Britain although now the identities are reversed where the central (Established) and periphery (Outsiders) have exchanged places in the consciousness of both. The fact remains that from the perspective of Irish nationalism, the unequal colonial relationship has generated a long-term traditional pattern of grievance against the English since the middle ages (Keenan 1983).

---

[108] De Valera enunciated the Irish sense of grievance against this racism. The first, in Dáil Éireann in 1921, he justified the Irish right to nationhood where he claimed that 'centuries of brutal and often ruthless injustice, and what is worse, centuries of insolence and insult, have driven the hatred of British rule into the very marrow of the Irish race' (De Valera 1921). The second was shortly after World War Two, when in his reply to Winston Churchill's Victory Speech rebuke on Irish neutrality, De Valera highlighted the unsuccessful efforts of the British to de-civilise the Irish nation 'Could he not find in his heart, the generosity to acknowledge that there is one small nation that stood alone, not for one year or two, but for several hundred years against aggression, endured spoilations, famine, massacres in endless succession, that was clubbed many times into insensibility…a small nation that could never be got to accept defeat and has never surrendered her soul?' (De Valera 1945).

An important point emerges from the above discussion in relation to our main concern, namely the impact of figurations on the development of an economic disposition. The position of Insider-Outsider since Irish independence has now been reversed, with the Irish now being on the inside track where the very characteristic of the minority of the worst set out by the British insiders, namely Catholicism and nationalism has now become transformed into the hallmarks of the new Irish insider group. Given the universal Catholic affiliation of Irish society, a British Protestant industrial disposition would therefore be unlikely to meet acceptable Catholic nationalist membership requirements and become transformed, from an Irish perspective into the chief characteristic that distinguishes the minority of the worst and to be avoided at all costs. A notable example of how this transformation excluded British Protestantism can be seen in the sporting arena. From 1880 to 1910 the Gaelic Athletic Association (GAA) and the Catholic Church were the most powerful organisations in the country and GAA field games were juxtaposed against the sentiment of British colonisers' games based on Protestant elitism and class (McDevitt 1994). The Irish version of Gaelic sports which were dominated by Catholic communalism, enabled 'the strong but dumb Paddy' to demonstrate scientific prowess through selflessness which was regarded as the most commendable action (McDevitt 1994).

While Gaelic football in pre-Great War Ireland reflected ideas of political and national autonomy and rugby the imperial aspirations of the Irish middle classes, association football was rejected outright by Irish nationalists because it lacked nationalist credentials for a variety of reasons (Garnham 2001).[109] In a nutshell, it was a foreign and colonial Outsider badge that failed to pass Catholic-Nationalist membership criteria. While sport provided a vehicle to accentuate the differences between an internal and external culture, the change in the occupational profile of the Irish political ruling class after independence re-aligned the internal institutional framework to complement the Catholic and nationalist world view.

Strand 2: The Emerging Occupational Profile of the Political Class in the Newly Emerging Irish State

Elias (1939) maintained that the moulding of the individual's disposition is dependent on his or her occupation and this moulding initiates change but is then itself subject to this very change process. Although norms are not absolute and are modified as a result of social and cultural developments, Elias and Dunning (1986)

---

[109] McDevitt explains that its main support came from unionist teams in the North of Ireland (supporting union with the UK) and therefore it was linked to an imperial centre London, was associated with the British military where their bands featured at many matches and was played mostly by 'unsavoury' lower ranks. Imported from English 'oppressors', it intrinsically promoted notions of servility and subjugation to an alien power by assisting with the development of an effeminate and unsuitable sport for the manly Irish, because it lacked civilising tendencies due to its highly commercialised and anti-heroic individualised bias.

stated that they provided a permanent key to measuring attitudinal shifts. Norms are what Elias and Scotson (1997) call

> sociological inheritance, the intergenerational transmission of social codes and attitudes. (Elias and Scotson 1997: 72)

Elias (1996) noted that almost all of the structural peculiarities of western societies could be explained in terms of a slow rise of the lower working urban occupations to political power in the form of the professional classes. In the previous chapter the occupational profile and social class of combatants and leaders involved in the state formation process was established. The subsequent change in the profile of the political class over a longer time frame should alert us then to the distinguishing features of Irish social structures and their impact on the Irish economic disposition.

To assist us apply Elias' insight into the rising movement of the urban occupations, four political snapshots were examined covering a period from the eve of Irish state formation to the high point of the Celtic Tiger. We used the occupational profile of Unionist and Sinn Féin MPs elected in the 1918 British General Election, the occupational profile of candidates presenting for the Free State General Election of 1927, a comparison of occupations of those elected in the 1918 British General Election, the 1927 Free State General Election and the 1998 Irish General Election and finally an occupational profile of prominent Irish politicians of the Celtic Tiger.

While the occupational titles used in the first two snapshots are not identical to modern ones they are nevertheless adequate for the purpose of establishing a *distinguishing* pattern of occupational change. Using the first snapshot as a baseline, the expected outcome using the occupational classification of Irish MPs elected in 1918 should indicate as Elias (1972) argued, the beginnings of a move from the dynastic and aristocratic elite towards an urban industrial middle class. We therefore find in the list of occupations of Irish MPs elected in the 1918 British General Election, three aristocrats, two gentlemen and six military occupations.[110] Overall the profile of those elected was predominantly upper middle class since it included the legal profession, writers, journalists, academics, doctors, proprietors and full time politicians. Most noticeable is the fact that working class occupations hardly feature.

A re-classification of the occupations of those elected in 1918 into the modern Irish Social Class Scale was completed following the three-step approach previously used in chapter seven to compress combatant and leadership occupations. As Table 8.1 now reveals, the elected representatives generally belonged to the higher social classes one, two and three and where one farmer only from class four and the absence of even one representative from the lower socio-

---

[110] Tabulated from Election Results *Irish Times 1918*, 5 December 1918, p. 5. According to the Irish Times, the status of sixteen elected Sinn Féin MPs occupationally categorised as unstated, signified that they were on the run, in prison or deported.

economic occupations in class five or class six, only succeeds in consolidating the higher class profile of this particular snapshot.

Table 8.1 Social Class of Irish MPs Elected in the 1918 British General Election

Class	Stratification of Occupations
1	academic, aristocrat, barrister, doctor, engineer, gentleman, magistrate, merchant, solicitor
2	civil servant (senior), foreman, pharmacist, proprietor, publican, teacher, tobacconist
3	city councillor, clerk, commercial traveller, journalist, Sinn Féin activist, union official
4	farmer
5	nil
6	nil

In the second snapshot, the candidate profile for the General Election of the Free State Government in 1927 shows that almost eighty six farmers had political ambitions.[111] This occupation is by far the most numerous, followed by Merchant with twenty four, Unstated with twenty one, Shopkeeper with twenty one, Barrister with nineteen, Union Official with seventeen, then followed by Academic, Doctor/Vet, and Craftworker. The occupations of Union Official and Craftworker are the only labour representatives in the top ten occupations of aspiring candidates. The high number of farmers reflected not only their occupational density in the economy but as Cairn and Richards (1988) point out, they were the group of paramount importance throughout the economic development of the Free State. In contrast, the two largest groups of combatants, the craftsmen and unskilled labourers belonged the industrial sector and accounted for a mere seven and a half per cent of the total number of prospective candidates. This trend would appear to suggest that while the majority of the lower social classes did the actual fighting, the middle and upper classes subsequently moved into position to secure power when hostilities ceased.

The continuing rise of the landed, entrepreneurial and professional classes becomes even more pronounced in the third snapshot which details the profile of successful candidates in the three elections of 1918, 1927 and 1998. Refer to Appendix C for this listing. The transformation in the profile of the top political occupations of farmer, barrister, union official and merchant in the 1927 Dáil, to managing director, teacher, politician, farmer, and barrister in the 1998 Dáil is striking. While the farmer and barrister are prominent in both periods, the union official and merchant have been eliminated and superseded by managing director, teacher and politician. The pattern of the rise to power of certain urban occupations

---

[111] Tabulated from *Irish Times*, 8 June, 1927.

and classes is now seen to be *generally* consistent with Elias' insight except that it is not lower urban but middle and upper-urban occupations that become prominent. Although farmer representation has declined over the period of the snapshots, it still remains at significant levels in the Celtic Tiger even though agriculture is now one of the smallest employment sectors, representing less than ten per cent of the Irish workforce and is inverse to that obtaining at independence. In 1927, the farming representative position was a fair reflection of its leading economic status because those in agricultural employment a year earlier accounted for sixty five per cent of the total workforce (Whelan 1998).

On the other hand the craftworker position inexorably declined reflecting their weak industrial economic status. In the 1920s the declining manufacturing sector accounted for a mere five per cent of total employment (O'Malley 1998) and by 1926, industrial occupations accounted for only ten per cent of employment (Kennedy Giblin and McHugh 1994). The reality in the Celtic Tiger was that the rise of the upper urban occupations continued and if anything became even more pronounced. In the data set for 1998, the demise of the craftworker (zero) and union official (four) are in marked contrast to the rise of the company director (eighteen) and accountant (nine). This represents further political consolidation of the business and professional class and may reflect the importance of the professional service sectors in the modern Irish economy. Only two years before the present Dáil was convened in 1998, the industrial and services sector accounted for almost eighty five per cent of stated occupations in the Irish workforce (FÁS/ESRI 1996). This trend can be observed in Table 8.2 where again we aggregate total of all occupations for those elected in the three elections is again compressed and reclassified using the Irish Social Class Scale.

Table 8.2 Social Class of Elected Representatives by Occupation in the 1918, 1927 and 1998 General Elections

Class	Stratification of Occupations
1	academic, accountant, aristocrat, company director, dentist, doctor, engineer, farmer, gentleman, landowner, lawyer
2	auctioneer, contractor, economist, employer representative, farmer, foreman, merchant, politician, publican, sheep breeder, shopkeeper, teacher, widow
3	civil servant, clerk, county councillor, farmer, farmer's union representative, health care worker, insurance official, journalist, land agent, military, public servant, political organiser, secretary, traveller, union official, writer
4	baker, craftsman, farmer, jeweller
5	agri-labourer, farmer, manual labourer, railway labourer, station-master
6	no occupations listed against unskilled
7	unstated

We then separate the numbers in each of the three general elections into the relevant social class and then calculate the numerical density of each. The results are presented below in Table 8.3.

Table 8.3 Social Class of Elected Representatives as a Percentage of Total Seats in 1918, 1927 and 1998 General Elections

Class	1918 Election (95 seats)	1927 (153 seats)	1998 (166 Seats)
1	28 (30%)	35 (23%)	60 (36%)
2	12 (13%)	42 (27%)	70 (42%)
3	39 (41%)	33 (22%)	25 (15%)
4	0	17 (11%)	6 (3.5%)
5	0	25 (17%)	5 (3.5%)
6	0	0	0
7*	16 (16%)	1	0
TOTAL	95 (100%)	153 (100%)	166 (100%)

* Where this is the number of unstated occupations

The absence of social classes four, five and six in the British General Election of 1918 has been transformed into a profile where approximately one third of those elected to the 1927 Irish Free State Dáil came from these very same classes. However, by 1998 their combined total had decreased to approximately seven per cent of elected members. On the other hand, the combined figures for social classes one and two has increased from fifty per cent in 1927 to approximately eighty per cent in the 1998 Dáil. There is no representative from class six in any of the three elections. Even presuming that all sixteen of the unstated politicians came from the unskilled social class six, it would fail to materially alter the underlying pattern observed in the class profile data.

Moreover, the profile of the most prominent occupations in the present Dáil can now be compared to the general occupational stratification of the modern Irish workforce to see if the elected occupations are representative of the overall stratification of the Irish workforce. For a listing of this occupational breakdown of the Celtic Tiger workforce now see Appendix D. The figures reveal the absence of an elected representative from the largest occupational group in the Celtic Tiger namely, craft/skilled worker. So from a position where they constituted one of the most important occupations to participate in the 1916 Rising and the War of Independence, they did not, unlike their American counterparts, rise into the ranks of the political class. On the other hand, while farmers are proportionately represented, teachers, managers, clerks and the legal profession are over represented. For example, the six thousand strong legal profession holds fifteen seats in the Dáil and while the legal profession and businessmen/women category constitute the smallest workforce occupational categories, they nevertheless hold eighteen of the one hundred and sixty six available parliamentary seats.

The importance of this stratification can be revealed when on the one hand, we learn that fifty per cent of those with leftist economic values (socialism) in the skilled manual class (the craftworker) support the republican and nationalist Fianna Fáil, while only eleven per cent support the Labour Party. On the other, approximately fifty six per cent of the skilled manual class with 'rightest' (capitalist) economic views also support Fianna Fáil while only four per cent support Labour (Hardiman and Whelan 1994). This would suggest that Irish craftworkers/skilled workers, the largest occupational group in the Celtic Tiger workforce, should exhibit a disposition characterised by non socialist, conservative, nationalist and republican sentiments.[112]

Since the evidence from chapter seven also suggests that the second largest occupational category, namely farmer, displays an inherently conservative disposition, we can argue with some confidence that significant sections of the Celtic Tiger workforce still carried a Catholic nationalist and anti-materialist economic disposition. The views expressed by many of the respondents including the farmers and craft workers in our research tends to confirm this and points to regularity of economic behaviour, that is to the presence of a durée.

Furthermore, the rise of teachers, accounting for one third of all serving TDs, is also a feature of this pattern and it therefore not alone places one social structure, namely education at the heart of the political institutions but through education the vast majority of occupations are linked directly to Catholic social teaching and economic objectives. Of course it goes without saying that it also places teachers in a prime position to shape government policy on education and on the economy. For example when the occupational and educational background of a number of prominent politicians from across the spectrum of Celtic Tiger political life is examined, it reveals the religious nature of their second level educational background. No less than eight religious teaching orders can be identified in Table 8.3. The higher class occupational profile of many of these prominent politicians which include the Celtic Tiger Taoiseach, two of his immediate predecessors and the Celtic Tiger Tánaiste can also be observed.

---

[112] This conservative disposition is precisely the one exhibited by workers in Domain C of our study.

Table 8.4 Selection of Senior Cross Party Modern Day Politicians, their Occupational and Educational Profile

Name	Portfolio	Occupation	Education Second Level[a]
Ahern, B.	Taoiseach	Accountant	CBS[b]
Haughey, C.J.	Former Taoiseach	Accountant	CBS
Brennan, S.	Chief Whip	Accountant	CBS
McCreevy, C.	Finance	Accountant	CBS
Ahern, D.	Social Welfare	Solicitor	Marist[c]
Cowen, B.	Health	Solicitor	Cistercians[d]
Fitzgerald, G.	Former Taoiseach	Academic	Jesuits[e]
Geoghegan-Quinn, M.	Retired Minister	Teacher	Mercy[f]
Harney, M.	Tánaiste and Minister for Enterprise Trade and Employment	Politician	Presentation[f]
O'Rourke, M	Public Enterprise	Politician	Loreto[f]

[a] Cairnduff, M. (1991), *The Most Influential 1000*, Hibernian Publishing, Dublin.
[b] CBS (Christian Brothers School) - Teaching Religious Order.
[c] Teaching Priests.
[d] Teaching Monks.
[e] Order of Priests involved in many aspects of Church work including teaching at second and third level.
[f] Teaching Nuns.

As we have already established in the previous chapter that the anti-materialist and charitable ethos of Catholic teaching would have infused in pupils a moderate economic objective of enough, so it now becomes feasible to suggest that Catholic education has had a pivotal role in successfully binding over present patterns of economic behaviour. [113]

Strand 3: Teachers and the Moulding of the Irish Economic Disposition

The value of education for Irish economic development is consistently affirmed by a cross section of the Irish political and academic elites.[114] However, Apple (1990) pointed out that a cosy arrangement usually exists between academics and the ruling class whereby intellectuals provide legitimacy for economic ideologies and these same ideologies then become reflected in the educational curriculum thus providing mutual legitimacy. Nevertheless, teachers are fighting hard against this advance of the business ethos into the school.[115] Moreover they have strong allies since the majority of teachers are subject to clerical-religious boards of management. According to Walshe (1999), the Churches, both Catholic and Protestant, regard the educational process as one that transcends beyond the secular into the spiritual sphere. He alerted us to the philosophy of Sister Eileen Randles, General Secretary of the Catholic Primary School Managers Association, who insisted at a 1996 Belfast conference on Pluralism in Education, that faith was the basis of an individuals outlook in all areas of life and consequently the Church sought through a Catholic education to create a synthesis of faith and culture that would then spill over into economic life.

This is not a new idea. The importance of embedding the religious ethos in the broader curriculum was previously spelt out to teachers in the mid 1960s. In the official Rules for National Schools for pupils aged five to twelve, the primacy of religious instruction over all other school subjects was highlighted and its core objective was to mould a disposition of charity, obedience and passivity in each pupil

> Of all the parts of a school curriculum...Religious Instruction is
> by far the most important, as its subject matter, is God's honour

---

[113] Based also on the revelations from contributors in National Domain A in our research that enough was the primary national economic aim and that it was also the individual economic target stated by the majority of respondents in the other three Domains.

[114] Including Harris (1989), Brennan (1992), Breathnach (1996), Barrett (1997), Breathnach (1997), Fitzgerald (1997), Mitchell (1997), Fitzgerald (1998), Fitzgerald Kearney Morgenroth and Smyth (1999) and the OECD (1999).

[115] This was one of the main institutional relationships identified by the career guidance teachers in our research when they articulated the close link between education and business To give a more recent example, the Chief Executive of Waterford Glass was appointed Chairman of the Waterford Institute of Technology (Irish Independent 11 February 2003). The strengthening of this relationship is seen by the teachers as an attempt to undermine the pastoral and holistic approach traditionally adopted in schools. The teachers also identified the widespread support in Irish society for the pastoral-religious holistic approach as opposed to the vocational one espoused by business and confirmed by the increase in registrations to theirs and other like-minded schools.

and service... the teacher should constantly inculcate the practice of charity. In this way he will fulfil the primary duty of an educator, the moulding to perfect form of his pupil's character, habituating them to observe, in their relations with God, and with their neighbour, the laws of God. (Govt 1965: 38)

Furthermore in the Primary Teachers Handbook, the transmission of *national* attitudes and social habits through the civics and history curriculum was also among the most important aims of Irish education (Govt 1994). Catholicism and nationalism (the Absolute Pre-supposition) are officially at the epicentre of Irish education. Here the Catholic spirit and practice of charity are identified as core *patriotic* sentiments to ensure the continued economic well-being of the nation (Govt 1994).[116] According to Walshe (1999) there was a recent attempt made to remove history as a core subject in the Junior Certificate Curriculum (lower second level cycle) but its status was successfully retrieved in 1999 following action by the History Teachers Association. The importance of national history is that it imparts to individuals a sense of belonging, a feeling of identity and solidarity with the group (Elias 1997). Moreover, these officially sanctioned dispositions which are inculcated by teachers through the religious, history and civics curricula, are unlikely then to dissolve in ones job or in institutional arrangements.[117]

The exposure to a set of Catholic manners was also an important and complementary support to the official position. Elias (1996) drew our attention to the role and power of manners when he asserted that they were more powerful in social control and more effective in inculcating lasting habits than either insults, mockery or threats of violence and were also highly effective in pacifying behaviour. For example, in the book Christian Politeness and Counsels for Youth used in many Irish schools, the ultimate purpose of toning down behaviour from noisy to silent in the sections entitled Table Manners and Recreation only becomes clear when both are linked to the overall spiritual purpose of the third extract Exhortation where pupils are expected to relegate the secular life in favour of the afterlife so that this-worldly trials and tribulations are to be regarded as opportunities to achieve Heaven in the next

> a long continuance of prosperity is often the greatest disaster alike to individuals and empire...still bitter as the bread of misfortune may be there is generally a wholesomeness about it that abundantly compensates its bitterness. (p. 114)

---

[116] For example the research responses in National Domain provided a good example of the infusion of Catholic tenets into political discourse when some acknowledged that Catholic Social Teaching underpins economic policy and national industrial relations.

[117] The Chairman of the Catholic Hierarchy's Education Commission Bishop Thomas Flynn 'was not concerned that the move...(to less Religious in control of schools)...might lead to greater State encroachment on Catholic education since the Church and the Government had recently drawn up an agreement outlining a Deed of Trust which would guarantee the ethos of the Catholic primary school'. See *Irish Times*, 11 January 1999, p. 1.

With this exhortation comes a clear warning that spiritual complacency can easily set in when one becomes wealthy, thus posing a serious threat to achieving the ultimate goal. Its tone is clearly anti-materialistic. Well established guidelines discussed in the previous chapter that were set out by the Papacy to inform individual Catholic economic behaviour would have insisted that loyal Catholics display an anti-materialist *and* a nationalist attitude. Moreover, this link between the Church and the nationalist republican struggle for self-determination has blurred the distinction between loyalty to the nation and loyalty to the Church making them one and the same thing (Williams 1999). Therefore the nub of the foregoing discussion is now fully exposed. The possession of a Protestant work ethic is likely to be regarded as traitorous and inimical to the achievement of an economic goal of moderation within a specifically Catholic socio-economic context. Moreover, a Catholic had already received the 'all clear' conscience wise from the Papacy to fully engage in a fight for Catholic, national and economically moderate ideals.

Strand 4: The Policing of Economic Behaviour

The significance of the role of conscience in comprehending the concrete world still remains undiminished in various world religions and in particular Roman Catholicism (Smith 1999). It is *the* indispensible factor underpinning moral decision making throughout the history of Roman Catholic moral teaching (Smith 1999). Conscience in the Catholic tradition not only has a role of evaluating past actions but determines the course of future action and can therefore be rightly regarded as a tool for constructing behavioural norms on foot of personal perceptions of reality (Hoose 1999). Conscience has therefore the potential to direct or re-align behaviour and should be included in any analysis of the interrelationship between religion and economic development. The importance of conscience is, that it is an inner voice that is listened to, sometimes called the voice of God, that not only makes an individual aware of his or her own guilt but compels subsequent action in a specific direction (Heiddeger 1949).

The Catholic notion of conscience embodies both synderesis and conscience, where the former can be regarded as a natural habitus or disposition that shapes and orientates human behaviour in readiness to act towards good, and the latter is the act itself that applies knowledge of right and wrong to enable the individual to pass a judgement on his or her actions (Smith 1999). Synderesis is an inborn disposition towards good (Leal 1999) and it is this disposition that all of the Catholic respondents displayed in our study through the expression of the Spirit of Charity and where the subsequent economic behaviour to achieve enough was the outcome.

The cause and effect between disposition and action was described by Saint Thomas Aquinas, the foremost official theologian of the Catholic Church, when he described how an individual can know that he or she has a particular disposition by actually exhibiting the correct behaviour so that the new self-knowledge of the presence of the disposition then further consolidates the required activity (Kenny 1994). When this required activity fails to follow a penalty is applied in the form of guilt (Costigane 1999). Because each individual has to account for his actions before God and since mistakes of judgement can occur because of our fallen nature usually described as original sin, a reliance on official teachings is therefore imperative (Costigane 1999).

Consequently, the traditional view is that conformity to Roman Catholic teaching is equivalent to having a good Catholic conscience and the most pre-eminent contemporary Catholic theologian, Haring, has asserted that using an informed conscience implies following the teachings of the Magisterium of the Church (Smith 1999). The Magisterium issues teaching statements on faith and morals and these teachings emphasise and facilitate the creation and exercise of a submissive or *passive* model of conscience (Hoose 1999). The Catholic is therefore religiously organised to display a Catholic economic disposition because by exhibiting the appropriate guiltless behaviour as demanded by the Popes, the approved economic disposition is confirmed and then further consolidated.

However, official teachings have the capacity to transform internalised free commitment to particular values implicit in the exercise of a conscience, into dependency on an external superego, explained in Freudian terms as the ego of another superimposed on an individual's own ego (Hoose 1999). This dependency regulates Catholic conduct by using guilt to compel individuals to conform to the expectations of those who are vital to that individual's development, namely the Pope and Bishops (Hoose 1999). This can explain the conforming force of the papal encyclicals and exhortations in relation to the 'isms' discussed in the previous chapter and the durability of the acceptable economic disposition of enough for Catholics.[118] Therefore conscience is not subjective at all because it becomes subservient to authority (Costigane 1999). Moreover, as conscience is not infallible it becomes the contested arena for making important moral decisions which are then reached following a well defined path of intention, followed by deliberation then by decision and finally by executing that decision (Leal 1999).

Yet, conscience is not just a Catholic notion because other religions have similar rules for adherents to engage with the economic order. For example, the eastern Orthodox view is that conscience is an innate capability to judge good and evil but this capability can be weakened because of our fallen human nature through original sin (Thomas 1999). Thomas (1999) argued that redemption is jeopardised if the individual succumbs to significant potential occasions of sin or bad passions such as the desire to accumulate possessions. Orthodoxy does not know the 'autonomous spirit of Protestantism' where conscience acts to overcome barriers such as material prosperity in order to attain a fuller understanding of and intimacy with God.

In Rabbinic Judaism conscience is perceived as two inclinations, namely the good or Yetzer Hatov and the bad or Yitzer Hara. Each individual is obliged to love God with both inclinations since the Yitzer Hara consists of the very energy that is chiefly responsible, for example, to engage in business to provide for the

---

[118] Hence the remark of one of the contributors in National Domain A that Catholic workers were fortunate to be able to leave ultimate questions to the priest as it allowed them to focus on more profane matters such as work.

family. It is only when that inclination becomes an end in itself does it then become bad (Gorsky 1999). Individual Jews also rely on teachings in exercising their conscience (Gorsky 1999).

Muslim conscience is concerned with discovering and carrying out the Divine Will as revealed in the Qur'an by the Prophet and because the issue of salvation and hell, 'the dreadful penalty' is so important, the individual does not leave room for possible error through subjective decision making (Greaves 1999). In fact the presence of God and of His two angels who draw up a balance sheet of good and evil actions, helps spur on individuals to accumulate pluses in the next life by silently assisting as many as possible in the community in this life, for example, by giving alms or building a mosque or a school. This giving leads to particular social values being internalised which shift the focus from accumulation to active disbursement (Greaves 1999).[119]

An exception is Buddhism which is not a revealed religion and does not consequently recognise a function for conscience because matching individual internal faculties in the absence of an external Higher Authority is absurd (Chryssides 1999). Yet Buddhism like Catholicism and Islam still endeavours to neutralise the cardinal evil of greed using the Buddha as the supreme example of how a balanced approach can be achieved.

So how does Catholic conscience impact on Irish economic behaviour? Broadly speaking we believe that an informed Catholic conscience still relies on Papal teachings. When these teachings support a particular attitude and an approved course of action, such as the moderate economic lifestyle and the Spirit of Charity, then there can be no guilt attached to the behaviour and so the individual is free from penalties. Nevertheless one might have rightly anticipated that, given the history of poor Irish economic development, when a wealth of economic opportunity actually arrived with the Celtic Tiger, it would have proven far too tempting for this moderate disposition and set off a generalized pattern of acquisition and accumulation. But not at all and the nub of the problem is revealed once again since our research findings highlighted the presence of an opposite distributive pattern or durée throughout the mosaic of Irish social life together with a limit placed on this acquisitive impulse.[120] We can now connect the Spirit of Charity, the acceptable enough measure of wealth and appropriate levels of work

---

[119] The Islamic leader in our research experienced difficulty in articulating an *acquisitive* economic vision for Irish Muslims and is similar to the Catholic Spirit of Charity.

[120] Certain forms of wealth accumulated through means other than work constitute a legitimate form of wealth such as the lotto mentioned by over half of the respondents in the research. Even at the national level there is a propensity to regard the EU as just another hugely successful and legitimate course of wealth accumulation for little or no effort where huge sums of 'support funding' accrue on foot of properly integrating into an insider group by observing their rules and regulations. Little wonder then that the Irish nation generally supports its integration into Europe, adopting an *instrumental* approach based on the received cultural tradition of deprivation (McQueen 1998) i.e. the passive and poor mouth begging bowl mentality taking a highly instrumental approach towards its EU integration as a recipient of EU largesse. This status is bound to come under threat as the eastern countries become full members of the EU.

commitment within the configuration of variables influenced by our Absolute Pre-supposition. We also now know that conscience plays a prominent role in policing the limits of acceptable economic behaviour and that the majority of respondents in our study displayed this behaviour.

Strand 5: The Impact of the Civilising Process on the Economic Disposition

The term civilisation is a concept that refers to a wide array of facts such as the level of technology, scientific knowledge, the nature of religion and the manners of western nation states and expresses their self conscious belief in their own superiority over earlier or contemporary primitive societies (Elias 1996). It also implies a more pacified and reasoned approach to interconnecting and competitive relationships such as economic ones. Elias (1996) described the civilising process as a movement towards the eventual supremacy of the secular over the ecclesiastical.[121]

Elias (1996) maintained that the civilising process did not happen through the purposive and rational education of individuals but that by and large it happened unplanned, although it is not without a specific type of order. The autonomous order comes about when an individual's plans compete with the plans of others, thus causing either conflict or integration of activities. The continuous overlapping of these competitive plans and the subsequent unplanned action of individuals is the reason why an apparent contradiction can co-exist with the presence of an underlying process initiating social change and a tendency to preserve social structures.

Although Giddens (1996) noted that Durkheim highlighted the propensity of strongly held religious beliefs to promote a static nature of society by promising a better afterlife, Inglis (1998) argued that Catholicism influenced the Irish personality towards a more civilised disposition. In contrast Connolly (1994) noted that prior to the emergence of the new Free State, it was British Protestantism that was actually the major civilising influence in Ireland.[122] Nevertheless as a necessary part of the civilising process, colonisation was often justified when in fact it was simply land grabbing and expulsion of the indigenous people (Elias 1996). Mennel (1998) identified the violent pre-condition of colonisation, pointing out that Western society had taken for granted that it had already reached the pinnacle of civilisation, implying that only natives of colonised lands required to be civilised and so these peoples underwent in the process of civilization some very serious phases of de-civilisation. Although it remains inappropriate to label behaviours or developmental processes as either civilised or barbarous because they do not lend themselves to easy categorisation (Burkitt 1996), the need to civilise the de-civilised Irish by getting them to adopt a

---

[121] This has not been our experience of examining the development of the Celtic Tiger.

[122] When he noted that the writer William Wilde in 1849 commented that the general tone of Irish society was becoming more Protestant and that even the Catholic priest's customs and manners were following suit.

strong Protestant work ethic to eliminate their inborn laziness, informed the central message of the Quarterly Review as early as 1840.

Despite McLysaght's (1950) warning that biased accounts of Ireland were common because of the misleading generalisations and half truths of gullible tourists, there was sufficient and consistent evidence from a variety of English, French and German travel writers and other non tourists to support the view that a serious phase of de-civilisation had occurred in Ireland as a result of colonisation. We only have to look at the chapter titles in DeLatocnayne's Travel Book on Ireland 1796-1797, to see how they provided a sense of the prevailing conditions of the population.

Chapter	Chapter Title
3	Night in a Poor Cabin - Wexford Ugly and Dirty
4	Wretchedness of the Poor
5	Fighting at a Funeral
6	Misery of Small Cultivators
7	Nakedness of the Poor - Decay of Commerce
14	Religious Differences and Quarrels - Excesses on Both Sides
15	Laziness and Beggary

In Mr. and Mrs. Halls' Tour of Ireland (1825), they noted the absence of a general level of steadiness and sobriety, typical Protestant virtues and instead found that the Irish trusted too much in God and were not sufficiently industrious.[123] Johnson in his Tour of Ireland (1844) found the people to be resigned and totally despondent. Gibbons (1996a) referred to Gustav de Beaumont, who had travelled widely in the Old and New Worlds and maintained in 1839 that the misery of both the chained Negro and savage Indian could not match the poverty of the Irish peasant. A request for assistance by the poor of a parish in Donegal in the Northwest of Ireland through a letter entitled the Facts of Gweedore sent by a local national school teacher Patrick McKye to the Lord Lieutenant of Ireland in 1837 (Estyn-Evans 1992), described a fundamental lack of material well-being in the local community.

> There is about 4,000 persons in the parish and all Catholics, and as poor as I shall describe having among them no more than 1 cart...1 plough...16 harrows...8 saddles...2 pillions...no other school...1 priest...no other resident gentleman...no bonnet...no clock...3 watches...7 table forks...93 chairs...243 stools...no

---

[123] They claimed that this put off liberal political cotton spinning manufacturers from setting up a facility in Ireland.

swine-pigs...no bog...27 geese...3 turkeys...2 feather beds...8
chaff beds...1 national school...no boots...no spurs...no fruit
trees...or any other garden vegetable except for potato and
cabbage...all families sleep together in the bare buff. (Estyn-
Evans 1992: 97-99)

A number of observations can be made regarding the level of civilisation
indicated in this letter. Firstly, the lack of eating utensils, with no eating knives or
spoons and only seven table forks among the whole population, strongly suggests
that the threshold of delicacy had receded to a level lower than that normally
encountered even in the barbarism of war. Elias (1996) pointed out that eating
knives for meals were a common feature of military life even under the most
appalling barbarism of war.

Secondly, sleeping arrangements confirmed that the distance between children
and adults was small since all of the family slept in one room in the bare buff. The
accepted norm in the time of Erasmus as early as 1530 was that children enjoyed
separate sleeping quarters (Elias 1939). Van Kriegen (1997) argued that one of the
crucial factors in the advancement of the civilising process is this very distance in
behaviour and psychical structure between adults and children. These close quarter
sleeping arrangements were apparently quite a common feature of Irish life since
Gibbons (1996a) argued that descriptions of the savage Indian were often couched
in Irish terms remarking of their sleeping habits that they resembled those of the
Irish with six to twenty lying stark naked on the ground in a house.

Thirdly, the level of cuisine could not possibly constitute the art form that
Featherstone (1987) highlighted as another signal of a move to a higher level in the
civilising process.

In actual fact the general condition of the population in the mid-nineteenth
century shocked travellers of all persuasions including English economists, Italian
Nationalists, Communist Internationalists, French nobility, Germans and
Americans (Manseragh 1965). In 1862 a city official described the conditions of
the poor in Dublin as a 'disgrace to modern civilisation' where the shortcomings of
public sanitation compelled citizens to relieve themselves in the main
thoroughfares (Robins 1995). Visitors to Ireland from 1896 to 1909, including the
Chief Secretary of Ireland George Wyndham and the author George Russell (AE),
attested to extreme poverty levels noting that exceptionally high levels of
deprivation were a feature of both rural and urban society (Mulhall 1999).
Endemic poverty also characterised the early developmental years of the Free State
where in the 1930s the deprivation and backwardness of rural Ireland in particular
was exceptional by Western standards (Foster 1988).

Whelan (1995) saw the whole English civilising process as a Protestant
industrial event in the early 1800s and the global imperative of becoming a world
industrial power required the Irish nationalist population to be 'civilised' because
they posed an immediate threat to the economic and political supremacy of the
British Protestant establishment. Native Gaelic structures and institutions had
already existed prior to colonisation and featured a centralised system of control,
an advanced education system operating up to 1660 with strong intellectual

insights, and a system of fosterage or training (O'Curry 1873), all hallmarks of a civilised society. The strength of the English reaction against Ireland's perceived lack of civility, stemmed partly from Protestantism partly from English nationalism, giving rise to the English policy of scorched earth, starvation leading to cannibalism, and theoretical suggestions for transferring the Irish population as a whole to England, a policy that even worried the 'bloodthirsty' Victorian and historian Froude (Foster 1989).

As Arnason (1987) pointed out, one of the most striking and unfortunate features of the civilising insights of Elias was the consistent refusal to examine or even to admit to the influence of specific traditions or combinations of traditions on the long-term dynamics of European history. Van Krieken (1997) pointed out that some critics like Stefan Breuer have remarked that a central problem with Elias' work overall, was that there appeared to be a reluctance to perceive the process of social integration as being also accompanied by processes of social disintegration and decomposition (Van Krieken 1997) and neither had Elias any distinctive interpretation of nationalism as an agent of social change.

In the consciousness of the Irish, the Protestant English 'civilising process' in Ireland could be turned on its head to strengthen the sentiment of nationalist identity. An example can be provided from an extract in a primary school reader used in the Christian Brothers schools in Marino, Dublin, at the end of the nineteenth century. The following excerpt highlights the anti-Catholic rather than the specifically nationalist criteria that emphasised Puritan intentions to extirpate both Catholic Irish *and* Catholic English communities so that even the label of English nationality would not be sufficient to save English Catholics. Again like the poetry of the combatant prisoners discussed in the previous chapter, this also points to a religious frame of reference for social change by force.

Second Period - Ireland and Her English Protestant Rule

AD 1583-AD 1878 - THE REFORMATION

Q.   Who were its leaders?
A.   In Germany the principal leader was Martin Luther, a Saxon Friar. In Switzerland, John Calvin, A Rigid Fanatic, In Scotland, John Knox, An Apostate Monk, and in England, Henry the Eight, a Voluptuous Tyrant.
Q.   Did the Irish People embrace the new doctrines?
A.   No! With the exception of five Bishops, three priests and a few laymen all continued to adhere to the ancient Faith.
Q.   Who were the Puritans?
A.   A set of fanatics who rose to power in England and Scotland in the reign of Charles I.
Q.   Where these threats made by those in authority?

A.   Yes! Lord Clarendon says that the Puritan Leaders 'had sworn to extirpate the whole Irish Nation...the Lord Justices had set their hearts on the extirpation, not only of the mere Irish, but likewise of all the English Families that were Roman Catholic'.

Source: Rev. J.J. Brennan, (1878), *The Catechism of Irish History - Ancient, Mediaeval and Modern*, Kelly Publishers, Barclay St., New York, p. 169 and p. 191.

In this passage the British Protestant authorities' intention to annihilate the Irish people is obvious and so fighting to preserve both Catholicism and a national identity could be easily conceived as an act of patriotism, defending as it did the civilised Irish Insider position. In other words, the undesirable traits of English Protestant civilisation where 'murderous' intent could easily be combined with an overtly greedy economic ethic and therefore could inform the basis of the incarnation of the anti-Catholic 'Other', i.e. the benchmarks to classify the minority of the worst and identify the majority of the best in the minds of the Irish Insiders.

Summary

In this chapter we have explored Elias's concept of Insider and Outsider within the figuration of the Irish and British colonial relationship. The qualifying membership criteria that applied to Irish national identity was also explored. The rise of certain urban occupations to political dominance was indeed consistent with Elias' insight into the nature of the dynamic underlining western development. Nationalist education inculcated a strongly charitable and anti-materialist economic disposition into Irish society and into its leadership.

A Catholic rather than a secular curriculum was a feature of Irish education where the Spirit of Charity featured prominently and where the transmission of these norms through the history, civics and Religious curricula shaped the nature of the Catholic economic disposition. This ethic was also underlined a patriotic disposition.

Manners textbooks also bolstered the prevailing religious orientation of the curriculum by infusing in their pupils expectations of adult economic behaviour based on enough and charity. The role of Catholic conscience to police non-conforming and unpatriotic economic behaviour was also explored.

The perception that exceptional and long-standing levels of poverty in Irish society were due to the English civilising process gave rise to an on-going national and traditional disposition of grievance against England for the lack of enough material well being. This grievance isolated the British and Protestant industrial ethic as one of the chief characteristics of the minority of the worst and thereby precluded it from surviving as part of the ethnic badge in the new Catholic and nationalist Irish state.

Chapter 9

Explaining the Profile using the Insights of Weber, Freud, Durkheim, Parsons and Giddens

> The Church asks not are the people rich but are they good, not are they clever, but are they chaste? Not is the nation powerful...but is it pious? And so when we hear the specious argument advanced...that Catholic countries are poor and Protestant countries are rich ...Catholics are not deceived by the glamour of success and the glitter of wealth...lay up not treasure on earth...what profiteth it a man if he gain the whole world and suffer the loss of his own soul?...these and other evangelical precepts are quite familiar and natural to Catholics. (Graham 1912)

Introduction

The theoretical analysis undertaken in the previous two chapters used contrasting yet complementary paradigms to explain many elements in the profile of the Irish economic disposition. When they were employed in this collaborative manner and featuring a stranding approach, it was then that the Marxist economic relations model and the figurational sociology of Elias increased our *general* understanding of the nature of the configuration of variables impacting on the economic disposition. Until this general understanding was fully explored, the question of whether the Absolute Pre-supposition, namely Catholicism-nationalism, de facto, precluded any rational economic behaviour at individual level remained an open one.

As Marxism underestimated the crucial impact that religion had in shaping economic behaviour and figurational sociology over-looked the central role of Catholicism and nationalism on the formation of the economic disposition, the challenge was now to apply additional complementary contributions that would add a specific focus on the reality of this religious and nationalist force. In this respect we employed insights from five sociologists who had already highlighted the nature of the connectivity between religious beliefs and economic behaviour and in particular their understanding of the level of rational intent underlining both the religious sentiment and the economic behaviour.

The first contribution used the insights of Max Weber because he was a sociologist of the impact of religious beliefs on the development of western capitalism and a theoretician of the nation state (Levy 1998). His insights supporting the central role of the Protestant Ethic and the subservient role of Catholicism in the rapid development of capitalism is explored in light of the emergence of the Celtic Tiger.

This is followed by a second contribution of Freudian insights, arguing that the embodiment of a tradition lies within great men, who then relegate the acquisitive and materialistic source of ideas in favour of the idealistic (Freud 1985). We test this insight in respect of an Irish leader Eamon De Valera and explore his ascetic vision for Irish society and its subsequent impact on the Irish economic disposition.

In the third contribution Durkheim's maintained that society alone shaped individuals dispositions (Morrison 1998) and his observation that suicide rates indicate a level of unhappiness in society that usually increases at the very moment of greatest economic development was also evaluated.[124]

The insights of Talcott Parsons are then used in the fourth contribution to argue that the norms and rules of conduct of a society emanate from religion. Religion regulates or equalises the conflicts and tensions that arise both within the individual and society during economic development. In other words, economic norms follow from religion and reflect a social need to secure and maintain a balanced society.

In the final contribution, we employ Giddens' Structuration Theory to examine the intentional nature of individual action and how the resultant choices of action can have both intended and unintended economic outcomes.

The Insights of Weber

Weber argued that an understanding of the social impact of religion was improved immeasurably if it was treated as an entity attached to both the social and economic process (Eaton 1999). He also argued that the religious factor was crucial to the development of capitalism since most cultures had a common economic infrastructure yet with different religious beliefs (Peters 1999). He also noted that capitalism failed to develop at all in some cultures, such as Islam for example, due to this-worldly accommodation of its doctrine (Peters 1999).

Yet Peters (1999) himself disagreed and argued that Islamic cultures possessed the same elements as those of Protestant Calvinist societies, namely predestination, worldly asceticism, rationalism, frugality and austerity. Therefore, capitalism must have developed due to a variable other than religion. Nevertheless, Weber concluded that religion wielded such significant transformative powers on society independent of a particular economic context mainly because the religious doctrine of predestination was the source of the capitalist mentality, compelling the individual to act as if he or she were already

---

[124] The puzzle was that our own research findings had indicated that all sections of Irish society evaluated their life as happy including most of the homeless and the unemployed.

ordained, thus giving rise to the puritanical and ethical pursuit of gain (Metcalfe 1999).

Weber acknowledged his dislike of rational thinking or the instrumentality prevalent in modern society being applied to values such as belief systems and conscience (Whimster 1998). Nevertheless, he remained accused of misinterpreting the effect of Catholicism on the development of western capitalism opting instead to make the case for the central role of the Protestant Work Ethic (Giddens 1996). Weber's Protestant Work Ethic (PWE) is distinguished by traits of industriousness, individualism, asceticism and the ranking of work as the most worthwhile way to spend one's time, and these traits correlated positively with conservative beliefs (Tang and Tzeng 1991). Yet the research in this thesis has already shown that in the Celtic Tiger, both Catholic and conservative beliefs prevailed and where the ranking of work by the respondents indicated that it was not regarded as the most worthwhile way to spend ones time.   Nor is an industrious disposition held in high esteem.

This particular constellation of Irish variables strongly suggests that the PWE could not have been a key factor in the economic success of the Celtic Tiger. Yet the absence of this particular correlation is not an unusual phenomenon. A meta-analysis of studies measuring the Protestant Work Ethic across thirteen countries, highlighted the contradiction that the richer countries such as the US, UK, New Zealand and Germany were ranked towards the lower end of the PWE scale i.e. seventh, ninth, thirteenth and last respectively, whereas the least industrialised countries like India, Ciskei (part of South Africa), Zimbabwe and Greece were ranked towards the higher end i.e. first, second, third and fourth respectively (Furnham, Bond, Heaven, Hilton, Lobel, Masters, Payne, Rajamanikam, Stacey, Van Daalen 1991). The study concluded that there appeared to be a correlation between strong PWE beliefs in societies that value collectivism over individualism. However, Niles (1999) maintained that many modern studies of the PWE tended to focus on a very narrow band of benchmarks, from a commitment to hard work to individualism whereas Weber's definition also included morality, willingness to defer self-gratification and asceticism. As a result most religions and cultures can easily demonstrate a work ethic close to the narrower definition of the PWE.

However, before the Reformation and the PWE there was another and different Christian approach to work. Pre-reformation Christian thought regarded work as a punishment where the accumulation of wealth was frowned upon and Divine Law insisted that the wealthy should give their excess wealth to charity (Hill 1996). Following from the Greco-Roman aversion to work the Judeo Christian culture then viewed work as having no intrinsic value at all and where contemplative work was the ideal and manual work the least acceptable because its main function was to meet the physical needs of one's family and to avoid idleness, long regarded as the source of sin (Hill 1996). This contrasted with the post

Reformation Protestant Work Ethic (PWE), which held that all types of labour had equal spiritual dignity, including manual labour.[125]

Consequently, there are two work ethics, the well known PWE and the much older but rarely articulated Catholic Work Ethic (CWE). The CWE is fundamentally different in that work is regarded as instrumental rather than transcendental i.e. where the emphasis is on work as a means to do more important things in this life (Tropman 1992). Moreover, in mature capitalist countries it can become even more influential than the PWE.[126] This echoes many of the enough measurements outlined by the majority of respondents in our research.

Weber (1930) also acknowledged that the propensity to earn just enough to live at that level to which the individual was accustomed, was naturally present in individuals and he regarded it as the greatest obstacle to the promotion of capitalist efficiency. Yet the Celtic Tiger economy with its target of enough was characterised by precisely this crucial inefficiency even where strong growth and high productivity became a consistent feature of the economic analyses presented in the early chapters of the study. The limitation of work as the most useful activity continuously surfaced in the individual contributions across the Domains and was consistently expressed in the Catholic worldview.

Given the paradox that Irish Catholicism was set against the rational and wealth seeking ethos of capitalism it was nevertheless, one of the most successful of the global Christian denominations to provide stability in a changing world for societies feeling a sense of alienation, although it generated the appearance of individuals being in but not of the industrialising process (Fahey 1995). Kalberg (1998) argued that the very same stability in relation to American democracy that Tocqueville ascribed to religion, was crucial in providing counterbalances of absolute fixed principles against a feature of capitalist development, namely indeterminate and apparently uncontrolled change. In other words, religion provided a stable counterbalance rather than acting in a subservient support to capitalism.[127] Weber (1999) maintained in his study 'Catholic Economic Life' that individuals frequently felt a deep sense of unease about economic life because

---

[125] Weber noted that Luther used the German word 'Beruf' to identify a significant change from the Catholic understanding of a calling. Luther understood the highest morality that an individual could attain was by fulfilling his duty in worldly affairs as it was the visible sign of brotherly love and was the only way to meet God's law because it was always the will of God to fulfil worldly duties. Therefore all callings were of equal value. In contrast, there are different degrees of calling in the Catholic Church, where for example, the religious and clerical vocation is more worthy than marriage, where the professions are higher than craft and farming.

[126] Novac maintains that Catholics have always had a moral imperative to actively engage and support the capitalist system as it provides the means to assist in the creation of a better world. He argues that being a capitalist is a Catholic's true vocation. However, we have shown from our research that the capitalist engagement is not the primary concern of Catholics and Weber's insight is still valid. Novak, M. (1993), *The Catholic Ethic and the Spirit of Capitalism*, Free Press.

[127] The very point highlighted in chapter four by the Taoiseach in his address to the Catholic Bishops of Ireland.

the Christian ideal of charity worked against the development of the rational business spirit. In 'Religions - the Jews, Catholic and Puritan', Weber (1999) pointed out that Catholics were dis-inclined to economic acquisition since it conflicted with Papal injunctions. Given our research findings this observation is only partially true, since the acquisitive impulse is quite strong but only to the point when enough is achieved. He also maintained that both Judaism and Puritanism were fundamentally different from Catholicism. The Jewish perspective regarded success in economics as not having done anything wrong in the sight of God whereas the Puritan

> and this is the crucial point, religiosity was demonstrated through absolutely reliable business relationships with everyone. (Weber 1999: K.1.d)

Both of these religions are almost non existent in Irish society and as Weber (1999) argued, Catholics were in any event preoccupied with a series of religious injunctions to ensure salvation and as a consequence the decisive outcome for them was indifference to the world.

Again this contrasts with the findings of the research where the Spirit of Charity co-existed with a strong focus on experiencing this world. From our own study, it is also apparent that the experience was governed by an instrumentalist focus that regards work as a means to an end. The priority is to secure both material and spiritual well-being and where a tailored measure of enough is likely to achieve that objective. The initial effort expended on achieving enough gives all the appearance of a PWE. However, when it is achieved, a weaker effort clicks in to maintain enough when the focus then switches to experiencing and enjoying life. This contrasts sharply with the directive of Calvin that one should not seek easy living but strive continuously to achieve maximum returns on work (Hill 1996).

Yet it would be unfortunate if the impression was given that wealth and Catholicism naturally repelled each other. On the contrary, both were surprisingly common features of everyday Irish life in the late nineteenth and early twentieth centuries, an observation that cast serious doubt on the taken for granted fact of the anti-industrial disposition the Irish (Kenny 1997). Moreover, the central role of the PWE as *the* underlying dynamic of capitalist development has continued to be problematical. One of the reasons is that the systematic self-control required by Calvin to limit worldly outcomes which was the basis of the Weber argument, functioned on the premise that Protestantism predated the entrepreneurial spirit (Bernstein 1997). This very pre-dating claim needs to be clarified because Von Kreitor (1999) noted that Sombart identified Judaism rather than Protestantism as the driving force behind the development of capitalism

> the Jewish ethic and Jewish psychology had uncanny parallels to the spirit of capitalism...[where]...all qualities are dissolved through purely quantitative exchange values. (Von Kreitor 1999: 3)

Moreover, as the business class already displayed a strong work ethic and an intense rationality built up over three hundred years, all Calvinism did was to validate their lives by re-enforcing their existing work ethic (Bernstein 1997). Around the year 1100, Italian mercatores (merchants) in Latin Christendom elevated money as a prime investment tool that could, with some risks attached, realise greater profits and therefore Duby (1974) argued

> let us have no hesitation in describing such an attitude as 'capitalist'. (Duby 1974: 261)

By the year 1200, both merchants and craftworkers in the cities of southern France and Northern Italy had already developed a strong sense of calling and an intense rationality out of a twin need to reconcile their pious asceticism while avoiding poverty (Cantor 1993).

Later and still well in advance of the Reformation capitalism and the market economy flourished in thirteenth century England (Cinnirella 2000). On mainland Europe, the Knights Templars were so adept at accumulating and using capital profitably, that they became the greatest bankers in Europe so that by the mid thirteenth century they were distinguished by their *ascetic* dedication to banking in the service of God and so they constituted a documented example of a direct link between Pre-Reformation Latin Christendom and the rise of capitalism (Cantor 1993). Their asceticism was striking because by taking the vow of chastity they were able to channel all their energies into work (Duby 1983).

By the sixteenth century, the emergence of capitalism had coincided with the proliferation of luxury retail stores and the competitive approach that they were then compelled to adopt in the marketplace (Sombart 1967). Furthermore, the spirit of capitalism manifested in the emergence of the specific relationship between capital and wage labour was also evident as early as the sixteenth century and this was well over two hundred years before the industrial revolution (Dobb 1958).

Not only can sixteenth century Pre-Reformation clothing merchants in England be considered nouveau riche capitalists fighting against labour demands but also devout Catholics who practised works of charity for the salvation of their souls (Power 1986). Because the first great capitalist upsurges occurred in Pre-Reformation Europe making economic development independent of the impact of Protestantism, Weber's thesis that a direct causal relationship existed between the Protestant-Calvinist ethic and the development of capitalism, is incorrect (Eisenstadt 1969). However, Greenwood (2002) argues that even if Weber's claim about Calvinism was wrong, it was 'only a minor point' as his main contribution was that he identified two crucial influences on the emergence of the modern economy, namely a new set of motivations and ethics and the way all work was transformed into a calling. The results of our research indicate that a high performing economy can emerge with an economic ethic that self-limits the acquisitive impulse and that utilizes work as a facilitation to rather than an out and out calling to support global capitalism.

Moreover, Kwang-Kuo (1995) contended that Weber, in his assessment of the impact of Confucianism on the individual's economic disposition, also incorrectly concluded that Confucian thought and ethics impeded the individual's ability to apply rational calculation to maximise profits. Because the Confusian 'rendao' or (way of humanity) was overlooked, Weber missed the significance of individuals working hard to acquire various social resources to satisfy the need of family members rather than as a private accumulation of wealth. This is the drive that has been responsible for the economic transformation of the East Asian countries after 1945 (Hwang-Kuo1995).

The drive also endowed intellectuals with a mission to benefit society and the state with DAO (way), so that they studied hard in the west and returned to use the technology of production previously imported from the west, to pursue wealth for their own families. In other words, there was a significant level of instrumentalism also in-built into their approach to work, which like Catholicism and Islam was also directed primarily towards the benefit of the community rather than the individual and yet it generated remarkable economic growth.

Nonetheless, the Catholic theologian Kung (1999) supported Weber's interpretation of the PWE, pointing out that the patriarchal and centralist structure of the Catholic Church and its close alignment with the nobility contrasted with the corporatist and federalist structure of Calvinism which made it (Calvinism) more amenable to capitalism. However, Schuck (1991) argued that the Popes actually favoured the development of a balanced entrepreneurial spirit most notably in the area of capital formation and the investment of excess income both of which were strongly recommended as virtuous economic activities.

There is been a longstanding tradition about the balanced message of Catholicism regarding wealth accumulation. In fact the economic position of Catholicism was enunciated as far back as the Council of Paris in 829, which held that commerce was not intrinsically bad, that no social stigma was attached to any merchant who acquired immense wealth by charging a just price, namely the market value as determined by supply and demand and this is contrary to what many commonly believed was the official Pre-Reformation Christian view on commerce and riches (Riché 1978).

Local clergy probably best captured the essence of the Catholic economic argument in Ireland. For example Hauville (1878) contended that capitalism and Irish Catholicism could flourish together but the reason that Catholic Ireland was not prosperous rested with the British government who compelled small landowners to subdivide their property unlike their British counterparts and was calculated

> to impoverish the Catholic population. Catholic nations are quite as well informed as others (Protestant) on the importance of capital and the value of labour but they possess an admirable intermediary between these two sources of riches...the Church. (De Hauville 1878: 282)

Fr. Graham (1912) later argued for the existence of two forms of prosperity, namely the social and material and the religious and moral, insisting that very wealthy Protestant nations such as Britain were only *materially* prosperous whereas 'poor' Ireland possessed high levels of *moral* prosperity. He also stated that Catholicism did not permit individual Catholics to exclusively focus on business and therefore it was obvious that Protestant Britain could subsequently excel in commerce but fail in morality, whereas Ireland perfectly illustrated the close connection between moral wealth and material poverty. This latter connection was also a recurring theme in the responses of contributors in Domains A, C and D of our research.

Then Fr. Bampton S.J. argued in Westminster Cathedral in the early 1920s that wealth achieved in business was acceptable provided that workers also shared in the profits. At the time Catholics were so enthusiastic in amassing so-called industrial wealth that the Catholic Social Guild of Oxford (1929) found it necessary to remind Catholic industrialists, to *consider* share holding by employees in their capitalist enterprises as a means of redistributing wealth.

Father Kevin Quinn (1958) Professor of Sociology at the Pontifical Gregorian University Rome delivered a sermon in the Jesuit controlled Catholic Workers' College in Dublin, where he stated that the Church's choice was for capitalism because of the fundamental perversities of Communism as revealed by Pope Pius XII. Later, the Catholic Bishop of Muenster Rt. Reverend Joseph Hoffner (1962) included economic activity within the Catholic Seven Fold Significance of Work Topology admittedly in the position of least importance behind the intellectual work of priests, educators, teachers, artists, the ancillary work of doctors nurses, and the regulatory work of politicians, the judiciary and the military.

The balanced approach is also a feature of another salvation religion, Islam. The responses of the Islamic leader in our study indicated that Muslims are concerned with achieving material and spiritual well-being through a balanced approach to economic development. Here the emphasis is to secure the Heavenly paradise through charitable works. However, Weber (1999) also argued that because of its primarily feudal economic ethos, where wealth, power and honour were esteemed in the here and now in anticipation of the soldiers sensual paradise in the next life, it made Islam antithetical towards a methodical conduct of life. Therefore the key difference that enabled rational capitalism to develop in the west and not in the Islamic world, was that the God of Islam only required the performance of the five pillars of Islam and consequently Islam could not transform the spirit of traditional economic life (Huff and Schlucter 1999).[128]

On the other hand, the Calvinist doctrine of predestination, namely a predetermined outcome in the next life requiring a sign in this one, gave rise to a tension that was based on a fear of a misspent life which then necessitated a life of sobriety and hard work (Huff and Schlucter 1999). The key differences based on a summary of Webers' insights into the nature, orientation and conditioning to this

---

[128] These are Faith-kalma, Prayer-namaz, Fasting-roza, Almsgiving-zakat and Pilgrimage-hajj. By fulfilling obligations in relation to these precepts, paradise would then be assured.

world evoked in individuals by the strength of their religious beliefs is provided in Table 9.1 below.

Table 9.1 Summary of Weber's Insights into the Effects of Four Early Religions on the Formation of This-Worldly Dispositions

Religious Idea	Early Judaism	Early Christianity	Early Islam	Early Calvinism
Mean and Paths to Salvation	Rituals No Magic	Otherworldly Asceticism (Faith) Sacramental Magic	No Asceticism Faith Indifference to the World	This Worldly Asceticism Faith
Religious Ethic	Legal Ethic	Ethic of Love	Legal Ethic	Ethic of Duty
Religiously Conditioned relationship to the World	Indifference	Indifference Transcendence	World mastery World Adjustment	World Mastery
Religious Ideal of Life	Intellectual Scriptural Scholar	Virtuoso of Faith	Hero (War)	Professional Man of Expertise

Source: Schlucter, W. (1999), 'Hindrances to Modernity: Max Weber on Islam' Toby Huff and Wolfgang Schluchter (eds.), *Max Weber and Islam*, Transaction Publishers, New Brunswick, USA, Paper 1, pp. 114-116.

Here the ethic of love or the Spirit of Charity for Catholics can be contrasted with the ethic of duty for Calvinists and the legal ethic for Muslims. The religiously conditioned relationship to this world for the Catholic is indifference to it, whereas for the Calvinist it is mastery of it. Yet we know from the responses in the research that Catholics are not indifferent to this world as they actively seek out enjoyment and experience of it. In fact they actually trade off higher levels of wealth to do so. Despite evidence of this trade off in the Celtic Tiger, Weber (1930) stated that Catholicism is always in constant tension with economic rationalism, one of the foundations of the capitalistic ethos so that Catholicism remains inimical to capitalism and hard work.

We know from our discussions in chapter seven on Marxism, in chapter eight on Figurational Sociology and from our own research findings, that it is not now appropriate to hold that Catholicism is inimical to capitalism. Rather, it conditionally mimics the spirit of capitalism and up to a point exhibits a very strong work ethic. In fact one could maintain that some of the respondents in our research initially exhibited the characteristics of a Protestant work ethic, until they had achieved their work related efficiency targets or their personal material goals.

Let us now re-examine the Catholic work ethic, identified by some commentators in chapter one of our study as still being problematic for Irish economic development during the Celtic Tiger. The myth of the lazy Irish Catholic work ethic is hard to dislodge and is again supported in a recent study where Blackburn (1997) contrasted the existence of the low occupational status and the spendthrift approach of Irish workers against the general dominance of Protestants in manufacturing and business sectors in Australia at the end of the nineteenth century. Yet an in-depth examination of Fitzpatrick's (1994) publication of letters to Australian emigrants from their families back *in* Ireland at roughly the same period covered by Blackburn's studies, reveals that both Catholic *and* Protestant families exhorted their relatives to apply the same economic behaviours, namely, sobriety, industriousness and honesty. These are the very values associated with the PWE (Weber 1930).

Evidence of the industrious Irish work ethic in Ireland, comes from none other than British Army Officers coordinating the Ordinance Survey in Co. Donegal in the north west region of Ireland in 1835-1836 as they collated numerous reports referring to the *industrious* disposition of the indigenous population (O'Day and McWilliams 1997). Hickman (1995) noted that even British employers in the mid nineteenth century, had to concede that the Irish had the capacity for long gruelling work for low pay.

The reason for the apparent contradiction in the lazy work ethic of Irish Catholics working in Ireland with those working abroad was revealed as early as 1850 when Joseph Kay of Cambridge University was appointed by the Senate of the university to travel through Western Europe to compare the social conditions of the poorer classes and establish their causes. The Dublin Review (1850) recorded that he uncovered a sense of sheer futility in Irish peasants because all their hard work brought little benefit to them while it kept the landlord very wealthy. Kay (1850) highlighted the formidable Irish work ethic that developed particularly in America and England where chances of wealth accumulation were much higher than in Ireland. This suggests that the local Irish environment worked against the development of an industrious disposition and of course this environment was fundamentally a colonial one.

If we accept Nafissi's (1998) argument that due to his sole reliance on an exclusively religious frame of reference, Weber then failed to take account of the role of colonialism and imperialism in the industrial development of colonised nations, then a more acute problem now arises. Given that the deliberate laziness of Irish workers in Ireland where it existed, was due to exceptionally low returns for their hard work within a colonised context, it seemed plausible enough that they would weaken their work effort at every opportunity. However, in the transformed economy of the Celtic Tiger where very high and favourable levels of return on labour were on offer it now appeared equally plausible that a strong acquisitive ethic such as that associated with the Protestant one would emerge. Yet on the contrary we now know from our study that almost all respondents displayed the Spirit of Charity and that both Tiger executives in Domain B and workers in Domain C *consciously* reduced their effort from the high level required to maximise returns to a lower one required to maintain customary levels of well-being. In order to address the idea that an individual may consciously reduce the work effort when its exertion is likely to produce rich dividends we now turn to the insights of Freud.

The Insights of Freud

Psychoanalysis is the study of conscious and unconscious mental forces of the mind where the unconscious aspect is regarded as being separate to and in conflict with the more social force of the conscious will, because this latter force is derived from primal desires and wishes (Strachey 1985). Cooper (1996) pointed out that the term psychoanalysis meant the examination of the soul, where the term soul is not used in the religious sense but as a label for the source of personal and communal morality in a post religious society. However, bad translations of Freud have left his writings abstract, highly theoretical and scientific and

> attempt to lure the reader into developing a scientific attitude
> towards man and his actions, a scientific understanding of the
> unconscious… [and this]…subverts Freud's intentions. (Cooper
> 1996: 70)

In other words, psychoanalysis should not be employed in a purely empirical manner but as an aid to understanding consciousness. Nevertheless, Oakley (1990) remained highly sceptical of the static and conservative 'ragbag' of Freud's ideas on psycho-analysis because they provided legitimacy for the accepted subservient role of women in western society. This subservience as we know from Leacocks (1986) argument in chapter one, drew upon the racialist inference that achieving western standards of skill and knowledge would successfully address the core problem of economic development in all societies.

Freud (1985) identified the dual source of attitudes and beliefs by pointing out that some are derived from the reality of life surrounding the individual while others lie much deeper and emanate from hidden sources usually of a sexual origin. Determining whether beliefs and attitudes are nature based or intellectual (free will) as Kenny (1994) argued or alternatively a learned behavioural function (connectionist theory) as Hill (1990) argued, remains difficult to determine. Yet the fact that these conscious and unconscious forces do exist indicates that they have the potential, at least, to impact directly on the economic disposition.

One of the most basic attitudes and values of a society is its code of morality and sexual morality in particular. According to Whelan (1994), strong traditional conservative values against divorce, abortion and sexual freedom are evident in Irish society yet paradoxically they co-exist alongside a high birth rate outside of marriage (twenty per cent), making it hard to establish if Ireland conforms to any orthodox notion of modernity at all. While Whelan and Fahey (1994) noted that sexual activity within marriage only was breaking down, Connell (1968) argued that Irish peasant society *reacquired* a trait towards longer and life-long celibacy from the early 1800s up to the late 1950s because of economic necessity and self-interest. In fact the majority of people, cottiers and labourers, always married early and that tendency to late marriage and celibacy of an extreme nature by European standards had occurred within a hundred years after the Great Famine (Inglis 1998). From the middle of the nineteenth until well into the twentieth century Catholic Ireland showed evidence of sexual control rather than sexual asceticism (Akenson 1991).

The important point is that sexual behaviour more often that not lays down the pattern for other modes of engagement including the economic (Freud 1991a). The economic consequence of enforced celibacy is that it promotes hoarding which is a behaviour *inimical* to the capitalist requirement to re-invest wealth (Sombart 1967). Furthermore, by foregoing sexual activity (abstinence) either through sublimation (to please God and be saved), or by displacement (to get more land), or by its restrictive use in marriage for procreation purposes, a society devoid of energy, self reliance, original thinkers and reformers is then created and replaced with weaklings and followers all too willing take their cue from a strong individual (Freud 1991a). Moreover, this passivity is passed on to each generation (Freud 1991a) and therefore it is highly probably that each Irish generation would, almost by default, possess this weak economic spirit.

Freud (1991b) also noted that norm or group consciousness is characterised by members being very credulous with little critical thinking and by not being open to reason or argument. Thus, ties with a religious or political leader were far more important than ties with other members of the group (Freud 1991c). Empathy underpins the bond with the leader (Freud 1991d) making it impossible therefore, to understand the nature of the group without recourse to defining the nature of its leader (Freud 1991e). The key now to deepening our understanding of how group dynamics impacts on the individuals economic disposition lies in grounding the abstraction of leadership in an individual such as Eamon De Valera.[129]

De Valera was among the world's great men, symbolising twentieth century nationalism rather than internationalism where his very being was almost exclusively focussed on his Catholicism, his romantic Gaelic ideals and with little or no interest in socio-economic matters (Manseragh 1997d). According to Lenski (1966), great men unduly influence culture and social organisation particularly in advanced horticultural and agricultural societies. From the data provided in chapter two, Ireland had traditionally been economically dependent on agriculture for its main source of employment and national wealth. From the analyses in chapters seven and eight, the economic and religious conservatism of the revolutionary leadership that included De Valera was also revealed.

---

[129] A reminder that he was a Founder Member of Fianna Fáil and Head of the Treaty negotiations with Britain's Prime Minister Lloyd George. Served three terms as Taoiseach 1932-1948, then 1951-1954 and finally 1957-1959. Then served two seven-year terms as President of Ireland from 1959 to 1973.

Furthermore, he also provides a link between the revolutionary leadership and the rise of the urban classes to political prominence as noted by Elias in chapter eight. De Valera cannot however be classified as a charismatic leader. The reason, is that a person with charisma is defined by Weber as a leader who works *against* the traditional social order (Parsons 1968a).[130] Nevertheless, his vision of a balanced industrial society highlighted the superior standing of religion over economic matters and was not per se an outright rejection of industrialism

> The Ireland which we dreamed of would be the home of a people
> who were satisfied with frugal comfort, and devoted their leisure
> to the things of the spirit, a land whose countryside would be
> bright with cosy homesteads, whose fields and villages would be
> joyous with the sounds of industry. It would, in a word, be the
> home of a people living the life that God desires that man should
> live. (De Valera 1943)

It is obvious that De Valera was not anti-industry as he approved of its joyous sounds mainly because it had the instrumental capacity to contribute to a balanced life of material self-sufficiency and allow spirituality to flourish.[131] Boyce (1996) confirmed the subservient role assigned by De Valera to the economic order on the Fiftieth Anniversary of the 1916 Rising. The achievement of his vision was meant to relieve pressure for material needs in order to advance the intellectual and spiritual well-being of Irish society. The target of enough wealth to allow Irish society achieve this balance is barely disguised.

On the other hand, Hornsby-Smith (1992) argued that De Valera's vision merely reflected the strong Catholic suspicion of industrial capitalism and the materialism that followed it. As the Church was fearful of the industrial city, She glorified the family farm and the village as the bedrock of social and economic life (Fahey 1994). The moulding of this anti-materialist disposition by De Valera, was aided by a concerted effort of politicians, historians, journalists, teachers and in rural areas by shop assistants (Goldring 1993). Again many respondents in our study regarded work in the same way as De Valera did, namely to achieve other more preferable non-economic objectives. Moreover, trying to compel individuals to work against their will has had a number of profound anti-capitalistic consequences. For example, it has only succeeded in turning the slave against work (DuBois 1899), forced the conditioning of human conduct towards obedience as a requirement for industrialisation (Weber 1918), caused the manipulation of

---

[130] The economic developmental debates pursued in chapter four clearly indicated that the conservative economic order barely changed during the formation and early development of the state.

[131] This capacity is also reflected in many of the contributions in our own study. The direction of subservience always favours 'other worldly' imperatives and in this respect Weber was correct. The resultant nature of the economic disposition and the subsequent impact on the dynamic of development is where we diverge.

the masses first by production then by consumption (Baudrilliard 1988) and fractured the process of socialisation needed for belonging (Fromm 1962).

But because subjugated peoples have a strong emotional attachment to their masters (Freud 1991f), substantial force is required to fracture it. On many occasions the individual compensates for the opposite true feeling by the process of displacement or substitution of impulses (Freud 1985a). This repressive force is sometimes called conscience

> whereby Faith becomes the enemy of the intellect and is the basis of what commentators call irrational behaviour. (Freud 1985b: 365)

Yet paradoxically the role of conscience as outlined by some Catholic respondents in the research can lead to highly industrious economic behaviour while also holding the Spirit of Charity and the measure of enough as paramount moral and economic objectives in this life. Because faith development is based on the hypotheses expressed by Freud that man cannot live a meaningless life, it permits meaning to be determined and maintained (Fowler 1996). Because a direct translation from thought to word is impossible (Vygotsky 1979) and as thought can only be represented in speech (Derrida 1997), the type of language an individual speaks can determine his or her thought processes (Garnham and Oakhill 1994). As words play a central part in the historical growth of consciousness (Vygotsky 1979) and this is the important point, the repeated use of the terms enough and charity in the research findings must therefore represent the conscious economic thoughts of the individual's Catholic faith. Moreover conscious religious forces compel the sublimation of unconscious material or profane ones. Because the channelling of instincts into constructive social behaviour (sublimation) forms the basis of culture and civilisation (Muuss 1996), then the Irish economic disposition channels the acquisitive impulse towards the opposing charitable ethic and is culturally manifested in the measure of enough. In other words the Absolute Pre-supposition Catholicism-nationalism gives the Irish economic disposition its rational, balanced and sacred imprint.

The Insights of Durkheim

According to Durkheim (1964) work is a profane activity and cannot co-exist with the religious life in the same place or at the same time. He conceded that the contagiousness of religion is bound to affect the profane world i.e. would have a marked influence on the individual's engagement with work. Individuals have two mutually exclusive forms of life, one toward the ego the other towards society, so that two distinct conscious states of mind direct individual behaviour towards the profane or the sacred (Durkheim 1964). Therefore, no economic system is devoid of sacred consciousness only by degrees of secularisation. Because the data presented in chapter one and the themes emerging from the research responses indicated that the level of secularisation in Ireland still remained low by European standards even if higher than previous years, then we can assume that a relatively high degree of sacred consciousness was a key feature of the Celtic Tiger economy.

Durkheim (1964) contended that each individual remained subject to the sacred and these religious and social sentiments were conditioned by education. In chapters seven and eight we have examined how education shaped the economic disposition and through it how an instrumental work ethic and an anti-materialist moderate and charitable ethos was imprinted on each pupil. Just like many of our respondents, everyday economic behaviour was consciously and unconsciously shaped by their faith and conscience.

Since the key to every salvation religion is belief in salvation by faith and because this faith is anything but illusory (Durkheim 1964) then two existences are simultaneously lived by each individual i.e. one governed by matter, the other by impersonal reason (Durkheim 1964). Because religion is in society's image, the ideal religious society is also part of the real society (Durkheim 1964). Therefore, each individual must embody both real and ideal reflections of that society at any particular moment. When the prevailing economic conditions then presents Irish society with inordinate acquisitive opportunities i.e. the Celtic Tiger, tension is bound to arise in balancing the profane and sacred needs of the individual. The results of this tension emerge in higher levels of unhappiness and become manifest in the increasing suicide rate.

Unhappiness levels increase during periods of high economic activity because the previously secure level of well-being or enough is breached

> people perform reasonably well as engines of necessity, they may
> face deep psychological and spiritual crises as they are relieved of
> this necessity and achieve an even more plentiful material state.
> (Marshall, Brigg and King 1984: 654)

Because suicide is linked to the social environment it increases with the development of the division of labour indicating that the general level of unhappiness is also increasing (Durkheim 1984). Yet suicide is symptomatic not of economic but of moral poverty (Bellah 1973). Therefore the causes of suicide must be found in society rather than in the individual. Because social facts are the collective beliefs of the group, suicide as a social fact expresses the unhappiness level in the group mind (Durkheim 1982).

Now in chapter four, we saw how all the economic benchmarks indicated that Irish society had moved from the threshold of necessity in a sudden and accidental fashion i.e. Irish society was totally unprepared to address the profound transformation in the actual and potential levels of material well-being on offer. Given this lack of preparedness, tension was bound to arise and Irish suicide rates displayed a marked increase at this very juncture on Irish economic development. Whereas a general pattern of increasing suicide levels is recorded for the five phases of economic development during the period 1971-1999, the highest level of group unhappiness emerged during the fifth Celtic Tiger phase. The data in the table below captures this longer term rising pattern.

Table 9.2 Suicide Figures in the Republic of Ireland 1971-2001

Year	Number	Variation	Year	Number	Variation
1971[a]	81	-	1997	345	38
1972	90	9	1988	266	21
1973	105	15	1989	278	12
1974	118	13	1990	334	56
1975	148	30	1991	346	12
1976	183	35	1992	363	17
1977	151	-32	1993	361	-2
1978	163	12	1994	353	-8
1979	193	30	1995[a]	383	30
1980	216	23	1996[b]	380	-3
1981	223	7	1997[c]	433	50
1982	241	18	1998[c]	500	68
1983	282	41	1999[d]	439	-61
1984	232	-50	2000[e]	413	-26
1985	276	44	2001[e]	448	35
1986	283	7			

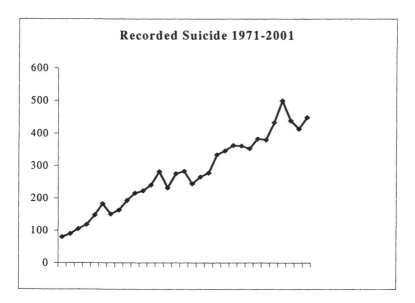

[a] For period 1971-1995 *National Task Force on Suicide Interim Report*, Department of Health, Government Publications Office, Dublin, p. 24.
[b] *Irish Times*, Home News, October 19 1998, p. 4.
[c] *Irish Independent*, 22 January 1999, p. 1.
[d] *Irish Times,* March 26 2001, p. 13.
[e] *Vital Statistics, Fourth Quarter and Yearly Summary Report 2001*, The Central Statistics Office, Dublin.

These figures reveal a *six-fold* increase in suicide numbers in Ireland in the period 1971-2001. This would appear to confirm the hypothesis of Durkheim that rates of suicide and levels of economic development appear to be strongly linked. Moreover, if we compare the average suicide rate per annum for an economic setback period (1970-1986), with the rate for an economic recovery period (1987-2001), it almost doubles from one hundred and eighty six per annum in the former to over three hundred and fifty per annum in the latter period. Moreover, in the Interim Report on Suicide 1976-1992, the rate in Ireland was lower than Finland, the US and Japan, even though the Irish rate was increasing as theirs was *decreasing*. It now appears that as a country becomes more industrially advanced individuals adapt and adjust more readily to the division of labour than a society in the early stages of accidental rapid economic growth.

Furthermore when the increased rate of suicide is compared with other demographic trends such as the lower overall mortality rate, then the level of unhappiness in the Celtic Tiger appears even more acute. Table 9.3 presents figures for mortality rates, suicide rates, educational enrolment rates and the population totals at the following intervals, 1971, 1981, 1991 and 1996 respectively.

Table 9.3 Suicide Rates and Concomitant Demographic Changes in the Republic of Ireland 1971-1996

Year	Pop[a]	Suicide rate per million[b]	Mortality rate per 1000[c]	Education Enrolments as a per cent of the total population[d]			
				Primary	Second	Tertiary	(nos)
1971	2,978,248	27	10.7	17.5	0.70	0.08	2,000
1981	3,443,405	65	9.6	16.6	0.80	0.10	
1991	3,525719	98	8.9	15.3	0.90	0.20	
1996	3,626,087	105	8.7	13.2	1.00	0.30	10,000

[a] Central Statistics Office - www.CSO.ie see 'Principal Statistics, Demography, Population'.
[b] Calculated using figures in Table 9.2 of CSO 'Principal Statistics, Demography, Population'.
[c] Department of Health and Children - www.doh.ie/statistics/index.html 'Health Statistics 1999' p. 24.
[d] Department of Education and Science www.gov.ie/educ/briefdescriptionirishedu/stats.html and in particular 'Brief Description of Irish Education System - Statistics'.

Despite an increase in excess of twenty one per cent in the population for the period 1971-1996, the increase in the rate of suicide per million increased by nearly four hundred per cent, a figure just slightly below the increase in absolute suicide numbers. Yet the overall mortality rate actually *decreased* from just over ten per cent to less than nine per cent per thousand at the very moment that the suicide rate jumped from twenty seven to one hundred and five per million. Both absolute numbers and increased levels of reported suicide are now seen to have *increased* against a backdrop of *decreasing* mortality rates. In other words while more people were living longer, more also committed suicide indicating the existence of even higher levels of unhappiness in Irish society.

Suicide had also increased in tandem with increased enrolments in primary, secondary and third level education. These enrolments occurred as a result of implementing the main recommendation of the OECD Report, 'Investment in Education' published in 1969, namely to implement a strategy to align education to the future needs of industry and to ensure increased participation in all three educational levels. We know that increased suicide rates are also an outcome of widespread education because the common faith is weakened and traditional beliefs are challenged thus giving rise to a lack of cohesion in society (Durkheim 1970). Because suicide rates reflect profound and abrupt changes in the social structure, it can take some time for the increased rates to filter through (Durkheim 1970). The delayed effect started to emerge during the Celtic Tiger. Moreover, the new and increased industrial emphasis in the curriculum, together with the increase in potential and actual wealth on offer in Celtic Tiger, may cause even more tension within the individual because it directly challenges the sacred, charitable and moderate ethos inculcated in the school.

Another reason for the increase in tension is that the rise in prosperity accentuates the desire to have *limitless* well-being something which is naturally insatiable and simultaneously unachievable and this tension becomes unbearable, leading to increased suicide rates (Durkheim 1970). The limit on individual material well-being that was traditionally imposed socially by the norms of society had the advantage of pre-determining the amount of luxury deemed acceptable for an individual in any particular occupation (Durkheim 1970). This enough amount of luxury successfully set a maximum material limit to be aspired to and as it was fixed, it was achievable and the outcome, happiness (Durkheim 1970). Moreover, Durkheim also argued that during periods of intense economic opportunity no social censure exists to curb the material desires of society because religion becomes powerless to influence the so-called supreme end of economic materialism. Yet our research strongly suggests that religion is not powerless in the face of global capitalism. While beliefs may remain, integration may weaken (Durkheim 1970), hence the existence in the Celtic Tiger of relatively high levels of Catholicism with high levels of group unhappiness.

Yet as Durkheim (1984) pointed out, the desire for happiness is the over-riding motivation that drives social progress. In our research findings almost all respondents had a strong belief in Heaven and this challenged each individual to seek out a strategy to ensure balanced material and spiritual well-being. However, one of the least susceptible groups noted by Durkheim in his studies, farmers, are *the* most susceptible Irish group together with veterinary surgeons and caring professionals (Irish Times 2001). In our study farmers were seen to be compelled to mix the industrial factory job with farming to ensure their viability and therefore had to develop a divided disposition, namely one for the industrial factory and the other for their co-operative and farm work.

This latter form of co-operation, namely mechanical solidarity, is fostered by mutual self-interest (Durkheim 1973). It exists at the expense of organic solidarity whereby specialisation of functions under the control of a central authority leads to further co-operation (Durkheim 1973a) such as that experienced in commerce and in industry. Giddens (1995a) identified the main difference between mechanical and organic solidarity. Mechanical solidarity is where each individual remains largely unconscious of his or her separateness due to the strength of the moral integration of the collective conscience such as that experienced in farming, while organic solidarity points to the nature of the attachment of the individual to the conscience collective, tying them together through dependency on other occupations, a feature that is characteristic of the industrial concern. The division of labour therefore tends to weakens social solidarity such as cultural norms and institutions and this in turn leads to a state of anomie (Durkheim 1973b).

Elias (1965) warned against a static notion of anomie as described by Merton who defined it as the antithesis of predictability and regularity and therefore something likely to be 'bad'. Durkheim saw anomie as a distinct and valid social structure in itself. The increasing suicide rate in Ireland particularly in times of prosperity challenges Halbwach's argument when reviewing Durkheim's conclusions on suicide – and remarked upon by Giddens (1996b) – that suicide rates tend to decline during boom periods. The opposite appears to be the case as the most significant increase is evident during the Celtic Tiger era and supports Durkheims insight as the more valid one.

Rapid social and economic change due to unprecedented increases in prosperity and industrialisation has also coincided with a remarkable increase in the levels of indictable and non indictable crime in the Republic in the period 1949-1999, and in particular after the mid 1960s (Redmond and Heanue 2000). For example, murder rates have increased by a factor of thirty eight, wounding by a factor of four, malicious damage by a factor of twenty nine and burglary by a factor of thirteen.

Table 9.4 A Selection of Indictable Offences 1949-1999

Indictable Offences	1949	1999	> by factor
Murder	1	38	38.0
Wounding	167	691	4.0
Other	310	1,162	3.7
(mostly Sexual)			
Malicious Damage	277	8,223	29.0
Burglary	2,065	28,626	13.0
Pickpocket	254	3202	12.0
Larceny (vehicles)	944	7688	8.0

Source: Redmond, A. and Heanue, M. (2000), 'Aspects of Society', Adrian Redmond (ed.), *That Was Then, This is Now - Change in Ireland 1949-1999*, Government of Ireland, Central Statistics Office, Dublin, February 2000, p. 55, p. 60.

Both the number and seriousness of the crimes committed has also increased significantly during all the five phases of Irish economic development. However, the overall national crime trend has been moving steadily downwards since the high drug related levels of the 1980s with only Spain within the EU having a lower recorded level (National Crime Council 2001).

The point about the increase in levels of anomie and unhappiness during strong economic development is, that Durkheim identified a religious factor in the proclivity for suicide. The spirit of free enquiry of Protestantism and its attendant lack of a Catholic collective credo caused unbearable tension because of the individual's doubt about their eternal salvation (Jones 1986). This contrasts with the very point highlighted by one of the contributors in Domain A, where it was pointed out that the responsibility to provide answers to ultimate questions lay with the clergy and this approach was an economically advantageous one as it allowed Catholic workers to concentrate on 'profane' work. However, Durkheim acknowledged the unifying role of collective and centralised Catholicism rather than individualistic Protestantism even if it promoted a static view of society and condemned the poor to accept poverty (Giddens 1971).

Again our research findings indicated that Catholicism remained *the* normative social influence on individual economic orientation during the Celtic Tiger. It is then reasonable to suggest that the common Catholic consciousness appeared resistant though by no means immune to the sudden and accidental occurrence of the Celtic Tiger and its attendant prosperity. In other words, the Absolute Presupposition Catholicism-nationalism working over the longer term demanded that the individual organise an adaptive strategy, namely the *limit* of enough which then acts as a counter balance to the sudden availability of unachievable and *unlimited* economic possibilities. This concept of balance forms a central theme throughout many of the sociological insights of Talcott Parsons.

The Insights of Parsons

Parsons is well known for his theory of structural functionalism. Structural functionalism is a unique method of conceptualising society. Modern structural-functionalists focus on society as whole and the impact of various parts on the whole and even though there is change in one part, the system eventually finds its equilibrium and the whole remains stable (Ritzer 1988). Parsons' functionalism is an action based system. Each system has four subsystems and each subsystem its own specialised function

> The organism [economy] directed towards adaptation, the personality system [polity] related to goal attainment, the social system [community] directed towards integration [solidarity] and the cultural system geared towards pattern maintenance [values and regulation]. (Baert 1998: 52)

Parsons' model of society assigned a central role to the internalisation of values and norms and their capacity to integrate society i.e. to increase social solidarity (Giddens 1995c). Mayhew (1982) argued that Parsons accepted that there were individuals who have ends that they pursue in a world out there full of obstacles and opportunities and where choices of action were governed by norms that do not rest exclusively on predictable positivistic relationships. Here the cultural system appears to drive the social system to the point where conformity with a value becomes a need in the individual's personality (Mayhew 1982). In our study there is the example of the Absolute Presupposition driving the individuals engagement with the economic system in conformance with the economic norm of enough.

Parsons (1982) maintained that different value systems embedded in different societies should be examined for relationships existing between those different systems. Different religious doctrines have a common feature, namely they are ingrained as part of the individuals attitude towards daily economic life. Here they embed themselves cognitively, giving rise to a religious sentiment crucial for the survival of a functioning social system because it enables the individual to make sense of difficult concepts such as evil and suffering (Parsons 1954).

Religion re-enforces sentiments that underpin the essential norms for the institutional integration of society (Parsons 1969) such as appropriate economic behaviour within the capitalist system. Parsons was committed to promoting social harmony in the capitalist nation state through the application of Calvinist principles whereby the individual and society are seen as instruments to build the Kingdom of God on earth and thereby contribute to the achievement of a good society (Buxton 1985).[132] In this respect, he rejects Marx's conception of social order, since Marx failed to address the issue of individuals pursuing their own self interest while acting according to a predetermined set of economic circumstances (Buxton 1985).

Marx could not explain through historical materialism how it was that the bourgeoisie with their ethical rejection of rampant self-interest were just as much condemned to suffering as the proletariat since both were obliged to work (Parsons 1999c). In contrast, Parsons acknowledged the central role of religious values in the development of modern industrial capitalism (Parsons 1999). He regarded Calvinism as a more privatised enhancement of the Christian individualistic principle already present in pre-Reformation Catholicism as the one that put a particularly Christian shape on society (Parsons 1999).

Parsons (1999a) acknowledged that tension had always existed in Christianity when the Christian engaged with this world since material well-being had never been seen as an absolute end in itself. The secular world has always been regarded as a gift from God and as such it had to be a holy rather than a profane thing. He then implied that Christianity must now be stronger than ever, since its main pre-occupation was in developing the secular world (Parsons 1999a). This view partially echoes the sentiments of the Catholic representative in Domain A, who pointed out that creating God's kingdom on earth was one official Catholic interpretation of the purpose of work. However, the difference between Parsons'

---

[132] This is the precisely the point made by Novak but about Catholicism. See ffn 127 in this chapter.

secular and Catholicism's instrumental position towards economic development is that in the former salvation is achieved through *acquiring* wealth whereas in the latter Heaven is primarily achieved by *experiencing* it.

Interestingly the concept of creating the Kingdom of God on Earth as part of the divine plan is also paralleled in Socialism (Parsons 1999b). Not only is man perceived in sin to be tied to a capitalistic regime but freedom can only be achieved by revolution (redemption)

> the analogue of Heaven is clearly the state of communism and only those who have made the transition from...the capitalistic society to the state of communism by way of socialism can be said in this sense to be saved...alienation being the equivalent to Christian sin. (Parsons 1999c: 91, 97:ffn 2)

Michael O'Riordan (2000) former General Secretary of the Irish Communist Party has indicated that there is strong Christian Marxist dialogue in Ireland where the relief of distress and poverty is both a common aim and a practical way of changing society for the better. This particular view of creating God's Kingdom on earth was also expressed in Domain A by the Catholic Hierarchy. Puritanism and Socialism both work to achieve an earthly paradise and this idea follows a long traditional belief in a pre-existent paradise where man's true being flourished (Parsons, Fox and Lidz 1999). Christians were eschatologically orientated to eternal life in a new paradise whereas Puritan Protestants focussed on a religious sanctification of life in *this* world and this kind of utopia or paradise had also dominated the desired outcome for Communists. Since life is a gift from God, it creates in the individual the need to reciprocate which can only be achieved through death since individual death is not only seen as the supreme sacrifice leading to paradise but the opportunity to give, in the redemptive sense, the gift of life to future generations (Parsons 1999d). Of course we are familiar with this concept of paradise and sacrifice in the poetry of Irish revolutionary prisoners previously discussed in chapter seven.

Although the religious orientation of Catholic prisoners, ascetic Protestants and Christian socialists may differ, their commitment to a set of core religious principles capable of restructuring society for the better, does not. Religion can be regarded as an evolutionary universal for embedding cultural patterns or dureés regulating social action (Parsons 1999d). Parsons saw all of society's norms and rules of conduct emanating from religion because it exercised the particular function of successfully motivating individuals in the face of evil when for example the virtuous cannot rise above their poverty threshold while at the same time affluence is achieved by corruption, and vice sometimes goes unpunished (Aldridge 2000).

The Absolute Pre-supposition appears to integrate different social institutions and make sense of work and the purpose of existence. For example, many of the respondents in National Domain A were clear that religious beliefs enabled them to comprehend and provide answers to these ultimate questions. Furthermore, because the individual is compelled to accept the orientations common to the society in which he lives (Parsons 1982b), Irish society developed a strongly Catholic orientation as part of the Irish personality system.

As the role of culture is defined as a system enabling individuals to conform to pre-defined behavioural patterns (Parsons 1982b) norms such as religion have the primary role of minimising conflict and maintaining stability and order (Parsons 1982d).   This explains the passivity of many respondents to the prevailing economic and social system.   However, Giddens argued that Parsons failed to recognise the conscious decisions of individuals in this maintenance of stability (Giddens 1995c).   Moreover, behaviourism, namely responding to a stimulus, failed to take account of biological pre-dispositions and internal thoughts and feelings as important individual motivators in their own right (Myers 1988).   As the implicit and distinct function of each system always borrowed to a greater or lesser degree the inherent functions of related systems (Parsons and Smelser 1982), then distinctly Catholic norms such as the Spirit of Charity act as a counterbalancing force to one such as global capitalism that promises unlimited and unachievable wealth.   The outcome is the acceptance of the measure of enough in national policy and in individual economic behaviour.

Yet Parsons and Platt (1982) argued that the American value system of individualism has changed very little since the Founding Fathers where instrumental activism or the cult of the individual had been the underlying pattern of western development.   However, the limitations of Parsons general abstract theory of structural functionalism is that its very abstraction was regarded as the primary purpose of sociology and the classification of society as being either traditional or modern automatically led to the analysis of social development with reference only to advanced industrialising nations (Giddens 1973).   This of course was a real concern in the informed interpretation of the profile of the Irish economic disposition and was also highlighted in the opening remarks of this study.

Moreover, this very concept of an underlying uni-directional western move towards a predetermined objective such as advanced industrialised society has presented significant problems in an Irish context particularly within liberal economic policies because it was not the industrialisng process that shaped Ireland but the external colonial interdependencies (Goldthorpe 1994).   This had the effect of positioning modernisation well ahead of industrialisation as a feature of recent Irish development.   In any event the uni-directional logic of industrialisation is flawed because prosperity depends on combining culture-specific traditional social and ethical habits with modern institutions (Fukyama 1995).   In other words, to generate a successful economy, a country specific adaptation of the economic order must incorporate its *traditional* cultural values and economic norms.   The fact that the Absolute Pre-supposition religion-nationalism remained a durable force at the height of the Celtic Tiger appears to support Parsons' insight that religion continues to have an important function in its own right in maintaining norms and values even within changing social structures.

The Insights of Giddens

Giddens (1996d) contrasted the relatively relaxed approach of Catholic religious based tolerance towards economic traditionalism, namely pre-modern economic activity, to that of the antagonism of the Puritan. The function of religion has been re-engineered from a centrally justified to an individually directed construction to tolerate the tensions that follow from western industrialisation patterns. The tension from being told what's right to do and outlined by teachings and encyclicals, as opposed to relying on an internalised 'choosing to do the right thing' approach, may generate psychological tension and explain the high levels of suicide noted in a previous section of this chapter. Giddens (1996e) supported the view that individuals purposive actions are restricted by the very structure of society but they can still decide on different courses of action. As a result they generate both intended and unintended consequences by their actions. This practical consciousness can be defined as the social survival tools such as language and time which are known and used by every individual but cannot be intuitively explained. They have the crucial function of making ordinary life more predictable (Giddens 1996e).[133]

This is an important insight since there was an erroneous view that individuals were more in control of their lives in traditional times of small communities when contrasted against the sense of powerlessness experienced within the dynamics of a large scale global market (Giddens 1991). The importance of the nature of this global market centres on the fact that because the self can only be expressed in terms of having wealth, the pursuit and facilitation of this objective is meant to trigger the consuming behaviour required by the market. Instead it only leads to a lasting frustration and a sense of unhappiness because the intrinsic needs of self-development are not met (Giddens 1991).

The importance of the Absolute Pre-supposition religion-nationalism within an Irish Catholic context is that it has shaped an economic disposition focussed on securing a predictable level of happiness in this life by not exceeding the boundary of enough and by applying the Spirit of Charity in modern economic life. In other words when economic activity is infused with the enlightenment of Catholic Social Teaching, apparently contradictory targets of competitiveness *and* equity become preferred social outcomes. While the overall developmental trends in western culture concentrate on rational purposive action (Giddens 1996f), our

---

[133] In his interview, Giddens, stated that 'scientists forget that most of what we do as human beings we do intentionally, and that we are aware of our reasons for doing so. Knowledgeability is always bounded [institutionally]. But recovering the notion of the knowledgeable human agent is quite fundamental to reformulating what the social sciences are all about. The recovery has to be based on practical consciousness. A flaw in the traditional conception of social science was the idea that it is possible to discover laws of social life more or less directly analogous to those existing in the natural sciences. Actors always know what they are doing, but the consequences of what they do characteristically escape what they intend so that perpetuation of social institutions involves some kind of mix of intended and unintended outcomes of action'.

research findings indicated that the religious instrumental approach also informs national economic policy as well as individual economic action. This latter approach of the individual may be quite effective to handle the global market illusion of igniting self-development. The reason is that Habermas sees future development being dependent on the recapture of the life world (Lebenswelt) i.e. the taken for granted ordinary daily life from the dominance of rationality, because further capitalist expansion and improved government interventionist strategies cannot now reproduce the required social culture necessary to resolve problems such as social equity (Giddens 1996f).

If Giddens (1996d) was correct when he noted that the past tenaciously searches for its expression in the present, then the Catholic standard of enough may be embodied in the conscious effort of all respondents in the Celtic Tiger to balance equity and competitiveness and material and spiritual well-being. Of course Giddens (1996a) highlighted that this was one of the main arguments against Functionalism, namely its very inability to satisfactorily explain this conscious intentional action In response Giddens used the concept of duality of structure to explain the reproductive qualities of social action using certain social structures such as language (Giddens 1995d). His theoretical model was based on the concept of structuration, which he defined as a skilled rational act of social reproduction by individuals but where the rational input is limited (Giddens 1996a). While on a visit to Dublin, Giddens (1998) explained it as follows

> I got it [Structuration] from a French context, I don't remember who used it, it wasn't used very often...meaning not just interacting with somebody but doing that interaction in a kind of active way. Parsons introduced this idea of the theory of action. But as critics always said it wasn't clear where the action was. But on the other side there were also various forms of what seemed to be quite deterministic Marxism. In none of the approaches did you get a worthwhile theory of agency...people capable of understanding themselves with reasons and intentions for what they do...people in general are pretty rational about what they do most of the time, if you understand the context of their actions and understand the emotions that move them. (Giddens 1998: 114-115)

Giddens (1998) stated that he was still opposed to the idea that many people still did not really know what they were doing when they acted in society.

The findings in our study appear to confirm Giddens' insight since we observed how Catholics went about their work and practised their religion with clear intentions and expectations of the outcomes both in this world and in the next. The profile of the Irish economic disposition revealed in the research was also an outcome of intentional and instrumental action based on a rational need to acquire limited amounts of material well-being within a given set of socio-economic circumstances. Nevertheless repressed and unconscious wants, structural conditions and unintended consequences can restrict rational action (Giddens

1996a). One of the ways to overcome these restrictions is to re-define reality (McGettigan 1998), where for example, poverty is seen in a positive light if it increases the likelihood of achieving Heaven.[134]

However, the reality of salvation is *already* known by Catholics and does not require re-definition. Not alone is there a high probability of achieving Heaven after death by invoking a disposition of enough and by practising the Spirit of Charity, but an inner Catholic conscience can compel the individual through the force of guilt to re-align behaviour if and when it does not conform to social norms. This 'certainty' challenges the argument of Giddens (1998) that

> you simply have to bracket out lots of questions that if you had any sense actually you would ask about your life…I mean why do all of us just go on with this struggle when you know you are going to die? It's not obvious is it? (Giddens 1998: 120)

Giddens (1990) conceded that religion provided both the reliability and the explanation for events as well as the assurance that a Heavenly provider would dispense material and spiritual well-being. By placing the Catholic Spirit of Charity at the core of the Irish economic disposition the individual objective of securing enough and the national objective of competitiveness with equity become the most rational and intentional course of national and individual economic behaviour.

Conclusion of Theme Three

The approach of employing a complementary array of diverse sociological insights has again exposed how the Absolute Pre-supposition impacts on the individual economic disposition. This approach went a long way towards explaining the intentional and rational purpose of the economic measure of enough, an instrumental work ethic, national economic policies infused with Catholic Social Teaching and the existence of a Spirit of Charity shaping national and individual engagement with global capitalism.

These insights were possible because we have brought together the complementary sociological paradigms of Historical Materialism and Figurational Sociology together with five diverse but interconnecting contributions from Weber, Freud, Durkheim, Parsons and Giddens to bear on the problem of exposing the interaction of the configuration of culture specific variables on economic behaviour. We have been able to show that religion-nationalism rather than materialism and its relations has shaped the Irish economic disposition. We have used the concept of Insider-Outsider to reveal how Irish nationalism inculcated an economic disposition that reflected a Catholic worldview that placed a premium on acquiring experiential capital as opposed to an all out acquisitive disposition.

---

[134] We have previously explained the Catholic understanding of the spirit of poverty as it unfolds in the Beatitudes (Sermon on the Mount). See ffn 105 p. 159.

The Protestant Work Ethic and secularisation remain relatively peripheral players in the economic development of Irish society.

Although Weber highlighted the profound religious impact on economic life, the central role of the PWE in the development of capitalism has been destabilised with a case for the adaptive and older Catholic Work Ethic (CWE) being more influential.

Freud's understanding of conscious and unconscious mental forces then highlighted how repressive sexual mores weakened the Irish acquisitive impulse. We also highlighted the weak nature of the Irish collective economic consciousness that resulted from the impact of De Valera's leadership, focussed as it primarily was on the ascetic rather than the material world.

From Durkheims insights we concluded that a high degree of sacred consciousness still existed within the Irish economic system during the height of the Celtic Tiger. Durkheim contended that levels of unhappiness and anomie, as indicated by levels of suicide, increased in tandem with economic development. This trend was confirmed in the Celtic Tiger. The unlimited and unachievable wealth on offer in the Celtic Tiger was seen to cause great tension in individuals. One of the effects of Catholicism was to provide a counter balancing alternative by elevating enough as the most preferable material and moral target.

Parsons argued that modern western society now demonstrated a more Christian value orientation than ever before. With its primary focus on creating wealth as a way of expanding God's kingdom on earth, the economic system was then seen to incorporate some of the norms of the religious system. In this respect the enough element characteristic of the Irish economic disposition could be explained as a counter-balancing force within the socio-economic system.

Finally, Giddens highlighted the importance of acknowledging that most individuals had choices on the type of rational economic action that they could take. The not so obvious reason why individuals carried on living and working, knowing full well that they will eventually die may be more rational to Catholics who regard salvation as the ultimate objective. It is this knowledgeability through the exercise of the logic of faith that establishes the intentional nature of Irish economic behaviour.

Chapter 10

Conclusion :
A Theory of Limits

The world of those who are happy is different from the world of
those who are not. (Wittgenstein 1989)

Introduction

The benefits of employing complementary sociological paradigms have already
been acknowledged. The original contradiction understood as the paradox of the
Catholic ethic actively engaging with global capitalism and defined by a macro
socio-economic backdrop of Tiger economic performance, relatively low levels of
secularisation and accidental development can now be re-evaluated. In this
concluding chapter the relevance and durability of these sociological insights are
revitalised into a new synthesis and presented as A Theory of Limits. In the sense
that it builds upon previous insights, this amended theory must be understood as a
valorised rather than an innovative one. Moreover, it must also be acknowledged
that only *now* has it been possible to take advantage of the emergence of the Celtic
Tiger to re-formulate this theory whereas none of the sociological insights
employed throughout this study could claim the benefits of such an unforeseen or
accidental advantage.

A New Species or a Different Variety?

The Celtic Tiger profile of the Irish economic disposition revealed in our study
contrasts sharply with the conclusions of a three year Princeton University Survey
on Religion and Economic Values where active employed Americans conceded
that enough would never be enough (Wuthnow 1993). It also differs from the
more recent study of Hoon and Lim (2001) on Thai, Singaporean and Chinese
attitudes to money and work. In this instance all three cultures displayed a strong
Protestant work ethic with the Chinese giving the highest endorsement to the PWE
and where the maxim *the more one has the better* is generally regarded as being
the most powerful stimulant for recent economic growth in Asia. Specifically, the
American and Asian unlimited economic objective of more, contrasts sharply with
the limited Catholic one of enough. A respected academic Peillon (2000) has even
called the excess wealth generated in the Celtic Tiger, the curse of affluence,

labeling it a danger to social harmony that needs to be dissipated or distributed in festivals and bank holidays in order not to endanger the well-being of Irish society. It is to this very concept of well-being that we now turn our attention.

Veenhoven (1984) stated that synonyms such as well-being, happiness, life satisfaction, and balance while being differentiated are often used interchangeably to mean

> the degree to which an individual's overall evaluation of his life
> as-whole concluded positively. (Veenhoven 1984: 36)

Moreover, there appears to be a strong positive relationship between the presence of Catholicism in society and higher levels of happiness (Veenhoven 2000). In a study of forty eight nations conducted in the early 1990s where Ireland was third happiest, a belief in God was identified as having a strong positive correlation (+0.40) on that level of happiness (Veenhoven 1997). Well over forty per cent of Irish Catholics at the height of the Celtic Tiger indicated that they were very happy with their life, the highest proportion in the world (Greeley and Ward 2000). Again recent research has concluded that job satisfaction, which promotes well-being reached the highest level in one of the poorest of the advanced nations, namely Ireland, but the reasons for this remained unclear (Blanchflower and Oswald 1999). Irish workers were particularly positive towards work but again for uncertain reasons (Oswald 1997).[135]

The key point here is that while the industrialised countries, Ireland included, may experience a slight rise in well-being as real national income grow, there is *no* correlation between economic growth and a feeling of well-being or between higher income and higher levels of happiness except in developing nations (Oswald 1997). Most important of all, better economic performance does not equal more happiness for a nation. What we do know is that unemployment is the single main contributor to low levels of happiness (Oswald 1997).

De Tella, McCulloch and Oswald (1997) provided evidence which showed that there is an apparent positive correlation between levels of employment and inflation with levels of well-being.[136] Yet paradoxically, during the Celtic Tiger era, the highest levels of suicide co-existed with an unemployment rate below four per cent, its lowest level for fifteen years (Central Statistics Office 2000a), and a similar low for inflation.[137] Despite the record levels of suicide, there still appears to be both an economic and religious basis for the 'happy' disposition of the Irish

---

[135] It is only when we place the instrumental emphasis of work characteristic of the Catholic worldview at the core of the economic disposition can we appreciate that other preferences such as enjoyment of life become paramount. The belief expressed by many contributors in our research that more money did not necessarily bring more happiness now appears to be a valid one.

[136] 250,000 randomly sampled Americans and Europeans from 1970s to 1990s using the US General Social Survey and the Euro-Barometer Survey Series.

[137] The data for this and other economic indicators is presented in chapter three of this study and the data for recorded suicide is presented in chapter nine of this study.

workforce, a disposition that was almost universally present in our research findings.

Yet only since the 1970s have scientific measurements of happiness been developed (Veenhoven 1997).[138] Many economists were still unused to and uncomfortable working with data on well-being and happiness and then applying it to economic matters (Di Tella, MacCulloch, Oswald 1997). For example, it was only in the last four years that a number of leading Irish economists openly conceded that GNP growth had little or nothing at all to do with well-being. The fact was that three of the leading industrial nations achieving high levels of economic growth could only generate a measure of national well-being that was barely three per cent above their 1950 levels (Douthwaite 2000).[139]

While terms such as well-being, happiness, welfare and quality of life do not have an unequivocal meaning, nevertheless, happiness or the length and degree of happiness experienced by the individual, remains the most inclusive summary of the quality of life (Veenhoven 2000).[140] It does not include a fourth measurement, usefulness of a person's life, as a life can be happy and not useful or useful and quite unhappy (Veenhoven 2000). Moreover, while a work ethic may motivate individuals and societies to increase material wealth, it does not automatically follow that they would be necessarily better off than a materially poorer but more leisurely society (Congleton 1991). Empirical research on happiness can only suggest that it has a *tendency* to correlate positively with economic affluence (Veenhoven 1998).

And there is a further problem with aggregating individual levels of well-being and happiness. Because no two individuals are psychically identical there are limitations to psychological interpretations of needs, wants and behaviour (Fromm (1978). Even at the individual level, increases in material wealth do not necessarily correlate with increased levels of happiness

> had Gallup or MORI been around say in the 1850s and 1860s…a sample of Irish people might well have declared themselves to be on average, as happy as a sample chosen today. (O'Gráda 1998: 22)

In fact, having more money brings little well-being or happiness and what actually impels people to strive for more money is to increase or maintain their income relative to others in society (Oswald 1997) i.e. striving to achieve a socially accepted norm, an acceptable limit. Still, people from the most global economy in the world, Ireland, just happened to be the happiest although any correlation

---

[138] Based on a three tier model, including national macro factors such as economic development, micro factors such as income and finally individual characteristics such as health and ability.

[139] Using Cobb's Index of Economic Sustainable Welfare measured against the GNP per annum of the US. The examples cited were the US, UK and Germany.

[140] Defined by measurements of livability in the environment, life ability of the person, and appreciation of life by the individual.

between globalisation and happiness is at best very fuzzy (AT Kearney/Foreign Policy 2002).[141] Yet in a earlier cross national study using subjective social criteria on perceived happiness and well-being levels in eight EU countries, it was found that the higher the income the higher the well-being expressed by the individual although again there was no direct correlation between national wealth and national well-being (Davis, Fine-Davis and Meehan 1982).[142] In other words only at an individual level is there some evidence for a positive correlation between income and happiness.

Although high levels of happiness do not appear to occur in economically poorer countries (Veenhoven 2000), there was evidence that the merriest Irish agricultural workers in the late nineteenth and early twentieth centuries were often those with the lowest level of income and cultural explanations for this phenomenon although quite difficult to verify cannot be overlooked (O'Gráda 1995). In fact one of the major complaints that the Dublin Review of 1850 had of the English attitude to working so intensely to accumulate wealth was, that they among all the nations of the world spent the least amount of time enjoying life. One explanation may be that Catholics had a duty in conscience

> to fight against any tendency to make a hardship of work.
> (Cardinal Lecaro 1960: 8)

Proudhon (1888) had contended that an increase in misery in society was proportional to the increase in wealth and the ideal to be sought after was the amount that maximised social well-being, and in this respect Catholicism appeared to be well placed to address this objective.[143] Furthermore more recent studies have highlighted a possible reason for this, suggesting that Mass attendance orientates Catholics to value leisure more highly than Protestants because the Catholic world-view regards this world as enchanted, full of mystery and therefore worthy of being enjoyed (Jeanrond 2001).

Therefore, different levels of enough are highly likely to emerge where individual comparisons and self-assessment of individual circumstances are measured against others in similar circumstances i.e. against accepted norms. This is consistent with the views of many of the respondents in our research. Even income inequality, where it does exist, is not positively correlated either with unhappiness or well-being (Di Tella, MacCulloch, Oswald 1997). Fromm identified the crux of the matter as follows

---

[141] In the second edition of the *A. T. Kearney/Foreign Policy Magazine Globalisation Index*. The Index follows changes in sixty advanced and emerging markets. It quantifies economic integration by using data on trade, portfolio capital flow, income payments and receipts, technology, political engagement in world affairs and the level of cross border contacts, telephone traffic and tourism.

[142] Ireland, Denmark, Germany, France, Italy, Netherlands, Belgium, UK.

[143] These self same sentiments were expressed by many of our contributors across each of the four domains that we researched as discussed in chapter five and six of this study.

> The alternative of having versus being does not appeal to common sense...to have so it would seem, is a normal function of our life. In order to live we must have things...it would seem that the very essence of being is having; that if one has nothing, one is nothing. (Fromm 1978: 25)

He said that because individuals had an intrinsic desire to escape selfishness, the economist's job was to re-assert it and replace humanity with the need to accumulate wealth and money. Moreover, most economic theory tended to be based on the benchmark of individual needs and wants rather than on social needs and desires (Schumpter 1908). The whole market system of western economies was therefore directed towards instilling this very need to buy ever more to confirm having as a true expression of the self, and is generally known as the commodification of society (Giddens 1991). The Jesuit, Quinn (1958), also argued that the ideal human existence was to be rather than to have because the impoverishment of man was caused by excessive preoccupation with his/her material welfare.

At a macro level, Tawney (1921) identified societies that were focused exclusively on achieving material well-being as acquisitive societies because their disposition was almost totally orientated towards acquiring *unlimited* amounts of wealth. Hobson (1914) argued that western society was so accustomed to regard wealth as the only desirable economic end that it then mistakenly concluded that a rise in wealth caused a rise in well-being and this was due to the arrogance of the industrial consciousness that precluded any other scale of values except quantitative ones. This in turn made the construction of qualitative social well-being standards almost impossible.

In the 1960s and 1970s there was some evidence to suggest that the Irish economic disposition was ill disposed towards this ever-increasing acquisitive impulse. In a review of the research on poor economic development at that time, Raven (1970) identified ten attitudes that would promote economic growth and change the Irish work ethic for the better. The importance of the list for our discussion lies in the fact that at that time, Raven did not consider material possessions and money as influential factors in fostering economic development because he understood that workers wanted to lead happier and more effective rather than wealthier lives. This contrasts with the studies of Goldthorpe, Lockwood, Bechhofer and Plat (1968) who studied affluent industrial workers in Luton England at about the same time and discovered that while they stated that work was not a central life interest as was the family, they nevertheless *relentlessly pursued maximum returns* on their work. Lesser (1965) concluded at the time that while industrialisation was neither a suitable nor a preferable objective in itself, happy Ireland somehow got to the top of the middle group of industrialised countries i.e. had passed the take off stage of development.[144] This made Irish industrial attitudes and behaviour appear totally incomprehensible when they were separated from the wider social structures (Whelan 1975).

---

[144] Using the definitions of manufacturing value added per capita or gross domestic product per capita or the ratio of consumer to capital goods output.

A highly innovative study of Irish social values and their impact on economic development had previously been undertaken by Hutchinson of the ESRI as early as 1968. In it he made a number of assertions that are directly related to our research findings because he too made a point of focusing on an *internal* set of social factors that had impacted on development. His hypothesis placed him firmly in the colonial school in the debates as discussed in chapter four, blaming the industrially advanced British establishment view of pre-independent Irish society on

> illegitimate and ethnocentric extension of a foreign system of values to a society differing in many fundamental respects from the society to which the critics themselves belonged...(consequently the people)...were blamed for failing to achieve materialist goals in which they were only marginally interested. (Hutchinson 1968: 5)

Central to his analysis is the argument that traditional Irish life may have been a non-materialist one where people were satisfied with a decent subsistence economy, as it left them free to pursue other preferred activities rather than increasing their level of wealth. Furthermore, the concept prevalent in industrial societies that if man was not working he was doing nothing of value, was actually a minority viewpoint in Ireland not least since leisure was an integral part of Irish traditional culture. Individuals only worked hard when the circumstances demanded it.[145]

More importantly, former social structures where the landlord class spent lavishly did not promote the idea of frugality and thrift for others to emulate and when they raised rents with every improvement to the farm and land by the Irish peasant occupier to support their own lifestyle, they made a mockery of an industrious ethos. This resulted in a divisiveness between landlord and peasant which reinforced the development of Irish tendencies such as laziness and visible poverty to avoid bringing them into conflict with the establishment.

Mutual aid, community and family values were more prized in Irish society than the individualism and the independence required for economic life. Community norms resulted in deference to senior family members which mitigated against technical innovation on the farm in particular, resulting in static economic conditions becoming socially acceptable. The late inheritance of the family farm and the mother's opposition to the son(s) marrying led to a comfortable life for the son(s), a consequent diminution of both the desire for the family farm and the will to initiate technical innovations with the subsequent loss of the imperative for hard work and enterprise.

Furthermore, small rural and urban family businesses – the majority of business in the Republic up to the 1950s and 1960s – were family affairs where family

---

[145] This view still dominates our own findings in the Celtic Tiger and is further support for the controlling impact of the Absolute Pre-supposition.

members were looked after by the father-owner often at the expense of hired help who may have worked on the farm for a considerable period of time yet often dismissed at short notice in favour of a family member. The security of tenure for the family on the one hand, coupled with the threat of dismissal and the related insecurity for the hired labourer on the other, failed to motivate either to develop a strong economic work ethic. With the Catholic Church contributing to almost universal social conformity in Irish society there was no social context available for enterprising individuals to flourish. Hutchinson then concluded that these characteristics were still a feature of Irish society and argued that there must have been a *raison d'être* for their continued existence. Unlike this study however, he had no further analysis to offer at that time.

Some of Hutchinson's observations were corroborated by American historians. They indicated that Irish Catholics were predisposed towards passivity, conformity, fatalism and dependence on others, having a disposition that mitigated directly against innovation, initiative, optimism and action (McCarthy 1990). Perhaps Adam Smith's (1776) argument that agriculture was the pre-eminent disposition of man despite changes in individual circumstances may explain the absence of the Protestant Work Ethic and underline Weber's (1930) argument that the peasant is unsuited to rational ascetic behaviour, conduct that was a key Protestant contribution to the development of the spirit of capitalism.

Even at local parish level work avoidance was also noted. For example, in the early 1960s, Kelly (1996) recorded that the level of distaste for work by parishioners shocked the local parish priest in Granard, County Longford, who summed up the prevailing attitude

> it is drudgery and slavery and the less of it one can get off with the better (what they do is) hold on to some sort of job for thirteen weeks and then draw the 'dole' or stamps for six months is the motto. (Kelly 1996: 43)

While it may understandable to expect lower material expectations during economic hardship, what could possibly be the cause of the apparent contradiction of not wanting more and more in the midst of the plenty that was the Celtic Tiger when it is self evident that this flies in the face of expected western norms in a global capitalist society?

Balancing Contradiction

Although modern science focuses on eliminating contradictions in theories as its modus vivendi, contradiction and conflict are not in themselves a sufficient reason against something being real (Heiddegar 1991). In other words, it is possible that the enough objective, the Spirit of Charity and a less than total work commitment can co-exist with sustained economic development. One of the reasons for this may lie in the fact that oppositions and dualities that arise from living in this world often compel individuals to adopt a functional and adaptive strategy called balance, to address metaphysical and secular contradictions (O'Donoghue 2000). Balance is about achieving richness rather than riches whereby self sufficiency is achieved without falling victim to commodification and where the emphasis as a society is on growth management rather than continuous growth promotion (Collins 2000), a sentiment revealed by some of the Celtic Tiger contributors in Domain A as the optimum economic strategy for Ireland. The OECD (1999) defined the ultimate measure of economic success as the ability of the nation to support the private consumption of its residents. As Ireland had experienced an average increase per annum in private consumption of approximately seven per cent during the Celtic Tiger, the conditions to create oppositions and dualities for Catholic society with a low materialist ethos in a Tiger economy were now in place. The need at an individual level for a balancing strategy to manage these dualities became even more immediate.

Hempton (1996) pointed out that the ethical and community based definition of Christian living that consisted of doing one's best and not doing harm to others had a long history in Christian religions and was based on the premise that, given this charitable behaviour, the individual would be rewarded in the next life. As the research findings have already shown, this is the view of many of the respondents. As Catholic tenets promoted the idea that adherence to its faith brought both spiritual and material well-being provided that material acquisitiveness did not exceed the limit of moderation or enough, then it was a foregone conclusion that the lob-sided potential material rewards of the industrial ethic would be superseded by the promised material *and* spiritual rewards of the Catholic ethic. The sensible thing then for a Catholic to do would be to achieve this balance. Moreover, this balanced approach is not an exclusively Catholic phenomenon.

Some Islamic nation states exhibited similarities to Ireland insofar as they shared a common post-colonial history and their state formation process took an almost identical route with parallel actors involved. For example, radical Islamic groups such as the Muslim Brothers in Egypt were also drawn from clerks, teachers, shopkeepers and small property owners (Gilsenan 1982). Here many revolutionary officers fighting against the British administration were also fiercely opposed to imperialist control, while being socially conservative with little or no time for Socialism (Gilsenan 1982). They were drawn mostly from the petty bourgeois and ended up controlling the national institutions of culture and education. Another parallel was the emergence in Egypt of a charismatic leader, Nasser who paralleled the stature of De Valera in Ireland.

The ethos of Islam in regard to the individual's engagement with the economic order is also of particular interest. Gumley and Redhead (1990) noted that there was a high economic opportunity cost involved in the amount of time needed to attend to the Five Pillars of Islam. Islamic history was constructed on the premise that excessive wealth led to moral weakness, hence the discomfort of most Muslims with American wealth, supremacy and individualism and their competitive disposition (Ahmed 1988). Islamic economics as opposed to capitalist or Marxist types tended to be defined in terms of achieving balance where conspicuous consumption was discouraged while the Quran and the Life of the Prophet strongly supported austerity.[146]

As Islamic scholarship in the social sciences was in a shambles (Ahmed 1988), it was not surprising that Islamic intellectual confrontation with a secularised and highly technological Europe in the nineteenth and twentieth centuries on how development and progress could be attained within the foundations of Islamic faith, failed to change a society that still regarded religion and the non secular government as the path to salvation (Endress 1994). Many tensions arose for practising Muslims in their dealing with the capitalist system and western paradigms appeared inappropriate to explain Muslim economic behaviour

> the western system is focussed almost exclusively on this-worldly life whereas the Islamic code merges both secular and Divine knowledge and activities and this merged perspective makes Western economic and sociological theoretical frameworks 'useless' to explain Islamic society. (Ashraf 1991: 133)

One Muslim intellectual, Bennabi, placed religion in a central position within his social theory framework and Tahir El-Masawi (1998) noted that Bennabi regarded religion as the independent force that determined culture, civilisation and development. This immediately grounded his thoughts within a theistic as opposed to a materialistic framework.

As religion is embedded in the psyche and nature of the human race and is the source of all social transformation, the real wealth of a nation was therefore not measured materially but by its ideational base, namely the norms, beliefs, and values woven into the fabric of social relations and institutions (Tahir El-Masawi 1998). The Marxist claim that social relations were determined by productive forces was therefore not applicable for most of the Arabic world (Tahir El-Masawi 1998).

This inappropriateness resonates strongly with our conclusions in chapter seven regarding Marxism and Irish economic development. If, as Islam teaches, the individual is subject to God's role then he must be both agent and witness in the real world. This is the secular mandate (Tahir El-Masawi 1998). If that then is correct, structuration theory required a third metaphysical factor which acts both as a restrictive force in relation to acquiring material wealth and as an expanding one in guiding the individual's spiritual frame of meaning (Tahir El-Masawi 1998).

The above insights imply that the individualistic ascetic vocation as described by Weber was superseded by an integrative set of priorities that included a sufficient degree of material well-being or enough. Tonnies (1957) on the other hand, argued that the simple fact of the matter was, that the very character of a nation and the intellectual attitude of its many individuals would eventually

---

[146] The Islamic Leader of the Irish Muslim Community re-enforced this view in his contribution to this study.

become less influenced by religion so that the importance of the spiritual would eventually be replaced by rational and scientific rules.

By contrast, in both Irish Catholic and in some Islamic cultures this rational and scientific force has not dominated the spiritual arena. Our study of the Celtic Tiger shows that Catholicism evokes an instrumental rationalism that seeks both enjoyment of this life through acquiring enough wealth and the application of a Spirit of Charity in daily and economic life to acquire spiritual well-being.

The Enough Principle

Evidence of strong Stoic and Platonic undercurrents in the Irish economic disposition was also revealed in our findings. Here, the tendency to privatism and a strategy to reconcile the tensions in attending to spiritual needs in the materialistic Celtic Tiger is activated by restricting the acquisitive impulse to a maximum limit of enough. In its relationship to modern economic activity, Baudrillard (1988) pointed out that Kenneth Galbraith maintained that the enough principle attempted to structure modern society so as to provide the maximum levels of well-being

> there exists in human nature...a tendency towards
> satisfaction...not viewed as optimising, but as harmonious...what
> is called economic development consists rather in no small part
> in devising strategies to overcome the tendency to place limits on
> their [men] objectives. (Baudrillard 1988: 41)

This inclination in individuals to limit acquisitiveness was also observed by Murphy (1999), while the objective of being able to secure enough was a significant factor in informing young adults on their vocational choice (Gottfredson 1981). Even in one of the world's most acquisitive societies, the US, over half of those interviewed in a study said that $100,000 would be enough to achieve all their dreams (Brown and Lauder 2001).[147] In other words most Americans could define a limit of enough in money terms and it was a relatively low amount at that.

Handy (1997) attempted to define a Theory of Limits that would incorporate this enough principle. He maintained that most people recognised when they had achieved enough and it was unnecessary to move beyond that point because it then became counter productive to the well-being of the individual. Strategies to optimise economic growth rather than generate unlimited growth should therefore

---

[147] A Roper Starch Survey conducted in 1995 where less than twenty per cent of Americans interviewed said that they wanted to be really rich. This appears to contradict the findings of the Princeton University Survey.

be the objective of society. Once the level of enough was guaranteed, this never-ending spiral of accumulation should cease.[148]

Handy also stated that enough invited the individual to reject materialism as the Puritans had done in favour of 'being' i.e. a continuous process of self-development through searching for the Good or God in this world. Handy argued that the lower the target of enough the higher the level of freedom that would be experienced by the individual. Unfortunately his personal affirmations about the value of enough were in fact spurious as they were not backed up with any conviction because he conceded that he was not committed to his own theory stating that it did not match the reality where *enough was never enough.*

By contrast, this thesis has consistently argued that the opposite was a reality in the Celtic Tiger, that many Catholics can decide when *enough is enough* and even in some cases when it is more than enough since many respondents in our research had chosen or intended to lower work effort after enough had been achieved. Our amended Theory of Limits is informed by O'Higgins' (1998) argument and supported by our own research findings that individuals are always aware of the inevitability of their own death and in one way or another this inevitability influences they way they live. In other words, the religious imperative of salvation determines the on-going attitude of the Irish individual towards the economic order because salvation is not pre-ordained as it was for the Puritan but contingent on favourable outcomes from each individual's intentional behaviour as measured against Catholic guidelines for the accumulation of wealth. This also appears to hold true for Islamic societies.

In specific terms we now know that Catholics exhibit two beliefs that impact on the nature of their economic orientation. Firstly, belief in Heaven and its attainment through the Spirit of Charity remain paramount and individuals' economic behaviour is policed by an inner voice called conscience. Secondly, the Catholic world-view holds that enjoyment of this life is an important and visible acknowledgement of God's existence and of His created universe. It is therefore rational to relegate work to an instrumental activity supporting this enjoyment. As the maximisiation of spiritual well-being is paramount then the *rational* strategy to work must be based adopting an instrumental approach to global capitalism. In other words, limits on labour inputs, on the acquisitive impulse and on the measure of enough are rational requirements.

Moreover, enough is not an intangible or abstract concept. The contributors in our study identified a series of standard norms that applied in reality. It is finite and reproduced through the material world as an object or an experience such as golf, alcohol (a jar), holidays, education for the kids, a home, money to buy clothes, etc. This approach however does not frown on good fortune or luck such as a win on the lotto so that an individual does not necessarily have to work in order to acquire. The vocational emphasis of work is not therefore, the most important one. Where

---

[148] Again this echoes the views of many of the respondents in all Domains. The Traveller Women were also concerned not alone about their unhappiness but more importantly about the spiritual dangers of excessive wealth.

happiness is experienced then the social and economic relations obtaining at the time are regarded as legitimate.

The primary role of the Absolute Pre-supposition Catholicism-Nationalism, is to motivate the individual to overcome the unlimited acquisitive impulse in favour of enough. In that sense it weakens the Spirit of Capitalism. The initial focus is to relentlessly generate whatever level of work effort is required to secure enough and only then reducing it to maintain enough. From that moment forward work is used as an instrument to sustain enough rather than generate ever-increasing levels of wealth. In that sense, the Catholic economic disposition strengthens the Spirit of Capitalism.

We can now state that our Theory of Limits defines the Catholic Ethic as essentially instrumental in character, actively assisting with economic development until the point when enough is reached i.e. when a sustaining rather than an acquisitive impulse informs the individual's economic activity. The Catholic worldview internalises this self-limiting economic effort to temper the acquisitive impulse to a level where a satisfactory balance between material and spiritual well-being can be achieved. Therefore, it tends to *conditionally* assist economic development within self-defined limits and as these limits are reached it then tends to preserve differentials rather than increase the preferred measure of enough in absolute terms. The achievement of enough pacifies the individual's acquisitive impulse and thereafter the individual adopts a detachment where a sense of being in but not of global capitalism applies. This frees him/her to place a premium on activities regarded as more rational than work such as enjoyment of life. In that sense alone global capitalism is imprinted with the stamp and approval of the Spirit of Charity.

Summary of this Study

We have concluded under theme one, that Ireland had experienced a so-called belated golden age of development, namely the Celtic Tiger. The tendency of both sociologists and economists to deploy universal insights that had been developed using larger more industrially advanced societies and where smaller countries such as Ireland or non conforming Islamic societies were often 'airbrushed' out of economic and sociological discourse. A set of debates then followed on the causes of poor economic development since independence and another set attempted to explain the underlying 'good' causes of the Celtic Tiger. We concluded that the Celtic Tiger phenomenon was an accident of circumstances where secularisation, the usual pre-requisite for economic development, was largely absent.

Under theme two we employed an original multi-faceted research approach and a tailor made instrument to capture the views of a unique array of respondents, representing the mosaic of Irish social life. Our research findings revealed that Irish economic policy was not only infused with Catholic Social Teaching but was distinguished by support for optimising rather than maximising growth. Furthermore, the findings were used as a basis to build up a unique profile capturing the essence of the Irish economic disposition where two durable sentiments religion and nationalism were active dureés or Absolute Pre-suppositions shaping that recurring economic disposition.

In theme three we successfully employed a stranding approach to throw light on the nature of the configuration of internal socio-cultural factors impacting on the economic disposition. Through a series of sociological analyses we established both the nature and force of the configuration. One of the most effective approaches used was to anchor Marxist and Eliasian insights in a real war of conflicting interests where the fire of the sentiments under scrutiny could be grounded in individuals and groups such as James Connolly and the craftworker combatants, and where the interrelationship between the configuration of variables was exposed at work shaping individual and national economic behaviour.

Finally, in theme four, a re-formulated Theory of Limits was presented to provide a more inclusive explanation of the research data that informed the profile of the Irish economic disposition and its impact on individual economic behaviour and on the dynamic of economic development. Moreover, we have achieved this while maintaining the fabric of Durkheim's, sociological approach i.e. we have gone back to basics and analysed how the economic disposition evolved and became complicated little by little until it reached its Celtic Tiger form. Our analysis of the empirical data confirmed our suspicion that the process of economic development is not really fully understood and that the various descriptive explanations to explain the emergence of the Celtic Tiger only compounded this analytical weakness. However, our research indicated that durable culture specific factors called Absolute Pre-suppositions play a central role in the dynamic of economic development and have demonstrated, we believe, the developmental process in action.

The accident of the Celtic Tiger was that Irish structures such as social partnership consensus and the Irish economic disposition, both heavily influenced by the tenets of Catholic social teaching, together with the non socialist economic environment, just happened to be the necessary pre-requisites or conditions conducive to the development of global capitalism where a so-called miracle of economic development was invoked. The strong Catholic ethos exhibited in the Celtic Tiger, contrasts sharply with many traditional views on the central role of the rational and scientific Protestant ethic in capitalist development, a relationship that is still widely regarded as almost divinely pre-determining western economic development. Our data shows that there is a parallel and equally valid alternative to this hypothesis.

This latter insight now highlights the real possibility that a significant analytical weakness is embedded in relying on a universal blueprint to understand developmental dynamics because of the need to factor Absolute Pre-suppositions into the equation. Of course this culture specific adaptation goes against the preferred one size fits all approach of global capitalism. Yet without these pre-suppositions it is difficult enough to explain developmental patterns of advanced societies and near impossible when examining non-secularised Islamic countries or Catholic countries like Ireland that have experienced accidental development. This means that in addition to the purely empirical approach there is now an imperative to accommodate within the industrial policy framework, culture specific expectations of material and religious levels of well-being largely driven by the absolute presupposition religion/nationalism. In many societies these expectations demand a *minimal* level of engagement with global capitalism because its intrinsic acquisitiveness is equated with economic imperialism and a material focus. De facto both are usually perceived to threaten other worldly sacred national norms and values. The tension between profane and sacred norms is often manifested through the 'fire' of religious/nationalist sentiment. We have seen in this study of Irish economic development just how powerful a socio-economic force this fiery sentiment can be, successful initiating a Catholic nationalist 'holy' war against an imperial Protestant infidel.

Secondly, the analysis of our data confounds the traditional position of many commentators that the Catholic ethic was and still is inimical to economic development and averse to global capitalism. The fact is that the Catholic ethic becomes temporarily aligned to rather than a bedfellow of global capitalism.

The instrumental outcome for successfully managing the contest and tensions between on the one hand, global capitalism that fosters unlimited wealth as its raison d'être and on the other, where Catholic religious beliefs endorse limited acquisition, is observed in the pursuit of an individualised tailor-made and conscience endorsed measure of enough. This temporary and committed work effort acts as a capitalist growth promoter. However, once enough has been achieved, the engagement level diminishes to a point where the individual can maintain what is already acquired and this maintenance ethos sets limits on the acquisitive impulse. At this point growth promoting engagement is diverted to generating increasing levels of enjoyment.

The evidence of our third line of inquiry, where we re-visited some of the sociological insights of Marx, Elias, Weber, Freud, Durkheim and Giddens was that that they had either overlooked, undervalued or even dismissed the influence of religion and nationalism as drivers of socio-economic development. Weber in particular, overestimated the growth inhibiting force of Catholicism while at the same time underestimated its growth promoting potential. The distinguishing mark between the Protestant Ethic and the Spirit of Capitalism and the Catholic Ethic and the Spirit of Charity is only tactical. The former promotes continuous unlimited accumulation to re-invest and limits enjoyment, whereas the latter sets limits to accumulating and promotes enjoyment. In fact, high levels of accidental growth made available by facilitating global capitalism provided an ideal solution for the Catholic to optimise personal well-being. It is this insight into the win-win focus of the Catholic dual mandate of securing material and spiritual well-being and the rationality behind the resultant instrumental and capitalist friendly economic behaviour, that ultimately eluded the fathers of sociology.

This dual mandate approach appears to be well disposed towards Tawney's (1961) recommendation that economic activity must remain subordinated to higher social purposes if the intention is to make a better life for everyone. Our study revealed that the Catholic ethic had the capacity to expand to accommodate the accidental birth of global capitalism incarnated as the Celtic Tiger and that it is demonstrating equal flexibility in contracting to accommodate its accidental death.

Appendix A

Economic Speeches of the Tánaiste and the Minister for Enterprise, Trade and Employment 1998-2000

Plenary Meeting of the Social Partners, Dublin Castle, 28 July 1998.

Address at the Northern Ireland Economic Conference, Galgorm Manor, Ballymena, Co. Antrim, 17 September 1998.

Address at the North Dublin Development Conference, Dublin City University, 24 September 1998.

Address to The Institute of Engineers Congress, Wellington, New Zealand, 5 February 1999.

Remarks at The Call Centres 1999 Exhibition and Conference, Burlington Hotel Dublin, 2 March 1999.

Remarks at the Limerick Chamber of Commerce EXPO'99, Business Lunch, Castletroy Hotel, 30 April 1999.

Remarks to members of the Foreign Press Association, London, 16 June 1999.

Remarks at the Irish National Organisation for the Unemployed, National Literacy Association Conference, 17 June 1999.

Remarks to the Dublin Chamber of Commerce Breakfast Meeting, Davenport Hotel, Dublin, 14 September 1999.

Launch of the Western Development Commission Report, 'Promoting Foreign Direct Investment in the West of Ireland', Carrick-on-Shannon, 8 October 1999.

Remarks at the Encounter Synposium. 'Managing our Economies', Berkeley Court Hotel, Dublin, 29 October 1999.

Address at the launch of the Government's National Development Plan, Dublin Castle, 15 November 1999.

Remarks at the 'Employment in the New Millennium Conference', Burlington Hotel, Dublin, 3 November 1999.

Remarks at the Co-Operative Organisation Society Ltd., National Co-Operative Conference, Burlington Hotel, Dublin, 1 November 1999.

Speaking at the Regional Consultative Forum, Ballaghaderreen '50% of IDA Jobs to go to Objective 1 Region', 19 January 2000.

Remarks at the Opening of the FÁS 'Opportunities 2000' Conference, Minerva Suite, Royal Dublin Society, 7 February 2000.

Address to the Fifth Annual Conference to the World Association of Investment Promotion Agencies (WAIPA) Bangkok, Thailand, 10 February 2000.

Speaking about Job Losses in Ballinasloe and Dundalk, 18 February 2000.

Government Press and Publicity Office Announcement, 'A New Labour Market Immigration Policy', 28 March 2000.

Appendix B

Stated Occupations of Captured Combatants 1916 and 1922

C1 Title of Occupation	C2 Dublin Area Combatants to Knutsford Jail, 1 May 1916[a]	C3 Dublin Area Combatants to Knutsford Jail, 3 May 1916[b]	C4 Country Combatants to Wakefield Prison, 13 May 1916[c]	C5 Roll Call E- Coy Dublin 2nd Battalion IRA, 31 June 1920[d]
Craftsman	58	77	42	47
Apprentice	2		4	2
Skilled Worker			1	
Apprentice	2	6		
Machinist		7	6	
Labourer	32	57	30	14
Shop Assistant/ Porter	16	19	37	15
Clerk	11	45	16	13
Farmer	4	4	45	
Engineer	2		2	
Profession Man				1
Teacher	2	1	10	
Merchant		2	6	
Insurance Inspector		1		
Inspector of Telephones		1		
Baker		2	3	
Civil Servant		2		
Chemist		1		1
3rd Level Student		4	2	
Private Means		1		
Van/Car Driver		5	10	
Pharmacist		1		
Cinematograph Operator		1		
Druggist		1		
Tailor		3		

C1 Title of Occupation	C2 Dublin Area Combatants to Knutsford Jail, 1 May 1916[a]	C3 Dublin Area Combatants to Knutsford Jail, 3 May 1916[b]	C4 Country wide Combatants to Wakefield Prison, 13 May 1916[c]	C5 Roll Call E-Coy Dublin 2nd Battalion IRA, 31 June 1920[d]
Foreman		2	1	
Seaman		2		
Gardener		1		
Artist		1		
Waiter		1		
Teapacker		2		
Groom		1		
Ex-Policeman		1		
Bookkeeper		1	1	
Postman		1	3	
Journalist			1	
News reporter			1	
Farm Manager			2	
Surveyor			1	
Banker			1	
Garage Owner			1	
Accountant			1	1
Undertaker			1	
Builder			1	
Butcher			1	
Forester			1	
Miscell/unstated.	71	53	42	58
TOTAL	200	308	273	152

[a] *Sinn Féin Rebellion Handbook 200, Dublin Area Sinn Féin Prisoners sent to Knutsford*, Cheshire, 1 May, 1916, p. 69.

[b] *Sinn Féin Rebellion Handbook 308 Dublin Area Sinn Féin Prisoners sent to Knutsford*, 3 May, 1916, p. 73.

[c] *Sinn Féin Rebellion Handbook 273 Countrywide (outsideDublin) sent to Wakefield Prison*, 13 May, 1916.

[d] *Roll Call E-Company Second Battalion, IRA 1 January-31 June 1920*, Allen Library, Dublin, presented by Commdt. Vincent Byrne through Mr. Brendan Kenny to the Allen Library, Nth Richmond St., Dublin 3. Volunteers from the following Dublin City Areas;- Nth. Wall, Parnell St., Nth. Earl St., Nth. King St., Grafton St., Ormond Quay, Sackville Place (all within 1 mile radius of GPO). Amiens St., Oriel St., Seville Place, Nth. Strand, Drumcondra, Fairview, Marino, Dorset St., Nth. William St., Jones Road, Glasnevin, Townsend St., Lr. Gardiner St., Harold's Cross (all within 3 mile radius of O'Connell St, City Centre).

Appendix C

Comparison of the Occupational Profiles of those Elected in 1918 British General Election, the 1927 Free State Election and the 1998 General Election in the Republic

Occupation	C1[a]	C2[b]	C3[c]	C4[d]
Academic		4	7	7
Accountant				9
Barrister/Lawyer/Solicitor	5	9	12	15
Politician			9	26
Contractor			4	
Union Official	2		12	4
Landowner			1	
Farmer		2	36	25
Engineer	1	3	9	
National School Teacher		2	3	10
Secondary School Teacher			2	14
Vocational Teacher				1
Other Teacher				3
Merchant	1	2	11	
Military	6		5	
Baker			2	
Gentleman	1	1	1	
Journalist	2	6	3	2
Widow			2	
Craftsman			7	
Dentist			1	
Shopkeeper		5	5	
Aristocrat	1	1	1	
Agri-Labourer			2	
Railway Labourer			1	
Station Master			1	
Doctor/Vet			3	
Farmers Union			1	
County Councillor		3	2	
Jeweller			1	
Publican		1	1	
Commercial Agent		1	1	
Civil Servant			2	

Occupation	C1[a]	C2[b]	C3[c]	C4[d]
Clerk/Clerical		1	1	14
Foreman		1		1
Public Servant			1	
Sheep Breeder			1	
Employer Representative			1	7
MD of Company	1	1		18
Secretary		2		
Sinn Féin Organiser		12		
Commercial Traveller		1		
Writer		1		
Health-Care				4
Auctioneer				4
Economist				2
Unstated	2	14	1	
TOTAL	22	73	153	166

Source: *Irish Times*, 5 September 1918, p. 5, and *Irish Times*, 17 June 1927, p. 3, and *Press & Publicity Office*, The Oireachtas Records 1998, Kildare St., Dublin 2.

[a] This Column represents occupations of Unionist MPs elected in the 1918 British General Election.

[b] This Column represents of Sinn Féin MPs elected in the 1918 British General Election.

[c] This Column represents occupation of TDs elected to Saorstát Éireann Elections in 1927.

[d] This Column represents occupations of those elected to Irish Parliament in 1998 Elections.

Appendix D

Profile of the Celtic Tiger Workforce Versus Profile of Elected Representatives

Occupation	000s[a]	TD[b]
Craftsman/Skilled Worker	146.7	0
Farmer	105.4	23
Clerical	81.1	12
Shop Assistant	75.3	
Typist/Bookkeeper	66.3	
Teacher	57.3	28
Manager/Company Secretary	56.6	18
Drivers of Bus, Train, Other	47.5	
Nurse	42.1	
Labourers	39.6	
Proprietors	32.1	
Domestic Servant	27.9	
Accountant	21.3	9
Commercial Traveller	18.5	
Waiter/Waitress	18.3	
Agri Labourer	17.8	
Cleaners	16.6	
Foremen/women	16.0	
Warehouse/Dispatch Clerks	15.3	
Engineers	14.7	9
Hospital Orderlies	14.3	
Barmen/Women	13.5	
Chef/Cook	12.6	
Barber/Hairdresser	11.3	
Computer Programmers	10.8	
Medical Practitioners	8.7.	
Clergy/Nuns/Religious	7.8	
Academic	6.9	6
Legal Professionals	6.0	15

[a] Sexton, J. and Frost, D. and Hughes G. (1998), *FÁS/ESRI Manpower Forecasting Studies - Aspects of Occupational Change in the Irish Economy: Recent Trends and Future Prospects*, ESRI, Dublin, Table 12, Report No 7, December 1998, pp. 96-97.
[b] *Press & Publicity Office*, The Oireachtas Records 1998, Kildare St., Dublin 2.

Bibliography

AHCPS (2000), *The Proposed Introduction of A Competency Based System of Performance Management for the Irish Civil Service*, The Association of Higher Civil and Public Servants, Dublin, February 2000 Edition, p. 6.

Ahern, B. (2000), 'Economic Values and the Common Good', Dublin, 5 February 2000, Address at the Irish Centre for Faith and Culture Conference.

Ahlstrom, D. (2000), 'Study Shows Young not Irreligious', *Irish Times*, 14 January, p. 7.

Ahmed, A. (1988), *Discovering Islam: Making Sense of Muslim History and Society*, Routledge, London, p. 155, pp. 208-210, p. 219.

Akenson, D. (1991), *Small Differences - Irish Catholics and Irish Protestants 1815-1922*, McGill University Press, Belfast, p. 13, pp. 16-19, p. 27, p. 35, pp. 140-143.

Aldridge, A. (2000), *Religion in the Contemporary World - A Sociological Introduction*, Polity Press in association with Blackwell Publishers, Cambridge, p. 2, p. 9, p. 92.

Allen, K. (1999), 'The Celtic Tiger, Inequality and Social Partnership', *Industrial Relations News*, Industrial Relations News, 26, July 1999, p. 16.

Allen, K. (2000), *The Celtic Tiger - The Myth of Social Partnership in Ireland*, Manchester University Press, Manchester, pp. 16-19, pp. 25-27, p. 160, p. 174.

Andrews, C. (1979), 'The Second City of the Empire: Colonial Dublin 1911', *Journal of Historical Geography*, No 23, 1997, p. 152.

Apple, M. (1997), *Ideology and Curriculum*, Routledge London 1990, second edition, p11.

Arkins, B. (1994), 'Sexuality in Fifth-Century Athens', *Classics Ireland*, Volume 1, University College Dublin, Dublin, p. 2.

Arnason, J. (1987), 'Figurational Sociology as a Counter-Paradigm', *Theory Culture and Society*, Sage, Volume 4, 1987, pp. 429-456.

Ashraf, S. (1991), *World Religions - Islam*, Stanley Thornes Publishers, Cheltenham.

Ashton, D. (1998), 'Linking Education and Training to Economic Development', Paper delivered by Professor David Ashton to CLMS Workshop, Mont Clare Hotel, Dublin, 25 April, 1998.

Ashton, D. and Green, F. (1996), *Education, Training and the Global Economy*, Elgar, Cheltenham, p. 65, p. 171.

Ashton, D. and Sung, J. (2000), *Adapting the Market for Skill Formation - Two Contrasting Approaches*, Centre for Labour Market Studies, University of Leicester, Leicester, p. 14.

Ashton, D. and Sung, J. (2001), *Lessons Learned from Overseas Experience*, Final Report Workforce Development, pp. 1-27, http/www.cabinet-office.gov.uk/innovation/2001/workforce/overseas.html

Augusteijn, J. (1998), 'Sinn Féin', S.J. Connolly (ed.), *The Oxford Companion to Irish History*, Oxford University Press, Oxford, p. 231, p. 513.

AT Kearney/Foreign Policy Magazine (2002), 'Globalisation's Last Hurray?', *Foreign Policy January/February 2002*, Carnegie Endowment for International Peace, pp. 38-51.

Baert, P. (1998), *Social Theory in the Twentieth Century*, Polity Press, Cambridge, p. 72, p. 74, p. 81.

Baker, T. and Duffy, D. and Shortall, F. (1998), *Quarterly Economic Commentary*, Economic and Social Research Institute, Dublin, April 1998, p. 31.

Ballymun Community Action Programme, (2001), *Ballymun: A Summary Introduction*, http://www.cap.ie, pp. 1-8.

Ballymun Regeneration, (2001), *Ballymun: A Bright New Future*, http://brl.ie/profile, pp. 1-3.

Bampton, Fr. (1923), *Christianity and Reconstruction-The Labour Question: A Series of Lectures Given by Fr. Bampton S.J. in Westminster Cathedral and Farm St. Church*, Sands and Co., London, p. 142, p. 159.

Barrett, S. (1997), 'Universities and Education', *Evening Herald*, Dublin, 2 August 1997, p. 13.

Barry, F. (1999), 'Irish Growth in Historical and Theoretical Perspective', Frank Barry (ed.), *Understanding Ireland's Economic Growth*, Macmillan Press, London, Essay 2, p. 1, pp. 25-26.

Barry, F and Bradley, J. and O'Malley, E. (1999), 'Indigenous and Foreign Industry: Characteristics and Performance', Frank Barry (ed.), *Understanding Ireland's Economic Growth*, Macmillan Press, London, Essay 3, p. 70.

Barry, F and Hannan, A. and Strobl, E. (1999), 'The Real Convergence of the Irish Economy and the Sectoral Distribution of Employment Growth', Frank Barry (ed.), *Understanding Ireland's Economic Growth*, Macmillan Press, London, Essay 2, pp. 14-15.

Bassanini, A. and Scarpetta, S (2001), *Does Human Capital Matter for Growth in OECD Countries? Evidence from Pooled Mean-Group Estimates*, OECD Economic Dept., Paris, Working Paper No 282, pp. 1-30.

Basset, E. (1978), 'The Suffering of Jesus', Elizabeth Basset (ed.) *Each in His Prison: An Anthology*, SPCK, London, with a foreword by Richard Hauser and Hephzibah Menuhin Hauser Co,, Directors of the Centre for Human Rights and Responsibilities, p. 159.

Baudrillard, J. (1988), 'Consumer Society', *Jean Baudrillard - Selected Writings*, Blackwell Press, in association with Polity Press, Oxford, p. 50.

Bellah, R. (1973), 'Introduction', Robert Bellah (ed.), *Emile Durkheim: On Morality and Society*, University of Chicago Press, Chicago, p. xxx.

Bernstein, P. (1997), *American Work Values Their Origin and Value*, State University of New York Press, Albany, p. 53, pp. 60-61.

Berresford Ellis, P. (1996), *A History of the Irish Working Class*, Pluto Press, London, p. 209.

Bielenberg, A. (1995), 'Enterprise and Investment in Ireland 1850-1900', Andrew Burke (Ed.), *Enterprise and the Irish Economy: Irish Studies in Management*, Oak Tree Press, Dublin, p. 21, p. 27.

Bielenberg, A. (2000), 'Career of William Martin Murphy', *Irish Economic and Social History*, Volume XXVII, 2000, pp. 25-43.

Billington, R and Hockey, J. and Strawbridge, S. (1998), *Exploring Self and Society*, Macmillan Press, London, p. 16, p. 34, p. 176, p. 250.

Black, B. (1994), 'British and Irish Work Related Values and Attitudes', *The International Journal of Human Resource Management*, Volume 5, No 4, December 1994, pp. 341-349.

Blackburn, K. (1997), 'The Protestant Work Ethic and the Australian Mercantile Elite, 1880-1914', *The Journal of Religious History*, Volume 21, No 2, June 1997, pp. 193-208.

Blanchflower, D. and Oswald A. (1999), 'Well Being, Insecurity and the Decline of American Job Satisfaction', paper presented in association with the American Bureau of Economic Research, at the Cornell University Conference, May 1999, p. 1 pp. 9-10.

Bottigheimer, K. (1982), *Ireland and the Irish - A Short History*, Columbia University Press, New York, p. 2.

Bould, G. (1991), *Conscience Be My Guide: An Anthology of Prison Writings*, Zed Books, London, p. vi, p. 56.

Bourke, E. (1997), 'The Irishman is no Lazzarone, German Travel Writer in Ireland 1828-1825', *History Ireland*, Volume V, No 3, Autumn 1997, pp. 21-36.

Boyce, D.G. (1996), 'Interpreting the Rising', D.G. Boyce and Alan O'Day (eds.), *The Making of Modern Irish History-Revisionism and the Revisionist Controversy*, Routledge, New York, Essay 9, p. 163.

Brabazon, T. and Stock, P. (1999), 'Riverdance and Stepping through Antipodean Memory', *Irish Studies Review*, Volume 7, Number 3, December 1999, pp. 301-313.

Bradford De Long, J. (1989), *The "Protestant Ethic" Revisited: A Twentieth Century Look*, Harvard University Press, USA, pp. 3-5.

Bradford, C. and Chakwin, N. (1993), *Alternative Explanations of Trade-Output Correlation in the East Asian Economies*, OECD, Paris, Technical Paper No 87.

Bradley, J. (2000), 'The Irish Economy in Comparative Perspective', Brian Nolan and Philip J. O'Connell and Christopher T. Whelan (eds.), *Bust or Boom - The Irish Experience of Growth and Inequality*, Institute of Public Administration, Dublin, p. 26.

Brady, C. (1999), 'Constructive and Instrumental: The Dilemma of Ireland's First New Historians', Ciarán Brady (ed.), *Interpreting Irish History - The Debate on Historical Revisionism*, Irish Academic Press, Dublin, Reading 1, pp. 3-34.

Breathneach, N. (1996), 'Investment in Education-the key to our future success as a nation', *Irish Times*, 30 July, 1996, p. 14.

Breathneach, N. (1997), *Government Action Plan on Skills*, Department of Enterprise and Employment, Press and Publicity Office, Dublin, 12 March 1997, p. 1.

Breen, R. and Hannan, D. and Rottman, D. and Whelan, C.T. (1990), *Understanding Contemporary Ireland - State, Class and Development in the Republic of Ireland*, Gill and Macmillan, Dublin, pp. 1-2, p. 27, p. 62, p. 108, p. 120, pp. 159-165, p. 219, p. 261.

Breen, R and Whelan, C.T. (1994), 'Social Class Origins and Political Partisanship in the Republic of Ireland', reprinted from *European Journal of Political Research*, No 26, pp. 117-133, ESRI Reprint Series 102, Dublin.

Brennan, S. (1992), *Education for a Changing World*, Government Publications Office, Dublin, Foreword.

Brewer, J.D. (2001), 'The Paradox of Northern Ireland', *Sociology*, British Sociological Association, Cambridge, Volume 35, No 3, August 2001, pp. 779-783.

British and Irish Communist Organisation, The (1977), *Communism in Ireland*, B and ICO, Belfast, pp. 12-25.

Broderick, E. (1994), 'The Corporate Labour Policy of Fine Gael 1934', *Irish Historical Studies*, No 113, May 1994, p. xxix, pp. 88-99.

Browett, J. (1983), 'Out of the Dependency Perspective', Peter Limqueco and Bruce McFarlane (eds.), *Neo-Marxist Theories of Development*, Croom Helm, London, p. 184.

Brown, P. and Lauder H. (2001), *Capitalism and Social Progress - The Future of Society in a Global Economy*, Palgrave, Basingstoke, p. 238.

Bryman, A. (1994), 'Quantitative and Qualitative Research', paper delivered to the Centre for Labour Market Studies, MSc Residential, Leicester, November 1994, pp. 1-6.

Burgess, R. (1984), *In the Field - An Introduction to Field Research*, Routledge, London, reprinted 1993.

Burke, A. (1995), 'Economic Integration and New Firm Formation: Britain's Impact on Irish Enterprise', Andrew Burke (ed.), *Enterprise and the Irish Economy: Irish Studies in Management*, Oak Tree Press, Dublin, p. 132.

Burkitt, I. (1996), 'Civilisation and Ambivalence', *Sociology*, Volume 47, No 1, March 1996, pp. 135-150.

Buxton, W. (1985), *Talcott Parsons and the Capitalist Nation State-Political Sociology as a Strategic Vocation*, University of Toronto Press, Toronto, p. 5, p. 56.

Cairncross, A. (1962), *Factors in Economic Development*, George Allen and Unwin, London, p, 26, p. 156.

Cairns, D. and Richards, S. (1988), *Writing Ireland - Colonialism, Nationalism and Culture*, Manchester University Press, Manchester, pp. 20-21, pp. 115-118, p. 139.

Calder, J. and Sapsford, R. (1996), 'Multivariate Analysis', Roger Sapsford and Victor Jupp (eds.), *Data Collection and Analysis*, Sage Publications, in association with the Open University, p. 273.

Callan, T. and Nolan, B. (1999), 'Income Inequality in Ireland in the 1980s and 1990s', Frank Barry (ed.), *Understanding Ireland's Economic Growth*, Macmillan Press, London, Essay 8, p. 180, p. 182, p. 188.

Cantor, N. F. (1993), *The Civilisation of the Middle Ages, A Completely Revised and Expanded Edition of Medieval History, The Life and Death of a Civilisation*, Harpur Collins Publishers, New York, p. 20, p. 135, p. 147, p. 383.

Carroll, J. (2000), 'US Saw Ties Weakening and Communism Growing', *Irish Times*, 11 January, p. 3.

Catholic Encyclopaedia, The (1908), *An International Work on the Constitution, Doctrine, Discipline and History of the Catholic Church*, Caxton, London, Volume III, p. 761b and Volume IX, p. 289.

Catholic Encyclopaedia, The (1911), *An International Work on the Constitution, Doctrine, Discipline and History of the Catholic Church*, Robert Appleton Company, London, Volume XII, Online Edition Copyright 1999, by Kevin Knight, Nihil Obstat, June 1, 1911, http://www.newadvent.org/cathen/12575a.htm

CEDEFOP (1998), *Approaches and Obstacles to the Evaluation of Investment in Continuing Vocational Training: Discussions and Case Studies from Six Member States of the European Union*, CEDEFOP, Brussels, p. 95, p. 157.

Central Statistics Office (1995), *Labour Force Survey*, Stationery Office, Government Publications, Dublin.

Central Statistics Office (1999), 'Statistical Abstract 1999', *Table 2.32: Persons Classified by Religious Denomination*, CSO, Dublin, p. 57.

Central Statistics Office (2000), *Economic Series September 2000*, Stationery Office, Government Publications, Dublin, p. 11.

Central Statistics Office (2000a), *Quarterly National Household Survey - 3rd Quarter*, CSO, Dublin, pp. 1-28.

Central Statistics Office (2001), *Quarterly National Household Survey - March 2001*, CSO, Dublin, pp. 1-24.

Central Statistics Office (2001a), *External Trade (Details), February 2001-March 2001, First Estimates*, CSO, Dublin, pp. 1-8.

Central Statistics Office (2001b), *Population and Migration Estimates*, CSO, Dublin, August 2001, pp. 1-8.

Central Statistics Office (2001c), *Quarterly National Household Survey - 3rd Quarter 2001*, CSO, Dublin, pp. 1-24.

Central Statistics Office (2001d), *Live Register Statement November 2001*, CSO, Dublin, pp. 1-8.

Central Statistics Office (2003), *Commentary to Principle Demographic Results Census 2002*, CSO, Dublin, pp. 1-24.

Channel 4, (2001), 'Testing God', 2 September 2001.

Chart, D.A. (1920), *An Economic History of Ireland*, Talbot Press, Dublin, pp. 97-98, p. 105, p. 147.

Christian Brothers, The (1934), *Christian Politeness and Counsels for Youth*, M.H. Gill and Son, O'Connell St. Upper, Dublin, pp. 94-107.

Christian Brothers, The (1946), *Fortifying Youth*, M.H. Gill and Son, O'Connell St. Upper, Dublin, p. 9, p. 94, p. 103.

Christian, H. (1994), *The Making of Anti-Sexist Men*, Routledge, London.

Christopher, A.J. (1997), 'The Second City of the Empire: Colonial Dublin 1911', *Journal of Historical Geography*, 23 Edition, Volume 2, 1997, pp. 150-155, pp. 160-161.

Cinnirella, M. (2000), 'Britain: A History of Four Nations', Louk Hagendoorn, Gyorgy Csepeli, Henk Dekker, Russell Farnen (eds.), *European Nations and Nationalism-Theoretical and Historical Perspectives*, Ashgate Research Migration and Ethnic Relations Series, Aldershot, p. 42.

Clancy, P. (1995), 'Education in the Republic of Ireland: The Project of Modernity?', Patrick Clancy, Sheelagh Drudy, Kathleen Lynch and Liam Dowd (eds.), *Modern Ireland: Irish Society, Sociological Perspectives*, IPA in association with The Sociological Association of Ireland, Dublin, pp. 467-491.

CLMS (1998), *Research Methods*, MSc in Training and HRM, University of Leicester, Leicester, Module 3, Unit 1, Section 2, p. 19, pp. 41-42.

CLMS (2000), *Demystifying Methodology - Introduction, Aims and Objectives*, Paper presented at the CLMS Workshop at Halbowline Naval Base, Cork, Ireland pp. 3-4.

Coakley, J. (1986), 'The Evolution of Irish Party Politics', Roland Sturm (ed.), *Politics and Society in Contemporary Ireland*, Gower Publishing Company, Aldershot p. 30, p. 40, p. 43.

Coakley, J. (1998), 'Blueshirts', 'Fianna Fáil', S.J.Connolly (ed.), *The Oxford Companion to Irish History*, Oxford University Press, Oxford, p. 48, p. 192.

Coleman, S. and Keep, E. (2001), 'Background Literature Review for Performance and Innovation Unit (PIU)', *Project on Workforce Development (UK)*, pp. 1-48, http/www.cabinet-office.gov.uk/innovation/2001/workforce/SKOPE.html

Collingwood, R.G. (1940), *An Essay on Metaphysics*, Oxford University Press, Oxford.

Collingwood, R.G. (1998), *An Essay On Metaphysics*, Clarendon Press, Oxford edited with an introduction by Rex Martin, first published in 1940, pp. xxvii-xxx, pp. 196-198, pp. 31-32.

Collins, R. (1998), 'Democratisation in World-Historical Perspective', Ralph Schroeder (ed.), *Max Weber, Democracy and Modernisation*, Macmillan Press, London.

Collins, T. (2000), 'Ireland The Challenges of Success', *Working Toward Balance-Our Society in the New Millenium*, Veritas, Dublin, pp. 88-98.

Collons, P. (1998),'Negotiating Selves: Reflections on Unstructured Interviewing', *Sociological Research Online*, Volume 3, No 3, http://www.socresonline.org.uk/socresonline/3/3/2.html

Combat Poverty Agency (1999), *Strategic Plan 1999-2001*, Combat Poverty Agency, Dublin, pp. 1-18.

Comiskey, B. (1998), 'Would you believe?', *RTE 1 Television*, 15 November.

Congleton, R. (1991), 'The Economic Role of a Work Ethic', *Journal of Economic Behaviour and Organisation*, Volume 15, pp. 365-385.

Connell, K.H. (1968), 'Catholicism and Marriage in the Century after the Famine', K.H. Connell (ed.), *Irish Peasant Society*, Irish Academic Press, Dublin, p. 113, p. 151.

Connolly, J. (1896), *Irish Socialist Republican Party-Minute Book 29th May 1896 to 18th September 1898*, Dublin, National Library of Ireland, MS16295, Reference 29/05/96, Reference 02/07/1896, Reference 05/11/1896, Reference 07/01/1897, Reference 24/02/1898, Reference 10/03/1898.

Connolly, J. (1898), *The Workers Republic*, National Library of Ireland, Dublin, Reel 22, Volume 1, No 2, 20 August 1898, p. 8.

Connolly, J. (1908), 'James Connolly on Socialism and Sinn Féin', Alan O'Day and John Stevenson (eds.), *Irish Historical Documents Since 1800*, Gill and Macmillan, Dublin, p. 145.

Connolly, J. (1909), *Reply of James Connolly to the Editor of the Daily People Dublin*, National Library of Ireland, William O' Brien Papers, MS 13929, p. 4.

Connolly, J. (1910), *Labour in Irish History*, Maunsel and Co., Dublin, pp. iii-xiv, p. 118, p. 215.

Connolly, J. (1910a), *Labour Nationality and Religion being a discussion of the Lenten Discourses against Socialism delivered by Father Kane S.J. in Gardiner St. Church, Dublin 1910*, Irish Transport and General Workers Union, Dublin, pp. i-xiii.

Connolly, J. (1911), 'Socialist Party of Ireland its Aims and Methods', *Socialism and Nationalism-a selection from the writings of James Connolly with introduction and notes by Desmond Ryan*, Sign of the Three Candles, Dublin, p. 191.

Connolly, J. (1914), 'Independent Labour Party of Ireland Appeal to the Irish Working Class', *Socialism and Nationalism-a selection from the writings of James Connolly*, with introduction and notes by Desmond Ryan, Sign of the Three Candles, Dublin, p. 181.

Connolly, J. (1914), *The Axe to the Root New Edition with Introduction and Old Wine in New Bottles-The Connolly Pamphlets*, Dublin, Irish Transport and General Workers Union, Bookcase S, Section 1, Shelf 5, Allen Library, O'Connell Schools North Richmond St. Dublin 1, Reprinted 1920, p. 209.

Connolly, J. (1934), *Labour in Ireland-II, The Re-Conquest of Ireland with an Introduction by Robert Lynd*, Irish Transport and General Workers Union, Dublin.

Connolly, J. (1941), *A Socialist and War*, Lawrence and Wishart, London, pp. 112-113, p. 328.

Connolly, S. (1994), *Religion and Society in Nineteenth Century Ireland - Studies in Irish Economic and Social History*, Dun Dalgan Press, Dundalk, Co. Louth, p. 1, p. 53, pp. 59-60.

Connolly, S.J. (1996), 'Nationalism', D.G. Boyce and Alan O'Day (eds.), *The Making of Modern Irish History - Revisionism and the Revisionist Controversy*, Routledge, New York.

Connolly S.J. (1998), 'Mother and Child Controversy', S.J. Connolly (ed.), *The Oxford Companion to Irish History*, Oxford University Press, Oxford, p. 370.

Connolly S.J. (1998a), 'Communist Party', S.J. Connolly (ed.), *The Oxford Companion to Irish History*, Oxford University Press, Oxford, p. 107.

Connolly, S.J. (1998b), 'Society of United Irishmen', S.J. Connolly (ed.), *The Oxford Companion to Irish History*, Oxford University Press, Oxford, pp. 67-568.

Conway, E. (2000), 'On This Rock', *RTE 1 Television*, 2 April 2000.

Conway, K. (1998), 'Doing God's Business is Getting Tougher', *Irish Independent*, 30 April, 1998.

Cooney, J. (1999), *John Charles McQuaid-Leader of Catholic Ireland*, O'Brien Press, Dublin, p. 252.

Cooper, H. (1996), 'The Cracked Crucible, Judaism and Mental Health', Dinesh Bhugra (ed.), *Psychiatry and Religion - Context, Consensus and Controversies*, Routledge, London, pp. 69-71.

Copi, I. and Cohen, C. (1998), *Introduction of Logic*, Prentice Hall, New Jersey, p. 187.

Corish, M. (1996), 'Aspects of the Secularisation of Irish Society 1968-1996', Eoin Cassidy (ed.), *Faith and Culture in the Irish Context*, Veritas, Dublin, p. 155.

Cornelius, P. (2002), *Global Competitiveness Report 2002-2003, Executive Summary*, World Economic Forum, Geneva, pp. 1-10.

Costigane, H. (1999), 'A History of the Western Idea of Conscience', Jane Hoose (ed.), *Conscience in World Religions*, Gracewing and the University of Notre Dame, Hertfordshire, p. 5, p. 48.

Cotterill, P. and Letherby, G. (1993), 'Weaving Stories: Personal Autobiographies in Feminist Research', *Sociology*, Volume 27, No 1, February 1993, pp. 67-79.

Coughlan, A. (1999), 'Irelands Marxist Historians', Ciarán Brady (ed.), *Interpreting Irish History - The Debate on Historical Revisionism*, Irish Academic Press, Dublin, Reading 19, pp. 288-305.

Cox, J. (1996), 'Psychiatry and Religion-A General Psychiatrist's Perspective', Dinesh Bhugra (ed.), *Psychiatry and Religion, Context, Consensus and Controversies*, Routledge, London, p. 157.

Craib, I. (1992), *Modern Social Theory from Parsons to Habermas*, Prentice Hall/Harvester Wheatsheaf, Hemel Hempstead, p. 87, p. 156, pp. 234-241.

Crone, P. (1999), 'Weber, Islamic Law and The Rise of Capitalism', Toby Huff and Wolfgang Schluchter (eds.), *Max Weber and Islam*, Transaction Publishers, New Brunswick, USA, p. 260.

Cronin, M. (1999), 'The Blueshirts in the Irish Free State, 1932-1935: the nature of socialist republican and governmental opposition', Tim Kirk and Anthony McElligott (eds.), *Opposing Facism - Community, Authority and Resistance in Europe*, Cambridge University Press, Cambridge pp. 80-96.

Crotty, R. (1986), *Ireland in Crisis - A Study in Capitalist Colonial Underdevelopment*, Brandon Book Publishers, Kerry, p. 10.

Chryssides, G. (1999), 'Buddism and Conscience', Jane Hoose (ed.), *Conscience in World Religions*, Gracewing, and the University of Notre Dame, Hertfordshire, p. 176, p. 185, p. 196, p. 197.

Cullen, L. (1995), *Irish National Income in 1911 and Its Context*, Dublin, the Economic and Social Research Institute, Working Paper 63. Compiled and tabulated from estimated Income/Receipts in Appendix A, pp. 1-12, the Censuses of Industrial and Agricultural Production, 1907 and 1908.

Cullen, P. (1999), 'Ireland's Poverty Level is Rated Second-Worst in Industrialised World', *Irish Times*, 12 July, p. 1.

Curtis, E. (1995), *A History of Ireland*, Routledge, London, pp. 2-8, pp. 421-423, p. 451.

Dáil Éireann, (1965), *Parliamentary Debate, Official Reports, Volume 217 Comprising the Period 29th June-21st July 1965*, Vote 3, Department of the Taoiseach, 13 July 1965, Dublin, Stationery Office, pp. 1148-1149.

Daly, M. (1998), 'Economic Development', S.J. Connolly (ed.), *The Oxford Companion to Irish History*, Oxford University Press, Oxford, p. 167.

Daly, M.B. (1994), 'The Formation of an Irish Nationalist Elite-Recruitment to the Irish Civil Service in the Decades Prior to Independence 1870-1920', *Paedagogica Historica*, Volume 30, pp. 281-301.

Davie, G. (2000), 'Religion in Modern Britain: Changing Sociological Assumptions', *Sociology*, Volume 34, No 1, February 2000, Cambridge University Press, pp. 113-115.

Davis, E. and Fine-Davis, M. and Meehan, G. (1982), *Demographic Determinants of Perceived Well-Being - Eight European Countries*, Economic and Social Research Institute, Dublin, p. 349, p. 353.

Davis, R. 1976: *Arthur Griffith in Irish History*, Irish Historical Association, Dundalk Series, No 10, p. 9, p. 13, p. 43.

De Bernoville, G. (1937), *The Jesuits*, Burns, Oates and Washbourne, London, p. 50.

Delaney, E. (2000), *Demography State and Society - Irish Migration to Britain 1921-1971*, Liverpool University Press, Liverpool, p. 29, p. 297.

Delaney, E. (2001), 'Irish Migration to Britain, 1929-1945' *Irish Economic and Social History*, Volume XXVIII, 2001, pp. 47-71.

Delanty, G. (1996a), 'Habermas and Post National Identity: Theoretical Perspectives on the Conflict in Northern Ireland', *Irish Political Studies*, Volume 11, pp. 20-32.

De Latocnayne (1917), *Promenade d'un Francais dans l'Irlande 1796-1797*, Hodges Figgis, Dublin.

De Markievicz, Countess (1920), *James Connolly - Policy and Catholic Doctrine, The Connolly Pamphlets Reprinted 1920*, Irish Transport and General Workers Union, Dublin, pp. 6-10.

De Nie, M. (1998), 'The Famine, Irish Identity and the British Press', *Irish Studies Review*, Volume 6, No 1, 1998, pp. 27-34.

Denny, K. and Harmon, C. and O'Connell J. (2000), *Investing in People-The Labour Market Impact of Human Resource Interventions Funded Under the 1994-1999 Community Support Framework in Ireland*, ESRI, Dublin, p. 23.

Department of Education (2001), *Statistical Report 1996/97*, Government Publications Office, Dublin, Figure B, p.vii, Figure F, p. ix, Figure H, p. x, and Figure N, p. xii.

Department of Foreign Affairs, (1998), *Ireland - The Economy Dublin*, The Department of Foreign Affairs, Dublin, p. 12.

Derrida, J. (1974), 'The Supplement to the Sources: The Alphabet and Absolute Representation' *Grammatology*, John Hopkins University Press, Liverpool, p. 295.

Desmond-Greaves, C. (1986), *The Life and Times of James Connolly*, Laurence and Wishart, London, p. 423, p. 431.

De Tocqueville, A. (1856), 'L'Ancien Regime', Angela Partington (ed.), *The Oxford Dictionary of Quotations*, Oxford University Press, Oxford, p. 698.

De Valera, E. (1921), 'A Separate Nation: Dáil Éireann: Public Session: 17th August 1921' Maurice Moynihan (ed.), *Speeches and Statements by Eamon De Valera*, Gill and Macmillan, Dublin, 1980.

De Valera, E. (1943), 'The Ireland that we dreamed of', Maurice Moynihan (ed.), *Speeches and Statements by Eamon De Valera*, Gill and Macmillan, Dublin, 1980.

De Valera, E. (1945), 'Reply to Winston Churchill' D.G. Hickey and J.E. Docherty (eds.), *A Dictionary of Irish History 1800-1980*, Gill and Macmillan, Dublin 1987, p. 123.

Devine-Wright, P. and Lyons, E. (1997), 'Remembering Pasts and Representing Places: The Construction of National Identities in Ireland', *The Journal of Environmental Psychology*, Academic Press, Volume 17, pp. 33-44.

Dewey, D. (1992), 'The Systems of Talcott Parsons', *The School of Sociology and Social Policy*, Middlesex University Online, p1-6,
http://www.sun.mdx.ac.uk/~malcol1 l/school/course/david/parsons.htm

Dey, I. (1993), *Qualitative Data Analysis - A User Friendly Guide for Social Scientists*, Routledge, London, pp. 98-99.

Dickson, D. (1987), *The Georgeous Mask Dublin 1700-1850*, Trinity College History Workshop, Dublin, pp. vii-viii.

Dinan, D. (1986), 'Constitution and Parliament' Brian Girvin and Roland Sturm (eds.), *Politics and Society in Contemporary Ireland*, Gower Publishing, Aldershot, p. 74.

Di Tella, R. and MacCulloch, R.J. and Oswald, A.J. (1997), 'The Macro Economics of Happiness', *The Labour Market: Consequences of Technical and Structural Change*, Coventry, Dept of Economics, University of Warwick, Discussion Paper Series No 19, pp. 1-16.

Dobb, M. (1958), *Capitalism Yesterday and Today*, Lawrence and Wishart, London, p. 20.

Donnelly, J. (2000), 'On This Rock', *RTE 1 Television*, 2 April 2000.

Donnelly, J. (2000a), 'A Church in Crises - The Irish Catholic Church Today', *History Ireland*, Volume 8, No 3, Autumn 2000, pp. 12-17.

Donnycarney Unemployment Action Group, (2001), *Hard Times*, Donnycarney Unemployment Action Group, Dublin Volume 6, Issue 5, July 2001, p. 1-4.

Douthwaite, R. (2000), 'The Growth Illusion' *Working Toward Balance - Our Society in the New Millennium*, Veritas, Dublin, pp. 116-139.

Drudy, P.J. (1995), From Protectionism to Enterprise: A Review of Irish Industrial Policy, Andrew Burke (ed.), *Enterprise and the Irish Economy Irish Studies in Management*, Oak Tree Press, University College Dublin and the Graduate School of Business, Dublin, p. 75.

Du Bois, W.E.B. (1899), *The Philadelphia Negro*, Lippincott, New York, p. 98.

Dublin Review, The (1850), Richardson and Son, London, Volume XXIX, September and December, pp. 462-467.

Duby, G. (1974), *The Early Growth of the European Economy*, Weidenfield and Nicholson, London, pp. 106-109, p. 233.

Duby, G. (1983), *The Knight the Lady and the Priest - the making of modern marriage in medieval France*, London, Penguin, p. 195.

Dudley Edwards, R. (1997), *James Connolly*, Gill and McMillan, Dublin, p. 28, p. 48, p. 56, p.141, p. 143.

Duffy, D. and Fitzgerald, J. and Kearney, I. and Hore, J. and MacCoille C. (2001), *Medium Term Review 2001-2007*, Dublin, ESRI, September 2001, Number 8, p. vii, p. 1, p. 116, p. 132.

Duffy, D and Williams, J. (2002), *Constructing a Consumer Sentiment Index for Ireland*, ESRI, Dublin, pp. 1-8.

Duggan, Br. B. (1948), *Christian Politeness and Counsels for Youth*, Halstead Press, Sydney, pp. 9-19.

Durkan, J. and Fitzgerald, D. and Harmon, C. (1999), 'Education and Growth in the Irish Economy', Frank Barry (ed.), *Understanding Ireland's Economic Growth*, Macmillan Press, London, Essay 6, pp. 119-130.

Durkheim, E. (1964), *The Elementary Forms of the Religious Life*, George Allen and Unwin London, p. 36, ffn 1, p. 317, p. 348, p. 398, pp. 418-419, pp. 421-422, p. 446.

Durkheim, E. (1970), *Suicide - A Study in Sociology*, Kegan Paul, London, pp. 46-47, p. 105, pp. 164-169, pp. 245-255, p. 270.

Durkheim, E. (1973), 'Progressive Preponderance of Organic Solidarity, The Evolution of Morality', *On Morality and Society: Emile Durkheim Selected Writings*, University of Chicago Press, Chicago, p. 86.

Durkheim, E. (1973a), 'Organic Solidarity and Contractual Solidarity: The Evolution of Morality' *On Morality and Society: Emile Durkheim Selected Writings*, University of Chicago Press Chicago, p. 69.

Durkheim, E. (1973b), 'Divisions of Labour in Society - Conclusions: The Evolution of Morality' *On Morality and Society: Emile Durkheim Selected Writings*, University of Chicago Press, Chicago, p. 139.

Durkheim, E. (1982), *The Rules of the Sociological Method*, Free Press, New York, pp. 50-59, pp. 55-57.

Durkheim, E. (1984), *The Division of Labour in Society*, Macmillan Press, London, p. 193, pp. 194-195, p. 212.

Durkheim, E. (1998), 'The Observation of Social Facts', Ian Marsh and Rosie Campbell and Mike Keating (eds.), *Classic and Contemporary Readings in Sociology*, Longman, Harlow, Reading 45, p. 288, p. 291.

Eaton, R. (1999), 'Islamization in the Late Medieval Bengal: The Relevance of Max Weber', Toby Huff and Wolfgang Schluchter (eds.), *Max Weber and Islam*, Transaction Publishers, New Brunswick, USA, p. 178.

Economist, The (1998), 'Asian Values Revisited - What Would Confucius Say Now?', *The Economist*, 25 July, 1998,
http://www.economist.com/editorial/freeforall/19980725/as5207.html
Economist Intelligence Unit, The (2001), *Country Report - Ireland*, EIU, London, February 2001, p. 11.
Eisenstadt, S.N. (1969), 'The Protestant Ethic Thesis', Roland Robertson (ed.), *Sociology of Religion*, Middlesex, Penguin Modern Sociology Readings, pp. 297-217.
EL Newsletter, (2001), 'Celtic Tiger Biting the Hands that Feeds It', *Education and Living*, 23 January 2001, pp. 1-16.
Elias, N. (1965), 'A Note on the Concepts "Social Structures" and "Anomie"', Elias. N. and Scotson, J.L. (eds.), *The Established and Outsiders - A Sociological Enquiry into Community Problems*, Frank Cass, London, Appendix 2, p. 178.
Elias, N. (1972), 'Processes of State Formation and Nation Building', *Transactions of the 7th World Congress of Sociology*, Sofia 1970, Volume 3, ISA, 1972, pp. 274-284.
Elias, N. (1987), 'The Retreat of Sociologists into the Present' *Theory Culture and Society*, Sage, London, Volume IV, pp. 223-247.
Elias, N. (1996), *The Civilising Process - The History of Manners*, Blackwell, Oxford, p. 5, p. 65, p. 120, p. 154, p. 229, p. 268, pp. 405-406, p. 443, p. 481, p. 509.
Elias, N. (1997), *The Germans*, Polity Press, Cambridge, p. 74, p. 351.
Elias, N. and Dunning, E. (1986), 'Leisure in the Spare Time Spectrum', Norbert Elias and Eric Dunning (eds.), *Quest for Excitement - Sport and Leisure in the Civilising Process*, Blackwell, Oxford, p. 103, p. 306.
Elias, N. and Scotson, J.L. (1965), *The Established and the Outsiders a Sociological Enquiry into Community Problems*, Frank Cass, London, pp. 166-167.
Ellingson, L. (1998), 'Then You Know How I Feel: Empathy, Identification and Reflexivity in Fieldwork', *Qualitative Inquiry*, December 1998, pp. 492-514.
Ellis, S.G. (1991), 'Historigraphical Debate: Representations of the Past in Ireland: Whose Past and Whose Present?', *Irish Historical Studies*, Volume 27, No 108, November 1991, pp. 289-308.
Endress, G. (1994), *An Introduction to Islam*, Edinburgh University Press, Edinburgh, pp. 273-275.
Engels, F. (1900), 'Engels to Marx in Brussels', *Die Neue Zeit*, Bd. 2, No 44, Stuttgart 1900-1901, and in full in Der Briefwechsel Zwischen F. Engels und K. Marx Bd. 1, Stuggart 1913, transcribed for the Internet by zodiac@interlog.com September 1996.
Engels, F. (1913), 'Engels to Marx in Argenteuil', *Der Briefwechsel Wischen F. Engels und K. Marx*, Bd. 1, Stuggart 1913, translated by P. and B. Ross, transcribed for the Internet by zodiac@interlog.com September 1996.
Engels, F. (1935), 'Engels to George Shipton in London', *Marx and Engels Works*, First Russian Edition Volume xxvii, Moscow, 1935, transcribed for the Internet by zodiac@interlog.com Sept 5, 1996.
Engels, F. (1993), *The Condition of the Working Class in England*, Oxford University Press, Oxford, pp. 101-105 p. 134.
Esmail, A. (1996), 'Islamic Communities and Mental Health', Dinesh Bhugra (ed.), *Psychiatry and Religion, Context, Consensus and Controversies*, Routledge, London, p. 150.
E.S.R.I (1997), 'The Economic and Social Research Institute's Medium Term Review 1997-2003, *Irish Times*, 30 April, 1997, p. 2.
E.S.R.I (2001), *Monitoring Poverty Trends and Exploring Poverty Dynamics in Ireland*, Policy Research Series Number 41, June 2001, pp. 1-23.
Estyn-Evans, E. (1992), *The Personality of Ireland - Habitat, Heritage and History*, Lilliput Press, Dublin.

European Commission, (2000), 'Irish Income Per Head Comes 2nd in EU Table', *Irish Times*, 7 July 2000, p. 5.

European Commission, (2002), *European Competitiveness Report 2002 Commission Staff Working Document (SEC (2002) 528)*, Luxembourg, Office for Official Publications of the European Communities, pp. 24-32, p. 37.

European Commission, (2002a), *Quality Indicators of Lifelong Learning Performance in Europe*, Brussels, 2 July 2002, IP/02/971, p. 13.

Fahey, T. (1994), 'Catholicism and Industrial Society in Ireland', J.H. Goldthorpe and C.T. Whelan (eds.), *The Development of Industrial Society in Ireland*, Oxford University Press, Oxford, pp. 261-262.

Fanning, C. (1983), *Enterprise and Entrepreneurs*, Economic and Social Research Institute Dublin, Reprint Series No 71, p. 8, ffn. 16.

Fanning, C (1983a), *Economic Development after 25 Years: Its Significance for the Current Crisis*, Economic and Social Research Institute, Dublin Memorandum Series No 162, p. 4.

Fanning, C. and McCarthy, T. (1983), *Hypotheses Concerning the Non - Viability of Labour - Directed Firms in Capitalist Economies*, The Economic and Social Research Institute, Dublin, Reprint Series No 76, p. 129.

FÁS, (2000), *Regional Aspects of Ireland's Labour Market*, FÁS/ESRI, Dublin, Labour Market Up-date Paper No 1/2000, pp. 1-17.

FÁS/ESRI (1996), *Labour Market Report*, Dublin, FÁS, Issue 1, January 1996, pp. 1-6.

Featherstone, M. (1987), 'Norbert Elias and Figurational Sociology: Some Prefatory Remarks' *Theory, Culture and Society*, SAGE, London, Volume IV, pp. 197-211.

Felstead, A. and Ashton, D. and Green, F. and Sung, J. (1994), 'Singapore', *International Study of Vocational Education and Training in the Federal Republic of Germany, France, Japan, Singapore and the United States*, Centre for Labour Market Studies, University of Leicester, Leicester, pp. 149-171.

Fenwick, P. (1996), 'The Neuro-physiology of Religious Experience', Dinesh Bhugra (ed.), *Psychiatry and Religion, Context, Consensus and Controversies*, Routledge, London pp. 168-169.

Fiddler, (1999), 'Childhood' Marsha Hunt (ed.), *The Junk Yard: Voices from an Irish Prison*, Mainstream Publishing, Edinburgh, p. 48.

Fine Gael, (1997), *Eire Ireland 1922-1997: A Salute to the Founders of a Free and Independent Ireland*, Fine Gael Political Party, Dublin.

Fingleton, E. (1999), *In Praise of Hard Industries - Why Manufacturing, Not The New Economy, is The Key to Future Prosperity*, Orion Business Books, London, p. 5, p. 50.

Firth, G.G. (1967), *The Economics of an Off-Shore Island - Some Aspects of Economic Development in the Irish Republic 1958-65*, Economic and Social Research Institute, Dublin Reprint No 15, pp. 427-428.

Fitzgerald, G. (1997), 'Some Easy Ways To Put Brake On Economic Growth', *Irish Times*, 28 June 1997, p. 13.

Fitzgerald, G. (1998), 'Sustained High Growth Rate Leading To Uncharted Waters', *Irish Times*, 6 June 1998, p. 12.

Fitzgerald, G. (2000), 'EEC Was Ally We Had Been Seeking For Centuries', *Irish Times*, Tuesday, 16 May, p. 14.

Fitzgerald, G. (2000a), 'Seven Ages: The Story of the Irish State', *RTE 1 Television*, Monday, 20 March 2000.

Fitzgerald, G. (2001), 'Right-Wing Policies Have Left Profound Inequalities', *Irish Times*, Saturday, 4 August, p. 14.

Fitzgerald, J. (1999), *Understanding Ireland's Economic Success*, The Economic and Social Research Institute, Dublin, Working Paper No 111, pp. 35-39.

Fitzgerald, J. (2000), 'The Story of Ireland's Failure and Belated Success', Brian Nolan, Philip J. O'Connell and Christopher T. Whelan (eds.), *Bust or Boom - The Irish Experience of Growth and Inequality*, Institute of Public Administration, Dublin, p. 28, pp. 55-57.

Fitzgerald, J. and Geary, J. and Lalor, T. and Nolan, B. and O'Malley, E. (1996), 'Industrial Policy', J.J. Sexton, and P.J. O'Connell (eds.), *Ireland - Labour Market Studies*, European Commission, Employment and Social Affairs Directorate, Employment and Labour Market, Brussells, Series No 1, p. xix.

Fitzgerald, J. and Kearney, I. and Morgenroth, E. and Smyth, D. (1999), *National Investment Priorities for the Period 2000-2006 - Executive Summary*, The Economic and Social Research Institute, Dublin in association with DKM Economic Consultants, Peter Bacon and Associates and the Departments of Economics and Geography, National University of Ireland, Maynooth, p. 8.

Fitzgerald, R. and Girvin, B. (2000), 'Political Culture, Growth and the Conditions for Success in the Irish Economy', Brian Nolan, Philip J. O'Connell and Christopher T. Whelan (eds.), *Bust or Boom - The Irish Experience of Growth and Inequality*, Institute of Public Administration, Dublin, pp. 268-270, p. 284.

Fitzpatrick, D. (1994), *Oceans of Consolation, Personal Accounts of Irish Migration to Australia*, Cornell University Press, Ithaca, p. 556.

Fitzpatrick, D. (1998), *Politics and Irish Life 1913-1921 - Provincial Experience of War and Revolution*, Cork University Press, Cork, pp. 192-198, p. 204, p. 218, pp. 229-233, p. 249, ffn. 12, p. 280, ffn. 22.

Fitzpatrick, J. and Kelly, J. (1985), 'Industry in Ireland: Policies Performance and Problems', Jim Fitzpatrick and John H. Kelly (eds.), *Perspectives on Irish Industry*, Irish Management Institute, Dublin, p. xvii, pp. 9-10.

Flanagan, K. (2001), 'Reflexivity, Ethics and the Teaching of the Sociology of Religion', *Sociology*, Cambridge University Press, Cambridge, Volume 35, No 1, February 2001, pp. 1-19.

Fletcher, J. (1997), *Violence and Civilisation, An Introduction to the Work of Norbert Elias*, Polity Press, Cambridge, pp. 60-61, p. 75.

Foley, A. and McAleese, D. (1991), *Overseas Industry in Ireland*, Gill and Macmillan, Dublin.

Ford, A. and Milne, K. (1998), 'The Church of Ireland', S.J.Connolly (ed.), *The Oxford Companion to Irish History*, Oxford University Press, Oxford, p. 92.

Forfás (1999), *Annual Employment Survey 1998*, Forfás - The Policy and Advisory Board for Industrial Development in Ireland, Dublin, pp. 10-12, pp. 17-18.

Forfás (2000), *The Second Report of the Expert Group on Future Skills Needs - Report to the Tánaiste and Minister for Enterprise, Trade and Employment and the Minister for Education and Science*, Forfás - The Policy and Advisory Board for Industrial Development in Ireland, Dublin p. 7.

Forfás (2000a), *Annual Survey of Irish Economic Expenditures - Results for 1998*, Forfás - The Policy and Advisory Board for Industrial Development in Ireland, Dublin, p. 6, p. 23.

Forfás (2000b), *Enterprise 2010 - A New Strategy for the Promotion of Enterprise in Ireland in the 21st Century*, Forfás, Dublin, pp 1-4.

Forfás (2001), *Overview of 2000*, Forfás - The Policy and Advisory Board for Industrial Development in Ireland, Dublin, p. 1.

Forfás (2001a), *Statement on Outward Direct Investment*, Forfás - The Policy and Advisory Board for Industrial Development in Ireland, Dublin, pp. 1-43.

Forfás (2001b), *Report on In-Company Training Responding to Ireland's Growing Skills Needs*, Dublin, Forfás - The Policy and Advisory Board for Industrial Development in Ireland, Dublin, pp. 1-32.

Forfás (2001c), *Forfás Employment Survey 2001*, Dublin, Forfás - The Policy and Advisory Board for Industrial Development in Ireland, Dublin.

Foskett, J. (1996), 'Christianity and Psychiatry', Dinesh Bhugra (ed.), *Psychiatry and Religion Context, Consensus and Controversies*, Routledge, London, p. 52.

Foster, R. F. (1988), *Modern Ireland 1600-1972*, Penguin, London, p. 34, p. 197, p. 519, pp. 548-550, pp. 562-563, p. 616.

Fowler, J. (1996), 'James Fowler's Theory of Faith Development with Emphasis on Adolescence', Rolf E. Muuss (ed.), *Theories of Adolescence*, McGraw Hill, New York, p. 266.

Francis (1999), 'Prison Life', Marsha Hunt (ed.), *The Junk Yard: Voices from an Irish Prison*, Mainstream Publishing, Edinburgh, p. 156.

Freud, S. (1985), 'If Moses was an Egyptian', *Sigmund Freud - The Origins of Religion, Totem and Taboo, Moses and Monotheism, and Other Works*, Penguin, London, p. 293, p. 335.

Freud, S. (1985a), 'Taboo and Emotional Ambivalence', *Sigmund Freud - The Origins of Religion, Totem and Taboo, Moses and Monotheism, and Other Works*, Penguin, London, p. 129.

Freud, S, (1985b), 'Renunciation of Instinct', *Sigmund Freud - The Origins of Religion, Totem and Taboo, Moses and Monotheism, and Other Works*, Penguin, London, p. 365.

Freud, S. (1991), 'Civilised Sexual Activity and Modern Nervous Illness', *Sigmund Freud - Civilisation, Society and Religion, Group Psychology Civilisation and its Discontents and other Works*, Penguin, London, pp. 33-55.

Freud, S. (1991a), 'The Disillusionment of the War - Thoughts for the Times on War and Death', *Sigmund Freud - Civilisation, Society and Religion, Group Psychology, Civilisation and its Discontents and other Works*, Penguin, London, reprinted 1991, p. 70.

Freud, S. (1991b), 'Le Bon's Description of the Group Mind, Group Psychology and the Analysis of the Ego', *Sigmund Freud - Civilisation, Society and Religion, Group Psychology Civilisation and its Discontents and other Works*, Penguin, London, p. 104, p. 107.

Freud, S. (1991c), 'Further Problems and Lines of Work, Group Psychology and the Analysis of the Ego', *Sigmund Freud - Civilisation, Society and Religion, Group Psychology, Civilisation and its Discontents and other Works*, Penguin, London, p. 129.

Freud , S. (1991d), 'Identification - Group Psychology and the Analysis of the Ego', *Sigmund Freud - Civilisation, Society and Religion, Group Psychology Civilisation and its Discontents and other Works*, Penguin, London, p. 137.

Freud, S. (1991e), 'The Herd Instinct - Group Psychology and the Analysis of the Ego', *Sigmund Freud - Civilisation, Society and Religion, Group Psychology, Civilisation and its Discontents and other Works*, Penguin, London.

Freud, S. (1991e), 'The Future of an Illusion', *Sigmund Freud - Civilisation, Society and Religion, Group Psychology, Civilisation and its Discontents and other Works*, Penguin, London.

Freud, S. (1991f), 'Identification', *Sigmund Freud - Civilisation, Society and Religion, Group Psychology, Civilisation and its Discontents and other Works*, Penguin, London, p. 192, p. 139, pp. 198-199, p. 200.

Freud, S. (1991g), 'Civilisation and It's Discontents', *Sigmund Freud - Civilisation, Society and Religion, Group Psychology, Civilisation and its Discontents and other Works*, Penguin, London, p. 251, p. 268.

Fromm, E. (1962), *Beyond the Chains of Illusion - My Encounter with Marx and Freud*, Abacus, London, p. 78.

Fromm, E. (1974), *On Psychological Experiments: The Anatomy of Human Destructiveness*, Pimlico, London, p. 79.

Fromm, E. (1978), *Erich Fromm - To Have or To Be?*, Abacus, London, p. 65, p. 91, p. 103, p. 155.

Fukuyama, F. (1995), *Trust, The Social Virtues and the Creation of Prosperity*, Penguin Books, London.

Fulford, K. (1996), 'Religion and Psychiatry', Dinesh Bhugra (ed.), *Psychiatry and Religion, Context, Consensus and Controversies*, Routledge, London, p. 8, p. 12.

Fulton, J. and Abela, A. and Borowik, I. and Dowling T. and Long Marler, P. and Tomasi, L. (2000), *Young Catholics at the New Millennium The Religion and Morality of Young Adults in Western Countries*, University College Press, Dublin.

Furnham, A. and Bond, M. and Heaven, P. and Hilton, D. and Lobel, T. and Masters, J. and Payne, M. and Rajamanikam, R. and Stacey, B. and Van Daalen, H. (1991), 'A Comparison of Protestant Work Ethic Beliefs in Thirteen Nations', *The Journal of Social Psychology*, No 133 (2), pp. 185-197.

Gagné, R and Medsker, K. (1996), *The Conditions of Learning*, Harcourt Brace, New York, p. 12.

Garfinkel, H. (1967), *Studies in Ethnomethodology*, Prentice Hall, Englewood Cliffs, USA.

Garnham A. and Oakhill, J. (1994), *Thinking and Reasoning*, Basil Blackwell, Oxford, p. 55.

Garnham, N. (2001), 'Football and National Identity in Pre-Great War Ireland', *Irish Economic and Social History*, Volume xxviii, 2001, pp. 13-31.

Garvin, T. (2000), 'A Quiet Revolution - The Remaking of Irish Political Culture', Ray Ryan (ed.), *Writing in the Irish Republic - Literature, Culture, Politics 1949-1999*, London, Routledge, pp. 187-203.

Garvin, T. (2001), *The Celtic Tiger - A Historical Journey*, Conference 2001, Ireland - A Euro Model, Dublin, FÁS Opportunities 2001.

Gaynor, F. (1999), 'An Irish Potatoe [sic] Seasoned with Attic Salt - The Reliques of Fr. Prout and Identity before the Nation', *Irish Studies Review*, Volume 7, Number 3, December 1999, pp. 313-325.

Gaynor, L. (no date), *A Civics Course for Young Students*, Fallons, Dublin, p. 8, p. 23.

Geary, F. (1995), *De-industrialisation in Ireland to 1851: Some Evidence from the Census*, Dublin, Economic and Social Research Institute Working Paper No 68, December 1995, pp. 7-19.

Geary, F. (1996), 'Regional Industrial Structure and Labour Force Decline 1841-51', *Irish Historical Studies*, Volume 30, No 118, November 1996, p. 193.

Geary, F. and Stark, T. (1996), *Examining Ireland's Post-Famine Economic Performance: The Distribution of Gross Domestic Product between the Countries of the United Kingdom1861-1911*, Economic and Social Research Institute, Dublin, p. 29, pp. 34-43.

Geoghegan, B. (1999), 'Ireland - The Challenges of Success', Paper delivered by Brian Geoghegan, Director of Economic Affairs, Irish Business and Employers Association, in Halifax, Nova Scotia, May 1999, p. 2.

Ghandi, I. (1948), 'Non Violence in Peace and War' Jonathan Green (ed.), *The Pan Dictionary of Contemporary Quotations*, Section 16, p. 391.

Gibbons, L. (1996), 'Labour and Local History: The Case of Jim Gralton, 1886-1945', Luke Gibbons (ed.), *Transformations in Irish Culture - Critical Conditions*, Cork University Press, Cork.

Gibbons, L. (1996a), 'Race Against Time - Racial Discourse and Irish History', Luke Gibbons (ed.), *Transformations in Irish Culture - Critical Conditions*, Cork University Press, Cork, pp. 151-152.

Giddens, A. (1971), *Capitalism and Modern Social Theory - An Analysis of the Writings of Marx, Durkheim and Max Weber*, Cambridge University Press, Cambridge, p. 42, p. 98, p. 116, p. 217, p. 226, p. 232.

Giddens, A. (1973), *The Class Structure of the Advanced Societies*, Hutchinson and Co. Publishers, London, p. 17, p. 273.

Giddens, A. (1976), 'Introduction' *The Protestant Ethic and the Spirit of Capitalism: Max Weber*, Routledge, London, pp. vii-xxvi.

Giddens, A. (1990), *The Consequences of Modernity*, Polity Press, Cambridge, pp. 103-104.

Giddens, A. (1991), *Modernity and Self-Identity: Self and Society in the Late Modern Age*, Stanford University Press, Stanford, pp. 187-201.

Giddens, A. (1995a), 'Durkheim and the Question of Individualism', *Politics, Sociology and Social Theory, Encounters with Classical and Contemporary Social Thought*, Polity Press, Cambridge, p. 118.

Giddens, A. (1995b), 'Marx, Weber and the Development of Capitalism', *Politics, Sociology and Social Theory, Encounters with Classical and Contemporary Social Thought*, Polity Press, Cambridge, p. 67, p. 74.

Giddens, A. (1995c), 'Habermas on Labour and Interaction', *Politics, Sociology and Social Theory, Encounters with Classical and Contemporary Social Thought*, Polity Press, Cambridge, pp. 257-258.

Giddens, A. (1995d), 'Garfinkel, Ethnomethodology and Hermeneutics', *Politics, Sociology and Social Theory, Encounters with Classical and Contemporary Social Thought*, Polity Press, Cambridge, p. 244.

Giddens, A. (1996), 'In Defence of Sociology', *Defence of Sociology - Essays Interpretations and Re-joinders*, Polity Press, Cambridge, p. 25, p. 114.

Giddens, A. (1996a), 'Functionalism - Apres La Lutte', *Defence of Sociology - Essays Interpretations and Re-joinders*, Polity Press, Cambridge, p. 96, p. 99, pp. 104-110.

Giddens, A. (1996b), 'The Suicide Problem in French Sociology', *Defence of Sociology - Essays Interpretations and Re-joinders*, Polity Press, Cambridge, p. 167.

Giddens, A. (1996c), 'Britishness and the Social Science', *Defence of Sociology - Essays Interpretations and Re-joinders*, Polity Press Cambridge, p. 114.

Giddens, A. (1996d), 'Living in Post Traditional Society', *Defence of Sociology - Essays Interpretations and Re-joinders*, Polity Press, Cambridge, p. 22, p. 61.

Giddens, A. (1996e), 'What is Social Science', *Defence of Sociology - Essays Interpretations and Re-joinders*, Polity Press, Cambridge, pp. 68-74.

Giddens, A. (1996f), 'Reason without Revolution? Habermas's Theory of Communicative', *Defence of Sociology - Essays Interpretations and Re-joinders*, Polity Press, Cambridge, p. 179, pp. 182-183, pp. 189-190.

Giddens, A. (1997), *Sociology*, Polity Press, Cambridge, p. 573.

Giddens A. (1998), 'An Interview with Anthony Giddens Dublin', *Irish Journal of Sociology*, Volume 8, 1998, pp. 113-123.

Gilsenan, M. (1982), *Recognising Islam, Religion and Society in the Modern Middle East*, Tauris Publishers, London, p. 37, p. 153, p. 222, pp. 261-262.

Girvin, B. (1984), 'Industrialisation and the Irish Working Class Since 1922', *Saothar: Document Studies Irish Labour History Society*, No 10, p. 31.

Girvin, B. (1986), 'National Identity and Conflict in Northern Ireland', Brian and Roland Sturm (eds.), *Politics and Society in Contemporary Ireland*, Gower Publishing, Aldershot, p. 7, p. 109.

Girvin, B. (1986a), 'Nationalism Democracy and Irish Political Culture', Brian Girvin and Roland Sturm (eds.), *Politics and Society in Contemporary Ireland*, Gower Publishing, Aldershot, p. 5.

Girvin, B. (1997), 'Political Culture, Political Independence and Economic Success in Ireland, *Irish Political Studies*, No 12, 1997, pp. 48-77.

Goffman, E. (1959), *The Presentation of Self in Everyday Life*, Penguin, London, p.57, p. 78, p. 85, p. 114, p. 211.

Goldring, M. (1993), *Pleasant the Scholar Life: Irish Intellectuals and the Construction of the Nation State*, Serif, London, p. 172.

Goldthorpe, J.H. (1994), 'The Theory of Industrialism and the Irish Case', J.H. Goldthorpe and C.T. Whelan (eds.), *The Development of Industrial Society in Ireland*, Oxford University Press, Oxford, p. 240, p. 416.

Goldthorpe, J.H and Lockwood, D. and Bechhofer, F. and Platt J. (1968), *The Affluent Worker: Industrial Attitudes and Behaviour: Cambridge Studies in Sociology*, Cambridge University Press, Cambridge, p. 180.

Goodwin, J. (1997), 'The Republic of Ireland and the Singaporean Model of Skill Formation and Economic Development', Centre for Labour Market Studies, Leicester University, Working Paper 14, pp. 11-12.

Goodwin, J. (1999), *Men's Work and Male Lives - Men and Work in Britain*, Ashgate, Aldershot, p. 193.

Goodwin, J. (1999a), 'The Celtic Tiger and Skill Formation: The Role of Training Policy in Addressing Social Exclusion in Ireland', Address at the Policy Institute, Trinity College Dublin, 28 September 1999.

Goodwin, J. (1999b), 'Men, Gender and Work in Dublin: Initial Findings on Work and Class', Centre for Labour Market Studies, University of Leicester, Working Paper No 24, p. 13.

Gorman, R.A. (1982), 'Neo-Marxism: The Meanings of Modern Radicalism Contributions', *Political Science Number 77*, Harvester Wheatsheaf, Conneticut, pp. 15-16.

Gorsky, J. (1999), 'Conscience in Jewish Tradition', Jane Hoose (ed.), *Conscience in World Religions*, University of Notre Dame, Hertfordshire, Gracewing, p. 133, p. 139, p. 150.

Gottfredson, L. (1981), 'Circumscription and Compromise - A Developmental Theory of Occupational Aspiration', *Journal of Counselling Psychology*, Monograph 28, pp. 545-579.

Govt of Ireland (1965), *An Roinn Oideachais - Oideachas Naisiúnta Rules for National Schools under the Department of Education*, The Stationery Office, Government Publications, Dublin.

Govt of Ireland (1990), *Bunreacht na hÉireann, Constitution of Ireland*, The Stationery Office, Government Publications, Dublin.

Govt of Ireland (1994), *An Roinn Oideachais, Primary School Curriculum Teacher's Handbook*, The Stationery Office, Government Publications, Dublin, p. 124, p. 128.

Govt of Ireland (1997), *Ireland - Constitution and Government*, Department of Foreign Affairs, Dublin, Fact Sheet 2/95.

Govt of Ireland (2000), *Statistical Abstract 1998-1999, Summary of Principle Statistics Ireland*, Dublin, p. 373.

Govt of Ireland (2000a), *Ireland - National Development Plan 2000-2006*, The Stationery Office, Government Publications, Dublin, pp. 28-29, pp. 94-95.

Govt of Ireland (2000b), *Statistical Report of the Revenue Commissioners Year ended 31st December 1999*, The Stationery Office, Government Publications, Dublin, p. 69.

Govt of Ireland (2000c), 'Tánaiste Appoints Brian Geoghegan as New Chairman of FÁS', *Government Press and Publicity Office*, 21 November 2000.

Govt of Ireland (2001), *Ireland's National Employment Action Plan 2000*, Department of Enterprise Trade and Employment, Stationery Office, Dublin, pp. 1-50.

Govt of Ireland (2001a), *The RAPID Brochure*, The Department for Tourism, Sport and Recreation, Government of Ireland, Dublin, pp. 1-5.

Govt of Singapore (2000), *Singapore Infomap - Religion*, Official Web Page of Singapore Government, www.sg/flavour/profile/html

Govt of Singapore (2001), *Labour Market Second Quarter 2001*, Ministry of Manpower, Manpower Research and Statistics Dept., Singapore, September 2001, pp. 1-14.

Govt of Singapore (2001a), *Manpower Statistics in Brief*, Ministry of Manpower, Manpower Research and Statistics Dept., Singapore, September 2001, pp. 1-5.

Graham, Father. (1912), *Prosperity, Catholic and Protestant - The Relation Between True Religion and Prosperity Examined*, Sands and Co. Glasgow, p. 6, p. 13, p. 15, p. 24, p. 33, p. 37, p. 54, p. 88, p. 103, p. 111.

Gray, B. (1999), 'Longings and Belongings - Gendered Spatialities of Irishness', *Irish Studies Review*, Volume 7, Number 2, August 1999, pp. 193-211.

Gray, P. (1995), 'Ideology and the Famine', Cathal Poirtéir (ed.), *The Great Irish Famine*, Mercier Press, Dublin, p. 98.

Greaves, R. (1999), 'Islam and Conscience', Jane Hoose (ed.), *Conscience in World Religions*, Gracewing and the University of Notre Dame, Hertfordshire pp. 157-159, p. 168.

Greeley, A. and Ward, C. (2000), 'How Secularised Is The Ireland We Live In?', *Doctrine and Life*, Dominican Publications, Dublin, December 2000, pp. 581-617.

Greenwood, L. (2001), *The Spirit of Capitalism: Nationalism and Economic Growth*, Massachusetts, Harvard University Press, pp. 2-6, pp. 57-58.

Guba, E. and Lincoln, Y. S. (1994), 'Competing Paradigms in Qualitative Research', Denzin, N. and Lincoln, Y.S. (eds.), *Handbook of Qualitative Research*, Sage, Thousand Oaks, CA, p. 110.

Gulalp, H. (1983), 'Frank and Wallerstein Revisited: A Contribution to Benner's Critique', Peter Limqueco and Bruce McFarlane (eds.), *Neo-Marxist Theories of Development*, Croom Helm, London, p. 114.

Gumley, F, and Redhead, B. (1990), *The Pillars of Islam - An Introduction to the Islamic Faith*, BBC Publishing, London, p. 34.

Haferkamp, H. (1987), 'From the Intra-State to the Inter-State Civilising Process?', *Theory, Culture and Society*, London, Sage, Volume 4, pp. 545-557.

Hagendoorn, L. and Pepels, J. (2000), 'European Nations and Nationalism: An Introductory Analysis', Louk Hagendoorn, Gyorgy Csepeli, Henk Dekker, Russell Farnen (eds.), *European Nations and Nationalism - Theoretical and Historical Perspectives*, Ashgate, Research Migration and Ethnic Relations Series, Aldershot, pp. 4-5, pp. 15-16.

Haggard, S. and Kim, E. (2001), 'The Sources of East Asia's Economic Growth', *Access Asia Review*, National Bureau of Asian Research Publications, Volume 1, No 1, Essay 2, pp. 1-28.

Hall, S.C. (1825), *Ireland - Its Scenery and Character Volume 1*, Virtue and Co., London, pp. 73-74, p. 311.

Hamilton, C. (1983), 'Capitalist Industrialisation in the Four Little Tigers of East Asia', Peter Limqueco and Bruce McFarlane (eds.), *Neo-Marxist Theories of Development*, Croom Helm, London, pp. 168-169, p. 173.

Hamilton, M. (1995), *The Sociology of Religion, Theoretical and Comparative Perspectives*, Routledge, London, p. 18, pp. 176-177, p. 217.

Handy, C. (1997), *The Hungry Spirit - Beyond Capitalism, a Quest for Purpose in the Modern World*, Hutchinson, London, pp. 113-121.

Hanley, B. (1999), 'The Storming of Connolly House', *History Ireland*, Volume 7, No 2, Summer 1999, pp. 5-7.

Hannigan, K. (2000), *Ireland's Economic Prospects - The Facts Behind Some Economic Myths*, Irish Management Institute, Economic Research Series, Dublin, April 2000, pp. 1-4.

Hansard, (1920), 'Orders of the Day, Government of Ireland: Vote of Censure Proposed', *Hansard*, Volume 133, August 9-Oct 29, 1920, p. 63.

Hardiman, N. (1994), 'The State and Economic Interests: Ireland in Comparative Perspectives', J.H. Goldthorpe and C.T. Whelan (eds.), *The Development of Industrial Society in Ireland*, Oxford University Press, Oxford, p. 356.

Hardiman, N. (2000), 'Social Partnership, Wage Bargaining and Growth', Brian Nolan, Philip J. O'Connell and Christopher T. Whelan (eds.), *Bust or Boom - The Irish Experience of Growth and Inequality*, Institute of Public Administration, Dublin, p. 307.

Hardiman, N. and Whelan, C.T. (1994), 'Values and Political Partisanship', Christopher Whelan (ed.), *Values and Social Change in Ireland*, Gill and Macmillan, Dublin, pp. 136-186.

Harney, M. (1999), *Enterprise 2010: A New Strategy for Enterprise in Ireland in the 21ˢᵗ Century*, Forfás - The Policy and Advisory Board for Industrial Development in Ireland, Dublin.

Harney, M. (2001), 'The 2001 Oldcastle Lecture', College of St. Rose, Albany, New York, U.S.A., 8 March, 2001.

Harris, J. (1989), 'The Policy Making Role of the Dept. of Education', D.G. Mulcahy and D. O'Sullivan (eds.), *Irish Education Policy: Process and Substance*, Institute of Public Administration, Dublin.

Harrison, B. and Lyon, S. (1993), 'A Note on Ethical Issues in the Use of Autobiography in Sociologial Research', *Sociology - The Journal of the British Sociological Association*, Volume 27, No 1, February 1993, pp. 101-109.

Hart, K. (1991), 'I Had Grown Up', Geoffrey Bould (ed.), *Conscience Be My Guide: An Anthology of Prison Writings*, Zed Books, London, p. 48.

Haughton, J. (1991), 'The Historical Background', John W. O'Hagan (ed.), *The Economy of Ireland - Policy and Performance*, IMI, Dublin, pp. 2-3, p. 23, p. 27, p. 29.

Haulleville, M. (1878), *Social Aspects of Catholicism and Protestantism in Their Civil Bearing Upon Nations*, Kegan Paul, London, p. 51, p. 282.

Healy, T. (2003) 'Education: Investing in our Future', paper delivered at the Department of Education Conference *'The Europe of Knowledge'*, Westbury Hotel, Dublin June 11, 2003

Heideggar, M. (1949), *Existence and Being*, Vision Press, London, p. 80, p. 84.

Heideggar, M. (1991), *The Principle of Reason*, Indiana University Press, Indianapolis, pp. 17-19.

Heller, F. (1986), *The Use and Abuse of Social Science*, Sage, London, pp. 461-462.

Hempton, D. (1996), *Religion and Political Culture in Britain and Ireland from the Glorious Revolution to the Decline of Empire*, Cambridge University Press, Cambridge, p. 90, p. 138, p. 178.

Herr, T. (1991), *Catholic Social Teaching - A Textbook of Christian Insights*, New City, Dublin, p. 68, p. 108.

Hickey, D.J. and Doherty J.E. (1980), *A Dictionary of Irish History 1800-1980*, Gill and Macmillan, Dublin, 1987.

Hickman, M. (1995), *Religion Class and Identity - The State, The Catholic Church and The Education of the Irish in Britain*, Avebury, Aldershot, p. 7, p. 10, p. 46, pp. 55-62, p. 127, p. 207, pp. 225-228, pp. 290-291.

Hickman, M.J. (1998), 'Reconstructing Deconstructing Race: British Political Discourses about the Irish in Britain, *Ethnic and Racial Studies*, Routledge, Volume 21, Number 2, March 1998, p. 64.

Hill, R. (1996), *The History of the Work Ethic*, Dept. of Occupational Studies, University of Georgia, http://www.coe.uga.edu/~rhill/workethic/hist.htm, pp. 1-14.

Hill, W.F. (1990), *Learning - A Survey of Psychological Interpretation*, Harper Collins, New York, pp. 184-185.

Hobbes, T. (1998), *De Cive - Cambridge Texts in the History of Political Thought*, Cambridge University Press, Cambridge.

Hobbes, T. (1651), 'On What is Necessary for Entry into The Kingdom of Heaven', *Leviathan*, Department of Philosophy Research School of Social Scientists, Australian National University, The Aphil Library Site, Chapter XVIII, http://coombs.anu.edu.au/Depts/RSSS/Philosophy/Texts/Leviathan.html

Hobson, J.A. (1914), *Work and Wealth - A Human Valuation*, pp. 38-43, http://www.soccsi.mcmaster.ca/~econ/ugcm/3113/hobson/workwealth.html

Hobson, J.A. (1988), *Imperialism: A Study*, Unwin Hyman, London, p. 5, pp. 14-16, pp. 114-115, pp. 137-161.

Hoffner, J. (1962), *Fundamentals of Christian Sociology*, The Mercier Press, Cork, p. 93.

Holdaway, S. (1998), 'Participant Observation (1): Inside the British Police', Ian Marsh, Rosie Campbell and Mike Keating (eds.), *Classic and Contemporary Readings in Sociology*, Longman, Harlow, Reading 51, pp. 318-323.

Hollaway, W. and Jefferson, T. (2000), *Doing Qualitative Research Differently - free association, narrative and the interview method*, Sage, London, p. 31, p.45, pp. 68-79, p. 152.

Hoon, L.S. and Lim, V.K.G (2001), 'Attitudes Towards Money and Work - implications for Asian management style following economic crisis', *Journal of Managerial Psychology*, Volume 16, No 2, pp. 159-172.

Hoose, J. (1999), 'Conscience in the Roman Catholic Tradition', Jane Hoose (ed.), *Conscience in World Religions*, Hertfordshire, Gracewing and the University of Notre Dame, p. 64, p. 66, p. 77, pp. 86-87, p. 93.

Horgan J. (1997), *Sean Lemass - The Enigmatic Patriot*, Gill and Macmillan, Dublin, p. 142.

Horgan, J. (2000), *Noel Brown - Passionate Outsider*, Gill and Macmillan, Dublin, p. 237.

Hornsby-Smith, M. (1992), 'Social and Religious Transformations in Ireland - A Case of Secularisation', J.H. Goldthorpe and C.T. Whelan (eds.), *The Development of Industrial Society in Ireland*, British Academy and Oxford University Press, New York, p. 273.

Hornsby-Smith, M. and Whelan, C.T. (1994), 'Religious and Moral Values', Christopher T. Whelan (ed.), *Values and Social Change in Ireland*, Macmillan Press, Dublin, p. 33.

Huff, T. (1993), *The Rise of Early Modern Science - Islam, China and the West*, Cambridge University Press, Cambridge, p. 18, pp. 329-330.

Huff, T. and Schlucter, W. (1999) 'Introduction', Toby Huff and Wolfgang Schluchter (eds.), *Max Weber and Islam*, Transaction Publishers, New Brunswick USA, pp. 30-32.

Humphrey, N. (1993), *A History of the Mind*, Vantage Books, London.

Humphreys, J. (1997), 'Religious change not dramatic priests are told', *Irish Times*, 16 September 1997, p. 8.

Hussey, G. (1993), *Ireland Today - Anatomy of a Changing State*, Townhouse, Viking, Dublin, p. 173.

Hutchinson, B. (1968), *Economic Development and Social Values in Ireland: A First Assessment*, The Economic and Social Research Institute, Dublin. Memorandum Series, Number 53, pp. 1-41.

Hyland, J.L. (1997), *James Connolly: The Historical Association of Ireland, Life and Times Series No: 11*, Dundalgan Press, Dundalk, p. 13, p. 29, p. 57.

Ignatieff, M. (2001), *Defining Moments - The Emotive Funerals of Sir Winston Churchill and Princess Diana*, Open University, BBC 2, 16 June 2001.

IMF (2000), *Ireland: Staff Report for the 2000 Article IV Consultation - Staff Country Report No: 00/97 August 2000*, Washington, International Monetary Fund, Public Information Notice Attachment, p. 43, and Annex 1, pp. 3-6.

IMI (1999), *Management Focus Newsletter*, Irish Management Institute, Dublin Volume 3, No 4, July-August 1999, pp. 1-4.

Inglehart, R and Baker, W. (2000) 'Modernisation, Cultural Change and the Persistence of Traditional Values', *American Sociological Review*, February 2000.

Inglis, T. (1987), *Moral Monopoly: The Catholic Church in Modern Irish Society*, Gill and Macmillan Press, Dublin, pp. 71-72.

Inglis, T. (1998), *Moral Monopoly: The Rise and Fall of the Catholic Church in Modern Ireland*, Gill and Macmillan, Dublin, revised edition, pp. 2-3, p. 8, p. 167.

Irish Times (1998), 'Taoiseach defends references to God', *Dáil Report*, 9 December, p. 10.

Irish Times (2000), 'Traveller Families on Roadside Increase', 6 October 2000, http://www.irish-times.ie

Irish Times (2000a), 'Number Sleeping Rough in Dublin Rises by 60%', 29 November, p. 3.

Irish Times (2001), 'As Economy Booms, the Deaths are Mounting', 26 March, p. 13.

Irish Times (2001), 'Budget will Hold No Big Tax Cuts', November 8, p. 1.

James, D. and Sung. J. (1997), *Education, Training and Economic Growth in Pacific Asia: A New Model of Skill Formation*, http://dialspace.dial.pipex.com/gsegal/papedu.htm

Jarvis, P. (1987), 'The Social Construction of the Person', Peter Jarvis (ed.), *Adult Learning in the Social Context*, Croom Helm, London, p. 40.

Jeanrond, W. (2001), 'What Makes Catholics Different? - Review of the Catholic Imagination by Andrew Greeley', *Doctrine and Life*, Dominican Publications, Dublin, February 2001, pp. 120-127.

Johnson, J. (1844), *A Tour in Ireland with Meditations and Reflections by James Johnson M.D. Physician to the Late King*, S. Highly, 32 Fleet St., London, p. 18.

Johnson, P. and Cassell, C. (2001), 'Epistemology and Work Psychology: New Agendas', *Journal of Occupational and Organisation Psychology*, June 2001, Volume 7, pp. 1-21.

Johnston, D. (1989), *The Inter-War Economy in Ireland: Studies in Irish Economic and Social History*, Dundalgan Press, Dundalk, pp. 5-15.

Jones, R. A. (1986), *Suicide (1897), Emile Durkheim: An Introduction to Four Major Works*, Beverly Hills, Sage Publications, pp. 92, http://eddie.cso.uiuc.edu/Durkheim/Summaries/suicide.html

Jung, C. (1985), *Man and Myth*, Paladin, London, 1980.

Jung, C. (1987), *Dictionary of Analytic Psychology*, Ark Paperbacks, London, pp. 135-136.

Jupp, V. (1996), 'Documents and Critical Research' Roger Sapsford and Victor Jupp (eds.), *Data Collection and Analysis*, Sage Publications, London, in association with the Open University, pp. 301-303.

Kalberg, S. (1998), 'Tocqueville and Weber on the Sociological Origins of Citizenship: The Political Culture of American Democracy', Ralph Schroeder (ed.), *Max Weber, Democracy and Modernisation*, Mac Millan Press, London, pp. 95-99.

Kane, R. (1910), *Lenten Lectures Delivered from Time to Time in the Church of St. Francis Xavier Dublin*, M.H. Gill and Son, Dublin.

Kavanagh, J. (1960), *Manual of Social Ethics*, M.H. Gill and Son, Dublin.

Kearns, K. (1996), *Dublin Tenement Life, An Oral History*, Gill and Macmillan, Dublin, p. 48, p. 52.

Keenan, B. (2000), 'Can the IDA make it two in a row?', *Irish Independent*, 13 January, p. 2.

Keith, T. (1997), *Religion and the Decline of Magic*, Oxford University Press, New York, p. 39, p. 60.

Kelly, F. (1996), *Window on a Catholic Parish: St. Mary's Granard Co. Longford, 1933-68 Maynooth Studies in Local History*, Irish Academic Press, Dublin.

Kelly, L. (1998), 'Feminist Principles (2), Researching Sexual Violence', Ian Marsh, Rosie Campbell and Mike Keating (eds.), *Classic and Contemporary Readings in Sociology*, Longman, Harlow, p. 345.

Kennedy, K. (1971), *Productivity and Industrial Growth - The Irish Experience*, Clarendon Press, Oxford, p. 28.

Kennedy, K. (1992), 'The Context of Economic Development', J.H. Goldthorpe and C.T. Whelan (eds.), *The Development of Industrial Society in Ireland*, British Academy and Oxford University Press, New York, p. 15.

Kennedy, K. (1994), *Irish National Accounts for the 19th and 20th Centuries*, Economic and Social Research Institute, Dublin, Memorandum Series No 187, December, p. 9, pp. 12-13, p. 19, p. 29.

Kennedy, K. (1995), 'Irish Enterprise in the 20th Century', Andrew Burke (ed.), *Enterprise and the Irish Economy: Irish Studies in Management*, Oak Tree Press, Dublin, p. 62.

Kennedy, K. and Giblin, T. and McHugh, D. (1994), *The Economic Development of Ireland in the Twentieth Century*, Routledge, London, p. 99, p. 254.

Kennedy, L. (1996), 'The Roman Catholic Church and Economic Development in Nineteenth Century Ireland', Liam Kennedy (ed.), *Colonialism, Religion and Nationalism in Ireland*, Institute of Irish Studies, Queen's University, Belfast, p. 111, p. 116.

Kennedy, L. (1996a), 'The Early Response of the Irish Catholic Clergy to the Co-operative Movement' Liam Kennedy (ed.), *Colonialism, Religion and Nationalism in Ireland*, Institute of Irish Studies, Queen's University, Belfast, p. 120, p. 132.

Kennedy, L. (1996b), 'Farmers Traders, and Agricultural Politics in Pre-Independence Ireland' Liam Kennedy (ed.), *Colonialism, Religion and Nationalism in Ireland*, Institute of Irish Studies, Queen's University, Belfast, p. 141, ffn. 36, p. 143, p. 164.

Kennedy, L. (1996c), 'Modern Ireland: Post Colonial Society or Post-Colonial Pretensions', Liam Kennedy (ed.), *Colonialism, Religion and Nationalism in Ireland*, Institute of Irish Studies, Queen's University, Belfast, pp. 176-177.

Kennedy, L. (1996d), 'Out of History: Ireland, That Most Distressful Country', Liam Kennedy (ed.), *Colonialism, Religion and Nationalism in Ireland*, Institute of Irish Studies, Queen's University, Belfast, pp. 200-201.

Kennedy, L. and Johnston, D.S. (1996), 'The Union of Ireland and Britain 1801-1921', D.G. Boyce and Alan O'Day (eds.), *The Making of Modern Irish History - Revisionism and the Revisionist Controversy*, Routledge, New York, Table 1, p. 58.

Kenny, A. (1994), 'The Freedom of the Will' John Marenbon (ed.), *Aquinas on Mind - Topics in Mediaeval Philosophy*, Routledge, London, p. 78, p. 121.

Kenny, B. (1998), 'The Message that Points to the Future Game Plan of Multinationals', *The Irish Independent*, p. 19.

Kenny, I. (1984), *Government and Enterprise in Ireland*, Gill and Macmillan, Dublin p. 69.

Kenny, M. (1997), *Goodbye to Catholic Ireland*, Sinclair-Stevenson, London, pp. 23-25, p. 62, p. 166, p. 181, p. 238.

Kilminster, J. (1987), 'Introduction to Elias', *Theory Culture and Society*, Sage, London Volume 4, 1987, pp. 213-222.

Kingston, W. (1995), 'Entrepreneurship or Rent Seeking?', Andrew Burke (ed.), *Enterprise and the Irish Economy: Irish Studies in Management*, Oak Tree Press, Dublin, p. 265.

Krugman, P. (1997), 'Good News form Ireland, A Geographical Perspective', Alan Gray (ed.), *International Perspectives on the Irish Economy*, Indecon, Dublin p. 51.

Kung, H. (1999), *Christianity, Its Essence and Its History - The Religious Situation of Our Time*, SCM Press, St. Albans, pp. 578-579, p. 584.

Kvale, S. (1996), *Interviews: An Introduction to Qualitative Research Interviewing*, Sage, London, p. 6, pp. 52-53.

Kwang-Kuo, H. (1995), 'Modernisation of the Chinese Family Business', Henry S.R. Kao, Durganand Sinha, and Ng Sek-Hong (eds.), *Effective Organisations and Social Values*, Sage Publications, New Dehli, pp. 39-41, p. 45.

Lafarge, J. (1928), *The Jesuits in Modern Times*, The America Press, New York, p. 73, p. 101. p. 138.

Lane, F. (1997), *The Origins of Modern Irish Socialism 1881-1896*, Cork University Press, Cork, pp. 22-26, p. 92, p. 109, p. 120, p. 153, p. 200, p. 206, p. 218.

Lane, F. (2000), 'William Morris and Irish Politics', *History Ireland*, Spring 2000, pp. 22-26.

Laney, M. (1999), *How is Communication Possible? From the Perspective of Harold Garfinkel*, p1, http://hss.fullerton.edu/sociology/laney5htm

Leacock, E. (1986), 'Implications for Organisation', Eleanor Leacock and Helen I. Safa (eds.), *Women's Work - Development and the Division of Labour by Gender*, Bergin and Garvey Publishers Inc, Massachusetts, Postscript.

Leal, D. (1999), 'Against Conscience - A Protestant View', Jane Hoose (ed.), *Conscience in World Religions*, Gracewing and the University of Notre Dame, Hertfordshire, p. 27, p. 34, p. 49.

Lecaro, G. (1960), *What is My Labour Worth? The Christian View*, The Catholic Social Guild, Oxford, p. 6.

Leddin, A. (2000), 'Redundant Wage Model Could Harm Economy's Growth', *Irish Times*, 11 February 2000, p. 6.

Leddin, A. and Walsh, B. (1998), *The Macro-Economy of Ireland*, Gill and Macmillan, Dublin, pp. 30-36, p. 48.

Lee, J.J. (1989), *Ireland 1912-1985 Politics and Society*, Cambridge University Press, Cambridge, p. 181, pp. 391-394, p. 522, p. 528.

Leitch, M. (1998), 'Closed Places of the Spirit, Maurice Leitch interviewed by Richard Mills', *Irish Studies Review*, Volume 6, Number 1, pp. 63-69.

Lenin, V.I. (1896), 'Fredrich Engels', *Miscellany Rabotnik No: 1-2*, Scanned and formatted by the Maoist Documentation Project, http://www.blythe.org/m/mlenin/f_engels.htm

Lenin, V.I. (1909), 'The Attitude of the Workers Party to Religion', *Lenin Collected Works Volume 15*, Progress Publishers, pp. 402-413.

Lenin, V.I. (1909a), 'Classes and Parties in Their Attitude to Religion and the Church', *Lenin Collected Works Volume 15*, Progress Publishers, pp. 414-432.

Lenin, V.I. (1916), 'Imperialism and the Split in Socialism', *Sbornik and Sotsial-Demokrata No: 2 and the Collected Works, Volume 23*, Progress Publishers, Moscow, USSR, 1966. translated transcribed for the Internet: Workers' Web ASCII Pamphlet project, 1997, p. 9.

Lenin, V.I. (1929), 'War and Revolution', *Lenin Collected Works, Volume 24*, Progress Publishers 1964, pp. 398-421, first published in Pravda No 93, 23 April 1929, translated from the Russian edited by Bernard Isaacs, transcribed LIA@marx.org 27 April 1997, p. 3, p. 10.

Lenski, G. (1966), *Power and Privilege: A Theory of Social Stratification*, McGraw Hill, New York, p. 115.

Lesser, C.E.V. (1965), *Industrialisation in Developing Countries*, Economic and Social Research Institute, Dublin, Memorandum Series No 40, p. 1, p. 9, p. 14.

Levy, C. (1998), 'Max Weber and European Integration', Ralph Schroeder (ed.), *Max Weber, Democracy and Modernisation*, Macmillan Press, Basingstoke, p. 113.

Littlewood, R. (1996), 'Psychopathology, Embodiment and Religious Innovation - an Historical Instance', Dinesh Bhugra *Psychiatry and Religion, Context, Consensus and Controversies*, Routledge, London, p. 181.

Lynch, P. (1968), 'The Economic Scene', Owen Dudley Edwards (ed.), *Conor Cruise O'Brien Introduces Ireland*, Andre Deutche, London, pp. 74-77, p. 81.

McAleese, D. (2000), 'Ireland's Economic Boom, The True Causes: A Reply to the OECD Economic Survey on Ireland', *OECD Observer*, 7 January 2000.

McBride, L. (1999), 'The Reynolds Letters - An Irish Emigrant Family in Late Victorian Manchester', David Fitzpatrick (ed.), *Irish Narratives*, Cork University Press, Cork.

McBrien, R. (1994), *Catholicism*, Geoffrey Chapman, London, pp. 8-9, p. 17, pp. 390-391.

McCarthy, J. (1990), 'Irelands Turnaround: Whitaker and the 1958 Plan for Economic Development', John F. McCarthy (ed.), *Planning Ireland's Future: The Legacy of T. K. Whitaker*, Glendale Press, Dublin, p. 13.

McCoy, D. and Duffy, D. and Hore, J. and MacCoille, C. (2001), *Quarterly Economic Commentary - October 2001 a Summary*, Economic and Social Research Institute, Dublin pp. 1-8.

McCreevy, C. (1998), *RTE 1 Television*, 6 One News, 2 July 1998.

McCreevy, C. (2000), *RTE 1 Television*, Nine O' Clock News, 14 June 2000.

McCrone, D. and Kiely, R. (2000), 'Nationalism and Citizenship', *Sociology*, Volume 34, No 1, February 2000, p. 21, p. 26.

McDevitt, P.F. (1997), 'Muscular Catholicism: Nationalism, Masculinity and Gaelic Team Sports 1884-1916', *Gender and History*, Volume 9, No 2, August 1997, pp. 262-284.

McGarry, F. (2001), 'Catholics First and Politicians Afterwards: The Labour Party and The Workers Republic, 1936-1939', *Saothar 25: Journal of the Irish Labour History Society*, Dublin pp. 57-65.

McGettigan, T. (1998), 'Redefining Reality: Epiphany as a Standard of Post Modern Truth', *Electronic Journal of Sociology 1998*, pp. 1-11,
http://www.sociology.org/content/vol1003.004/mcgettigan.html

McGuire, M. (1992), *Religion - The Social Context*, Wadsworth Publishing, California, p. 222.

McHugh, N. (1998), *Urban Poverty in the Shadow of Privilege: Drogheda before the Famine Maynooth Studies in Local History*, Irish Academic Press, Dublin, p. 36, p. 39.

McKendree, D. (1995), *Barbed Wire and Rice - Poems and Songs from Japanese Prisoner of War Camps*, Cornell University, New York.

McLoughlin, B. (1999), 'Delegated to the New World Irish Communists at Moscow's International Lenin School, 1927-1937', *History Ireland*, Volume 7, No 4, Winter 1999, pp. 37-40.

McLysaght, S. (1950), 'Meithal', Anne O'Dowd (ed.), *A Study of Co-Operative Labour in Rural Ireland*, UCD Folklore Dept., Dublin, p. 222.

McQueen, N. (1998), 'European Union', S.J. Connolly (ed.), *The Oxford Companion to Irish History*, Oxford University Press, Oxford, p. 180.

MacRaild, D. (1999), *Irish Migrants in Modern Britain 1750-1922*, Macmillan Press, Basingstoke, pp. 1-7, p. 12.

Mac Réamoinn, S. (2000), 'Secularisation not Secularism', *Doctrine and Life*, Dominican Publications, Dublin, December 2000, pp. 655-662.

MacSharry, R. and White, P. (2000), *The Making of the Celtic Tiger; The Inside Story of Ireland's Boom Economy*, Mercier Press, Cork, p. 377.

Machin, S. and Vignoles A. (2001), *The Economic Benefits of Training to the Individual, the Firm and the Economy: The Key Issues*, The Centre for the Economics of Education, pp. 1-25.

Madden, J. (2000), 'The Services Sector', Adrian Redmond (ed.), *That Was Then, This is Now - Change in Ireland 1949-1999*, Central Statistics Office, Dublin, February 2000, pp. 147-149.

Magee, B. (1998), *The Story of Philosophy*, Dorling Kindersey, London, pp. 165-167, p. 211.

Mair, P. (1992), 'Explaining the Absence of Class Politics in Ireland', J.H. Goldthorpe and C.T. Whelan (eds.), *The Development of Industrial Society in Ireland*, British Academy and Oxford University Press, New York, p. 395.

Malcolm, E. (1986), *Ireland Sober Ireland Free - Drink and Temperance in Nineteenth Century Ireland*, Gill and Macmillan, New York, pp. 52-53, p. 210, p. 225, p. 234, p. 263.

Malcolm, E. (1998), 'Printing and Publishing', S.J.Connolly (ed.), *The Oxford Companion to Irish History*, Oxford University Press, Oxford, p. 462.

Manning, M. (1999), *James Dillon - A Biography*, Wolfhound Press, Dublin, p. 217.

Manning, M. (1970), *The Blueshirts*, Gill and Macmillan, Dublin, p. 3, p. 11, pp. 30-36, pp. 240-249.

Manseragh, N. (1965), 'The State of Ireland in the Early Years of the Union', N. Manseragh (ed.), *The Irish Question 1840-1921, A Commentary on Anglo-Irish Relations and on Social and Political Forces in Ireland in the Age of Reform and Revolution*, George Allen and Unwin, London p. 21, p. 30.

Manseragh, N. (1965a), 'The Communist International and The Irish Question - Some Reflections on the Marxist Interpretation of the Irish Question', N. Manseragh (ed.), *The Irish Question 1840-1921, A Commentary on Anglo-Irish Relations and on Social and Political Forces in Ireland in the Age of Reform and Revolution*, George Allen and Unwin, London, p. 104, p. 110.

Manseragh, N. (1965b), 'European and Irish Nationalisms: The View of Italian Nationalists on the Nature of the Irish Question', N. Manseragh (ed.), *The Irish Question 1840-1921, A Commentary on Anglo-Irish Relations and on Social and Political Forces in Ireland in the Age of Reform and Revolution*, George Allen and Unwin, London, p. 21, p. 30.

Manseragh, N. (1965c), 'The Communist International and The Irish Question - Some Reflections on the Marxist Interpretation of the Irish Question', N. Manseragh (ed.), *The Irish Question 1840-1921, A Commentary on Anglo-Irish Relations and on Social and Political Forces in Ireland in the Age of Reform and Revolution*, George Allen and Unwin, London, p. 71.

Manseragh, N. (1997), 'From British Commonwealth towards European Community' Dinagh Manseragh (ed.), *Nationalism and Independence - Selected Irish Papers*, Cork University Press, Cork, p. 201, p. 208.

Manseragh, N. (1997a), 'Ireland - The Republic Outside the Commonwealth', Dinagh Manseragh (ed.), *Nationalism and Independence - Selected Irish Papers*, Cork University Press, Cork, p. 171 pp. 181-182.

Manseragh, N. (1997b), 'Political Parties at the 1948 General Election', Dinagh Manseragh (ed.), *Nationalism and Independence - Selected Irish Papers*, Cork University Press, Cork, p. 142.

Manseragh, N. (1997c), 'The Prelude to Partition Concepts and Aims in Ireland and India', Dinagh Manseragh (ed.), *Nationalism and Independence - Selected Irish Papers*, Cork University Press, Cork, p. 35.

Manseragh, N. (1997d), 'Eamon De Valera - Life and Irish Times', Dinagh Manseragh (ed.), *Nationalism and Independence - Selected Irish Papers*, Cork University Press, Cork, pp. 220-228.

Marcuse, H. (1987), *Eros and Civilisation: A Philosophical Inquiry into Freud*, ARK Paperbacks, London p. 36.

Marshall, F.R. and Briggs, V.M. and King, A.G. (1984), *Labour Economics: Wages, Employment, Trade Unionism and Public Policy*, Irwin Publications in Economics, Illinois.

Marx, K. (1843), 'On the Jewish Question' David McLellan (ed.), *Karl Marx Selected Writings*, Oxford University Press, Oxford, First published 1977, p. 48.

Marx, K. (1844), 'Towards a Critique of Hegel's Philosophy of Right: Introduction', David McLellan (ed.), *Karl Marx Selected Writings*, Oxford University Press, Oxford, first published 1977, pp. 63-74.

Marx, K. (1844a), 'Economic and Philosophical Manuscripts - critique of Hegel's Dialectic and General Philosophy', David McLellan (ed.), *Karl Marx Selected Writings*, Oxford University Press, Oxford, first published 1977, pp. 75-112.

Marx, K. (1845), 'The Holy Family', David McLellan (ed.), *Karl Marx Selected Writings*, Oxford University Press, Oxford, first published 1977, pp. 131-155.

Marx, K. (1849), 'Wage Labour and Capital', David McLellan (ed.), *Karl Marx Selected Writings*, Oxford University Press, Oxford first published 1977, p. 248.

Marx, K. (1857), 'Grundrisse', David McLellan (ed.), *Karl Marx Selected Writings*, Oxford University Press, Oxford, first published 1977, pp. 345-387.

Marx, K. (1864), 'Inaugural Address to the First International', David McLellan (ed.), *Karl Marx Selected Writings*, Oxford University Press, Oxford, first published 1977, p. 531 p. 536.

Marx, K. (1867), 'On Ireland, Marx to Engels 30th November 1867', David McLellan (ed.), *Karl Marx Selected Writings*, Oxford University Press, Oxford, first published 1977, p. 590.

Marx, K. (1869), 'On Ireland Marx to Kugelmann 29 Nov. 1869', David McLellan (ed.), *Karl Marx Selected Writings*, Oxford University Press, Oxford, first published 1977, p. 590.

Marx, K. (1870), 'On Ireland Marx to Meyer and Vogt 9th April 1870', David McLellan (ed.), *Karl Marx Selected Writings*, Oxford University Press, Oxford, first published 1977, p. 591.

Marx, K. (1902), 'The Poverty of Philosophy', David McLellan (ed.), *Karl Marx Selected Writings*, Oxford University Press, Oxford, first published 1977, p. 209.

Marx, K. (1963), 'Peasants and Artisans in Capitalist Society in Theories of Surplus Value Moscow 1963-68, David McLellan (ed.), *Karl Marx Selected Writings*, Oxford University Press Oxford, first published 1977, pp. 396-397.

Marx, K. (1998), 'Bourgeoise and Proletarians' Ian Marsh, Rosie Campbell and Mike Keating (eds.), *Classic and Contemporary Readings in Sociology*, Longman, Essex, p. 77.

Mason, J. (1996), *Qualitative Researching*, Sage, London.

Mayhew, L. (1982), 'Introduction' Leon H. Mayhew (ed.), *Talcott Parsons On Institutional and Social Evolution - Selected Writings*, University of Chicago Press, Chicago p. 7, p. 13, p. 61.

Mead, H. (1934), *Social Attitudes and the Physical World in Mind, Self, and Society*, Chicago University Press, Chicago, pp. 1-6.

Meenan, J.F. (1970), *The Irish Economy Since 1922*, Liverpool University Press, Liverpool, p. 62.

Mennell, S. (1997), *A Biographical Sketch of Norbert Elias (1897-1990)*, p. 1, http://www.ucd.ie/~figurate/concepts.html

Mennell, S. (1998), *Norbert Elias - An Introduction*, University College Dublin Press, Dublin p. 2, p. 35, p. 158.

Mercier, L.S. 'Tableau de Paris Amsterdam 1783-88, XI pp. 41042', cited in Sombart, W. 1967: *Luxury and Capitalism*, University of Michigan Press, p. 115, p. 155.

Merton, R. (1957), *Social Theory and Social Structure*, Free Press, Glencoe IL, pp. 60-69.

Metcalf, B. (1999), 'Weber and Islamic Reform', Toby Huff and Wolfgang Schluchter (eds.), *Max Weber and Islam*, Transaction Publishers, New Brunswick, p. 227.

Mezirow, J. (1990), *Fostering Critical Reflection in Adulthood - A Guide to Transformative and Emancipatory Learning*, Jossey Bass, San Francisco, p. 297.

Milotte, M. (1984*), Communism in Modern Ireland - The Pursuit of the Workers Republic Since 1916*, Gill and Macmillan, Dublin, p. 97, p. 107.

Minister for Finance, (2000a), 'The Last Word', *Today FM Radio*, 10 January 2000.

Mitchell, T. (1997), 'Tackling the Vicious Cycle of Poverty', *Irish Times*, 23 July 1997, p. 11.

Mjoset, L. (1993), 'The Irish Economy in a Comparative Institutional Perspective Report No: 93 National Economic and Social Council', Patrick Clancy, Sheelagh Drudy, Kathleen Lynch and Liam Dowd (eds.), *Modern Ireland: Irish Society - Sociological Perspectives*, Institute of Public Administration, Dublin, in association with the Sociological Society of Ireland, p. 118.

Moehler, J. (1894), *Doctrinal Differences Between Catholics and Protestants As Evidenced By Their Symbolical Writings*, Gibbings and Co., London, p. 152, p. 167.

Morgan, H. and Graham, T. (2000), 'The Catholic Church Through the Ages', *History Ireland*, Volume 8, No 3, Autumn 2000, Editorial, p. 5.

Morrison, K. (1995), *Marx Durkheim Weber; Formations of Modern Social Thought*, Sage, London, p. 99, pp. 112-115, p. 125, p. 213.

Mouzelis, N. (2000), 'The Subjectivist-Objectivist Divide: Against Transcendence', *Sociology*, Cambridge University Press, Cambridge, Volume 34, No 4, November 2000, pp. 741-762.

Movie-Tone News, (1999), 'Ireland in the 1930s', *Treo*, RTE 1, 20 April 1999.

Mulhall, D. (1999), *A New Day Dawning - A Portrait of Ireland in 1900*, The Collins Press, Cork, pp. 52-58.

Murphy, A. (1999), 'Ireland and Ante/Anti-Colonial Theory', *Irish Studies Review*, Volume 7, No 2, August 1999, pp. 153-163.

Murphy, D. (1997), 'Success Against The Odds: Catholic Schools in the USA', Daniel Murphy and Valentine Rice (eds.), *Studies in Education - A Journal of Education Research*, Volume 13, Number 1, Spring 1997, Dublin.

Muuss, R. (1996), 'The Psychoanalytic Theory of Adolescent Development', *Theories of Adolescence*, McGraw-Hill, New York, p. 18.

Myers, D.G. (1988), 'Learning', D.G. Myers (ed.), *Psychology*, Worth 1988, pp. 229-252.

Myers, K. (1999), 'An Irishman's Diary', *The Irish Times*, 22 December 1999, p. 15.

Nash, R. (1956), *Jesuits - Biographical Essays*, M.H. Gill and Son, Dublin, p. 24.

National Competitiveness Council (1999), *Report on Social Partnership*, Chapter 1, pp. 1-9, Chapter 4, p. 7.

National Crime Council (2001), *Crime in Ireland: Trends and Patterns 1950 to 1998*, Institute of Criminology, Faculty of Law, University College Dublin, Dublin, p. v, pp. xii-xiii.

NCCA, (1999), *From Junior to Leaving Certificate - A Longitudinal Study of 1994 Junior Certificate Candidates who took the Leaving Certificate Examination in 1997 - Final Report*, The National Council For Curriculum and Assessment, Educational Research Centre, St. Patrick's College, Dublin, p. 52.

Neary, T. and O'Grada, C. (1991), 'Protection, Economic War and Structural Change: The 1930s in Ireland', *Irish Historical Studies*, Volume xxvii, No 107, May 1991, pp. 250-266.

Nelson, R.R. and Pack, H. (1997), *The Asian Miracle and Modern Growth Theory*, World Bank, Washington, p. 4, p. 33.

Newman, J. (1965), *Change and the Catholic Church - An Essay in Sociological Ecclesiology*, Helicon, Dublin, p. 251.

Newsinger, J. (1993), 'The Devil It Was Who Sent Larkin To Ireland - The Liberator, Lakinism and the Dublin Lockout of 1913', *Saothar: Document Studies Irish Labour History Society*, No 18, 1993, pp. 101-105.

Newsinger, J. (1995), 'The Curse of Larkinism - Patrick McIntyre, The Toiler and the Dublin Lockout of 1913', *Éire-Ireland: A Journal of Irish Studies*, The Irish American Cultural Institute, Autumn, 1995, pp. 90-102.

Ni Bhrolchain, M. (1998), 'Is Ireland Underpopulated?', Kieran A. Kennedy (ed.), *From Famine to Feast - Economic and Social Change in Ireland 1847-1997*, Institute of Public Administration, Dublin, p. 28.

Nic Ghiolla Phadraig, M. (1995), 'The Power of the Catholic Church', Patrick Clancy, Sheelagh Drudy, Kathleen Lynch and Liam Dowd (eds.), *Modern Ireland: Irish Society, Sociological Perspectives*, IPA in association with the Sociological Association of Ireland, Dublin, pp. 594-598.

Nifissi, M. (1998), 'Reframing Orientalism: Weber and Islam', Ralph Schroeder (ed.), *Max Weber, Democracy and Modernisation*, Macmillan Press, London, p. 183.

Niles, F.S. (1999), 'Towards a Cross Cultural Understanding of Work-Related Beliefs', *Human Relations*, Volume 52, No 7, July 1999, pp. 855-867.

Nolan, B. (2000), 'Relative Poverty Deepens Despite Celtic Tiger', *Irish Times,* 19 May, p. 14.

Nolan, B (2002), 'Why does Ireland do so badly on the UN's Human Poverty Index?', *Quarterly Economic Commentary Autumn 2002*, ESRI, Dublin, pp. 38-48.

Nolan, B. and O'Connell, P.J. and Whelan T. (2000), 'The Irish Experience of Growth and Inequality', Brian Nolan, Philip J. O'Connell and Christopher T. Whelan (eds.), *Bust or Boom, The Irish Experience of Growth and Inequality*, Institute of Public Administration, Dublin, p. 341.

Nolan, B and O'Connell, P.J. and Whelan T. (2000a), 'Introduction', Brian Nolan, Philip J. O'Connell and Christopher T. Whelan (eds.), *Bust or Boom - The Irish Experience of Growth and Inequality*, Institute of Public Administration, Dublin, p. 1.

Oakley, A. (1990), *Housewife - High Value-Low Cost*, Penguin Books, London, p. 190.

O'Brien, G. (1918), *The Economic History of Ireland in the Eighteenth Century*, Maunsel and Company, Dublin, p. 304, p. 412.

O'Carroll, J, (1987), 'Contemporary Attitudes Towards the Homeless Poor 1725-1775', David Dickson (ed.), *The Georgeous Mask Dublin 1700-1850*, Trinity College History Workshop, Dublin, p. 73.

O'Connell, P.J. (2000), 'The Dynamics of the Irish Labour Market in Comparative Perspective', Brian Nolan, Philip J. O'Connell and Christopher T. Whelan (eds.), *Bust or Boom - The Irish Experience of Growth and Inequality*, Institute of Public Administration, Dublin, p. 62.

O'Curry, E. (1873), *Manners and Customs of the Ancient Irish Volumes I and II*, Williams and Norgate, London. And J.F. Fowler 3 Crow St. Dublin, p. 73, p. 353, p. 392.

O'Day, A. and McWilliams, P. (1997), *Ordinance Survey Memoirs of Ireland Volume 39, Parishes of County Donegal II 1835-6*, Institute of Irish Studies in association with Royal Irish Academy, Belfast, pp. 8-9, p. 55, p. 61, p. 98, p. 144, p. 150.

O'Donnell J.D. (1978), *How Ireland is Governed?*, Institute of Public Administration, Dublin, pp. 71-72.

O'Donoghue, J. (2000), 'Is Balance a Myth?, Creativity Awakens Only At The Edge', *Working Toward Balance - Our Society in the New Millennium*, Veritas, Dublin, pp. 140-157.

OECD (1969), *Investment in Education: Report by the Survey team appointed by the Minister for Education in October 1962*, Government of Ireland and OECD, Paris and Dublin, Appendix 12.

OECD (1999), *Economic Survey of Ireland - May 1999*, OECD, Paris, p. 2, pp. 27-31.

OECD (1999a), *Economic Outlook No: 66 Ireland*, OECD, Paris, December 1999, pp. 92-94.

OECD (1999b), *Employment Outlook*, OECD, Paris, June 1999, p. 135.

OECD (2001), *Economic Survey of Ireland - Policy Brief*, OECD, Paris, May 2001, p. 1.

OECD (2001a), *The Development Dimensions of Trade*, OECD Observer, Paris, pp. 1-85.

O'Gráda, C. (1995), *Ireland - A New Economic History 1780-1939*, Clarendon Press, Oxford, p. 44, p. 69, p. 74, pp. 207-242.

O'Gráda, C. (1997), *A Rocky Road: The Irish Economy Since the 1920s*, Manchester University Press, Manchester, pp. 1-4, p. 44, p. 216, p. 224, pp. 230-231.

O'Gráda, C. (1998), 'The Rise in Living Standards', Kieran A. Kennedy (ed.), *From Feast to Famine Economic and Social Change in Ireland 1847-1997*, Institute of Public Administration, Dublin.

O'Hagan. J. and Murphy, P. and Redmond, A. (2000), 'The Economy', Adrian Redmond (ed.), *That Was Then, This is Now - Change in Ireland 1949-1999*, Central Statistics Office, Dublin, February 2000, p. 8, p. 92.

O'Hare, A and Whelan, C.T. and Commins, P. (1991), *The Development of an Irish Census Based Social Class Scale*, The Economic and Social Research Institute, Dublin, Series No: 92, p. 139, p. 142.

O'Hare, D. (1999), 'Building on the Boom: Investment at Third Level Vital to Fuel Economic Growth', *Irish Times*, January 5, 1999, p. 14.

O'Hearn, D. (1995), 'Global Restructuring and the Irish Political Economy in Ireland' Patrick Clancy, Sheelagh Drudy, Kathleen Lynch and Liam Dowd (eds.), *Modern Ireland: Irish Society, Sociological Perspectives*, IPA in association with the Sociological Association of Ireland, Dublin, p. 118.

O'Hearn, D. (1998), *Inside the Tiger: The Irish Economy and the Asian Model*, Pluto Press, London, p. 12.

O'Herlihy, D and Griffin, A and O'Donnell, S and Devereaux, K. (1995), *To the Cause of Liberality - A History of the O'Connell Schools and the Christian Brothers, North Richmond Street*, Allen Library Project, Dublin, p. 15, p. 24, pp. 53-54.

O'Higgins, K. (1998), 'Hoping Against the Odds - On the Third Day', *The Sacred Heart Messenger*, Jesuit Publications, Dublin, May 1998, p. 24.

Olson, R. (1993), *The Emergence of the Social Sciences 1642-1792*, Macmillan Publishing Co., New York, p. 44.

O'Mahony, D. (2000), 'Even Blind Pigs Can Find an Acorn', *Sunday Independent*, 13 August 2000, p. 8, p. 141.

O'Malley, E. (1989), *Industry and Economic Development - The Challenge for the Latecomer*, Gill and Macmillan, Dublin, pp. 3-4, pp. 34-55, pp. 210-214, p. 265.

O'Malley, E. (1998), 'The Revival of Irish Indigenous Industry 1987-1997', T.J. Baker, David Duffy, Fergal Shortall (eds.), *Quarterly Economic Commentary April 1998*, ESRI, Dublin, pp. 35-60.

Oppenheim, A.N. (1997), *Questionnaire Design, Interviewing and Attitude Measurement*, Pinter, London, p. 83, p. 210.

O'Riain, S. (2001), 'Soft Solutions to Hard Times', Eamonn Slater and Michel Peillon (eds.), *Memories of the Present: A Sociological Chronicle of Ireland, 1997-1998 Volume II*, Institute of Public Administration, Dublin, pp. 237-245.

O'Riordan, M. (2000), 'Linking Marx and Religion', *Irish Times*, Opinion Section, 7 February 2000.

Orwell, G. (1986), *The Road to Wigan Pier*, Penguin, London, p. 122 pp. 150-151.

Oser, J. (1967), *Promoting Economic Development*, East Africa Publishing House, Nairobi, p. 4.

O'Sullivan, M. (1995), 'Manufacturing and Global Competition', J.W.O'Hagen (ed.), *The Economy of Ireland: Policy and Performance of a Small European Country*, Gill and Macmillan, Dublin, p. 373.

Oswald, J.A. (1997), *Happiness and Economic Performance in The Labour Market Consequences of Technical and Structural Change*, Department of Economics, University of Warwick, Coventry, Discussion Paper Series No 18, pp. 1-19.

O'Toole, D. (1987), 'The Employment Crisis of 1826', David Dickson (ed.), *The Georgeous Mask: Dublin 1700-1850*, Trinity College History Workshop, Dublin, pp. 153-154.

O'Toole, F. (1999), 'The Treason of the Elite in a Culture of Corruption', *Irish Times*, 1 October 1999, p. 14.

O' Toole, F. (2000), 'Does Power Erode Ethics', *Working Towards Balance - Our Society in the New Millennium*, Veritas, Dublin, pp. 17-29.

O'Toole, F. (2001), 'How Celtic Tiger's Cubs Find SF (Sinn Fein), Reassuring', *Irish Times*, 13 January 2001, p. 8.

O'Tuathaigh, G. (1998), 'Life on the Land', Kieran A. Kennedy (ed.), *From Famine to Feast - Economic and Social Change in Ireland 1847-1997*, Institute of Public Administration, Dublin, p. 38, p. 42.

O'Tuathaigh, G. (1999), 'Irish Historical Revisionism: State of the Art or Ideological Project?', Ciarán Brady (ed.), *Interpreting Irish History, The Debate on Historical Revisionism 1938-1994*, Irish Academic Press, Dublin, pp. 306-326.

Pareto, V. (1935), 'Circulation of the Elites', Arthur Livingston *The Mind and Society*, Harcourt Brace and Co., New York, pp. 2026–2029, pp. 2233-2236.

Parsons, T. (1968), *The Structure of Social Action - A Study in Social Theory with Special Reference to a Group of Recent European Writers Volume 1, Marshall, Pareto, Durkheim*, The Free Press, New York, p. 288, p. 440.

Parsons, T. (1968a), *The Structure of Social Action - A Study in Social Theory with Special Reference to a Group of Recent European Writers Volume 2, Weber*, The Free Press, New York, p. 663.

Parsons, T. (1969), 'Religion and Problem of Meaning', Roland Robertson (ed.), *Sociology of Religion*, Middlesex, Penguin, pp. 204-210.

Parsons, T. (1982), The Place of Ultimate Values in Sociological Theory;Sociological Theory and the Action Frame of Reference', Leon H. Mayhew (ed.), *Talcott Parsons On Institutions and Social Evolution - Selected Writings*, Chicago University Press, Chicago, p. 89.

Parsons, T (1982a), 'Integration and Institutionalisation in the Social System; Institutionalisation, Sociological Theory and the Action Frame of Reference', Leon H. Mayhew (ed.), *Talcott Parsons On Institutions and Social Evolution - Selected Writings Chicago*, University Press, Chicago, p. 119, p. 128.

Parsons, T. (1982b), 'The Superego and the Theory of Social Systems; Institutionalisation, Sociological Theory and the Action Frame of Reference', Leon H. Mayhew (ed.), *Talcott Parsons On Institutions and Social Evolution - Selected Writings*, Chicago University Press, Chicago, pp. 130-131, pp. 137-139.

Parsons T. (1982c), 'Illness and the Role of the Physician; Sociological Theory and the Action Frame of Reference', Leon H. Mayhew (ed.), *Talcott Parsons On Institutions and Social Evolution - Selected Writings*, Chicago University Press, Chicago, pp. 132-133, pp. 150-151.

Parsons T. (1982d), 'The Hierarchy of Control; Institutionalisation, Sociological Theory and the Action Frame of Reference', Leon H. Mayhew (ed.), *Talcott Parsons On Institutions and Social Evolution - Selected Writings*, Chicago University Press, Chicago, p. 159.

Parsons T. (1982e), 'Durkheim on Organic Solidarity; Institutionalised Exchange', Leon H. Mayhew (ed.), *Talcott Parsons On Institutions and Social Evolution - Selected Writings*, Chicago University Press, Chicago, pp. 208-209.

Parsons, T. (1999), 'Christianity and Modern Industrial Society - Religion and Modern Society', Bryan S. Turner (ed.), *The Talcott Parsons Reader*, Blackwell, Cambridge, p. 4, p. 24, p. 33, p. 40, p. 46, p. 49, p. 63.

Parsons, T. (1999a), 'Belief, Unbelief and Disbelief - Religion and Modern Society', Bryan S. Turner (ed.), *The Talcott Parsons Reader*, Blackwell, Cambridge, pp. 55-57, p. 73.

Parsons, T. (1999b), 'Religious Symbolisation and Death - Religion and Modern Society', Bryan S. Turner (ed.), *The Talcott Parsons Reader*, Blackwell, Cambridge, p. 85.

Parsons, T. (1999c), 'The Symbolic Environment of Modern Economies - Religion and Modern Society', Bryan S. Turner (ed.), *The Talcott Parsons Reader*, Blackwell, Cambridge, p. 96, p. 256.

Parsons, T. (1999d), 'Evolutionary Universal - Sociological Theory', Bryan S. Turner (ed.), *The Talcott Parsons Reader*, Blackwell, Cambridge, pp. 158-159, p. 167.

Parsons, T. and Fox, R. and Lidz, V. (1999), 'The "Gift of Life" and Its Reciprocation - Life, Sex and Death', Bryan S. Turner (ed.), *The Talcott Parsons Reader*, Blackwell, Cambridge, p. 125, pp. 130-131, p. 134.

Parsons, T. and Platt, G. (1982), 'American Values and American Society;Change Evolution and Modern Society', Leon H. Mayhew (ed.), *Talcott Parsons On Institutions and Social Evolution - Selected Writings*, Chicago University Press, Chicago, pp. 327-335.

Parsons, T. and Smelser, N. (1982), 'Double Interchanges in Economy and Society; Institutionalised Exchange', Leon H. Mayhew (ed.), *Talcott Parsons On Institutions and Social Evolution - Selected Writings*, Chicago University Press, Chicago, pp. 219-223.

Peillon, M. (1995), 'Interest Groups and the State in the Republic of Ireland', Patrick Clancy, Sheelagh Drudy, Kathleen Lynch and Liam Dowd (eds.), *Modern Ireland: Irish Society, Sociological Perspectives*, IPA, in association with the Sociological Association of Ireland, Dublin, pp. 358-362.

Peillon, M. (2000), 'Carnival Ireland', Eamonn Slater and Michel Peillon (eds.), *Memories of the Present:A Sociological Chronicle of Ireland, 1997-1998 Volume II*, Institute of Public Administration, Dublin, pp. 133-143.

Peillon, M. (2003) 'Material Inequalities' in *Introduction to Modern Irish Society* Lecture 4 Sociology 2002/2003.

Peschke, K. (1997), *Christian Ethics: Moral Theology in the Light of Vatican II Volume 2, Special Moral Theology*, Goodlife Neale, Alcester, p. 195, p. 199, p. 209.

Peters, R. (1999), 'Paradise or Hell? The Religious Doctrine of Election in Eighteenth and Nineteenth Century Islamic Fundamentalism and Protestant Calvinism', Toby Huff and Wolfgang Schluchter (eds.), *Max Weber and Islam*, Transaction Publishers, New Brunswick, USA, p. 205, pp. 211-215.

Peters, S. (1996), *Bernard Shaw, the Ascent of Superman*, Yale University Press, New Haven, pp. 90-95.

Pettigrew, J. (1981), 'Reminiscences of Fieldwork Among the Shikhs', H Robert (ed.), *Doing Feminist Research*, Routledge, London.

Pissarides, C. (2000), *Human Capital and Growth: A Synthesis Report*, OECD Development Centre, Paris, Technical Paper No 168, pp. 1-35.

Plunkett, H. (1905), *Ireland in the New Century*, Academic Press, Dublin, pp. 108.

Plunkett, J. (1968), 'People and Places, Dublin: Streets Broad and Narrow', Owen Dudley Edwards (ed.), *Conor Cruise O'Brien Introduces Ireland*, Andre Deutche, London, p. 192.

Pollio, H and Henley, T and Thompson, C. (1997), *The Phenomenology of Everyday Life*, The Press Syndicate of the University of Cambridge, Cambridge, p. 8, p. 30.

Polsky, N, (1998), 'Participant Observation (2): Deviant Lives and Careers', Ian Marsh, Rosie Campbell and Mike Keating (eds.), *Classic and Contemporary Readings in Sociology*, Longman, Harlow, p. 325.

Pope Benedict XIV (1751), *On Jews and Christians living in the Same Place; A Quo Primum Rome*, encyclical promulgated on 14 June 1751,
http://listserv.american.edu/catholic/franciscan/justice/sfopjgo.html

Pope John XXIII (1961), *Mater Et Magistra*, Rome, Encyclical promulgated on 15 May 1961, p. 21, http://listserv.american.edu/catholic/church/papal/john.xxiii/j23mater.txt

Pope Leo XIII (1878), *Inscrutabili Dei Consilio, On the Evils of Society*, Rome, Encyclical promulgated on 21 April 1878, pp. 1-7,
http://listserv.american.edu/catholic/church/papal/leo.xiii/inscrutabili.html

Pope Leo XIII (1878a), *Quod Apostolici Muneris - On Socialism*, Rome, Encyclical promulgated on 28 December 1878, p. 5,
http://listserv.american.edu/catholic/church/papal/leo.xiii/l13socsm.txt

Pope Leo XIII (1888), *Libertas; On the Nature of Human Liberty*, Rome, Encyclical promulgated on 20 June 1888, p. 8, p. 13,
http://listserv.american.edu/catholic/church/papal/leo.xiii/l13liber.txt

Pope Leo XIII (1888a), *Exeunte Iam Anno: On the Right Ordering of Christian Life*, Rome, Encyclical promulgated on 25 December 1889, pp. 3-7,
http://listserv.american.edu/catholic/church/papal/leo.xiii/l13rgt.txt

Pope Leo XIII (1889), *On Devotion to St. Joseph; QuamQuam Pluries*, Rome, Encyclical promulgated on 15 August 1889,
http://listserv.american.edu/catholic/church/papal/leo.xiii/l13jos.txt

Pope Leo XIII (1891), *Rerum Novarum; On the Condition of the Working Classes*, Rome, Encyclical letter issued on 15 May 1891, pp. 7-9, p. 19,
http://listserv.american.edu/catholic/church/papal/leo.xiii/rerum.novarum.html

Pope Pius IX (1864), *Condemning Current Errors, Quanta Cura*, Rome, Encyclical promulgated 8 December 1864, p. 4,
http://listserv.american.edu/catholic/church/papal/pius.ix/p9quanta.html

Pope Pius XI (1931), *Quadragessimo Anno; On the Reconstruction of the Social Order*, Rome, Encyclical issued on 15 May 1931, p. 7, p. 14,
http://listserv.american.edu/catholic/church/papal/pius.xi/p11quad.txt

Pope Pius XI (1937), *Divini Redemptoris;Atheistic Communism*, Rome, encyclical promulgated 19 March 1937, p. 1, p. 13,
http://listserv.american.edu/catholic/church/papal/pius.xi/p11-divi.txt

Potter, J. (1996), *Representing Reality, Discourse, Rhetoric and Social Construction*, Sage, London, p. 49.

Powell, T. (1995), 'The Idea of the Three Orders of Society and Social Stratification in Early Mediaeval Ireland', *Irish Historical Studies*, Volume 29, No 116, Nov 1995, pp. 476-482.

Power, E. (1986), 'Thomas Paycocke of Coggeshall, an Essex Clothier in the days of Henry VII', *Medieval People*, Essay VII, pp. 152-173.

Prothero, I. (1997), *Radical Artisans in England and France, 1830-1870*, Cambridge University Press, Cambridge, pp 2-5, p. 24, p. 101, p. 103, pp. 190-198, pp. 248-249, p. 270, p. 305, p. 316.

Proudhon, P.J. (1888), *A System of Economical Contradictions: Or the Philosophy of Misery*, Cambridge University Press and John Wilson and Son, Boston, p. 33, p. 43, p. 68, http://socserv2.socsci.mcmaster.ca/~econ/ugcm/3113/Proudhon/index.html.

Quarterly Review (1840), Cited in Joseph O'Connor *Sweet Liberty: Travels in Irish America*, Picador, London, p. 126

Quinn, K. (1958), *Pope Pius XII and The Worker*, Dublin, Irish Messenger Office, Catholic Workers Series 2, pp. 4-7, p. 19, p.15.

Raven, J. (1970), *Social and Economic Development*, Economic and Social Research Institute, Dublin, Memorandum Series No 62, pp. 2-10.

Redmond, A. and Heanue, M. (2000), 'Aspects of Society', Adrian Redmond (ed.), *That Was Then, This is Now Change in Ireland 1949-1999*, Government of Ireland, Central Statistics Office, Dublin, February 2000, p. 55, p. 60.

Reuters (1998), 'Pope calls on Catholics to keep God part of Sunday', *Irish Times*, 8 July 1998.

Rex, J. (1996), 'National Identity in the Democratic Multi-cultural State', *Sociological Online*, Volume 1, No 2, http//: www.socresonline.org.uk/socresonline/1/2/1.html

Ribbens, J. (1993), 'Facts or Fictions? Aspects of the Use of Autobiographical Writing in Undergraduate Sociology', *Sociology*, February 1993, Volume 27, No 1, pp. 81-92.

Riché, P. (1978), *Daily Life in the World of Charlemange*, Liverpool University Press, Liverpool, p. 120.

Ritzer, G. (1988), *Sociological Theory*, Alfred Knopf, New York, p. 16, pp. 39-42, p. 204, p. 301, p. 350.

Robins, J. (1995), *The Miasma - Epidemic and Panic in Nineteenth Century Ireland*, Dublin, IPA, p. 233.

Robinson, M. (1997), 'Daniel O'Connell - A Tribute', *History Ireland*, Volume V, No 4, Winter 1997, pp. 26-32.

Robinson, S. (1999), 'The Critical Theory of Jurgen Habermas', *English 980: Studies in Rhetoric*, Michigan State University, Michigan, http://www.msu.edu/user/robins11/habermas/main.html

Robson, C. (1995), *Real World Research: A Resource for Social Scientists and Practitioner Researchers*, Blackwell, Oxford, pp. 140-141, p. 168, pp. 256-263, p. 452, Appendix 2.

Rorabough, W.J. (1986), *The Craft Apprentice; From Franklin to the Machine Age in America*, Oxford University Press, Oxford, pp. 23-24.

Roth, G. and Wittich, C. (1968), *Max Weber, Economy and Society*, Bedminister Press, New York, Volume No 1, p. 8.

Roynane, T. (2001), *Ballymun Employment Report 2K*, WRC Social and Economic Consultants in association with the Ballymun Partnership 2001, Dublin, pp. 1-27.

RTÉ (2000), *Radio Telefis Éireann*, Nine O'Clock Television News, 7 December 2000.

RTÉ (2000a), *Radio Telefis Éireann Radio 1*, Morning Ireland, 17 November 2000.

Ryan, D. (1948), *Socialism and Nationalism - A Selection from the Writings of James Connolly*, Sign of the Three Candles, Dublin, pp. 2-3, p. 10.

Ryan, J.A. (1908), 'Charity and Charities', *The Catholic Encyclopedia Volume: III*, Robert Appleton Company, London, Nihil Obstat, November 1, 1908 Remy Lafort, S.T.D. Censor, Imprimatur+,John Cardinal Farley, Archbishop of New York, online edition copyright, Kevin Knight 1999, http://wwwnewadvent.org

Ryan, J.G. (1995), *Apprenticeship in Ireland - An Historical Analysis*, St. Patrick's College National University of Ireland, Maynooth, Co. Kildare, unpublished PhD Thesis, p. 129, p. 136, p. 158.

Sandford, A. (1987), *The Mind of Man: Models of Human Understanding*, Yale University Press, New Haven, p. 59.

Sapsford, R. (1996), 'Extracting and Presenting Statistics', Roger Sapsford and Victor Jupp (eds.), *Data Collection and Analysis*, Sage, in association with the Open University, London, p. 228.

Sapsford, R. and Abbott, P. (1996), 'Ethics, Politics and Research', Roger Sapsford and Victor Jupp (eds.), *Data Collection and Analysis*, Sage, in association with the Open University, London, pp. 318-319.

Sapsford, R. and Jupp, V. (1996), 'Validating Evidence', Roger Sapsford and Victor Jupp (eds.), *Data Collection and Analysis*, Sage, in association with the Open University, London, pp. 1-24.

Schlucter, W. (1999), 'Hindrances to Modernity: Max Weber on Islam', Toby Huff and Wolfgang Schluchter (eds.), *Max Weber and Islam*, Transaction Publishers, New Brunswick USA, p. 120, ffn 54, p. 130.

Schuck, M.J. (1991), *That They Be One - The Social Teachings of the Papal Encyclicals 1740-1989*, Georgetown University Press, Washington, p. 65, p. 100, ff 44, p. 111.

Schumpter, J. (1908), 'On the Concept of Social Value', *Quarterly Journal of Economics*, Volume 23, 1908/1909, p. 1,
http://socserv2.socsci.mcmaster.ca/~econ/ugcm/3113/schumpter/index.html

Sexton, J.J. (1998), *A Perspective on the Irish Labour Market Opportunities '98: Skills for the New Millenium*, Dublin, FÁS Paper No 3, pp. 1-6.

Shaw, G.B. (1920), *Irish Nationalism and Internationalism*, The Labour Party, London, pp. 8-9, p. 13.

Shuttleworth, I. and Kitchen, R. and Shirlow, P. and McDonagh, J. (2000), 'The Tail of the Tiger: Experiences and Perceptions of Unemployment and Inactivity in Donegal', *Irish Geography*, Volume 33, 2000, pp. 56-73.

Siltanen, J. and Stanworth, M. (1984), 'The Politics of Private Woman and Public Man', Janet Siltanen and Michelle Stanworth (eds.), *Women and the Public Sphere - A Critique of Sociology and Politics*, Hutchinson, London.

Singh, A. (1994), 'Global Economic Changes, Skills and International Competitiveness', *The International Labour Review*, Volume 133, No 2, 1994, pp. 168-181.

Smith, A. (1776), *An Inquiry into the Nature and Causes of the Wealth of Nations Book 3 - Of the Different Progress of Opulence in Different Nations*, p. 2, p.17,
http://socserv2.socsci.mcmaster.ca/~econ/ugcm/3113/smith/index.html.

Smith, R.J. (1999), *Conscience and Catholicism - The Nature and Function of Conscience in Contemporary Roman Catholic Moral Theology*, University Press of America, New York, pp. xii-xvii, pp. 5-6, pp. 10-11, p. 64, p. 135.

Social Guild of Oxford (1929), 'A Code of Social Principles', *The Catholic Social Year Book 1929*, The Catholic Social Guild, Oxford.

Sombart, W. (1967), *Luxury and Capitalism*, University of Michigan Press, Michigan, p. 25, p. 91, p. 94, p. 116, p. 132, pp. 169-170.

Stanley, L. and Wise, S. (1998), 'Feminist Principle (1): A Reflexive Approach', Ian Marsh, Rosie Campbell and Mike Keating (eds.), *Classic and Contemporary Readings in Sociology*, Longman, Harlow, pp. 152-63, p. 338.

Stark, R. and Glockman, C. (1969), 'Dimensions of Religious Commitment', Roland Robertson (ed.), *Sociology of Religion*, Penguin Modern Sociology Readings, Middlesex, pp. 253-261.

Stewart, A. (1997), *Michael Collins The Secret File*, Blackstaff Press, Belfast, p. 22.

Stewart, B. (1998), 'Inside Nationalism: A Meditation upon Inventing Ireland', Paul Hyland and Neil Sammells (eds.), *Irish Studies Review*, Volume 6, No 1, April 1998, pp. 5-16.

Storey, J. (1993), *An Introductory Guide to Cultural Theory and Popular Culture*, Harvester Wheatsheaf, Hertfordshire, p. 98.

Strachey, J. (1985), Sigmund Freud - A Sketch of his Life and Ideas, J. Strachey (ed.), *Sigmund Freud - Civilisation, Society and Religion*, Penguin, London, pp. 11-23.

Strauss, A. and Corbin, J. (1998), *Basics of Qualitative Research - Techniques and Procedures for Developing Grounded Theory*, Sage Publications, London, pp. 30-31, p. 147.

Suiter, J. (2000), 'US Investment in Ireland - A Commercial Report', *Irish Times*, 27 September 2000.

Sullivan, K. (1968), 'Literature in Modern Ireland', Owen Dudley Edwards (ed.), *Conor Cruise O'Brien Introduces Ireland*, Andre Deutche, London, p. 140.

Sunday Times (2000), 'Irish Telecoms Tycoon Tops Pay List with £IR184m', *The Sunday Times*, 19 November, Front Page.

Swanson, G. (1969), 'Experience of the Supernatural', Roland Roberston (ed.), *Sociology of Religion*, Penguin, Middlesex, pp. 237-252.

Sweeney, A. (1999), *Irrational Exuberance - The Myth of the Celtic Tiger*, Blackhall Publishing, Dublin, pp. 60-63.

Sweeney, G. (1992), 'The Role of Vocational Training in Endogenous Economic Growth', Joseph Davis (ed.), *Education Training and Local Economic Development*, The Regional Studies Association (Dublin Branch), Dept. of Surveying, Bolton St. Dublin, p. 66.

Sweeney, P. (1998), *The Celtic Tiger: Ireland's Economic Miracle Explained*, Oak Tree Press, Dublin, p. 1, p. 203.

Tahir El-Mesawi, M. (1998), *A Muslim Theory of Human Society - An Investigation Into the Sociological Thought of Malik Bennabi*, Thinkers Library, Selangor Darul Ehsan, p. 11 p. 37, pp. 58-59, p. 65, p. 80, p. 85, pp. 95-99, p. 112, p. 158.

Tang, T.L. and Tzeng, J.Y. (1991), 'Demographic Correlates of the Protestant Work Ethic', *Journal of Psychology*, Volume 126, pp. 163-169.

Tansey, P. (1998), *Ireland at Work - Economic Growth and the Labour Market 1987-1997*, Oak Tree Press, Dublin, p. 12, p. 35, p. 56, p. 155.

Tawney, R.H. (1921), *The Acquisitive Society*, Wheatsheaf Books, Brighton, p. 21, p. 44.

Tawney, R.H. (1961), *The Acquisitive Society*, Collins, London, p. 191.

Tennant, M. (1997), *Psychology and Adult Learning*, Routledge, London, p. 130.

Thomas, S. (1999), 'Conscience in Orthodox Thought', Jane Hoose (ed.), *Conscience in World Religions*, Gracewing and the University of Notre Dame, Hertfordshire, p. 106, p. 112, p. 122, ffns 23 and 24, p. 132.

Thomas, W.I. (1951), *Social Behavior and Personality Contributions of W.I. Thomas to Theory and Social Research*, Social Science Research Council, New York, p. 5, p. 15.

Tonnies, F. (1957), *Community and Society: Gemeinschaft und Gesellschaft*, The Michigan State University Press, p. 226.

Travers, J. (1999), 'Employment on Increase in Financial Services', *Irish Times*, 20 July 1999, p. 17.

Treacy, J. and O'Connell, N. (2000), 'Labour Market', Adrian Redmond (ed.), *That Was Then, This is Now - Change in Ireland 1949-1999*, Government of Ireland, Central Statistics Office, Dublin, February 2000, p. 108.

Treanor, P. (1997), 'Structures of Nationalism', *Sociological Research Online*, Volume 2, No 1, pp. 1-9, http://www.socresonline.org.uk/socresonline/2/1/8.html

Tripoli, A. (1998) 'Employee Voice and Involvement in Non-union Companies' in W.K. Roche, K. Monks and J. Walsh (eds.), *Human Resource Strategies, Policy and Practice in Ireland*, Oak Tree Press, Dublin, pp. 24-65.

Tropman, J.E. (1992), 'The Catholic Work Ethic', *The International Executive*, Volume 34, July/August 1992, pp. 297-304.

Trotsky, L. (1937), *Revolution Betrayed - What is the Soviet Union and Where is it Going?*, translated by Max Eastman and transcribed for the Internet by zodiac@interlog.com between August 1993 and March 1996, Chapter 3, p. 10, Chapter 9, p. 4, Chapter 10, pp. 3-4, Chapter 11, pp. 6-8.

Trotsky, L. (1939), *'Marxism in Our Times'*, p. 2, p. 11, http://www.marxist.com/theory/Miot.html

Tuck, R. and Silverthorne, M. (1998), *De Cive - On the Citizen Cambridge Texts in the History of Political Thought*, Cambridge University Press, Cambridge, edited and translated by Richard Tuck and Michael Silverthorne.

Turner, B.S. (1999), *The Talcott Parsons Reader*, Blackwell, Oxford, p. 10.

Tynan, M. (1985), *Catholic Instruction in Ireland 1720-1950: The O'Reilly/Donleavy Catechetical Tradition*, Four Courts Press, Dublin.

UN (1999), *Understanding Changes in the Human Development Index in Ireland: Human Development Report 1999, Briefing Notes for Ireland*, UN, Geneva pp. 1-8.

Valarasan-Twoomey, M. (1998), *The Celtic Tiger - From the Outside Looking In*, Blackhall Publishing, Dublin, p. 74.

Van Krieken, R. (1997), *Norbert Elias - Key Sociologist*, pp. 1-14, http://www.usyd.edu.au/su/social/elias/book/content.html

Van Maanen, J. (1979), *Reclaiming Qualitative Methodology for Organisational Research*, Sage, London.

Veblen, T. (1906), 'The Socialist Economics of Karl Marx and His Followers', *The Quarterly Journal of Economics*, Volume 20, pp. 3-4, http://socserv2.socsci.mcmaster.ca

Veblen, T. (1953), *The Theory of the Leisure Class*, New American Library, New York, pp. 182-192.

Veenhoven, R. (1984), *Conditions of Happiness*, Kluwer Academic, Boston.

Veenhoven, R. (1997), 'Advances in Understanding Happiness', *Revue Quèbècoise de Psychologie*, Volume 18, pp. 29-79, English Translation Erasmus University Rotterdam.

Veenhoven, R. (1998), 'Quality of Life and Happiness - Not Quite the Same', G. De Girolamo et al (eds.), *Health and the Quality of Life*, Rome Il Pensierro Scientificio, http://www.eur.nl/gsw/personeel/soc/veenhoven/Pub1990s/95b-ab.htm

Veenhoven, R. (2000), 'The Four Qualities of Life', *Journal of Happiness Studies*, Volume 1, Issue 1, 2000, pp. 1-39.

Viney, M. and Dudley Edwards, O. (1968), 'Parties and Power', Owen Dudley Edwards (ed.), *Conor Cruise O'Brien Introduces Ireland*, Andre Deutche, London, p. 99.

Von Kreitor, N. (1999), *Christian Gemeinschaft and Jewish Gesellshaft*, vonkreitor@euroseek.com

Vygotsky, L. (1979), *Thought and Language*, The MIT Press, Massachusetts, p. 89, p. 150, p.153.

Vygotsky, L. (1994), 'The Problem of Cultural Development of the Child', Rene van der Vere and Jaan Valsiner (eds.), *The Vygotsky Reader*, Blackwell, Oxford, p.57.

Walsh, B. (1999), 'What's in Store for the Celtic Tiger?', *Irish Banking Review*, Spring 1999 pp. 2-8.

Walsh, B. (1999a), 'The Persistence of High Unemployment in a Small Open Labour Market: The Irish Case', Frank Barry (ed.), *Understanding Ireland's Economic Growth*, Macmillan Press, London, p. 223.

Walsh, B, (2000), 'Economists Differ on How to Make Most of the Economy', *Irish Times*, 7 April 2000.

Walsh, E. (1987), 'Sackville Mall: The First One Hundred Years', David Dickson (ed.), *The Georgeous Mask: Dublin 1700-1850*, Trinity College History Workshop, p. 36.

Walshe, J (1999), *A New Partnership in Education; From Consultation to Legislation in the Nineties*, Dublin, Institute of Public Administration , Dublin, p. 174.

Walter, B. (1986), 'Ethnicity and Irish Residential Distribution', in Hickman, M. (ed.), *Religion, Class and Identity: The State, The Catholic Church and The Education of the Irish in Britain*, Avebury, Aldershot, p. 207.

Weber, M. (1918), 'Politik als Beruf Gesammelte Politische Schriften Muenchen 1921' H.H. Gerth and C. Wright Mills (eds.), *Max Weber: Essays in Sociology*, Oxford University Press, New York, 1946 p. 79.

Weber, M. (1930), *The Protestant Ethic and the Spirit of Capitalism*, Routledge, London, p. 27, p. 40, p. 52, p. 60, p. 64, p. 262.

Weber, M. (1968), *Economy and Society*, Bedminister Press, New York.

Weber, M. (1969), 'Major Features of World Religions', Roland Robertson (ed.), *Sociology of Religion*, Penguin, Modern Sociology Readings, Middlesex pp. 19-41.

Weber, M. (1999), *The Sociology of Religion*, Sociology Department, University of Amsterdam, 11 January 1999, p. J2.1, p. J.2.J, p. K.1.h, p.K.5.c, p. K.2.a., http://www.asahi-net.or.jp/~hw8m-mrkm/weber/society/socio_relig_frame.html

Weinz, W. (1986), 'Economic Development and Interest Groups', Brian Girvin and Roland Sturm (eds.), *Politics and Society in Contemporary Ireland*, Gower Publishing, Aldershot, pp. 88-89, p. 94.

Whelan B.J. (1998), 'Changing Work Patterns', Kieran A. Kennedy (ed.), *From Famine to Feast - Economic and Social Change in Ireland 1847-1997*, Institute of Public Administration, Dublin.

Whelan, C.T. (1975), *Orientations to Work: Some Theoretical and Methodological Problems*, Economic and Social Research Institute, Dublin, Series No 44, p. 156.

Whelan, C.T. (1994), 'Irish Social Values, Traditional or Modern', Christopher Whelan (ed.), *Value and Social Change in Ireland*, Gill and Macmillan, Dublin, p. 39, pp. 213-215.

Whelan, C.T. and Fahey, T. (1994), 'Marriage and The Family', Christopher T. Whelan (ed.), *Value and Social Change in Ireland*, Gill and Macmillan, Dublin, pp. 58-68.

Whelan, I. (1995), 'The Stigma of 'Souperism'', Cathal Portéir (ed.), *The Great Famine*, Dublin, Mercier Press, p. 36.

Whitaker, T.K. (1976), 'From Protection to Free Trade - The Irish Experience', *Administration*, No 24, p. 406.

Whitaker, T.K. (2001), 'Whitaker Lecture Highlights Poverty', *The Drogheda Independent Extra*, 26 October 2001, p. 3.

White, B. (1998), 'The Inferior Sort of the Kingdom of Ireland: Irishmen and Tyburn Tree', *Irish Studies Review*, Volume 6, No 1, April 1998, pp. 11-27.

Whyte, J.H. (1980), *Church and State in Modern Ireland 1923-1979*, Gill and Macmillan, Dublin, p. 4.

Wickham, J. (2000), *Changing Times - Working Time in Ireland 1983-2000*, Employment Research Centre, Labour Market Observatory, Trinity College, Dublin, p. 2, p. 8.

Williams, J.W. (1967), 'New Zealand's Economic Development', W. Bermingham and A. G. Ford (eds.), *Planning and Growth in Rich and Poor Countries*, George Allen and Unwin, London, p. 243.

Williams, K. (1999), 'Faith and the Nation: Education and Religious Identity in the Republic of Ireland', *British Journal of Educational Studies*, Volume 47, No 4, December 1999, pp. 317-331.

Williams, M. and May, T. (1997), *Introduction to the Philosophy of Social Research*, UCL Press, London.

Williams, R. (1987), 'The Practice of Possibility', *New Statesman*, 7 August 1987, p. 20.

Wilson, B.R. (1969), 'Religion in Secular Society', Roland Robertson (ed.), *Sociology of Religion*, Penguin, Middlesex, pp. 152-162.

Wilson, M. (1996), 'Asking Questions', Roger Sapsford and Victor Jupp (eds.), *Data Collection and Analysis*, Sage, London, in association with the Open University, pp. 94-120.

Wimster, S. (1998), 'The Nation State, The Protestant Ethic and Modernisation', Ralph Schroeder (ed.), *Max Weber, Democracy and Modernisation*, Macmillan Press, London, p. 63.

Winston, N. (2000), *Between Two Places - A Case Study of Irish-born People Living in England*, Irish National Committee of the European Cultural Foundation, Dublin, pp. 1-10, p. 22.

Wittgenstein, L. (1989), *The Pan Dictionary of Contemporary Quotations*, Pan Books, London, p. 148.

Woods, A. and Grant, T. (1994), 'The Relevance of Marxism Today', *Marxism in Our Time*, p. 1, p. 26, http://www.marxist.com/theory/Miotintro.html

Woods, A. and Grant, T. (1999), 'Philosophy and Religion', *Reason in Revolt - Marxism and Modern Science*, http://easyweb.easynet.co.uk/˜ zac/maindex.htm

Woods, A. and Grant, T. (2001), *Marxism and the National Question - Part 2, Marx and Engels and the National Question*, pp. 1-12, http://marxist.com/Theory/national_question.html

WRC Social and Economic Consultants (2000), *Combating Unemployment and Raising the Level and Quality of Employment: An Evaluation of the Employment Services Strategy of the Ballymun Partnership*, WRC Social and Economic Consultants, Dublin pp. 1-45.

Wren, M.A. (2000), 'The Decades of Growth - The Roller Coaster Decades', *Irish Times*, 6 May, p. 14.

Wright Mills, C. (1957), *The Power Elite*, Harpur, New York, p. 218.

Wuthnow, R. (1993) 'Pious Materialism: How Americans View Faith and Money', *The Christian Century*, 3 March 1993, pp. 239-242.

Index

For Product Safety Concerns and Information please contact our EU
representative GPSR@taylorandfrancis.com Taylor & Francis Verlag GmbH,
Kaufingerstraße 24, 80331 München, Germany

Printed and bound by CPI Group (UK) Ltd, Croydon, CR0 4YY

01/05/2025

01858351-0009